Edward FitzGerald, William Aldis Wright

Letters and Literary Remains of Edward Fitzgerald

Vol. II.

Edward Fitzgerald, William Aldis Wright

Letters and Literary Remains of Edward Fitzgerald
Vol. II.

ISBN/EAN: 9783744765831

Printed in Europe, USA, Canada, Australia, Japan

Cover: Foto © Thomas Meinert / pixelio.de

More available books at www.hansebooks.com

LETTERS

AND

LITERARY REMAINS

OF

EDWARD FITZGERALD

EDITED BY

WILLIAM ALDIS WRIGHT

IN THREE VOLUMES.

VOL. II.

London:

MACMILLAN AND CO.

AND NEW YORK.

1889

𝕮𝖆𝖒𝖇𝖗𝖎𝖉𝖌𝖊:

PRINTED BY C. J. CLAY, M.A. AND SONS,

AT THE UNIVERSITY PRESS.

TABLE OF CONTENTS.

EUPHRANOR.

Dᴜʀɪɴɢ the time of my pretending to practise Medicine at Cambridge, I was aroused, one fine forenoon of May, by the sound of some one coming up my staircase, two or three steps at a time it seemed to me ; then, directly after, a smart rapping at the door; and, before I could say, "Come in," Euphranor had opened it, and, striding up to me, seized my arm with his usual eagerness, and told me I must go out with him—"It was such a day—sun shining—breeze blowing —hedges and trees in full leaf.—He had been to Chesterton, (he said,) and pull'd back with a man who now left him in the lurch ; and I must take his place." I told him what a poor hand at the oar I was, and, such walnut-shells as these Cambridge boats were, I was sure a strong fellow like him must rejoice in getting a whole Eight-oar to himself once in a while. He laughed, and said, "The pace, the pace was the thing—However, that was all nothing, but—in short, I must go with him, whether for a row, or a walk in the fields, or a game of Billiards at Chesterton—whatever I liked— only go I must." After a little more banter, about some possible Patients, I got up ; closed some very weary medical Treatise I was reading ; on with coat and hat ; and in three minutes we had run downstairs, out into the open air ; where both of us calling out together "What a day !" it was, we

F.   I

struck out briskly for the old Wooden Bridge, where Euphra-
nor said his boat was lying.

"By-the-by," said I, as we went along, "it would be a
charity to knock up poor Lexilogus, and carry him along
with us."

Not much of a charity, Euphranor thought—Lexilogus
would so much rather be left with his books. Which I
declared was the very reason he should be taken from them;
and Euphranor, who was quite good-humour'd, and wish'd
Lexilogus all well, (for we were all three Yorkshiremen,
whose families lived no great distance asunder,) easily con-
sented. So, without more ado, we turn'd into Trinity Great
gate, and round by the right up a staircase to the attic where
Lexilogus kept.

The door was *sported*, as they say, but I knew he must
be within; so, using the privilege of an old friend, I shouted
to him through the letter-slit. Presently we heard the sound
of books falling, and soon after Lexilogus' thin, pale, and
spectacled face appear'd at the half-open'd door. He was
always glad to see me, I believe, howsoever I disturb'd him ;
and he smiled as he laid his hand in mine, rather than
return'd its pressure : working hard, as he was, poor fellow,
for a Fellowship that should repay all the expense of sending
him to College.

The tea-things were still on the table, and I asked him
(though I knew well enough) if he were so fashionable as
only just to have breakfasted ?

"Oh—long ago—directly after morning Chapel."

I then told him he must put his books away, and come
out on the river with Euphranor and myself.

"He could not possibly," he thought ;—"not so early,
at least—preparing for some Examination, or course of
Lectures——"

"Come, come, my good fellow," said Euphranor, "that is the very reason, says the Doctor; and he will have his way. So make haste."

I then told him (what I then suddenly remember'd) that, beside other reasons, his old Aunt, a Cambridge tradesman's widow whom I attended, and whom Lexilogus help'd to support out of his own little savings, wanted to see him on some business. He should go with us to Chesterton, where she lodged; visit her while Euphranor and I play'd a game or two of Billiards at the Inn; and afterwards (for I knew how little of an oars-man he was) we would all three take a good stretch into the fields together.

He supposed "we should be back in good time"; about which I would make no condition; and he then resign'd himself to Destiny. While he was busy changing and brushing his clothes, Euphranor, who had walk'd somewhat impatiently about the room, looking now at the books, and now through the window at some white pigeons wheeling about in the clear sky, went up to the mantelpiece and call'd out, "What a fine new pair of screens Lexilogus had got! the present, doubtless, of some fair Lady."

Lexilogus said they were a present from his sister on his birthday; and coming up to me, brush in hand, asked if I recognised the views represented on them?

"Quite well, quite well," I said—"the old Church—the Yew tree—the Parsonage—one cannot mistake them."

"And were they not beautifully done?"

And I answer'd without hesitation, "they were;" for I knew the girl who had painted them, and that (whatever they might be in point of Art) a still finer spirit had guided her hand.

At last, after a little hesitation as to whether he should wear cap and gown, (which I decided he should, for this time only, *not*,) Lexilogus was ready : and calling out on the staircase to some invisible Bed-maker, that his books should not be meddled with, we ran downstairs, crossed the Great Court—through the Screens, as they are call'd, perpetually travers'd by Gyp, Cook, Bed-maker, and redolent of perpetual Dinner;—and so, through the cloisters of Neville's Court, out upon the open green before the Library. The sun shone broad on the new-shaven expanse of grass, while holiday-seeming people saunter'd along the River-side, and under the trees, now flourishing in freshest green—the Chestnut especially in full fan, and leaning down his white cones over the sluggish current, which seem'd indeed fitter for the slow merchandise of coal, than to wash the walls and flow through the groves of Academe.

We now consider'd that we had miss'd our proper point of embarkation; but this was easily set right at a slight expense of College propriety. Euphranor calling out to some one who had his boat in charge along with others by the wooden bridge, we descended the grassy slope, stepp'd in, with due caution on the part of Lexilogus and myself, and settled the order of our voyage. Euphranor and I were to pull, and Lexilogus (as I at first proposed) to steer. But seeing he was somewhat shy of meddling in the matter, I agreed to take all the blame of my own awkwardness on myself.

"And just take care of this, will you, Lexilogus?" said Euphranor, handing him a book which fell out of the pocket of the coat he was taking off.

"Oh, books, books!" I exclaimed. "I thought we were to steer clear of them, at any rate. Now we shall have Lexilogus reading all the way, instead of looking about him, and inhaling the fresh air unalloy'd. What is it—Greek, Algebra, German, or what?"

"None of these, however," Euphranor said, "but only Digby's Godefridus;" and then asking me whether I was ready, and I calling out, "Ay, ay, Sir," our oars plash'd in the water. Safe through the main arch of Trinity bridge, we shot past the Library, I exerting myself so strenuously (as bad rowers are apt to do), that I almost drove the boat upon a very unobtrusive angle of the College buildings. This danger past, however, we got on better; Euphranor often looking behind him to anticipate our way, and counteracting with his experienced oar the many misdirections of mine. Amid all this, he had leisure to ask me if I knew those same Digby books?

"Some of them," I told him—"the 'Broad Stone of Honour,' for one; indeed I had the first Protestant edition of it, now very rare."

"But not so good as the enlarged Catholic," said Euphranor, "of which this Godefridus is part."

"Perhaps not," I replied; "but then, on the other hand, *not* so Catholic; which you and Lexilogus will agree with me is much in its favour."

Which I said slyly, because of Euphranor's being rather taken with the Oxford doctrine just then coming into vogue.

"You cannot forgive him that," said he.

"Nay, nay," said I, "one can forgive a true man any-thing."

And then Euphranor ask'd me, "Did I not remember Digby himself at College?—perhaps know him?"

"Not *that*," I answer'd, "but remember'd him very well. A grand, swarthy Fellow, who might have stept out of the canvas of some knightly portrait in his Father's hall—perhaps the living image of one sleeping under some cross-legg'd Effigies in the Church."

"And, Hare says, really the Knight at heart that he represented in his Books."

"At least," I answered, "he pull'd a very good stroke on the river, where I am now labouring so awkwardly."

In which and other such talk, interrupted by the little accidents of our voyage, we had threaded our way through the closely-packt barges at Magdalen; through the Locks; and so for a pull of three or four miles down the river and back again to the Ferry; where we surrender'd our boat, and footed it over the fields to Chesterton, at whose Church we came just as its quiet chimes were preluding Twelve o'clock. Close by was the humble house whither Lexilogus was bound. I look'd in for a moment at the old lady, and left him with her, privately desiring him to join us as soon as he could at the Three Tuns Inn, which I preferr'd to any younger rival, because of the many pleasant hours I had spent there in my own College days, some twenty years ago.

When Euphranor and I got there, we found all the tables occupied; but one, as usual, would be at our service before long. Meanwhile, ordering some light ale after us, we went into the Bowling-green, with its Lilac bushes now in full bloom and full odour; and there we found, sitting alone upon a bench, Lycion, with a cigar in his mouth, and rolling the bowls about lazily with his foot.

"What! Lycion! and all alone!" I call'd out.

He nodded to us both—waiting, he said, till some men had finish'd a pool of billiards upstairs—a great bore—for it was only just begun! and one of the fellows "a man I particularly detest."

"Come and console yourself with some ale, then," said I. "Are you ever foolish enough to go pulling on the river, as we have been doing?"

"Not very often in hot weather; he did not see the use," he said, "of perspiring to no purpose."

"Just so," replied I, "though Euphranor has not turn'd a hair, you see, owing to the good condition he is in. But here comes our liquor; and 'Sweet is Pleasure after Pain,' at any rate."

We then sat down in one of those little arbours cut into the Lilac bushes round the Bowling-green; and while Euphranor and I were quaffing each a glass of Home-brew'd, Lycion took up the volume of Digby, which Euphranor had laid on the table.

"Ah, Lycion," said Euphranor, putting down his glass, "there is one would have put you up to a longer and stronger pull than we have had to-day."

"Chivalry——" said Lycion, glancing carelessly over the leaves; "Don't you remember,"—addressing me—"what an absurd thing that Eglinton Tournament was? What a complete failure! There was the Queen of Beauty on her throne —Lady Seymour—who alone of all the whole affair was *not* a sham—and the Heralds, and the Knights in full Armour on their horses—they had been practising for months, I believe—but unluckily, at the very moment of Onset, the rain began, and the Knights threw down their lances, and put up their umbrellas."

I laugh'd, and said I remembered something like it had occurr'd, though not to that umbrella-point, which I thought was a theatrical, or Louis Philippe Burlesque on the affair. And I asked Euphranor "what he had to say in defence of the Tournament"?

"Nothing at all," he replied. "It *was* a silly thing, and fit to be laughed at for the very reason that it *was* a sham, as Lycion says. As Digby himself tells us," he went on, taking the Book, and rapidly turning over the leaves—

"Here it is"—and he read: "'The error that leads men to doubt of this first proposition'—that is, you know, that Chivalry is not a thing past, but, like all things of Beauty, eternal—'the error that leads men to doubt of this first proposition consists in their supposing that Tournaments, and steel Panoply, and Coat arms, and Aristocratic institutions, are essential to Chivalry; whereas, these are, in fact, only accidental attendants upon it, subject to the influence of Time, which changes all such things.'"

"I suppose," said Lycion, "your man—whatever his name is—would carry us back to the days of King Arthur, and the Seven Champions, whenever they were—that one used to read about when a Child? I thought Don Quixote had put an end to all that long ago."

"Well, *he*, at any rate," said Euphranor, "did not depend on fine Accoutrement for his Chivalry."

"Nay," said I, "but did he *not* believe in his rusty armour—perhaps even the paste-board Visor he fitted to it —as impregnable as the Cause——"

"And some old Barber's bason as the Helmet of Mambrino," interposed Lycion——

"And his poor Rocinante not to be surpass'd by the Bavieca of the Cid; believed in all this, I say, as really as in the Windmills and Wine-skins being the Giants and Sorcerers he was to annihilate?"

"To be sure he did," said Lycion; "but Euphranor's Round-table men—many of them great rascals, I believe— knew a real Dragon, or Giant—when they met him—better than Don Quixote."

"Perhaps, however," said I, who saw Euphranor's colour rising, "he and Digby would tell us that all such Giants and Dragons may be taken for Symbols of certain Forms of Evil which his Knights went about to encounter and exterminate."

"Of course," said Euphranor, with an indignant snort, "every Child knows that : then as now to be met with and put down in whatsoever shapes they appear as long as Tyranny and Oppression exist."

"Till finally extinguisht, as they crop up, by Euphranor and his Successors," said Lycion.

"Does not Carlyle somewhere talk to us of a 'Chivalry of Labour'?" said I; "that henceforward not '*Arms* and the Man,' but '*Tools* and the Man,' are to furnish the Epic of the world."

"Oh, well," said Lycion, "if the 'Table-Round' turn into a Tailor's Board—'Charge, Chester, charge!' say I—only not exorbitantly for the Coat you provide for us—which indeed, like true Knights, I believe you should provide for us gratis."

"Yes, my dear fellow," said I, laughing, "but then *You* must not sit idle, smoking your cigar, in the midst of it; but, as your Ancestors led on mail'd troops at Agincourt, so must you put yourself, shears in hand, at the head of this Host, and become what Carlyle calls 'a Captain of Industry,' a Master-tailor, leading on a host of Journeymen to fresh fields and conquests new."

"Besides," said Euphranor, who did not like Carlyle, nor relish this sudden descent of his hobby, "surely Chivalry will never want a good Cause to maintain, whether private or public. As Tennyson says, King Arthur, who was carried away wounded to the island valley of Avilion, returns to us in the shape of a 'modern Gentleman' who may be challenged, even in these later days, to no mock Tournament, Lycion, in his Country's defence, and with something other than the Doctor's shears at his side."

To this Lycion, however, only turn'd his cigar in his mouth by way of reply, and look'd somewhat superciliously at his Antagonist. And I, who had been looking into the leaves of the Book that Euphranor had left open, said :

"Here we are, as usual, discussing without having yet agreed on the terms we are using. Euphranor has told us, on the word of his Hero, what Chivalry is *not:* let him read what it *is* that we are talking about."

I then handed him the Book to read to us, while Lycion, lying down on the grass, with his hat over his eyes, composed himself to inattention. And Euphranor read :

"'Chivalry is only a name for that general Spirit or state of mind, which disposes men to Heroic and Generous actions; and keeps them conversant with all that is Beautiful and Sublime in the Intellectual and Moral world. It will be found that, in the absence of conservative principles, this Spirit more generally prevails in Youth than in the later periods of men's lives : and, as the Heroic is always the earliest age in the history of nations, so Youth, the first period of human life, may be considered as the Heroic or Chivalrous age of each separate Man ; and there are few so unhappy as to have grown up without having experienced its influence, and having derived the advantage of being able to enrich their imaginations, and to soothe their hours of sorrow, with its romantic recollections. The Anglo-Saxons distinguished the period between Childhood and Manhood by the term 'Cnihthade,' Knighthood : a term which still continued to indicate the connexion between Youth and Chivalry, when Knights were styled 'Children,' as in the historic song beginning

"Child Rowland to the dark tower came :"

an excellent expression, no doubt ; for every Boy and Youth is, in his mind and sentiments, a Knight, and essentially a Son of Chivalry. Nature is fine in him. Nothing but the

circumstance of a singular and most degrading system of
Education can ever totally destroy the action of this general
law. Therefore, as long as there has been, or shall be, a
succession of sweet Springs in Man's Intellectual World; as
long as there have been, or shall be, Young men to grow up
to maturity; and until all Youthful life shall be dead, and
its source withered for ever; so long must there have
been, and must there continue to be, the spirit of noble
Chivalry. To understand therefore this first and, as it were,
natural Chivalry, we have only to observe the features of
the Youthful age, of which examples surround us. For, as
Demipho says of young men:

"Ecce autem similia omnia : omnes congruunt :
Unum cognoris, omnes noris."

Mark the courage of him who is green and fresh in this Old
world. Amyntas beheld and dreaded the insolence of the
Persians; but not so Alexander, the son of Amyntas, ἅτε
νέος τε ἐών, καὶ κακῶν ἀπαθὴς (says Herodotus) οὐδαμῶς ἔτι
κατέχειν οἷός τε ἦν. When Jason had related to his com-
panions the conditions imposed by the King, the first im-
pression was that of horror and despondency : till Peleus
rose up boldly, and said,

Ὥρη μητιάασθαι ὅ κ' ἔρξομεν· οὐ μὲν ἔολπα
Βουλῆς εἶναι ὄνειαρ, ὅσον τ' ἐπὶ κάρτεῖ χειρῶν.

'If Jason be unwilling to attempt it, I and the rest will
undertake the enterprise; for what more can we suffer than
death?' And then instantly rose up Telamon and Idas,
and the sons of Tyndarus, and Œnides, although

οὐδέ περ ὅσσον ἐπανθιόωντας ἰούλους
Ἀντέλλων.

But Argus, the Nestor of the party, restrained their im-
petuous valour."

"Scarce the Down upon their lips, you see," said I, "Freshmen;—so that you, Euphranor, who are now Bachelor of Arts, and whose upper lip at least begins to show the stubble of repeated harvests, are, alas, fast declining from that golden prime of Knighthood, while Lycion here, whose shavings might almost be counted——"

Here Lycion, who had endured the reading with an occasional yawn, said he wish'd "those fellows upstairs would finish their pool."

"And see again," continued I, taking the book from Euphranor's hands—"after telling us that Chivalry is mainly but another name for Youth, Digby proceeds to define more particularly what *that* is—'It is a remark of Lord Bacon, that "for the Moral part, Youth will have the pre-eminence, as Age hath for the Politic;" and this has always been the opinion which is allied to that other belief, that the Heroic (the Homeric age) was the most Virtuous age of Greece. When Demosthenes is desirous of expressing any great and generous sentiment, he uses the term νεανικὸν φρόνημα' —and by the way," added I, looking up parenthetically from the book, " the Persians, I am told, employ the same word for Youth and Courage—'and it is the saying of Plautus, when surprise is evinced at the Benevolence of an old man, "Benignitas hujus ut Adolescentuli est." There is no differ- ence, says the Philosopher, between Youthful Age and Youthful Character; and what this is cannot be better evinced than in the very words of Aristotle : "The Young are ardent in Desire, and what they do is from Affection ; they are tractable and delicate ; they earnestly desire and are quickly appeased ; their wishes are intense, without com- prehending much, as the thirst and hunger of the weary ; they are passionate and hasty, and liable to be surprised by anger ; for being ambitious of Honour, they cannot endure to be despised, but are indignant when they suffer injustice: they love Honour, but still more Victory; for Youth desires superiority, and victory is superiority, and both of these they love more than Riches; for as to these, of all things, they care for them the least. They are not of corrupt manners, but are Innocent, from not having beheld much wickedness; and they are credulous, from having been seldom deceived; and Sanguine in hope, for, like persons who are drunk with wine, they are inflamed by nature, and from their having had but little experience of Fortune. And they live by Hope, for Hope is of the future, but Memory of the past, and to Youth the Future is everything, the Past but little; they hope all things, and remember nothing: and it is easy to deceive them, for the reasons which have been given; for they are willing to hope, and are full of Courage, being passionate and hasty, of which tempers it is the nature of one not to fear, and of the other to inspire confidence; and they are easily put to Shame, for they have no resources to set aside the precepts which they have learned: and they have lofty souls, for they have never been disgraced or brought low, and they are unacquainted with Necessity; they prefer Honour to Advantage, Virtue to Expediency; for they live by Affection rather than by Reason, and Reason is concerned with Expediency, but Affection with Honour: and they are warm friends and hearty companions, more than other men, because they delight in Fellowship, and judge of nothing by Utility, and therefore not their friends; and they chiefly err in doing all things over much, for they keep no medium. They love much, and they dislike much, and so in everything, and this arises from their idea that they know everything. And their faults consist more in Insolence than in actual wrong; and they are full of Mercy, because they regard all men as good, and more virtuous than they are; for they measure others by their own Innocence; so that they suppose every man suffers wrongfully."' So that Lycion, you see," said I, looking up from the book, and tapping on the top of his hat, "is, in virtue of his eighteen Summers only, a Knight of Nature's own dubbing—yes, and here we have a list of the very qualities which constitute him one of the Order. And all the time he is pretending to be careless, indolent, and worldly, he is really bursting with suppressed Energy, Generosity, and Devotion."

"I did not try to understand your English any more than your Greek," said Lycion; "but if I can't help being the very fine Fellow whom I think you were reading about, why, I want to know what is the use of writing books about it for my edification."

"O yes, my dear fellow," said I, "it is like giving you an Inventory of your goods, which else you lose, or even fling away, in your march to Manhood—which you are so eager to reach. Only to repent when gotten there; for I see Digby goes on—'What is termed *Entering the World*'— which Manhood of course must do—'assuming its Principles and Maxims'—which usually follows—'is nothing else but departing into those regions to which the souls of the Homeric Heroes went sorrowing—

"'ὃν πότμον γοόωσα, λιποῦσ' ἀδροτῆτα καὶ ἥβην.'"

"Ah, you remember," said Euphranor, "how Lamb's friend, looking upon the Eton Boys in their Cricket-field, sighed 'to think of so many fine Lads so soon turning into frivolous Members of Parliament!'"

"But why 'frivolous'?" said Lycion.

"Ay, why 'frivolous'?" echoed I, "when entering on

the Field where, Euphranor tells us, their Knightly service may be call'd into action."

"Perhaps," said Euphranor, "entering before sufficiently equipp'd for that part of their calling."

"Well," said Lycion, "the Laws of England determine otherwise, and that is enough for me, and, I suppose, for her, whatever your ancient or modern pedants say to the contrary."

"You mean," said I, "in settling Twenty-one as the Age of 'Discretion,' sufficient to manage, not your own affairs only, but those of the Nation also?"

The hat nodded.

"Not yet, perhaps, accepted for a Parliamentary Knight complete," said I, "so much as Squire to some more experienced, if not more valiant, Leader. Only providing that Neoptolemus do not fall into the hands of a too politic Ulysses, and under him lose that generous Moral, whose Inventory is otherwise apt to get lost among the benches of St Stephen's—in spite of preliminary Prayer."

"Aristotle's Master, I think," added Euphranor, with some mock gravity, "would not allow any to become Judges in his Republic till near to middle life, lest acquaintance with Wrong should harden them into a distrust of Humanity: and acquaintance with Diplomacy is said to be little less dangerous."

"Though, by-the-way," interposed I, "was not Plato's Master accused of perplexing those simple Affections and Impulses of Youth by his Dialectic, and making premature Sophists of the Etonians of Athens?"

"By Aristophanes, you mean," said Euphranor, with no mock gravity now; "whose gross caricature help'd Anytus and Co. to that Accusation which ended in the murder of the best and wisest Man of all Antiquity."

"Well, perhaps," said I, "he had been sufficiently punish'd by that termagant Wife of his—whom, by-the-way, he may have taught to argue with him instead of to obey. Just as that Son of poor old Strepsiades, in what you call the Aristophanic Caricature, is taught to rebel against parental authority, instead of doing as he was bidden ; as he would himself have the Horses to do that he was spending so much of his Father's money upon: and as we would have our own Horses, Dogs, and Children,—and young Knights."

"You have got your Heroes into fine company, Euphranor," said Lycion, who, while seeming inattentive to all that went against him, was quick enough to catch at any turn in his favour.

"Why, let me see," said I, taking up the book again, and running my eye over the passage—"yes,—'*Ardent of desire,*'—'*Tractable,*'—some of them at least—'*Without comprehending much*'—'*Ambitious*'—'*Despisers of Riches*'—'*Warm friends and hearty Companions*'—really very characteristic of the better breed of Dogs and Horses. And why not ? The Horse, you know, has given his very name to Chivalry, because of his association in the Heroic Enterprises of Men,—*El mas Hidalgo Bruto*, Calderon calls him. He was sometimes buried, I think, along with our heroic Ancestors—just as some favourite wife was buried along with her husband in the East. So the Muse sings of those who believe their faithful Dog will accompany them to the World of Spirits—as even some wise and good Christian men have thought it not impossible he may, not only because of his Moral, but——"

"Well," said Euphranor, "we need not trouble ourselves about carrying the question quite so far."

"Oh, do not drop your poor kinsman just when you are going into good Company," said Lycion.

" By-the-way, Lycion," said I, " has not your Parliament a 'Whipper-in' of its more dilatory members—or of those often of the younger ones, I think, who may be diverting themselves with some stray scent elsewhere ?"

To this he only replied with a long whiff from his Cigar; but Euphranor said :

"Well, come, Lycion, let us take the Doctor at his word, and turn it against himself. For if you and I, in virtue of our Youth, are so inspired with all this Moral that he talks of—why, we—or, rather, you—*are* wanted in Parliament, not only to follow like Dog and Horse, as he pretends, but also to take the lead; so as the Generous counsel, the νεανικὸν φρόνημα, of Youth, may vivify and ennoble the cold Politic of Age."

"Well, I remember hearing of a young Senator," said I, " who, in my younger days, was celebrated for his faculty of Cock-crowing by way of waking up his more drowsy Seniors, I suppose, about the small hours of the morning—or, perhaps, in token of Victory over an unexpected Minority."

" No, no," said Euphranor, laughing, " I mean seriously; as in the passage we read from Digby, Amyntas, the Man of Policy, was wrong, and his son Alexander right."

But oddly enough, as I remember'd the story in Herodotus, by a device which smack'd more of Policy than Generosity. " But in the other case, Argus, I suppose, was not so wrong in restraining the impetuosity of his Youthful Crew, who,—is it not credibly thought ?—would have fail'd, but for Medea's unexpected magical assistance."

Euphranor was not clear about this.

" Besides," said I, " does not this very νεανικὸν φρόνημα of yours result from that νεανικόν condition—ἔθος, do you call it ?—of Body, in which Youth as assuredly profits as in the Moral, and which assuredly flows, as from a Fountain of

F.   2

'Jouvence that rises and runs in the open' Field rather than in the Hall of St Stephen's, where indeed it is rather likely to get clogg'd, if not altogether dried up? As, for instance, *Animal Spirit, Animal Courage, Sanguine Temper,* and so forth—all which, by the way, says Aristotle, inflame Youth not at all like Reasonable people, but '*like persons drunk with wine*'—all which, for better or worse, is fermented by Cricket from good Roast Beef into pure Blood, Muscle— and Moral."

"Chivalry refined into patent Essence of Beef!" said Euphranor, only half-amused.

"I hope you like the taste of it," said Lycion, under his hat.

"Well, at any rate," said I, laughing, "those young Argonauts needed a good stock of it to work a much heavier craft than we have been pulling to-day, when the wind fail'd them. And yet, with all their animal Inebriation— whencesoever derived—so tractable in their Moral as to submit at once to their Politic Leader—Argus, was it not?"

"'The Nestor of the Party,' Digby calls him," said Euphranor, "good, old, garrulous, Nestor, whom, somehow, I think one seems to feel more at home with than any of the Homeric Heroes."

"Aye, *he* was entitled to crow in the Grecian Parliament, fine 'Old Cock' as he was, about the gallant exploits of his Youth, being at threescore so active in Body as in Spirit, that Agamemnon declares, I think, that Troy would soon come down had he but a few more such Generals. Ah yes, Euphranor! could one by so full Apprenticeship of Youth become so thoroughly season'd with its Spirit, that all the Reason of Manhood, and Politic of Age, and Experience of the World, should serve not to freeze, but to direct, the genial Current of the Soul, so that—

"'Ev'n while the vital Heat retreats below,
Ev'n while the hoary head is lost in Snow,
The *Life* is in the leaf, and still between
The fits of falling Snow appears the streaky Green'—

that Boy's Heart within the Man's never ceasing to throb
and tremble, even to remotest Age—then indeed your Senate
would need no other Youth than its Elders to vivify their
counsel, or could admit the Young without danger of cor-
rupting them by ignoble Policy."

"Well, come," said Euphranor gaily, after my rather
sententious peroration, "Lycion need not be condemn'd to
enter Parliament—or even 'The World'—unless he pleases,
for some twenty years to come, if he will follow Pythago-
ras, who, you know, Doctor, devotes the first forty years of
his Man's allotted Eighty to Childhood and Youth; a dis-
pensation which you and I at least shall not quarrel with."

"No, nor anyone else, I should suppose," said I.
"Think, my dear Lycion, what a privilege for you to have
yet more than twenty good years' expatiation in the Elysian
Cricket-field of Youth before pent up in that Close Borough
of your Father's! And Euphranor, whom we thought fast
slipping out of his Prime as his Youth attained a beard, is
in fact only just entering upon it. And, most wonderful of
all, I, who not only have myself enter'd the World, but
made my bread by bringing others into it these fifteen years,
have myself only just ceased to be a Boy!"

What reply Lycion might have deign'd to all this, I
know not; for just now one of his friends looked out again
from the Billiard-room window, and called out to him, "the
coast was clear." On which Lycion getting up, and mut-
tering something about its being a pity we did not go back
to Trap-ball, and I retorting that we could carry it forward
into Life with us, he carelessly nodded to us both, and

2—2

with an "*Au Revoir*" lounged with his Cigar into the house.

Then Euphranor and I took each a draught of the good liquor which Lycion had declined to share with us; and, on setting down his tumbler, he said:

"Ah! you should have heard our friend Skythrops commenting on that Inventory of Youth, as you call it, which he happen'd to open upon in my rooms the other day."

"Perhaps the book is rather apt to open there of its own accord," said I. "Well—and what did Skythrops say?"

"Oh, you may anticipate—'the same old Heathen talk,' he said—'very well for a Pagan to write, and a Papist to quote'—and, according to you, Doctor, for Horse and Dog to participate in, and for Bullock to supply."

"But I had been mainly bantering Lycion," I said; "as Euphranor also, I supposed, with his Pythagorean disposition of Life. Lycion would not much have cared had I derived them from the angels. As for that Animal condition to which I had partly referr'd them, we Doctors were of old notorious on that score, not choosing your Moralist and Philosopher to carry off all the fee. But, 'The Cobbler to his Last'—or, the Tailor to his Goose, if I might be call'd in, as only I profess'd, to accommodate the outer Man with what Sterne calls his Jerkin, leaving its Lining to your Philosopher and Divine."

"Sterne!" ejaculated Euphranor; "just like him—Soul and Body all of a piece."

"Nay, nay," said I, laughing; "your Lining is often of a finer material, you know."

"And often of a coarser, as in Sterne's own case, I believe."

"Well, then, I would turn Mason, or Bricklayer," I said;

"and confine myself to the House of Clay, in which, as the Poets tell us, the Soul is Tenant—'The Body's Guest'—as Sir Walter Raleigh calls him; would that do?"

"Better, at any rate, than Jerkin and Lining."

But here the same difficulty presented itself. For, however essentially distinct the Tenant from his Lodging, his Health, as we of the material Faculty believed, in some measure depended on the salubrity of the House, in which he is not merely a Guest, but a Prisoner, and from which I knew Euphranor thought he was forbidden to escape by any violent self-extrication. Dryden indeed tells us of—

> "'A fiery Soul that, working out his way,
> Fretted the pigmy Body to decay,
> And o'er-informed this Tenement of Clay.'"—

"But *that* was the Soul of an Achitophel," Euphranor argued, "whose collapse, whether beginning from within or without, was of less than little moment to the world. But the truly grand Soul possesses himself in peace, or, if he suffer from self-neglect, or over-exertion in striving after the good of others—why, that same Dryden—or Waller, it may be—says that such an one becomes, not weaker, but stronger, by that Bodily decay, whether of Infirmity, or of Old Age, which lets in new light through the chinks of dilapidation— if not, as my loftier Wordsworth has it, some rays of that Original Glory which he brought with him to be darken'd in the Body at Birth."

"But then," I said, "if your crazy Cottage won't fall to pieces at once, but, after the manner of creaking gates, go creaking—or, as the Sailors say of their boats 'complaining' on—making the Tenant, and most likely all his Neighbours, complain also, and perpetually calling on the Tenant for repairs, and this when he wants to be about other more

important Business of his own? To think how much time
—and patience—a Divine Soul has to waste over some little
bit of Cheese, perhaps, that, owing to bad drainage, will
stick in the stomach of an otherwise Seraphic Doctor."

Euphranor laughed a little; and I went on: "Better
surely, for all sakes, to build up for her—as far as we may—
for we cannot yet ensure the foundation—a spacious, airy,
and wholesome Tenement becoming so Divine a Tenant, of
so strong a foundation and masonry as to resist the wear and
tear of Elements without, and herself within. Yes; and a
handsome house withal—unless indeed you think the hand-
some Soul will fashion that about herself from within—like
a shell—which, so far as her Top-storey, where she is
supposed chiefly to reside, I think may be the case."

"Ah," said Euphranor, "one of the most beautiful of all
human Souls, as I think, could scarce accomplish that."

"Socrates?" said I. "No; but did not he profess that
his Soul was naturally an ugly soul to begin with? So, by
the time he had beautified her within, it was too late to
re-front her Outside, which had case-hardened, I suppose.
But did not he accompany Alcibiades, not only because of
his Spiritual, but also of his Physical Beauty, in which, as in
the Phidian statues, the Divine Original of Man was sup-
posed to reflect Himself, and which has been accepted as
such by Christian Art, and indeed by all Peoples who are
furthest removed from that of the Beast?"

"Even of Dog and Horse?" said Euphranor, smiling.

"Even my sturdy old Philosopher Montaigne—who, by
the way, declares that he rates 'La Beauté à deux doigts de
la Bonté...non seulement aux hommes qui me servent, mais
aux bêtes aussi;' quotes your Aristotle, saying that we owe
a sort of Homage to those who resemble the Statues of the
Gods as to the Statues themselves. And thus Socrates

may have felt about Alcibiades, who, in those earlier and better days when Socrates knew him, might almost be taken as a counterpart of the Picture of Youth, with all its Virtues and defects, which Aristotle has drawn for us."

"Or, what do you say, Doctor, to Aristotle's own Pupil, Alexander, who turned out a yet more astonishing Phenomenon?—I wonder, Doctor, what you, with all your theories, would have done had such an 'Enfant terrible' as either of them been put into your hands."

"Well, at any rate, I should have the advantage of first laying hold of him on coming into the World, which was not the case with Aristotle, or with the Doctors of his time, was it?"

Euphranor thought not.

"However, I know not yet whether I have ever had an Infant Hero of any kind to deal with; none, certainly, who gave any indication of any such 'clouds of glory' as your Wordsworth tells of, even when just arrived from their several homes—in Alexander's case, of a somewhat sulphureous nature, according to Skythrops, I doubt. No, nor of any young Wordsworth neither under our diviner auspices."

"Nay, but," said Euphranor, "he tells us that our Birth is but a 'Sleep and a Forgetting' of something which must take some waking-time to develope."

"But which, if I remember aright, is to begin to darken 'with shades of the Prison-house,' as Wordsworth calls it, that begin to close about 'the growing Boy.' But I am too much of a Philistine, as you Germans have it, to comprehend the Transcendental. All I know is, that I have not yet detected any signs of the 'Heaven that lies about our Infancy,' nor for some while after—no, not even peeping through those windows through which the Soul is said more immediately to look, but as yet with no more speculation in them than those of the poor whelp of the Dog we talked of—in spite of a nine days' start of him."

"Nevertheless," said Euphranor, "I have heard tell of another Poet's saying that he knew of no human out-look so solemn as that from an Infant's Eyes; and how it was from those of his own he learn'd that those of the Divine Child in Raffaelle's Sistine Madonna were not over-charged with expression, as he had previously thought they might be."

"I think," said I, "you must have heard of that from me, who certainly did hear something like it from the Poet himself, who used to let fall—not lay down—the word that settled the question, æsthetic or other, which others hammer'd after in vain. Yes; that was on occasion, I think, of his having watch'd his Child one morning *'worshipping the Sun-beam on the Bed-post'*—I suppose the worship of Wonder, such as I have heard grown-up Children tell of at first sight of the Alps, or Niagara; or such stay-at-home Islanders as ourselves at first sight of the Sea, from such a height as Flamborough Head."

"Some farther-seeing Wonder than dog or kitten are conscious of, at any rate," said Euphranor.

"Ah, who knows? I have seen both of them watching that very Sunbeam too—the Kitten perhaps playing with it, to be sure. If but the Philosopher or Poet could live in the Child's or kitten's Brain for a while! The Bed-post Sun-worship, however, was of a Child of several months— and Raffaelle's—a full year old, would you say?"

"Nay, you know about such matters better than I," said Euphranor, laughing.

"Well, however it may be with young Wordsworth, Raffaelle's child certainly *was* 'drawing Clouds of Glory' from *His* Home, and we may suppose him conscious of it—yes, and of his Mission to dispense that glory to the World. And I remember how the same Poet also noticed the Attitude of the Child, which might otherwise seem somewhat too magisterial for his age."

Euphranor knew the Picture by Engraving only; but he observed how the Divine Mother's eyes also were dilated, not as with Human Mother's Love, but as with awe and Wonder at the Infant she was presenting to the World, as if silently saying, "Behold your King!"

"Why," said I, "do not some of you believe the 'Clouds of Glory' to have been drawn directly from herself?"

"Nonsense, nonsense, Doctor—you know better, as did Raffaelle also, I believe, in spite of the Pope."

"Well, well," said I, "your Wordsworth Boy has also his Divine Mission to fulfil in confessing that of Raffaelle's. But, however it may be with that Mother and Child, does not one—of your Germans, I think—say that, with us mortals, it is from the Mother's eyes that Religion dawns into the Child's Soul?—the Religion of Love, at first, I suppose, in gratitude for the flowing breast and feeding hand below."

"Perhaps—in some degree," said Euphranor. "As you were saying of that Sun-worshipper, one cannot fathom how far the Child may see into the Mother's eyes any more than all that is to be read in them."

"To be developed between them thereafter, I suppose," said I, "when the Mother's lips interpret the Revelation of her Eyes, and lead up from her Love to the perception of some Invisible Parent of all."

"Ah," said Euphranor, "how well I remember learning to repeat after her, every morning and night, 'Our Father which art in Heaven.'"

"In your little white Surplice, like Sir Joshua's little

Samuel—on whom the Light is dawning direct from Heaven,
I think—from Him to whom you were half-articulately
praying to 'make me a dood Boy' to them. And, by-and-
by, Watts and Jane Taylor's, of the Star Daisy in the grass,
and the Stars in Heaven,

> "'For ever singing as they shine,
> The Hand that made us is Divine.'"

"Ah," said Euphranor, "and beautiful some of those
early things of Watts and Jane Taylor are. They run in my
head still."

"As why should they not?" said I, "you being yet in
your Childhood, you know. Why, I, who have left it some
way behind me, to be sure, am constantly reminded of
them in the nurseries I am so often call'd into from which
they are not yet banisht by more æsthetic verse. As also,
I must say, of some yet more early, and profane, such as
'Rock-a-bye Baby on the Tree-top,' with that catastrophe
which never fail'd to 'bring the House down' along with
the Bough which is,—Mother's Arms. Then there was
'Little Bopeep' whose stray flock came back to her of them-
selves, carrying their tails behind them—and 'Little Boy
Blue' who was less fortunate. Ah, what a pretty little
picture he makes 'under the haycock'—like one of your
Greek Idylls, I think, and quite 'suitable to this present
Month of May,' as old Izaak says. Let me hear if you
remember it, Sir."

And Euphranor, like a good boy, repeated the verses *.

> * "Little Boy Blue come blow your horn;
> The Cow's in the meadow, the Sheep in the corn.
> Is this the way you mind your Sheep,
> Under the haycock fast asleep?"

"The '*meadow*'" said I, by way of annotation, "being, you know,
of grass reserved for meadowing, or mowing."

"And then," said I, "the echoes of those old London
Bells whose Ancestors once recall'd Whittington back to
be their Lord Mayor; and now communicating from their
several Steeples as to how the account with St Clement's
was to be paid—which, by-the-by, I remember being thus
summarily settled by an old College Friend of mine—

> "'"Confound you all!"
> Said the Great bell of Paul;'

only, I am afraid, with something more Athanasian than
'Confound'—though he was not then a Dignitary of the
Church. Then that Tragedy of 'Cock Robin'—the Fly
that saw it with that little Eye of his—and the Owl with
his spade and '*Showl*'—proper old word that too—and the
Bull who the Bell could pull—and—but I doubt whether
you will approve of the Rook reading the Burial Service,
nor do I like bringing the Lark, only for a rhyme's sake,
down from Heaven, to make the responses. And all this
illustrated by appropriate—'Gays,' as they call them in
Suffolk—and recited, if not intoned, according to the dif-
ferent Characters."

"Plato's 'Music of Education,' I suppose," said Euphra-
nor.

"Yes," said I, warming with my subject; "and then,
beside the True Histories of Dog and Horse whose example
is to be followed, Fables that treat of others, Lions, Eagles,
Asses, Foxes, Cocks, and other feather'd or four-footed
Creatures, who, as in Cock Robin's case, talk as well as act,
but with a Moral—more or less commendable—provided
the Moral be dropt. Then as your punning friend Plato,
you told me, says that *Thaumas*—Wonder—is Father of
Iris, who directly communicates between Heaven and Earth
—as in the case of that Bed-post-kissing Apollo—you, being

a pious man, doubtless had your Giants, Genii, Enchanters, Fairies, Ogres, Witches, Ghosts——"

But Euphranor was decidedly against admitting any Ghost into the Nursery, and even Witches, remembering little Lamb's childish terror at Her of Endor.

"Oh, but," said I, "*She* was a real Witch, you know, though represented by Stackhouse; who need not figure among the Musicians, to be sure. You, however, as Lycion says, have your Giants and Dragons to play with—by way of Symbol, if you please—and you must not grudge your younger Brethren in Arms that redoubtable JACK who slew the Giants whom you are to slay over again, and who for that very purpose climb'd up a Bean-stalk some way at least to Heaven—an Allegory that, as Sir Thomas Browne says, ' admits of a wide solution.'"

"Ah," said my companion, "I remember how you used to climb up the Poplar in our garden by way of Bean-stalk, looking out upon us now and then, till lost among the branches. You could not do that now, Doctor."

"No more than I could up Jack's own Bean-stalk. I was a thin slip of a Knight then, not long turned of Twenty, I suppose—almost more like a Giant than a Jack to the rest of you—but Children do not mind such disproportions. No—I could better play one of the three Bears growling for his mess of porridge now. But, in default of my transcendental illustration of Jack, he and his like are well represented in such Effigies as your friend Plato never dream'd of in his philosophy, though Phidias and Praxiteles may have sketcht for their Children what now is multiplied by Engraving into every Nursery."

"Not to mention Printing, to read about what is represented," said Euphranor.

"I do not know what to say about *that*," said I.

"Does not your Philosopher repudiate any but Oral instruction?"

"Notwithstanding all which, I am afraid we must learn to read," said Euphranor, "in these degenerate days."

"Well, if needs must," said I, "you may learn in the most musical way of all. Do you not remember the practice of our Forefathers?

"'To Master John, the Chamber-maid
A Horn-book gives of Ginger-bread;
And, that the Child may learn the better,
As he can name, he eats the Letter.'"

"Oh, how I used to wish," said Euphranor, "there had been any such royal road to Grammar which one had to stumble over some years after."

"Well," said I, "but there is now, I believe, a Comic Grammar—as well as a Comic History of Rome—and of England."

"Say no more of all that, pray, Doctor. The old 'Propria quæ maribus' was better Music, uncouth as it was, and almost as puzzling as an Oracle. I am sure it is only now—when I try—that I understand the meaning of the rule I then repeated mechanically—like a Parrot, you would say."

"Sufficiently intelligible, however," said I, "to be mechanically applied in distinguishing the different parts of Speech, and how related to one another; how a verb governs an accusative, and an adjective agrees with a noun; to all which you are guided by certain terminations of *us*, *a*, *um*, and *do*, *das*, *dat*, and so on; till you are able to put the scattered words together, and so ford through a sentence. And the old uncouth Music, as you call it, nevertheless served to fix those rules in the memory."

"But all that is changed now!" said Euphranor;

"Nominative and Accusative are turned into Subjective and Objective, and what not."

"Darkening the unintelligible to Boys," said I, "whatever it may afterwards to men. 'Floreat Etona!' say I, with her old Lily, and 'Propria quæ maribus,' always providing there be not too much of it—even could it be construed, like the Alphabet, into Gingerbread."

"Well," said Euphranor, "I think you took pretty good care that we should not suffer an indigestion of the latter, when you were among us at home, Doctor. What with mounting that Bean-stalk yourself, and clearing us out of the Schoolroom into the Garden, wet or dry, regardless of Aunt's screaming from the window for us to come in, when a Cloud was coming up in the Sky——"

"Or a little dew lying on the Grass."

"Why, I believe you would have a Child's shoes made with holes in them on purpose to let in water, as Locke recommends," said Euphranor, laughing.

"I wouldn't keep him within for having none, whole shoes, or whole clothes—no, nor *any*—only the Police would interfere."

"But the Child catches cold."

"Put him to bed and dose him."

"But he dies."

"Then, as a sensible woman said, 'is provided for.' Your own Plato, I think, says it is better the weakly ones should die at once; and the Spartans, I think, kill'd them off."

"Come, come, Doctor," said Euphranor. "I really think you gave us colds on purpose to be called in to cure them."

"No, no; that was before I was a Doctor, you know. But I doubt that I was the Lord of Mis-rule sometimes, though, by the way, I am certain that I sometimes recommended a remedy, not when you were sick, but when you were sorry—without a cause—I mean, obstinate, or self-willed against the little Discipline you had to submit to."

Euphranor looked comically at me.

"Yes," said I, "you know—a slap on that part where the Rod is to be applied in after years—and which I had, not long before, suffered myself."

"*That* is almost out of date now, along with other Spartan severities even in Criminal cases," said Euphranor.

"Yes, and the more the pity in both cases. How much better in the Child's than being shut up, or additionally tasked—revenging a temporary wrong with a lasting injury. And, as for your public Criminal—my wonder is that even modern squeamishness does not see that a public application of the Rod or Lash on the bare back in the Market-place would be more likely to daunt the Culprit, and all Beholders, from future Misdemeanour than months of imprisonment, well-boarded, lodged, and cared for, at the Country's cost."

"Nevertheless," said Euphranor, "I do not remember your Advice being taken in our case, much as I, for one, may have deserved it."

"No," said I; "your Father was gone, you know, and your Mother too tender-hearted—indulgent, I might say."

"Which, with all your Spartan discipline, I know you think the better extreme," said Euphranor.

"Oh, far the better!" said I—"letting the *Truth* come to the surface—the ugliest Truth better than the fairest Falsehood which Fear naturally brings with it, and all the better for determining outwardly, as we Doctors say, than repressed to rankle within. Why, even without fear of spank or Rod, you remember how your Wordsworth's little

Harry was taught the practice of Lying, who, simply being teased with well-meaning questions as to *why* he liked one place better than another, caught at a Weather-cock for a reason *why*. Your mother was wiser than that. I dare say she did not bother you about the meaning of the Catechism she taught you, provided you generally understood that you were to keep your hands from picking and stealing, and your tongue from evil-speaking, lying, and slandering. She did not insist, as Skythrops would have had you, on your owning yourselves Children of the Devil."

"No, no!"

"I should not even wonder if, staunch Churchwoman as she was, she did not condemn you to go more than once of a Sunday to Church—perhaps not to be shut up for two hours' morning Service in a Pew, without being allowed to go to sleep there; nor tease you about Text and Sermon afterward. For, if she had, you would not, I believe, have been the determined Churchman you are."

"Ah, I remember so well," said Euphranor, "her telling a stricter neighbour of ours that, for all she saw, the Child generally grew up with clean opposite inclinations and ways of thinking, from the Parent."

"Yes," said I, "that is the way from Parent to Child, and from Generation to Generation; and so the World goes round."

"And we—Brothers and Sister, I mean"—said Euphranor, "now catch ourselves constantly saying how right she was in the few things we ever thought her mistaken about. God bless her!"

He took a long pull at his glass, and was silent some little while—she had died a few years ago—and then he said:

"However, even she began in time to find 'the Boys too much for her,' as she said—for which you, Doctor, as you say, are partly accountable; besides, we should have our livelihood to earn, unlike your born Heroes; and must begin to work sooner rather than later. Our Friend Sky-throps' *ipse* had already warned her of our innate, and steadily growing, Depravity, and, when I was seven or eight years old, came to propose taking me under his wing, at what he called his 'Seminary for young Gentlemen.'"

"I see him," said I, "coming up the shrubbery walk in a white tie, and with a face of determined asperity—the edge of the Axe now turned *toward* the Criminal. Aye, I was gone away to Edinburgh by that time; indeed I think he waited till I was well out of the way. Well, what did he say?"

"Oh, he explained his scheme, whatever it was——"

"And—oh, I can tell you—some eight or ten hours a day of Grammar and Arithmetic, Globes, History, and as Dickens says, 'General Christianity'; and, by way of Recreation, two hours' daily walk with himself and his sallow Pupils, two and two along the High-road, improved with a running commentary by Skythrops—with perhaps a little gymnastic gallows in his gravel Play-ground, with-out room or time for any generous exercise. Your Mother, I hope, gave him a biscuit and a glass of Sherry, and, with all due thanks, let him go back the way he came."

"His Plan does not please you, Doctor?"

"And if it did—and it only wanted reversing—*he* would not. No Boy with any Blood in his veins can profit from a Teacher trying to graft from dead wood upon the living sapling. Even the poor Women's '*Preparatory Establish-ments*' for 'Young Gentlemen' are better; however narrow their notions and routine, they do not at heart dislike a little of the Devil in the other sex, however intolerant of him in their own."

"Well, we were committed to neither," said Euphranor,

"but to a nice young Fellow who came to be Curate in the Parish, and who taught us at home, little but well—among other things—a little Cricket."

"Bravo!" said I.

"Then Uncle James, you know, hearing that I was rather of a studious turn—'serious,' he called it—took it into his head that one of his Brother's family should be a Parson, and so undertook to pay my way at Westminster, which he thought an aristocratic School, and handy for him in the City. In which, perhaps, you do not disagree with him, Doctor?"

"No," said I; "though not bred up at any of them myself, I must confess I love the great ancient, Royal, aye, and aristocratic Foundations—Eton with her 'Henry's holy Shade'—why, Gray's verses were enough to endear it to me—and under the walls of his Royal Castle, all reflected in the water of old Father Thames, as he glides down the valley; and Winchester with her William of Wykeham entomb'd in the Cathedral he built beside his School—"

"And *West*minster, if you please, Doctor, under the Shadow of its glorious old Abbey, where Kings are crown'd and buried, and with Eton's own River flowing beside it in ampler proportions."

"Though not so sweet," said I. "However, excepting that fouler water—and fouler air—and some other less wholesome associations inseparable from such a City, I am quite ready to pray for your Westminster among those other 'Royal and Religious Foundations' whom the Preacher invites us to pray for at St. Mary's. But with Eton we began, you know, looking with Charles Lamb and his Friend at the fine Lads there playing; and there I will leave them to enjoy it while they may, 'strangers yet to Pain'—and Parliament—to sublime their Beefsteak into Chivalry in

that famous Cricket-field of theirs by the side of old Father
Thames murmuring of so many Generations of chivalric
Ancestors."

"We must call down Lycion to return thanks for *that*
compliment," said Euphranor; "he is an Eton man, as
were his Fathers before him, you know, and, I think, proud,
as your Etonians are, of his School, in spite of his affected
Indifference."

"Do you know what sort of a Lad he was while there?"
said I.

"Oh, always the Gentleman."

"Perhaps somewhat too much so for a Boy."

"No, no, I do not mean that—I mean essentially
honourable, truthful, and not deficient in courage, I be-
lieve, whenever it was called for; but indolent, and perhaps
fonder too of the last new Novel, and the Cigar and Easy-
chair, to exert himself in the way you like."

"Preparing for the Club, Opera, Opera-glass, '*Déjeuner
dansant*,' etcetera, if not for active service in Parliament.
Eton should provide for those indolent Children of hers."

"Well, she has provided her field, and old Father Thames,
as you say, and Boys are supposed to take pretty good care
of themselves in making use of them."

"Not always, however, as we see in Lycion's case, nor
of others, who, if they do not 'sacrifice the Living Man to
the Dead Languages,' dissipate him among the Fine Arts,
Music, Poetry, Painting, and the like, in the interval. Why,
did not those very Greeks of whom you make so much—
and, as I believe, your modern Germans—make Gymnastic
a necessary part of their education?"

"But you would not have Eton Boys compelled to climb
and tumble like monkeys over gymnastic poles and gallows
as we saw with Skythrops' 'Young Gentlemen'?"

"Perhaps not; but what do you say now to some good
Military Drill, with March, Counter-march, Encounter,
Bivouac 'Wacht am Rhein'—Encampment—that is, by
Father Thames—and such-like Exercises for which Eton
has ample room, and which no less a Man—although a
Poet—than John Milton, enjoin'd as the proper preparation
for War, and, *I* say, carrying along with them a sense of
Order, Self-restraint, and Mutual Dependence, no less
necessary in all the relations of Peace?"

"We might all of us have been the better for that, I
suppose," said Euphranor.

"And only think," said I, "if—as in some German
School—Fellenberg's, I think—there were, beside the Play-
ground, a piece of Arable to *work in*—perhaps at a daily
wage of provender according to the work done—what illumin-
ation might some young Lycion receive, as to the condition
of the Poor, 'unquenchable by logic and statistics,' says
Carlyle, 'when he comes, as Duke of Logwood, to legislate
in Parliament.'"

"Better Log than Brute, however," answer'd Euphranor.
"You must beware, Doctor, lest with all your Ploughing
and other Beef-compelling Accomplishments you do not
sink the Man in the Animal, as was much the case with our
'Hereditary Rulers' of some hundred years ago."

"'Μηδὲν ἄγαν,'" said I; "let us but lay in—when only
laid in it can be—such a store of that same well-concocted
stuff as shall last us all Life's journey through, with all its
ups and downs. Nothing, say the Hunters, that Blood and
Bone won't get over."

"Be there a good Rider to guide him!" said Euphranor ;
"and *that*, in Man's case, I take it is—if not yet the Reason
we talked of—a Moral such as no Beast that breathes is
conscious of. You talk of this Animal virtue, and that—

why, for instance, is there not a *moral*, as distinguisht from an *animal* Courage, to face, not only the sudden danger of the field, but something far-off coming, far foreseen, and far more terrible—Cranmer's, for instance——"

"Which," said I, "had all but failed—all the more honour for triumphing at last! But Hugh Latimer, I think, had wrought along with his Father's hinds in Leicestershire. Anyhow, there is no harm in having two strings to your Bow, whichever of them be the strongest. The immortal Soul, obliged, as she is, to take the Field of Mortality, would not be the worse for being mounted on a good Animal, though I must not say with the Hunters, till the Rider seems 'part of his horse.' As to your Reason—he is apt to *crane* a little too much over the hedge, as they say, till, by too long considering the '*How*,' he comes to question the '*Why*,' and, the longer looking, the less liking, shirks it altogether, or by his Indecision brings Horse and Rider into the Ditch. Hamlet lets us into the secret—luckily for us enacting the very moral he descants on—when he reflects on his own imbecility of action :

> "'Whether it be
> Bestial oblivion, or some craven scruple
> Of thinking too precisely on the Event,
> A thought which, quarter'd, hath but one part Wisdom,
> And ever three parts Coward—I do not know
> Why yet I live to say, '*This thing's to do*,'
> Sith I have Cause, and Will, and Strength, and Means,
> To do't.'

Not in his case surely '*oblivion*,' with such reminders, supernatural and other, as he had : nor as in our case, with the Ditch before our Eyes : nor want of Courage, which was his Royal inheritance ; but the *Will*, which he reckon'd on as surely as on Strength and Means—was he so sure of *that?* He had previously told us how 'The native hue of Resolution'—how like that glow upon the cheek of healthy Youth !—

"'The native hue of Resolution
Is sicklied o'er with the pale cast of Thought,
And Enterprizes of great pith and moment
With this regard their currents turn awry,
And lose the name of Action.'

He had, he tells his College Friends, foregone his '*Custom of Exercises*'—among others, perhaps, his Cricket, at Wittenberg too soon, and taken to reasoning about 'To be, or not to be'—otherwise he would surely have bowl'd his wicked uncle down at once."

"Though not without calling 'Play !' I hope," said Euphranor, laughing.

"At any rate, not while his Adversary's back was turned, and so far prepared, inasmuch as he was engaged in repentant Prayer. And that is the reason Hamlet gives for not then despatching him, lest, being so employ'd, he should escape the future punishment of his crime. An odd motive for the youthful Moral to have *reasoned* itself into."

"His Father had been cut off unprepared, and perhaps, according to the Moral of those days, could only be avenged by such a plenary Expiation."

"Perhaps ; or, perhaps—and Shakespeare himself may not have known exactly why—Hamlet only made it an excuse for delaying what he had to do, as delay he does, till vengeance seems beyond his reach when he suffers himself to be sent out of the country. For you know the *Habit* of Resolving without Doing, as in the Closet, gradually snaps the connexion between them, and the case becomes chronically hopeless."

Euphranor said that I had stolen that fine Moral of

mine from a Volume of "Newman's Sermons" which he had lent me, as I agreed with him was probably the case; and then he said:

"Well, Bowling down a King is, I suppose, a ticklish Business, and the Bowler may miss his aim by being too long about taking it: but, in Cricket proper, I have most wonder'd at the Batter who has to decide whether to block, strike, or tip, in that twinkling of an eye between the ball's delivery, and its arrival at his wicket."

"Yes," said I, "and the Boxer who puts in a blow with one hand at the same moment of warding one off with the other."

"'Gladiatorem in arenâ,'" said Euphranor.

"Yes; what is called '*Presence of mind*,' where there is no time to '*make it up*.' And all the more necessary and remarkable in proportion to the Danger involved. As when the Hunter's horse falling with him in full cry, he braces himself, between saddle and ground, to pitch clear of his horse—as Fielding tells us that brave old Parson Adams did, when probably thinking less of his horse than of those Sermons he carried in his saddle-bags."

"Ah!" said Euphranor, "Parson Adams was so far a lucky man to have a Horse at all, which we poor fellows now can hardly afford. I remember how I used to envy those who—for the fun, if for nothing else—followed brave old Sedgwick across country, through brier, through mire. Ah! *that* was a Lecture after your own heart, Doctor; something more than peripatetic, and from one with plenty of the Boy in him when over Seventy, I believe."

"Well, there again," said I, "your great Schools might condescend to take another hint from abroad where some one—Fellenberg again, I think—had a Riding-house in his much poorer School, where you might learn not only to sit

your horse if ever able to provide one for yourself, but also
to saddle, bridle, rub him down, with the *ss'ss-s'ss'* which I
fancy was heard on the morning of Agincourt—if, by the
way, one horse was left in all the host."

"Well, come," said Euphranor, "the Gladiator, at any
rate, is gone—and the Boxer after him—and the Hunter,
I think, going after both; perhaps the very Horse he rides
gradually to be put away by Steam into some Museum
among the extinct Species that Man has no longer room or
business for."

"Nevertheless," said I, "War is *not* gone with the
Gladiator, and cannon and rifle yet leave room for hand-to-
hand conflict, as may one day—which God forbid!—come
to proof in our own sea-girt Island. If safe from abroad,
some Ruffian may still assault you in some shady lane—
nay, in your own parlour—at home, when you have nothing
but your own strong arm, and ready soul to direct it.
Accidents will happen in the best-regulated families. The
House will take fire, the Coach will break down, the Boat
will upset;—is there no gentleman who can swim, to save
himself and others? no one do more to save the Maid
snoring in the garret, than helplessly looking on—or turning
away? Some one is taken ill at midnight; John is drunk in
bed; is there no Gentleman can saddle Dobbin—much
less get a Collar over his Head, or the Crupper over his tail,
without such awkwardness as brings on his abdomen the
kick he fears, and spoils him for the journey? And I do
maintain," I continued, "having now gotten 'the bit be-
tween my teeth'—maintain against all Comers that, inde-
pendent of any bodily action on their part, these, and the
like Accomplishments, as you call them, do carry with them,
and, I will say, with the Soul incorporate, that habitual
Instinct of Courage, Resolution, and Decision, which, to-

gether with the Good Humour which good animal Condition goes so far to ensure, do, I say, prepare and arm the Man not only against the greater, but against those minor Trials of Life which are so far harder to encounter because of perpetually cropping up; and thus do cause him to radiate, if through a narrow circle, yet, through that, imperceptibly to the whole world, a happier atmosphere about him than could be inspired by Closet-loads of Poetry, Metaphysic, and Divinity. No doubt there is danger, as you say, of the Animal overpowering the Rational, as, I maintain, equally so of the reverse; no doubt the high-mettled Colt will be likeliest to run riot, as may my Lad, inflamed with Aristotle's 'Wine of Youth,' into excesses which even the virtuous Berkeley says are the more curable as lying in the Passions; whereas, says he, 'the dry Rogue who sets up for Judgment is incorrigible.' . But, whatever be the result, VIGOUR, of Body, as of Spirit, one must have, subject like all good things to the worst corruption—Strength itself, even of Evil, being a kind of *Virtus* which Time, if not good Counsel, is pretty sure to moderate; whereas Weakness is the one radical and Incurable Evil, increasing with every year of Life.—Which fine Moral, or to that effect, you will also find somewhere in those Sermons, whose Authority I know you cannot doubt."

"And thus," said Euphranor, "after this long tirade, you turn out the young Knight from Cricket on the World."

"Nay," said I, "did I not tell you from the first I would not meddle with your Digby any more than your Wordsworth? I have only been talking of ordinary mankind so as to provide for Locke's '*totus, teres,*' and—except in the matter of waistband—'*rotundus*' man, sufficiently accoutred for the campaign of ordinary Life. And yet, on second

thought, I do not see why he should not do very fairly well
for one of the 'Table round,' if King Arthur himself is to be
looked for, and found, as the Poet says, in the 'Modern
Gentleman,' whose 'stateliest port' will not be due to the
Reading-desk or Easy-chair.   At any rate, he will be suffi-
ciently qualified, not only to shoot the Pheasant and hunt
the Fox, but even to sit on the Bench of Magistrates—or
even of Parliament—not unprovided with a quotation or
two from Horace or Virgil."

Euphranor could not deny that, laughing.

"Or if obliged, poor fellow—Younger son, perhaps—to
do something to earn him Bread—or Claret—for his Old
Age, if not prematurely knocked on the head—whether not
well-qualified for Soldier or Sailor?"

"Nor that."

"As for the Church, (which is your other Gentlemanly
Profession,) you know your Bishop can consecrate Tom or
Blifil equally by that Imposition——"

"Doctor, Doctor," broke in Euphranor, "you have been
talking very well; don't spoil it by one of your grimaces."

"Well, well," said I,—"Oh, but there is still THE LAW,
in which I would rather trust myself with Tom than Blifil,"
added I.   "Well, what else?   Surgery?   which is said to
need 'the Lion's Heart.'"

"But also the Lady's Hand," replied he, smiling.

"Not in drawing one of the Molares, I assure you.
However, thus far I do not seem to have indisposed him
for the Professions which his Rank usually opens to him;
or perhaps even, if he had what you call a Genius in any
direction, might, amid all his Beef-compelling Exercises,
light upon something, as Pan a-hunting, and, as it were
'unaware,' says Bacon, discover'd that Ceres whom the
more seriously-searching Gods had looked for in vain."

"Not for the sake of *Rent*, I hope," said Euphranor, laughing.

"Or even a turn for looking into Digby and Aristotle, as into a Mirror—could he but distinguish his own face in it."

Euphranor, upon whose face no sign of any such self-consciousness appeared, sat for a little while silent, and then said :

"Do you remember that fine passage in Aristophanes' Clouds—lying libel as it is—between the Δίκαιος and Ἄδικος Λόγος?"

"I had forgotten," I said, "my little Latin and less Greek:" and he declared I must however read this scene over again with him. "It is, you see, Old Athens pleading against Young; whom after denouncing, for relinquishing the hardy Discipline and simple severe Exercises that reared the Μαρα-θωνομάχους Ἄνδρας, for the Warm Bath, the Dance, and the Law Court; he suddenly turns to the Young Man who stands hesitating between them, and in those Verses, musical—

’Αλλ’ οὖν λιπαρός γε καὶ εὐανθής—"

"Come, my good fellow," said I, "you must interpret." And Euphranor, looking down, in undertone repeated :

"O listen to me, and so shall you be stout-hearted and fresh as a Daisy:
Not ready to chatter on every matter, nor bent over books till you're hazy:
No splitter of straws, no dab at the Laws, making black seem white so cunning:
But scamp'ring down out o' the town, and over the green Meadow running.
Race, wrestle, and play with your fellows so gay, like so many Birds of a feather,

All breathing of Youth, Good-humour, and Truth, in the time
    of the jolly Spring weather,
In the jolly Spring-time, when the Poplar and Lime dishe-
    vel their tresses together."

"Well, but go on," said I, when he stopp'd, "I am sure
there is something more of it, now you recall the passage to
me—about broad shoulders and——"

But this was all he had cared to remember.

I then asked him who was the translator; to which he
replied with a shy smile, 'twas more a paraphrase than a
translation, and I might criticize it as I liked. To which I
had not much to object, I said—perhaps the trees "dishe-
velling their tresses" a little Cockney; which he agreed it
was *. And then, turning off, observed how the degradation
which Aristophanes satirized in the Athenian youth went on
and on, so that, when Rome came to help Greece against
Philip of Macedon, the Athenians, says Livy, could con-
tribute little to the common cause but declamation and
despatches—'quibus solum valent.'

"Aye," said I, "and to think that when Livy was so
writing of Athens, his own Rome was just beginning to go
downhill in the same way and for the same causes: when,
says Horace, the Boy of gentle blood, adept enough at feats
of trivial dexterity, had no seat on the Horse, nor courage to
follow the Hounds: unlike those early times, when Heroic
Father begot and bred Heroic Son; Generation following
Generation, crown'd with Laurel and with Oak; under a

---

* On a subsequent reference to the original, We expanded the
last line into the following Couplet—whether for better or worse:

Until with a cool reed drawn from the pool of a neighbouring
    Water-nymph crown'd, you
Lie stretcht at your ease in the shade of the trees that whisper
    above and around you.

system of Education, the same Livy says, handed down, as it were an Art, from the very foundation of Rome, and filling her Parliament with Generals, each equal, he rhetorically declares, to Alexander.—But come, my dear fellow," said I, jumping up, "here have I been holding forth like a little Socrates, while the day is passing over our heads. We have forgotten poor Lexilogus, who (I should not wonder) may have stolen away, like your fox, to Cambridge."

Euphranor, who seemed to linger yet awhile, nevertheless follow'd my example. On looking at my watch I saw we could not take anything like the walk we had proposed and yet be at home by their College dinner* ; so as it was I who had wasted the day, I would stand the expense, I said, of dinner at the Inn : after which we could all return at our ease to Cambridge in the Evening. As we were leaving the Bowling-Green, I called up to Lycion, who thereupon appeared at the Billiard-room window with his coat off, and asked him if he had nearly finish'd his Game. By way of answer, he asked us if we had done with our Ogres and Giants ; whom, on the contrary, I said, we were now running away from that we might live to fight another day—would he come with us into the fields for a walk? or, if he meant to go on with his Billiards, would he dine with us on our return? "Not walk with us," he said ; and when I spoke of dinner again, seemed rather to hesitate ; but at last said, "Very well ;" and, nodding to us, retired with his cue into the room.

Then Euphranor and I, leaving the necessary orders within, return'd a little way to look for Lexilogus, whom we soon saw, like a man of honour as he was, coming on his way to meet us. In less than a minute we had met ; and

* Then at 3.30 p.m.

he apologized for having been delay'd by one of Aunt Martha's asthma-fits, during which he had not liked to leave her.

After a brief condolence, we all three turn'd back; and I told him how, after all, Euphranor and I had play'd no Billiards, but had been arguing all the time about Digby and his books.

Lexilogus smiled, but made no remark, being naturally little given to Speech. But the day was delightful, and we walk'd briskly along the road, conversing on many topics, till a little further on we got into the fields. These—for it had been a warm May—were now almost in their Prime, (and that of the Year, Crabbe used to say, fell with the mowing,) crop-thick with Daisy, Clover, and Buttercup; and, as we went along, Euphranor, whose thoughts still ran on what we had been talking about, quoted from Chaucer whom we had lately been looking at together:

> "'Embrouded was he as it were a Mede,
> Alle ful of fresshe Floures, white and rede,'"

and added, "What a picture was that, by the way, of a young Knight!"

I had half-forgotten the passage, and Lexilogus had never read Chaucer: so I begg'd Euphranor to repeat it; which he did, with an occasional pause in his Memory, and jog from mine.

> "'With him ther was his Sone, a yonge Squier,
> A Lover, and a lusty Bacheler,
> With Lockes crull, as they were laide in presse;
> Of Twenty yere of age he was, I gesse;
> Of his Stature he was of even lengthe,
> And wonderly deliver, and grete of Strengthe;
> And he hadde be somtime in Chevachie,
> In Flaundres, in Artois, and in Picardie,

And borne him wel, as of so litel space,
In hope to stonden in his Ladies grace.
Embrouded was he as it were a Mede,
Alle ful of fresshe Floures, white and rede;
Singing he was, or floyting alle the day;
He was as fresshe as is the moneth of May:
Short was his Goune, with sleves long and wide,
Wel coude he sitte on Hors, and fayre ride;
He coude Songes make, and well endite,
Juste, and eke dance, and wel pourtraie and write.
So hote he loved, that by nightertale
He slep no more than doth the Nightingale.
Curteis he was, lowly, and servisable,
And carf before his Fader at the table.'

"Chaucer, however," said Euphranor, when he had finished the passage, "credited his young Squire with other Accomplishments than you would trust him with, Doctor. See, he dances, draws, and even indites songs—somewhat of a Dilettante, after all."

"But also," I added, "is of 'grete Strengthe,' 'coude fayre ride,' having already 'borne him wel in Chevachie.' Besides," continued I, (who had not yet subsided, I suppose, from the long swell of my former sententiousness,) "in those days, you know, there was scarce any Reading, which now, for better or worse, occupies so much of our time; Men left that to Clerk and Schoolman; contented, as we before agreed, to follow their bidding to Pilgrimage and Holy war. Some of those gentler Accomplishments may then have been needed to soften manners, just as rougher ones to strengthen ours. And, long after that, Sir Philip Sidney might well indulge in a little Sonneteering, amid all those public services which ended at Zutfen; as later on, in the Stuart days, Lord Dorset troll off—' *To all you Ladies now on Land*,' from the Fleet that was just going into Action off the coast of Holland."

"Even Master Samuel Pepys," said Euphranor, laughing, "might sit with a good grace down to practise his '*Beauty retire*,' after riding to Huntingdon and back, as might Parson Adams have done many years after."

"They were both prefigured among those Canterbury Pilgrims so many years before," said I. "Only think of it! Some nine-and-twenty, I think, 'by aventure yfalle in feleweship,' High and Low, Rich and Poor, Saint and Sinner, Cleric and Lay, Knight, Ploughman, Prioress, Wife of Bath, Shipman, hunting Abbot-like Monk, Poor Parson—(Adams' Progenitor)—Webster (Pepys')—on rough-riding 'Stot' or ambling Palfrey, marshall'd by mine Host of the Tabard to the music of the Miller's Bag-pipes, on their sacred errand to St. Thomas'; and one among them taking note of all in Verse still fresh as the air of those Kentish hills they travelled over on that April morning four hundred years ago."

"Lydgate too, I remember," said Euphranor, "tells of Chaucer's good-humour'd encouragement of his Brother-poets—I cannot now recollect the lines," he added, after pausing a little*.

"A famous Man of Business too," said I, "employ'd by Princes at home and abroad. And ready to fight as to write; having, he says, when some City people had accused

---

* The verses Euphranor could not remember are these :

"For Chaucer that my Master was, and knew
    What did belong to writing Verse and Prose,
Ne'er stumbled at small faults, nor yet did view
    With scornful eyes the works and books of those
That in his time did write, nor yet would taunt
At any man, to fear him or to daunt."

him of Untruth, 'prepared his body for Mars his doing, if any contraried his saws.'"

"A Poet after your own heart, Doctor, sound in wind and limb, Mind and Body. In general, however, they are said to be a sickly, irritable, inactive, and solitary race."

"Not our 'Canterbury Pilgrim' for one," said I; "no, nor his successor, William Shakespeare, who, after a somewhat roving Knighthood in the country, became a Player, Play-wright, and Play-manager in London, where, after managing (as not all managers do) to make a sufficient fortune, he returned home again to settle in his native Stratford—whither by the way he had made occasional Pilgrimages before—on horseback, of course—putting up— for the night—at the Angel of Oxford—about which some stories are told——"

"As fabulous as probably those of his poaching in earlier days," said Euphranor.

"Well, however that may be—and I constantly believe in the poaching part of the Story—to Stratford he finally retired, where he built a house, and planted Mulberries, and kept company with John-a-Combe, and the neighbouring Knights and Squires—except perhaps the Lucys—as merrily as with the Wits of London; all the while supplying his own little 'Globe'—and, from it, 'the Great globe itself,' with certain manuscripts, in which (say his Fellow-players and first Editors) Head and hand went so easily together as scarce to leave a blot on the pages they travell'd over."

."Somewhat resembling Sir Walter Scott's, I think," said Euphranor, "in that love for Country home, and Country neighbour—aye, and somewhat also in that easy intercourse between Head and hand in composition which those who knew them tell of—however unequal in the result. Do you

F. 4

remember Lockhart's saying how glibly Sir Walter's pen was heard to canter over the paper, before 'Atra Cura' saddled herself behind him?"

"Ah, yes," said I; "'Magician of the North' they call'd him in my own boyish days; and such he is to me now; though maybe not an Archi-magus like him of Stratford, to set me down in Rome, Athens, Egypt, with their Heroes, Heroines, and Commoners, moving and talking as living men and women about me, howsoever 'larger than human' through the breath of Imagination in which he has clothed them."

"Somebody—your Carlyle, I believe," said Euphranor, "lays it down that Sir Walter's Characters are in general fashioned from without to within—the reverse of Shakespeare's way—and Nature's."

"What," said I, "according to old Sartor's theory, beginning from the over-coat of temporary Circumstance, through the temporary Tailor's 'Just-au-corps,' till arriving at such centre of Humanity as may lie within the bodily jerkin we talk'd of?"

"Something of that sort, I suppose," said Euphranor; "but an you love me, Doctor, no more of that odious old jerkin, whether Sterne's or Carlyle's."

"Well," said I, "if the Sartor's charge hold good, it must lie against the Heroes and Heroines of the later, half-historical, Romances; in which, nevertheless, are scenes where our Elizabeth, and James, and Lewis of France figure, that seem to me as good in Character and Circumstance as any in that Henry the Eighth, which has always till quite lately been accepted for Shakespeare's. But Sartor's self will hardly maintain his charge against the Deanses, Dumbiedykes, Ochiltrees, Baillies, and others of the bonâ-fide *Scotch* Novels, with the likes of whom Scott

fell 'in feleweship' from a Boy, riding about the country—
'born to be a trooper,' he said of himself; no, nor with the
Bradwardines, Balfours, Maccombicks, Macbriars, and others,
Highlander, Lowlander, Royalist, Roundhead, Churchman,
or Covenanter, whom he animated with the true Scottish
blood which ran in himself as well as in those he lived
among, and so peopled those Stories which are become
Household History to us. I declare that I scarce know
whether Macbeth's blasted heath would move me more
than did the first sight of the Lammermoor Hills when I
rounded the Scottish coast on first going to Edinburgh; or
of that ancient 'Heart of Mid-Lothian' when I got there.
But the domestic Tragedy naturally comes more nearly
home to the bosom of your Philistine."

"Sir Walter's stately neighbour across the Tweed," said
Euphranor, "took no great account of his Novels, and none
at all of his Verse—though, by the way, he did call him
'Great Minstrel of the Border' after revisiting Yarrow in
his company; perhaps he meant it only of the Minstrelsy
which Scott collected, you know."

"Wordsworth?" said I—"a man of the Milton rather
than of the Chaucer and Shakespeare type—without humour,
like the rest of his Brethren of the Lake."

"Not but he loves Chaucer as much as you can, Doctor,
for those fresh touches of Nature, and tenderness of Heart—
insomuch that he has re-cast the Jew of Lincoln's Story into
a form more available for modern readers."

"And successfully?"

"Ask Lexilogus—Ah! I forget that he never read Chaucer;
but I know that he loves Wordsworth next to his own Cowper."

Lexilogus believed that he liked the Poem in question,
but he was not so familiar with it as with many other of
Wordsworth's pieces.

4—2

"Ah, you and I, Euphranor," said I, "must one day teach Lexilogus the original before he is become too great a Don to heed such matters."

Lexilogus smiled, and Euphranor said that before that time came Lexilogus and he would teach me in return to love Wordsworth more than I did—or pretended to do. Not only the Poet, but the Man, he said, who loved his Home as well as Shakespeare and Scott loved theirs—aye, and his Country Neighbours too, though perhaps in a sedater way; and, as so many of his Poems show, as sensible as Sir Walter of the sterling virtues of the Mountaineers and Dalesmen he lived among, though, maybe, not of their humour.

"Was he not also pretty exact in his office of stamp-distributor among them?" asked I.

"Come, you must not quarrel, Doctor, with the Business which, as with Chaucer and Shakespeare, may have kept the Poetic Element in due proportion with the rest—including, by the way, such a store of your Animal, laid in from constant climbing the mountain, and skating on the lake, that he may still be seen, I am told, at near upon Eighty, travelling with the shadow of the cloud up Helvellyn."

"Bravo, Old Man of the Mountains!" said I. "But, nevertheless, it would not have been amiss with him had he been sent earlier, and further, from his mountain-mother's lap, and had some of his—conceit, I must not call it— Pride, then—taken out of him by a freer intercourse with men."

"I suppose," said Euphranor, again laughing, "you would knock a young Apollo about like the rest of us common pottery?"

"I think I *should* send young Wordsworth to that Military Drill of ours, and see if some rough-riding would not draw some of that dangerous Sensibility which 'young Edwin' is apt to mistake for poetical Genius."

"Gray had more than that in him, I know," said Euphranor; "but I doubt what might have become of his poetry had such been the discipline of his Eton day."

"Perhaps something better—perhaps nothing at all— and *he* the happier man."

"But not *you*, Doctor—for the loss of his Elegy—with all your talk."

"No; I am always remembering, and always forgetting it; remembering, I mean, the several stanzas, and forgetting how they link together; partly, perhaps, because of each being so severally elaborated. Neither Yeomanry Drill— nor daily Plough—drove the Muse out of Burns."

"Nor the Melancholy neither, for that matter," said Euphranor. "Those 'Banks and braes' of his could not bestow on him even the 'momentary joy' which those Eton fields 'beloved in vain' breathed into the heart of Gray."

"Are you not forgetting," said I, "that Burns was not then singing of himself, but of some forsaken damsel, as appears by the second stanza? which few, by the way, care to remember. As unremember'd it may have been," I continued, after a pause, "by the only living—and like to live—Poet I had known, when, so many years after, he found himself beside that 'bonnie Doon' and—whether it were from recollection of poor Burns, or of 'the days that are no more' which haunt us all, I know not—I think he did not know—but, he somehow 'broke' as he told me, 'broke into a passion of tears.'—Of tears, which during a pretty long and intimate intercourse, I had never seen glisten in his eye but once, when reading Virgil—'dear old Virgil,' as he call'd him—together: and then of the burning of Troy in the Second Æneid—whether moved by the catastrophe's

self, or the majesty of the Verse it is told in—or, as before,
scarce knowing why. For, as King Arthur shall bear
witness, no young Edwin he, though, as a great Poet, com-
prehending all the softer stops of human Emotion in that
Register where the Intellectual, no less than what is call'd
the Poetical, faculty predominated. As all who knew him
know, a Man at all points, Euphranor—like your Digby, of
grand proportion and feature, significant of that inward
Chivalry, becoming his ancient and honourable race; when
himself a 'Yongé Squire,' like him in Chaucer 'of grete
strength,' that could hurl the crow-bar further than any of
the neighbouring clowns, whose humours, as well as of
their betters,—Knight, Squire, Landlord and Land-tenant,—
he took quiet note of, like Chaucer himself. Like your
Wordsworth on the Mountain, he too, when a Lad, abroad
on the Wold; sometimes of a night with the Shepherd;
watching not only the Flock on the greensward, but also

> "'The fleecy Star that bears
> Andromeda far off Atlantic seas'

along with those other Zodiacal constellations which Aries,.
I think, leads over the field of Heaven. He then observed
also some of those uncertain phenomena of Night: unsur-
mised apparitions of the Northern Aurora, by some shy
glimpses of which no winter—no, nor even summer—night,.
he said, was utterly unvisited; and those strange voices,
whether of creeping brook, or copses muttering to them-
selves far off—perhaps the yet more impossible Sea—to-
gether with 'other sounds we know not whence they come,'
says Crabbe, but all inaudible to the ear of Day. He was
not then, I suppose, unless the Word spontaneously came
upon him, thinking how to turn what he saw and heard into
Verse; a premeditation that is very likely to defeat itself,.

previously breathing, as it were, upon the mirror which is to
receive the Image that most assuredly flashes Reality into
words." *

Something to this effect I said, though, were it but for
lack of walking breath, at no so long-winded a stretch of
eloquence. And then Euphranor, whose lungs were in so
much better order than mine, though I had left him so
little opportunity for using them, took up where I left off,
and partly read, and partly told us of a delightful passage
from his Godefridus, to this effect, that, if the Poet could
not invent, neither could his Reader understand him, when
he told of Ulysses and Diomed listening to the crane clang-
ing in the marsh by night, without having *experienced* some-
thing of the sort. And so we went on, partly in jest, partly
in earnest, drawing Philosophers of all kinds into the same
net in which we had entangled the Poet and his Critic—
How the Moralist who worked alone in his closet was apt to
mismeasure Humanity, and be very angry when the cloth
he cut out for him would not fit—how the best Histories
were written by those who themselves had been actors in
them—Gibbon, one of the next best, I believe, recording
how the discipline of the Hampshire Militia he served as
Captain in—how odd he must have looked in the uniform!—
enlighten'd him as to the evolutions of a Roman Legion—
And so on a great deal more; till, suddenly observing how
the sun had declined from his meridian, I look'd at my
watch, and ask'd my companions did not they begin to feel
hungry, like myself? They agreed with me; and we turn'd

---

* The sentence originally stood thus:
" For is not what we call *Poetry* said to be an inspiration, which,
if not kindling at the sudden collision, or recollection, of Reality, will
yet less be quicken'd by anticipation, howsoever it may be controll'd
by after-thought?"

homeward : and as Lexilogus had hitherto borne so little part in the conversation, I began to question him about Herodotus and Strabo, (whose books I had seen lying open upon his table,) and drew from him some information about the courses of the Nile and the Danube, and the Geography of the Old World : till, all of a sudden, our conversation skipt from Olympus, I think, to the hills of Yorkshire—our own old hills—and the old friends and neighbours who dwelt among them. And as we were thus talking, we heard what seemed to us the galloping of Horses behind us, (for we were now again upon the road,) and, looking back as they were just coming up, I recognised Phidippus for one of the riders, with two others whom I did not know. I held up my hand, and call'd out to him as he was passing ; and Phidippus, drawing up his Horse all snorting and agitated with her arrested course, wheel'd back and came alongside of us.

I ask'd him what he was about, galloping along the road ; I thought scientific men were more tender of their horses' legs and feet. But the roads, he said, were quite soft with the late rains ; and they were only trying each other's speed for a mile or so.

By this time his two companions had pulled up some way forward, and were calling him to come on ; but he said, laughing, " they had quite enough of it," and address'd him-self with many a " Steady !" and " So ! So !" to pacify Miss Middleton, as he called her, who still caper'd, plung'd, and snatch'd at her bridle ; his friends shouting louder and louder—" Why the Devil he didn't come on ? "

He waved his hand to them in return ; and with a " Confound " and " Deuce take the Fellow," they set off away toward the town. On which Miss Middleton began afresh, plunging, and blowing out a peony nostril after her flying fellows; until, what with their dwindling in distance, and some expostulation address'd to her by her Master as to a fractious Child, she seem'd to make up her mind to the indignity, and composed herself to go pretty quietly beside us.

I then asked him did he not remember Lexilogus,—(Euphranor he had already recognised,)—and Phidippus, who really had not hitherto seen who it was, (Lexilogus looking shyly down all the while,) call'd out heartily to him, and wheeling his mare suddenly behind us, took hold of his hand, and began to inquire about his family in Yorkshire.

"One would suppose," said I, "you two fellows had not met for years."

"It was true," Phidippus said, "they did not meet as often as he wish'd; but Lexilogus would not come to his rooms, and he did not like to disturb Lexilogus at his books; and so the time went on."

I then inquired about his own reading, which, though not much, was not utterly neglected, it seemed; and he said he had meant to ask one of us to beat something into his stupid head this summer in Yorkshire.

Lexilogus, I knew, meant to stop at Cambridge all the long Vacation; but Euphranor said he should be at home, for anything he then knew, and they could talk the matter over when the time came. We then again fell to talking of our County; and among other things I asked Phidippus if his horse were Yorkshire,—of old famous for its breed, as well as of Riders,—and how long he had had her, and so forth.

Yorkshire she was, a present from his Father, "and a great pet," he said, bending down his head, which Miss Middleton answered by a dip of hers, shaking the bit in her mouth, and breaking into a little canter, which however was easily suppress'd.

"Miss Middleton?" said I—"what, by Bay Middleton out of Coquette, by Tomboy out of High-Life Below-Stairs, right up to Mahomet and his Mares?"

"Right," he answered, laughing, "as far as Bay Middleton was concerned."

"But, Phidippus," said I, "she's as black as a coal!"

"And so was her Dam, a Yorkshire Mare," he answered; which, I said, saved the credit of all parties. Might she perhaps be descended from our famous "Yorkshire Jenny," renowned in Newmarket Verse? But Phidippus had never heard of "Yorkshire Jenny," nor of the Ballad, which I promised to acquaint him with, if he would stop on his way back, and dine with us at Chesterton, where his Mare might have her Dinner too—all of us Yorkshiremen except Lycion, whom he knew a little of. There was to be a Boat-race, however, in the evening, which Phidippus said he must leave us to attend, if dine with us he did; for though not one of the Crew on this occasion, (not being one of the best,) he must yet see his own Trinity keep the head of the River. As to that, I said, we were all bound the same way, which indeed Euphranor had proposed before; and so the whole affair was settled.

As we went along, I began questioning him concerning some of those Equestrian difficulties which Euphranor and I had been talking of: all which Phidippus thought was only my usual banter—"he was no Judge—I must ask older hands," and so forth—until we reach'd the Inn, when I begg'd Euphranor to order dinner at once, while I and Lexilogus accompanied Phidippus to the Stable. There, after giving his mare in charge to the hostler with due directions as to her toilet and table, he took off her saddle and bridle himself, and adjusted the head-stall. Then, follow'd out of the stable by her flaming eye and pointed ears, he too pausing a moment on the threshold to ask me, "was she not a Beauty?" (for he persisted in the delusion of my knowing more of the matter than I chose to confess,) we cross'd over into the house.

There, having wash'd our hands and faces, we went up into the Billiard-room, where we found Euphranor and Lycion playing,—Lycion very lazily, like a man who had already too much of it, but yet nothing better to do. After a short while, the girl came to tell us all was ready; and, after that slight hesitation as to precedence which Englishmen rarely forget on the least ceremonious occasions,— Lexilogus, in particular, pausing timidly at the door, and Euphranor pushing him gently forward,—we got down to the little Parlour, very airy and pleasant, with its windows opening on the bowling-green, the table laid with a clean white cloth, and upon that a dish of smoking beef-steak, at which I, as master of the Feast, and, as Euphranor slyly intimated, otherwise entitled, sat down to officiate. For some time the clatter of knife and fork, and the pouring of ale, went on, mix'd with some conversation among the young men about College matters : till Lycion began to tell us of a gay Ball he had lately been at, and of the Families there ; among whom he named three young Ladies from a neighbouring County, by far the handsomest women present, he said.

"And very accomplish'd too, I am told," said Euphranor.

"Oh, as for that," replied Lycion, "they *Valse* very well." He hated "your accomplished women," he said.

"Well, there," said Euphranor, "I suppose the Doctor will agree with you."

I said, that certainly *Valsing* would be no great use to me personally—unless, as some Lady of equal size and greater rank had said, I could meet with a concave partner.

"One knows so exactly," said Lycion, "what the Doctor would choose,—a woman

> "'Well versed in the Arts
>   Of Pies, Puddings, and Tarts,'

as one used to read of somewhere, I remember."

"Not forgetting," said I, "the being able to help in compounding a pill or a plaister; which I dare say your Great-grandmother knew something about, Lycion, for in those days, you know, Great ladies studied Simples. Well, so I am fitted,—as Lycion is to be with one who can *Valse* through life with him."

> "'And follow so the ever-rolling Year
>   With profitable labour to their graves,'"

added Euphranor, laughing.

"I don't want to marry her," said Lycion testily.

"Then Euphranor," said I, "will advertise for a 'Strong-minded' Female, able to read Plato with him, and Wordsworth, and Digby, and become a Mother of Heroes. As to Phidippus there is no doubt—Diana Vernon—"

But Phidippus disclaimed any taste for Sporting ladies.

"Well, come," said I, passing round a bottle of sherry I had just call'd for, "every man to his liking, only all of you taking care to secure the accomplishments of Health and Good-humour."

"Ah! there it is, out at last!" cried Euphranor, clapping his hands; "I knew the Doctor would choose for us as Frederick for his Grenadiers."

"So you may accommodate me," said I, "with a motto from another old Song whenever my time comes;

> "'Give Isaac the Nymph who no beauty can boast,
>   But Health and Good-humour to make her his toast.'

Well, every man to his fancy—Here's to mine!—And when we have finish'd the bottle, which seems about equal to one more errand round the table, we will adjourn, if you like, to the Bowling-green, which Euphranor will tell us was the goodly custom of our Forefathers, and I can recommend as a very wholesome after-dinner exercise."

"Not, however, till we have the Doctor's famous Ballad about Miss Middleton's possible Great-Great-Grandmother," cried Euphranor, "by way of Pindaric close to this Heroic entertainment, sung from the Chair, who probably composed it——"

"As little as could sing it," I assured him.

"Oh, I remember, it was the Jockey who rode her!"

"Perhaps only his Helper," answered I; such bad grammar, and rhyme, and altogether want of what your man—how do you call him—G. O. E. T. H. E.—'Gewty,' will that do?—calls, I believe, *Art.*"

"Who nevertheless once declares," said Euphranor, "that the Ballad was scarcely possible but to those who simply saw with their Eyes, heard with their Ears—and, I really think he said, fought with their fists,—I suppose also felt with their hearts—without any notion of '*Art*'—although Goethe himself, Schiller, and Rückert, and other of your æsthetic Germans, Doctor, have latterly done best in that line, I believe."

"Better than Cowper's 'Royal George,'" said I, "where every word of the narrative *tells*, as from a Seaman's lips?"

"*That* is something before our time, Doctor."

"Better then than some of Campbell's which follow'd it? or some of Sir Walter's? or 'The Lord of Burleigh,' which is later than all? But enough that my poor Jock may chance to sing of his Mare as well as Shenstone of his Strephon and Delia."

"Or more modern Bards of Cocles in the Tiber, or
Regulus in the Tub," said Euphranor.—"But come! Song
from the Chair!" he call'd out, tapping his glass on the
table, which Phidippus echoed with his.

So with a prelusive "Well then," I began—

"'I'll sing you a Song, and a merry, merry Song'—
By the way, Phidippus, what an odd notion of merriment is
a Jockey's, if this Song be a sample.   I think I have ob-
served they have grave, taciturn faces, especially when old,
which they soon get to look.   Is this from much wasting, to
carry little Flesh—and large—Responsibility?"

"Doctor, Doctor, leave your—faces, and begin!" inter-
rupted Euphranor.   "I must call the Chair to Order."

Thus admonish'd, with some slight interpolations, (to
be jump'd by the Æsthetic,) I repeated the poor Ballad
which, dropt I know not how nor when into my ear, had
managed, as others we had talk'd of, to chink itself in some
corner of a memory that should have been occupied with
other professional jargon than a "Jockey's."

I.

"I'll sing you a Song, and a merry, merry Song,
    Concerning our Yorkshire Jen;
Who never yet ran with Horse or Mare,
    That ever she cared for a pin.

II.

When first she came to Newmarket town,
    The Sportsmen all view'd her around;
All the cry was, 'Alas, poor wench,
    Thou never can run this ground!'

III.

When they came to the starting-post,
    The Mare look'd very smart;
And let them all say what they will,
    She never lost her start—

—which I don't quite understand, by the way: do you, Lycion?"—No answer.

IV.

"When they got to the Two-mile post,
　　Poor Jenny was cast behind·:
She was cast behind, she was cast behind,
　　All for to take her wind.

V.

When they got to the Three-mile post,
The mare look'd very pale—

(Phidippus!"—His knee moved under the table—)

"SHE TAID DOWN HER EARS ON HER BONNY NECK,
AND BY THEM ALL DID SHE SAIL;

VI.　　(*Accelerando.*)

'Come follow me, come follow me,
　　All you who run so neat;
And ere that you catch me again,
　　I'll make you well to sweat.'

VII.　　(*Grandioso.*)

When she got to the Winning-post,
　　The people all gave a shout:
And Jenny click'd up her Lily-white foot,
　　And jump'd like any Buck.

VIII.

The Jockey said to her, 'This race you have run,
　　This race for me you have got;
You could gallop it all over again,
　　When the rest could hardly trot!'

"They were Four-mile Heats in those days, you see, would pose your modern Middletons, though Miss Jenny, laying back her ears—away from catching the Wind, some think—and otherwise '*pale*,' with the distended vein and starting sinew of that Three-mile crisis, nevertheless on coming triumphantly in, click'd up that lily-white foot of hers, (of which *one*, I have heard say, is as good a sign, as all four white are a bad,) and could, as the Jockey thought, have gallop'd it all over again—Can't you see him, Phidippus, for once forgetful of his professional stoicism, (but I don't think Jockeys were quite so politic then,) bending forward to pat the bonny Neck that measured the Victory, as he rides her slowly back to the—*Weighing-house*, is it—? follow'd by the scarlet-coated Horsemen and shouting People of those days?—all silent, and pass'd away for ever now, unless from the memory of one pursy Doctor, who, were she but alive, would hardly know Jenny's head from her tail— And now will you have any more wine?" said I, holding up the empty decanter.

Phidippus, hastily finishing his glass, jump'd up; and, the others following him with more or less alacrity, we all sallied forth on the Bowling-green. As soon as there, Lycion of course pull'd out his Cigar-case, (which he had eyed, I saw, with really good-humoured resignation during the Ballad,) and offer'd it all round, telling Phidippus he could recommend the contents as some of Pontet's best. But Phidippus did not smoke, he said; which, together with his declining to bet on the Boat-race, caused Lycion, I thought, to look on him with some indulgence.

And now Jack was rolled upon the green; and I bowl'd after him first, pretty well; then Euphranor still better; then Lycion, with great indifference, and indifferent success; then Phidippus, who about rivall'd me; and last of all, Lexilogus, whom Phidippus had been instructing in the mystery of the bias with some little side-rolls along the turf, and who, he said, only wanted a little practice to play as well as the best of us.

Meanwhile, the shadows lengthen'd along the grass, and

after several bouts of play, Phidippus, who had to ride round by Cambridge, said he must be off in time to see his friends start. We should soon follow, I said; and Euphranor asked him to his rooms after the race. But Phidippus was engaged to sup with his crew.

"Where you will all be drunk," said I.

"No; there," said he, "you are quite mistaken, Doctor."

"Well, well," I said, "away, then, to your race and your supper."

"Μετὰ σώφρονος ἡλικιώτου," added Euphranor, smiling.

"Μετὰ, 'with,' or 'after,'" said Phidippus, putting on his gloves.

"Well, go on, Sir," said I,—"Σώφρονος?"

"A temperate—something or other—"

"'Ηλικιώτου?"

"Supper?"—he hesitated, smiling—"'After a temperate supper?'"

"Go down, Sir; go down this instant!" I roar'd out to him as he ran from the bowling-green. And in a few minutes we heard his mare's feet shuffling over the stable threshold, and directly afterwards breaking into a retreating canter beyond.

Shortly after this, the rest of us agreed it was time to be gone. We walk'd along the fields by the Church, (purposely to ask about the sick Lady by the way,) cross'd the Ferry, and mingled with the crowd upon the opposite shore; Townsmen and Gownsmen, with the tassell'd Fellow-commoner sprinkled here and there—Reading men and Sporting men—Fellows, and even Masters of Colleges, not indifferent to the prowess of their respective Crews—all these, conversing on all sorts of topics, from the slang in *Bell's Life* to the last new German Revelation, and moving in ever-changing groups down the shore of the river, at whose

F. 5

farther bend was a little knot of Ladies gathered up on a green knoll faced and illuminated by the beams of the setting sun. Beyond which point was at length heard some indistinct shouting, which gradually increased, until "They are off—they are coming!" suspended other conversation among ourselves; and suddenly the head of the first boat turn'd the corner; and then another close upon it; and then a third; the crews pulling with all their might compacted into perfect rhythm; and the crowd on shore turning round to follow along with them, waving hats and caps, and cheering, "Bravo, St John's!" "Go it, Trinity!"—the high crest and blowing forelock of Phidippus's mare, and he himself shouting encouragement to his crew, conspicuous over all—until, the boats reaching us, we also were caught up in the returning tide of spectators, and hurried back toward the goal; where we arrived just in time to see the Ensign of Trinity lowered from its pride of place, and the Eagle of St John's soaring there instead. Then, waiting a little while to hear how the winner had won, and the loser lost, and watching Phidippus engaged in eager conversation with his defeated brethren, I took Euphranor and Lexilogus under either arm, (Lycion having got into better company elsewhere,) and walk'd home with them across the meadow leading to the town, whither the dusky troops of Gownsmen with all their confused voices seem'd as it were evaporating in the twilight, while a Nightingale began to be heard among the flowering Chestnuts of Jesus.

SIX DRAMAS

OF

CALDERON.

ADVERTISEMENT.

In apologizing for the publication of so free translations of so famous a poet as Calderon, I must plead, first, that I have not meddled with any of his more famous plays; not one of those on my list being mentioned with any praise, or included in any selection that I know of, except the homely Mayor of Zalamea. Four of these six indeed, as many others in Calderon, may be lookt on as a better kind of what we call melodramas. Such plays as the *Magico Prodigioso* and the *Vida es Sueño* (I cannot rank the *Principe Constante* among them) require another translator, and, I think, form of translation.

Secondly, I do not believe an exact translation of this poet can be very successful; retaining so much that, whether real or dramatic Spanish passion, is still bombast to English ears, and confounds otherwise distinct outlines of character; Conceits that were a fashion of the day; or idioms that, true and intelligible to one nation, check the current of sympathy in others to which they are unfamiliar; violations of the probable, nay *possible*, that shock even healthy romantic licence; repetitions of thoughts and images that Calderon used (and smiled at) as so much stage properties—so much, in short, that is not Calderon's own better self, but concession to private haste or public taste by one who so often

relied upon some striking dramatic crisis for success with a
not very accurate audience, and who, for whatever reason,
was ever averse from any of his dramas being printed.

Choosing therefore such less famous plays as still seemed
to me suited to English taste, and to that form of verse in
which our dramatic passion prefers to run, I have, while
faithfully trying to retain what was fine and efficient, sunk,
reduced, altered, and replaced, much that seemed not;
simplified some perplexities, and curtailed or omitted scenes
that seemed to mar the breadth of general effect, supplying
such omissions by some lines of after-narrative; and in
some measure have tried to compensate for the fulness of
sonorous Spanish, which Saxon English at least must forego,
by a compression which has its own charm to Saxon ears.

That this, if proper to be done at all, might be better
done by others, I do not doubt. Nay, on looking back over
these pages, I see where in some cases the Spanish indi-
viduality might better have been retained, and northern
idiom spared; and doubtless there are many inaccuracies I
am not yet aware of. But if these plays prove interesting
to the English reader, I and he may be very sure that,
whatever of Spain and Calderon be lost, there must be a
good deal retained; and I think he should excuse the licence
of my version till some other interests him as well at less
expense of fidelity.

I hope my *Graciosos* will not be blamed for occasional
anachronisms not uncharacteristic of their vocation.

THE

PAINTER OF HIS OWN DISHONOUR.

DRAMATIS PERSONÆ.

FEDERIGO,	*Prince of Orsino.*
CELIO,	*his Friend.*
DON LUIS,	*Governor of Naples.*
PORCIA,	*his Daughter.*
ALVARO,	*his Son.*
FABIO,	
BELARDO,	*their Servants.*
JULIA,	
DON JUAN ROCA.	
SERAFINA,	*his Wife.*
DON PEDRO,	*his Father-in-law.*
LEONELO,	*their Servants.*
FLORA,	

MASKERS, MUSICIANS, SAILORS, &c.

PAINTER OF HIS OWN DISHONOUR.

ACT I.

SCENE I. *A Room in* DON LUIS' *palace at Naples.—Enter*
DON LUIS *and* DON JUAN *meeting.*

Luis. Once more, a thousand times once more, Don Juan,
Come to my heart.
   Juan.   And every fresh embrace
Rivet our ancient friendship faster yet!
   Luis. Amen to that! Come, let me look at you—
Why, you seem well—
   Juan.   So well, so young, so nimble,
I will not try to say how well, so much
My words and your conception must fall short
Of my full satisfaction.
   Luis.   How glad am I
To have you back in Naples!
   Juan.   Ah, Don Luis,
Happier so much than when I last was here,
Nay, than I ever thought that I could be.
   Luis. How so?

Juan.   Why, when I came this way before,
I told you (do you not remember it?)
How teased I was by relatives and friends
To marry—little then disposed to love—
Marriage perhaps the last thing in my thoughts—
Liking to spend the spring time of my youth
In lonely study.
     Luis.   Ay, ay, I remember:
Nothing but books, books, books—still day and night
Nothing but books; or, fairly drowsed by them,
By way of respite to that melancholy,
The palette and the pencil—
In which you got to such a mastery
As smote the senseless canvas into life.
O, I remember all—not only, Juan,
When you were here, but I with you in Spain,
What fights we had about it!
     Juan.   So it was—
However, partly wearied, partly moved
By pity at my friends' anxieties,
Who press'd upon me what a shame it were
If such a title and estate as mine
Should lack a lineal inheritor,
At length I yielded—
Fanned from the embers of my later years
A passion which had slept in those of youth,
And took to wife my cousin Serafina,
The daughter of Don Pedro Castellano.
     Luis. I know; you showed me when you last were here
The portrait of your wife that was to be,
And I congratulated you.
     Juan.   Well now
Still more congratulate me—as much more

As she is fairer than the miniature
We both enamoured of. At the first glance
I knew myself no more myself, but hers,
Another (and how much a happier!) man.

 Luis. Had I the thousand tongues, and those of brass,
That Homer wished for, they should utter all
Congratulation. Witty too, I hear,
As beautiful?

 Juan. Yourself shall judge of all,
For even now my lady comes; awhile
To walk the Flora of your shores, and then
Over your seas float Venus-like away.

 Luis. Not *that*, till she have graced our gardens long,
If once we get her here. But is she here?

 Juan. Close by—she and her father, who would needs
See her abroad; and I push'd on before
To apprize you of our numbers—so much more
Than when I first proposed to be your guest,
That I entreat you—

 Luis. What?

 Juan.   —to let us go,
And find our inn at once—not over-load
Your house.

 Luis. Don Juan, you do me an affront—
What if all Naples came along with you?—
My heart—yes, and my house—should welcome them.

 Juan. I know. But yet—

 Luis. But yet, no more "but yets"—
Come to my house, or else my heart shall close
Its doors upon you.

 Juan. Nay, I dare not peril
A friendship—

 Luis. Why, were't not a great affront

To such a friendship—when you learn besides,
I have but held this government till now
Only to do you such a courtesy.

Juan. But how is this?

Luis.   Sickness and age on-coming,
I had determined to retire on what
Estate I had—no need of other wealth—
Beside, Alvaro's death—my only son—

Juan. Nay, you have so felicitated me,
I needs must *you*, Don Luis, whose last letter
Told of a gleam of hope in that dark quarter.

Luis. A sickly gleam—you know the ship he sail'd in
Was by another vessel, just escaped
The selfsame storm, seen to go down—it seem'd
With all her souls on board.

Juan.   But how assured
'Twas your son's ship?—

Luis.   Alas, so many friends
Were on the watch for him at Barcelona,
Whither his ship was bound, but never came—
Beside the very messenger that brought
The gleam of hope, premised the tragedy—
A little piece of wreck,
That floated to the coast of Spain, and thence
Sent to my hands, with these words scratcht upon't—
" *Escaped alive, Alvaro.* "

Juan.   When was this?

Luis. Oh, months ago, and since no tidings heard,
In spite of all inquiry. But we will hope.
Meanwhile, Serafina—when will she be here?

Juan. She must be close to Naples now.

Luis.   Go then,
Tell her from me—

I go not forth to bid her welcome, only
That I may make that welcome sure at home.
   Juan. I'll tell her so. But—
   Luis.   What! another "*But*"?
No more of that. Away with you.—Porcia! [*Exit* JUAN.

Enter PORCIA.

Daughter, you know (I have repeated it
A thousand times, I think) the obligation ··
I owe Don Juan Roca.
   Porcia.   Sir, indeed
I've often heard you talk of him.
   Luis.   Then listen.
He and his wife are coming here to-day—
Directly.
   Por. Serafina!
   Luis.   Yes.
To be our guests, till they set sail for Spain;
I trust long first—
   Por.   And I. How glad I am!
   Luis. You! what should make you glad?
   Por.   That Serafina,
So long my playmate, shall be now my guest.
   Luis. Ay! I forgot—that's well, too—
Let us be rivals in their entertainment.
See that the servants, Porcia, dress their rooms
As speedily and handsomely as may be.
   Por. What haste can do (which brings its own excuse)
I'll do—'tis long a proverb hereabout
That you are Entertainer-general,
Rather than Governor, of Naples.
   Luis.   Ay,
I like to honour all who come this way.

Enter LEONELO.

Leonelo. Peace to this house!—and not only that, but
a story beside.—A company of soldiers coming to a certain
village, a fellow of the place calls out for *two* to be billeted
on him. "What!" says a neighbour, "you want a double
share of what every one else tries to shirk altogether?"
"Yes," says he, "for the more nuisance they are while they
stay, the more glad one is of their going." In illustration of
which, and also of my master's orders, I crave your Lord-
ship's hand, and your Ladyship's foot, to kiss.

Luis. Welcome, good Leonelo. I was afraid I had over-
looked you in receiving your master.

Por. And how does marriage agree with you, Leonelo?

Leon. One gentleman asked another to dine: but such
an ill-ordered dinner that the capon was cold, and the wine
hot. Finding which, the guest dips a leg of the capon into
the wine. And when his host asks him what he's about—
"Only making the wine heat the capon, and the capon cool
the wine," says he. Now just this happened in my marriage.
My wife was rather too young, and I rather too old; so, as
it is hoped—

Por. Foolery, foolery, always!—tell me how Serafina is—

Leon. In a coach.

Por. What answer is that?

Leon. A very sufficient one—since a coach includes hap-
piness, pride, and (a modern author says) respectability.

Por. How so?

Leon. Why, a certain lady died lately, and for some rea-
son or other, they got leave to carry her to the grave in
a coach. Directly they got her in,—the body, I mean,—it
began to fidget—and when they called out to the coachman
—"Drive to St Sepulchre's!"—"No!" screams she,—"I

won't go there yet.   Drive to the Prado first; and when I
have had a turn there, they may bury me where they
please."

Luis. How can you let your tongue run on so!

Leon. I'll tell you.   A certain man in Barcelona had five
or six children : and he gave them each to eat—

(*Voices within.*)   "Way there ! way !"

Por. They are coming.

Leon. And in so doing, take that story out of my mouth.

Enter JULIA.

Julia. Signor, your guests are just alighting.

Luis. Come, Porcia—

Leon. (No, no, stop you and listen to me about those
dear children.)

Por. They are coming upstairs—at the door—

Enter DON JUAN *leading* SERAFINA, DON PEDRO, *and* FLORA—*all in travelling dress.*

Luis. Your hand, fair Serafina, whose bright eyes
Seem to have drawn his lustre from the sun,
To fill my house withal ;—a poor receptacle
Of such a visitor.

Por.   Nay, 'tis for me
To blush for that, in quality of hostess ;
Yet, though you come to shame my house-keeping,
Thrice welcome, Serafina.

Serafina.   How answer both,
Being too poor in compliment for either !
I'll not attempt it.

Pedro.   I am vext, Don Luis,
My son-in-law should put this burden on you.

Luis. Nay, vex not me by saying so.—What burden ?

The having such an honour as to be
Your servant?—

    Leon.   Here's a dish of compliments!

    Flora. Better than you can feed your mistress with.

                          (*Guns heard without.*)

    Juan. What guns are those?

Enter FABIO.

    Fabio.   The citadel, my lord,
Makes signal of two galleys in full sail
Coming to port.

    Luis.   More guests! the more the merrier!

    Ped. The merrier for them, but scarce for you,
Don Luis.

    Luis.   Nay, good fortune comes like bad,
All of a heap. What think you, should it be,
As I suspect it is, the Prince Orsino
Returning; whom, in love and duty bound,
I shall receive and welcome—

    Juan.   Once again,
Don Luis, give me leave—

    Luis.   And once again.
And once for all, I shall *not* give you leave.
Prithee, no more—
All will be easily arranged. Porcia,
You know your guest's apartments—show her thither:
I'll soon be back with you.

    Ped.   Permit us, sir,
To attend you to the port, and wait upon
His Highness.

    Luis.   I dare not refuse that trouble,
Seeing what honour in the prince's eyes
Your company will lend me.

Leon. And methinks
I will go with you too.
Juan. What, for that purpose?
Leon. Yes—and because perhaps among the crowd ·
I shall find some to whom I may relate
That story of the children and their meat.

[*Exeunt* DON LUIS, PEDRO, JUAN, LEONELO, FABIO, &c.

Ser. Porcia, are they gone?
Por. They are.
Ser. Then I may weep.
Por. Tears, Serafina!
Ser. Nay, they would not stay
Longer unshed. I would not if I could
Hide them from you, Porcia. Why should I,
Who know too well the fount from which they flow?
Por. I only know you weep—no more than that.
Ser. Yet 'tis the seeing you again, again
Unlocks them—is it that you do resent
The discontinuance of our early love,
And that you *will* not understand me?
Por. Nay,—
What can I say!
Ser. Let us be *quite* alone.
Por. Julia, leave us.
Ser. Flora, go with her.
Julia. Come, shall we go up to the gallery,
And see the ships come in?
Flora. Madame, so please you.

[*Exeunt* FLORA *and* JULIA.

Ser. Well, are we *quite* alone?
Por. Yes, quite.
Ser. All gone,
And none to overhear us?

F. 6

Por.   None.

Ser.   Porcia,

You knew me once when I was happy!

Por.   Yes,

Or thought you so—

Ser.   But now most miserable!

Por. How so, my Serafina?

Ser.   You shall hear.

Yes, my Porcia, you remember it,—

That happy, happy time when you and I

Were so united that, our hearts attun'd

To perfect unison, one might believe

That but one soul within two bodies lodg'd.

This you remember?

Por.   Oh, how could I forget!

Ser. Think it not strange that so far back I trace

The first beginnings of *another* love,

Whose last sigh having now to breathe, whose last

Farewell to sigh, and whose deceased hopes

In one last obsequy to commemorate,

I tell it over to you point by point

From first to last—by such full utterance

My pent up soul perchance may find relief.

Por. Speak, Serafina.

Ser.   You have not forgot

Neither, how that close intimacy of ours

Brought with it of necessity some courtesies

Between me and your brother, Don Alvaro—

Whose very name, oh wretched that I am!

Makes memory, like a trodden viper, turn,

And fix a fang in me not sharp enough

To slay at once, but with a lingering death

Infect my life—

Por.　　　Nay, calm yourself.

Ser.　　　　　　We met,
Porcia—and from those idle meetings love
Sprang up between us both—for though 'tis true
That at the first I laugh'd at his advances,
And turn'd his boyish suit into disdain,
Yet true it also is that in my heart
There lurk'd a lingering feeling yet behind,
Which if not wholly love, at least was liking;
In the sweet twilight of whose unris'n sun
My soul as yet walk'd hesitatingly.
For, my Porcia, there is not a woman,
Say what she will, and virtuous as you please,
Who, being lov'd, resents it: and could he
Who most his mistress's disfavour mourns
Look deeply down enough into her heart,
He'd see, however high she carries it,
Some grateful recognition lurking there
Under the muffle of affected scorn.
You know how I repell'd your brother's suit:
How ever when he wrote to me I tore
His letters—would not listen when he spoke—
And when, relying on my love for you,
Through you he tried to whisper his for me,
I quarrell'd with yourself—quarrell'd the more
The more you spoke for him. He wept—I laugh'd;
Knelt in my path—I turn'd another way;
Though who had seen deep down into my heart,
Had also seen love struggling hard with pride.
Enough—at last one evening as I sat
Beside a window looking on the sea,
Wrapt in the gathering night he stole unseen
Beside me. After whispering all those vows

6—2

Of love which lovers use, and I pass by,
He press'd me to be his. Touch'd by the hour,
The mask of scorn fell from my heart, and Love
Reveal'd himself, and from that very time
Grew unconceal'd between us—yet, Porcia,
Upon mine honour, (for I tell thee *all*,)
Always in honour bounded. At that time
In an ill hour my father plann'd a marriage
Between me and Don Juan—yours, you know,
Came here to Naples, whence he sent your brother,
I know not on what business, into Spain;
And we agreed, I mean Alvaro and I,
Rather than vex two fathers at one time
By any declaration of our vows,
'Twere best to keep them secret—at the least,
Till his return from Spain. Ah, Porcia,
When yet did love not thrive by secrecy?
We parted—he relying on my promise,
I on his quick return. Oh, mad are those
Who, knowing that a storm is up, will yet
Put out to sea. Alvaro went—my father
Urged on this marriage with my cousin. Oh!—
   Por. You are ill, Serafina!
   Ser.   Nothing—nothing—
I reason'd—wept—implor'd—excus'd—delay'd—
In vain—O mercy, Heaven!
   Por.   Tell me no more:
It is too much for you.
   Ser.   Then suddenly
We heard that he was dead—your brother—drown'd—
They married me—and now perhaps he lives.
They· say—Porcia, can it be?—I know not
Whether to hope or dread if that be true:—

And every wind that blows your father hope
Makes my blood cold; I know that I shall meet him,
Here or upon the seas—dead or alive—
Methinks I see him now!—Help! help!　　　[*Swoons.*
　Por.　　　　　　　　　　　　Serafina!—
She has fainted!—Julia! Flora!—

Enter ALVARO.

　Alvaro.　.　　　　　　　　My Porcia!
　Por. Alvaro! (*They embrace.*)
　Alv.　　　　I have outrun the shower of compliment
On my escapes—which you shall hear anon—
To catch you to my heart.
　Por.　　　　　　　　Oh joy and terror!
Look there!—
　·*Alv.*　　　　Serafina!
And sleeping too!
　Por.　　　　Oh, swooning! see to her
Till I get help.　　　　　　　　　　[*Exit.*
　Ser. (*in her swoon*). Mercy, mercy!
Alvaro, slay me not!—I am not guilty!—
Indeed I am not!—
　Alv. She dreams—and dreams of me—but very strangely—
Serafina!—
　Ser. (*waking*). Dead!—or return'd alive to curse and
　　slay me!—
But I am innocent!—I could not help—
They told me you were dead—and are you not?—
And I must marry him—
　Alv.　　　　　　Must marry?—whom?—
Why, you are dreaming still—
Awake!—'tis your Alvaro—　　(*Offers to embrace her.*)
　Ser.　　　　　　　No, no, no—

I dare not—
 Alv.   Dare not!

Enter PORCIA, FLORA, JULIA.

Por. Quick, quick!
Flora. My lady!
Julia. My lord alive again!
Alv. Porcia, come hither—I am not alive,
Till I have heard the truth—nay, if't be true
That she has hinted and my heart forebodes,
I shall be worse than dead—   ·

[*Retires with* PORCIA *to back of Stage.*

Enter JUAN *and* PEDRO.

Juan.   What is the matter?—
My Serafina!
Pedro. We have hurried back,
Told of your sudden seizure—What is it?
Ser. The very heart within me turn'd to ice.
Juan. But you are better now?—
Ser.   Yes—better—pray,
Be not uneasy for me.
Alv. (*to* PORCIA *in the rear*). This is true then!
Por. Nay, nay, be not so desperate, Alvaro, ·
Hearing but half the story—no fault of hers—
I'll tell you all anon. Come, Serafina,
I'll see you to your chamber.
Pedro. She will be better soon—
Juan. Lean upon me, my love—so—so.
Alv.   Oh, fury!
Ser. Oh, would to heaven these steps should be my last,
Leading not to my chamber, but my grave!

Por. (*to* ALVARO).   Wait here—compose yourself—I shall·
    be back
Directly.   [*Exeunt* PORCIA, SERAFINA, *and* JUAN.
    Alv.   She is married—broke her troth—
And I escaped from death and slavery
To find her—but the prince !—Oh weariness ! ·

Enter the PRINCE ORSINO, CELIO, DON LUIS, *and Train.*

Prince. Each day, Don Luis, I become your debtor
For some new courtesy.
    Luis.   My lord, 'tis I
Who by such small instalments of my duty
Strive to pay back in part the many favours
You shower upon your servant.   And this last,
Of bringing back Alvaro to my arms,
Not all my life, nor life itself, could pay.
    Prince. Small thanks to me, Don Luis ; but indeed
The strangest chance—two chances—two escapes—
First from the sinking ship upon a spar,
Then from the Algerine who pick'd him up,
Carried him captive off—
He first adroitly through their fingers slipping
That little harbinger of hope to you,
And then, at last, himself escaping back
To Barcelona, where you know I was—
If glad to welcome, house, and entertain
Any distrest Italian, how much more,
Both for his own sake and for yours, your son,
So making him, I trust, a friend for life.
    Alv. Rather a humble follower, my lord.
    Luis. I have no words to-thank you—we shall hear
The whole tale from Alvaro by and by—

To make us merry—once so sad to him.
Meanwhile, Alvaro, thou hast seen thy sister?
  Alv. Yes, sir—
  Luis.   Oh what a joy 'tis to see thee!
  Prince. A day of general joy.
  Alv. (*aside*).   Indeed!—
  Prince.   Especially
To her, Alvaro—
  Alv.   Sir?
  Prince.   I mean your sister.
  Alv. Yes, my lord—no—I am not sure, my lord—
A friend of hers is suddenly so ill,
My sister is uneasy—
  Luis.   Serafina!
Indeed!—I know your Highness will forgive
My seeing to her straight.   [*Exit.*
  Alv.   And I, my lord,
Would fain see some old faces once again
As soon as may be.
  Prince.   Nay, no more excuse—
Follow your pleasure.
  Alv. (*aside*).   'Tis no friend I seek,
But my one deadliest enemy—myself.   [*Exit.*
  Prince. Celio, I think we have well nigh exhausted
The world of compliment, and wasted it:
For I begin to doubt that word and deed
Are wasted all in vain.
  Celio.   How so, my lord?
  Prince. Why, if I never am to see Porcia
Whom I have come so far and fast to see—
  Cel. Never, my lord! her father's guest is ill,
And she for a few minutes—
  Prince.   *Minutes*, Celio!

Knowest thou not minutes are years to lovers?

Cel. I know that lovers are strange animals.

Prince. Ah, you have never loved.

Cel.   No, good my lord,
I'm but a looker-on; or in the market
Just give and take the current coin of love—
Love her that loves me; and, if she forget,
Forget her too.

Prince.   Ah, then I cannot wonder --
You wonder so at my impatience;
For he that cannot love, can be no judge
Of him that does.

Cel.   How so?

Prince.   I'll tell thee, Celio.
He who far off beholds another dancing,
Even one who dances best, and all the time
Hears not the music that he dances to,
Thinks him a madman, apprehending not
The law that rules his else eccentric action.
So he that's in himself insensible
Of love's sweet influence, misjudges him
Who moves according to love's melody:
And knowing not that all these sighs and tears,
Ejaculations, and impatiences,
Are necessary changes of a measure,
Which the divine musician plays, may call
The lover crazy; which he would not do
Did he within his own heart hear the tune
Play'd by the great musician of the world. ⌋

Cel. Well, I might answer, that, far off or near
Hearing or not the melody you tell of,
The man is mad who dances to it. But
Here is your music.

Enter PORCIA.

Porcia. I left my brother here but now.
Prince. ˙But now,
Sweet Porcia, you see he is not here—
By that so seeming earnest search for him
Scarce recognising me, if you would hint
At any seeming slight of mine toward you,
I plead not guilty—
Por. You mistake, my lord—
Did I believe my recognition
Of any moment to your Excellency,
I might perhaps evince it in complaint,
But not in slight.
Prince. Complaint !—
Por. Yes, sir—complaint.
Prince. Complaint of what? I knowing, Porcia,
And you too knowing well, the constant love
That I have borne you since the happy day
When first we met in Naples—
Por. No, my lord—
You mean my love to you, not yours to me—
Unwearied through your long forgetful absence.
Prince. How easily, Porcia, would my love
Prove to you its unchanged integrity,
Were it not that our friends—
Por. Your friends indeed,
Who stop a lame apology at the outset.

Enter SERAFINA.

Serafina. I cannot rest, Porcia, and am come
To seek it in your arms—but who is this?
Por. The Prince Orsino.

Ser.   Pardon me, my lord—
I knew you not—coming so hurriedly,
And in much perturbation.
    Prince.   ·   Nay, lady,
I owe you thanks for an embarrassment
Which hides my own.
    Ser.   Let it excuse beside
What other courtesies I owe your Highness,
But scarce have words to pay.   Heaven guard your High-
    ness—
Suffer me to retire.   [*Exit.*
    Por. I needs must after her, my lord.   But tell me,
When shall I hear your vindication?—
To-night?
    Prince. Ay, my Porcia, if you will.
    Por. Till night farewell, then.   [*Exit.*
    Prince.   Farewell.—Celio,
Didst ever see so fair an apparition,
As her who came and went so suddenly?
    Cel. Indeed, so sweetly mannered when surprised,
She must be exquisite in her composure.
    Prince. Who is she?
    Cel.   Nay, my lord, just come with you,
I know as little—
What! a new tune to dance to?—
    Prince.   In good time,
Here comes Alvaro.

Enter ALVARO.

Alvaro. How restless is the sickness of the soul!
I scarce had got me from this fatal place,
And back again—
    Prince.   Alvaro!

Alv. My lord—

Prince. Who is the lady that was here anon?

Alv. Lady, my lord—what lady?—

Prince. She that went
A moment hence—I mean your sister's guest.

Alv. (This drop was wanting!)
My lord, the daughter of a nobleman
Of very ancient blood—
Don Pedro Castellano.

Prince. And her name?

Alv. Serafina.

Prince. And a most seraphic lady!

Alv. You never saw her, sir, before?

Prince. No, surely.

Alv. (*aside*). Would I had never done so!

Prince. And in the hasty glimpse I had,
I guess her mistress of as fair a mind
As face.

Alv. Yes, sir—

Prince. She lives in Naples, eh?

Alv. No—on her way
To Spain, I think—

Prince. Indeed!—To Spain. Why that?

Alv. (How much more will he ask?)
My lord, her husband—

Prince. She is married then?—

Alv. Torture!

Prince. And who so blest to call her his,
Alvaro?

Alv. Sir, Don Juan Roca, her cousin.

Prince. Roca? Don Juan Roca? Do I know him?

Alv. I think you must; he came, sir, with my father
To wait upon your Grace.

Prince.   Don Juan Roca!
No; I do not remember him—should not
Know him again.

Enter DON LUIS.

Luis.   My lord, if my old love
And service for your Highness may deserve
A favour at your hands—
Prince.   They only wait
Until your tongue has named it.
Luis.   This it is then—
The captain of the galleys, good my lord,
In which your Highness came,
Tells me that, having landed you, he lies
Under strict orders to return again
Within an hour.
Prince.   'Tis true.
Luis.   Now, good my lord,
The ships, when they go back, must carry with them
Some friends who, long time look'd for, just are come,
And whom I fain—
Prince.   Nay, utter not a wish
I know I must unwillingly deny.
Alvaro. Confusion on confusion!
Prince.   I have pledg'd
My word to Don Garcia of Toledo,
The galleys should not pass an hour at Naples.
I feel for you,—and for my self, alas!
So sweet a freight they carry with them. But
I dare not—and what folly to adore
A Beauty lost to me before I found it!
                    [*Exeunt* PRINCE *and* CELIO.
Luis. And those I so had long'd for, to avenge

Their long estrangement by as long a welcome,
Snatcht from me almost ere we'd shaken hands !—
Is not this ill, Alvaro ?
    Alv.   Ill indeed.
    Luis. And, as they needs must go, my hospitality,
Foil'd in its spring, must turn to wound myself
By speeding their departure. (*Going.*)
    Alv.   Sir, a moment.
Although his Highness would not, or could not,
Grant you the boon your services deserv'd,
Let not that, I beseech you, indispose you
From granting one to me.
    Luis.   What is't, Alvaro ?
Twere strange could I refuse you anything.
    Alv. You sent me, sir, on state affairs to Spain,
But being wreckt and captur'd, as you know,
All went undone.
Another opportunity now offers ;
The ships are ready, let me go and do
That which perforce I left undone before.
    Luis. What else could'st thou have askt,
In all the category of my means,
Which I, methinks, had grudg'd thee ! No, Alvaro,
The treacherous sea must not again be trusted
With the dear promise of my only son.
    Alv. Nay, for that very reason, I entreat you
To let me go, sir. Let it not be thought
The blood that I inherited of you
Quail'd at a common danger.
    Luis.   I admire
Your resolution, but you must not go,
At least not now.
Beside, the business you were sent upon

Is done by other hands, or let go by
For ever.
    Alv.   Nay, sir—
    Luis.   Nay, Alvaro.   *[Exit.*
    Alv. He is resolved. And Serafina,
To whose divinity I offered up
My heart of hearts, a purer sacrifice
Than ever yet on pagan altar blaz'd,
Has play'd me false, is married to another,
And now will fly away on winds and seas,
As fleeting as herself.
Then what remains but that I die? My death
The necessary shadow of that marriage !
Comfort !—what boots it looking after that
Which never can be found? The worst is come,
Which 'twere a blind and childish waste of hope
To front with any visage but despair.
Ev'n that one single solace, were there one,
Of ringing my despair into her ears,
Fails me. Time presses ; the accursed breeze
Blows foully fair. The vessel flaps her sails
That is to bear her from me. Look, she comes—
And from before her dawning beauty all
I had to say fades from my swimming brain,
And chokes upon my tongue.

    Enter SERAFINA, *drest as at first, and* PORCIA.

    Porcia. And must we part so quickly?—
    Serafina.   When does happiness
Last longer?
    Alv.   Never !—who best can answer that?
I standing by, why ask it of another?
At least when speaking of such happiness

As, perjur'd woman, thy false presence brings!

Ser. Alvaro, for Heaven's sake spare me the pang
Of these unjust reproaches.

Alv.   What! unjust!

Ser. Why, is it not unjust, condemning one
Without defence?

Alv.   Without defence indeed!

Ser. Not that I have not a most just defence,
But that you will not listen.

Alv.   Serafina,
I listen'd; but what wholly satisfies
The criminal may ill suffice the judge;
And in love's court especially, a word
Has quite a different meaning to the soul
Of speaker and of hearer. Yet once more,
Speak.

Ser. To what purpose? I can but repeat
What I have told your sister, and she you,—
What on the sudden waking from my swoon,
I, who had thought you dead so long, Alvaro,
Spoke in my terror, suddenly seeing you
Alive, before me.

Alv.   I were better, then,
Dead than alive?

Ser.   I know not—were you dead
I might in honour weep for you, Alvaro;
Living, I must not.

Alv.   , Nay then, whether you
Forswear me living or lament me dead,
Now you must hear me; if you strike the wound,
Is it not just that you should hear the cry?

Ser. I must not.

Alv.   But I say you must.

Ser.   Porcia,
Will you not help me when my life and honour
Are thus at stake?
    Alv.   Porcia's duty lies
In keeping watch that no one interrupt us.
    Porcia. Between the two confus'd, I yield at last
To him, both as my brother, Serafina,
And for his love to you. Compose yourself;
I shall be close at hand, no harm can happen.
And let him weep at least who has lost all. .   [*Exit.*
    Ser. If I am forc'd to hear you then, Alvaro,
You shall hear me too, once more, once for all,
Freely confessing that I loved you once;
Ay, long and truly loved you. When all hope
Of being yours with your reported death
Had died, then, yielding to my father's wish,
I wed another, and am—what I am.
So help me Heaven, Alvaro, this is all!
    Alv. How can I answer if you weep?
    Ser.   No, no,
I do not weep, or, if I do, 'tis but
My eyes,—no more, no deeper.
    Alv. Is 't possible you can so readily
Turn warm compassion into cold disdain!
And are your better pulses so controll'd
By a cold heart, that, to enhance the triumph
Over the wretched victim of your eyes,
You make the fount of tears to stop or flow
Just as you please? If so, teach me the trick,
As the last courtesy you will vouchsafe me.
    Ser. Alvaro, when I think of what I was,
My tears will forth; but when of what I am,
My honour bids them cease.

    F.   7

Alv. You *do* feel then—

Ser.   Nay, I'll deny it not.

Alv. That, being another's—

Ser.   Nay, no argument—

Alv. These tears—

Ser.   What tears?

Alv.   Are the relenting rain
On which the Iris of my hope may ride;
Or a sweet dew—

Ser.   Alvaro—

Alv.   That foretells
That better day when in these arms again—

Ser. Those arms! Alvaro, when that day shall come
May heaven's thunder strike me dead at once!

                    (*Cannon within.*)

Mercy, what's that?

                 Enter PORCIA.

Porcia.   A signal from the ship,
'Tis time: your father and Don Juan now
Are coming for you.

Alv.   O heavens!

Por.   Compose yourself,
And you, Alvaro— (*Motions him back.*)

      Enter DON JUAN, LUIS, PEDRO, LEONELO, &c.

Luis. Lady, believe how sadly I am come
To do you this last office.

Juan.   Trembling still?—
But come, perhaps the sea-breeze, in requital
Of bearing us away from those we love,
May yet revive you.

Luis.   Well, if it must be so,
Lady, your hand. Porcia, come with us.

            [*Exeunt all but* ALVARO.

ACT II.

SCENE I. *A room in* DON JUAN'S *house at Barcelona: he is discovered painting* SERAFINA. *It gradually grows dusk.*

Juan. Are you not wearied sitting?
Serafina.   Surely-not
Till you be wearied painting.
  Juan.   Oh, so much
As I have wish'd to have that divine face
Painted, and by myself, I now begin
To wish I had not wish'd it.
  Ser.   But why so?
  Juan. Because I must be worsted in the trial
I have brought on myself.
  Ser.   You to despair,
Who never are outdone but by yourself!
  Juan. Even so.
  Ser.   But *why* so?
  Juan.   Shall I tell you why?
Painters, you know, (just turn your head a little,)
Are nature's apes, whose uglier semblances,
Made up of disproportion and excess,
Like apes, they easily can imitate:
But whose more gracious aspect, the result
Of subtlest symmetries, they only outrage,
Turning true beauty into caricature.
The perfecter her beauty, the more complex
And hard to follow; but her perfection
Impossible.
  Ser.   That I dare say is true,

But surely not in point with me, whose face
Is surely far from perfect. ·
　　Juan.　　　　　　Far indeed
From what is perfect call'd, but far beyond,
Not short of it; so that indeed my reason
Was none at all.
　　Ser.　　　　　Well now then the true reason
Of your disgust.
　　Juan.　　　　Yet scarcely my disgust,
When you continue still the cause of it.
Well then, to take the matter up again—
The object of this act, (pray, look at me,
And do not laugh, Serafina,) is to seize
Those subtlest symmetries that, as I said,
Are subtlest in the loveliest; and though
It has been half the study of my life
To recognise and represent true beauty,
I had not dreamt of such excess of it
As yours; nor can I, when before my eyes,
Take the clear image in my trembling soul;
And therefore if that face of yours exceed
Imagination, and imagination
(As it must do) the pencil; then my picture
Can be but the poor shadow of a shade.
Besides,—
　　Ser.　Can there be any thing besides?
　　Juan. 'Tis said that fire and light, and air and snow,
Cannot be painted; how much less a face
Where they are so distinct, yet so compounded,
As needs must drive the artist to despair!
I'll give it up.—(*Throws away his brushes, &c.*)　The light
　　begins to fail too.
And Serafina, pray remember this,

If, tempted ever by your loveliness,
And fresh presumption that forgets defeat,
I'd have you sit again, allow me not,—
It does but vex me.

   Ser.   Nay, if it do that
I will not, Juan, or let me die for it,—
Come, there's an oath upon't.

   Juan.   A proper curse
On that rebellious face.

Enter LEONELO.

   Leonelo.   And here comes in a story :—
A man got suddenly deaf, and seeing the people about
him moving their lips, quoth he, "What the devil makes
you all dumb?" never thinking for a moment the fault
might be in himself. So it is with you, who lay the blame
on a face that all the world is praising, and not on your
own want of skill to paint it.

   Juan. Not a very apt illustration, Leonelo, as you would
admit if you heard what I was saying before you came in.
But, whose soever the fault, I am the sufferer. I will no
more of it, however. Come, I will abroad.

   Ser. Whither, my lord?

   Juan. Down to the pier, with the sea and the fresh air,
to dispel my vexation.

   Ser. By quitting me?

   Juan. I might indeed say so, since the sight of you is
the perpetual trophy of my defeat. But what if I leave
you in order to return with a double zest?

   Ser. Nay, nay, with no such pretty speeches hope to de-
lude me; I know what it is. The carnival with its fair
masks.

   Juan. A mask abroad when I have that face at home !

Ser. Nay, nay, I know you.

Juan. Better than I do myself?

Ser. What wife does not?

Leon. Just so. A German and the priest of his village coming to high words one day, because the man blew his swine's horn under the priest's window, the priest calls out in a rage, "I'll denounce your horns to the parish, I will!" which the man's wife overhearing in the scullery, she cries out, "Halloa, neighbour, here is the priest revealing my confession!"

Ser. What impertinence, Leonelo!

Leon. Very well then, listen to this; a certain man in Barcelona had five or six children, and one day—

Juan. Peace, foolish fellow.

Leon. Those poor children will never get the meat well into their mouths.

Juan. Farewell, my love, awhile.

　　　　　　　　　　　　[*Exeunt* JUAN *and* LEONELO.

Ser.　　　　　　　　　　　Farewell, my lord.
Thou little wicked Cupid,
I am amused to find how by degrees
The wound your arrows in my bosom made,
And made to run so fast with tears, is healing.
Yea, how those very arrows and the bow
That did such mischief, being snapt asunder—
Thyself art tamed to a good household child.

　　　　　　Enter FLORA, *out of breath.*

Flora. O madam!

Ser. Well, Flora, what now?

Flora. O madam, there is a man down-stairs!

Ser. Well?

Flora. Drest sailor-like.

Ser. Well?

Flora. He will not go away unless I give this letter into your hands.

Ser. Into my hands? from whom?

Flora. From the lady Porcia he says, madam.

Ser. From Porcia, well, and what frightens you?

Flora. Nothing, madam, and yet—

Ser. And yet there is something.

Flora. O, my lady, if this should be Don Alvaro!

Ser. Don Alvaro! what makes you think that?

Flora. I am sure it is he.

Ser. But did you tell him you knew him?

Flora. I could not help, madam, in my surprise.

Ser. And what said he then?

Flora. That I must tell you he was here.

Ser.   Alvaro!—
Flora, go back, tell him you dared not tell me,
Fearful of my rebuke, and say beside,
As of your own advice, that it is fit,
Both for himself and me,
That he depart immediately.

Flora.   Yes, madam.

As she is going, enter ALVARO, *as a Sailor.*

Alvaro. No need. Seeing Don Juan leave his house,
I have made bold to enter, and have heard
What Flora need not to repeat.

Ser.   Nay, sir,
Rather it seems as if you had not heard;
Seeing the most emphatic errand was
To bid you hence.

Alv.   So might it seem perhaps,
Inexorable beauty: but you know

How one delinquency another breeds ;
And having come so far, and thus disguised,
Only to worship at your shrine, Serafina,
(I dare not talk of love,) I do beseech you
Do not so frown at my temerity,
As to reject the homage that it brings.

 Ser. Don Alvaro,
If thus far I have listen'd, think it not
Warrant of further importunity.
I could not help it—'tis with dread and terror
That I have heard thus much ; I now beseech you,
Since you profess you came to honour me,
Show that you did so truly by an act
That shall become your honour well as mine.

 Alv. Speak, Serafina.

 Ser.   Leave me so at once,
And without further parley,
That I may be assured *you* are assured
That lapse of time, my duty as a wife,
My husband's love for me, and mine for him,
My station and my name, all have so changed me,
That winds and waves might sooner overturn
Not the oak only,
But the eternal rock on which it grows,
Than you my heart, though sea and sky themselves
Join'd in the tempest of your sighs and tears.

 Alv. But what if I remember other times
When Serafina was no stubborn oak,
Resisting wind and wave, but a fair flower
That open'd to the sun of early love,
And follow'd him along the golden day :
No barren heartless rock,
But a fair temple in whose sanctuary

Love was the idol, daily and nightly. fed
With sacrifice of one whole human heart.
   Ser. I do not say 'twas not so ;
But, sir, to carry back the metaphor
Your ingenuity has turn'd against me,
That tender flower, transplanted it may be
To other skies and soil, might in good time
Strike down such roots and strengthen such a stem
As were not to be shook : ·the temple, too, _
Though seeming slight to look on, being yet
Of nature's fundamental marble built,
When once that foolish idol was dethroned,
And the true God set up into his place,
Might stand unscathed in sanctity and worship,
For ages and for ages.
   Alv.   Serafina,
Why talk to me of ages, when the account
Of my misfortune and your cruelty
Measures itself by hours, and not by years !
It was but yesterday you loved me, yes,
Loved me, and (let the metaphor run on)
I never will believe it ever was,
Or is, or ever can be possible
That the fair flower so soon forgot the sun
To which so long she owed and turn'd her beauty,
To love the baser mould in which she grew :
Or that the temple could so soon renounce
Her old god, true god too while he was there,
For any cold and sober deity
Which you may venerate, but cannot love,
Newly set up.
   Ser.   I must leave metaphor,
And take to sober sense ; nor is it right,

Alvaro, that you strive
To choke the virtuous present with the past,
Which, when it was the past, was virtuous too,
But would be guilty if reiterate.
Nor is it right, nor courteous, certainly,
Doubting what I declare of my own heart;
Nay, you who do yourself affirm, Alvaro,
How well I loved you when such love was lawful,
Are bound to credit me when I declare
That love is now another's.

Alv.   Serafina—
Juan (*speaking within*).   Light, light, there!

Enter FLORA *hurriedly.*

Flora.   Madam, my lord, my lord.
Alv. Confusion!
Ser.   O ye heavens!
Flora.   The old lover's story.
Brother or husband sure to interrupt.
Juan (*within*). A light there, Flora! Serafina! night
Set in, and not a lamp lit in the house?
Alv. He comes.
Ser.   And I am lost!
Flora.   Quick, Don Alvaro,
Into this closet, till my lord be gone
Into his chamber; in, in, in!
Alv.   My fears
Are all for you, not for myself.   [*Hides in the closet.*
Flora.   In, in!   [*Exit*
Juan (*entering*). How is it there's no light?
Ser.   She had forgot—
But here it comes.

Enter FLORA *with lights.*

'Twas kind of you my lord,—
So quickly back again—
Sooner than I expected.
    Juan.   Yes, a friend
Caught hold of me just as I reach'd the pier,
And told me to get home again.
    Ser. (aside).   My heart !_
    Juan. And wherefore do you think?
    Ser.   Nay, I know not.
    Juan. To tell you of a festival, Serafina,
Preparing in your honour.
    Ser. (aside).   I breathe again.
    Juan. The story's this.   It is the carnival,
You know, and, by a very ancient usage,
To-morrow all the folk of Barcelona,   '
Highest as well as lowest, men and women,
Go abroad mask'd to dance and see the shows.
And you being newly come, they have devised
A dance and banquet for you, to be held
In Don Diego's palace, looking forth
So pleasantly (do you remember it?)
Upon the sea.   And therefore for their sakes,
And mine, my Serafina, you must for once
Eclipse that fair face with the ugly mask;
I'll find you fitting dress,—what say you?
    Ser.   Nay,
What should I say but that your will is mine,
In this as evermore?
And now you speak of dress, there are ev'n now
Some patterns brought me in the nick of time
To choose from, in my chamber; prithee come,

And help me judge.

Juan.   I would that not your robe
Only, but all the ground on which you walk
Were laced with diamond.

Ser.   What not done yet
With compliment? Come—come.   (*She takes. a light.*)

Juan.   But wherefore this?

Ser. My duty is to wait upon you.

Juan.   No.
Take the lamp, Flora.

Ser.   Flora waits on me,
And I on you.

Juan.   What humour's this?
But be it as you will.   [*Exeunt* JUAN *and* SERAFINA.

Flora (*letting out* ALVARO).   Now is the time, Signor Al-
    varo! hist!
The coast is clear, but silently and swiftly—
Follow—but, hush! stop! wait!

Alv.   What now?

Flora.   A moment!
Back, back, 'tis Leonelo.

Alv. Put out the light, I can slip past him.

Flora (*falls putting out light*).   No sooner said than done.
    O Lord, Lord, Lord!

Enter LEONELO.

Leonelo. What is the matter?

Flora. The matter is, I have fallen.

Leon. Into temptation?

Flora. It is well, sir, if I have not broken my leg; here,
sir, cease your gibing, and get this lamp lighted directly.

Leon. (*stumbling over* ALVARO).   Halloa!

Flora. What now?

Leon. I've fallen now, and on your temptation I think, for it has got a beard.

Alv. (*groping his way*).   The fool! but I can find the door.   [*Exit.*

Leon. There goes some one!

Flora. The man's mad!

Leon. Am I? Halloa! halloa, there!

Enter JUAN *with light.*

Juan. What is the matter?

Flora. Nothing, nothing, my lord.

Leon. Nothing? I say it is something, a great—

Flora. My lord, going to shut the door, I stumbled, fell, and put out the light, that's all.

Leon. And I stumbled too.

Juan. Well?

Leon. Over a man.

Juan. In this chamber?

Leon. Yes, and—

Flora. Nonsense! my lord, he stumbled against *me*, as we both floundered in the dark.

Leon. You! What have you done with your beard then?

Juan. Are you mad? or is this some foolery?

Leon. My lord, I swear I stumbled over a fellow here.

Juan (*aside*).   And she so anxious to light me to her chamber! what is all this? Take the lamp, Leonelo. Though partly I think you have been dreaming, I will yet search the house; come with me.   I will draw the sting of suspicion at once, come what come may.

                                        [*Draws sword and exit.*

Flora (*to* LEON.).   All of your work. A murrain on your
     head,
Making this pother.

Leon.   Minx! what is said, is said.

[*Exeunt severally.*

SCENE II.—*The garden of* DON LUIS' *palace at Naples; a
window with a balcony on one side, or in front:—night
Enter the* PRINCE *and* CELIO *muffled up.*

Celio. Still sighing? pardon me, your Highness, but
This melancholy is a riddle to me.

Prince. Ah, Celio, so strange a thing is love,
The sighs you think are melancholy sighs,
Yet are not so; I have indeed drunk poison,
But love the taste of it.

Cel.   I used to think
'Twas all of being away from your Porcia;
But now when better starr'd, her brother absent,
Her father unsuspicious, at her bidding
Night after night you come beneath her lattice,
And yet—

Prince. If Porcia be not the cause
Of my complaint she cannot be the cure:
Yet (such is love's pathology) she serves
To soothe the wound another made.

Cel. Who then was she, my lord, for whose fair sake
You cannot either love this loving lady,
Nor leave her?

Prince.   I would tell you, Celio,
But you would laugh at me.

Cel.   Tell me, however.

Prince. Rememberest not the lady whom we saw
For a few minutes, like some lovely vision,
In this same house a little while ago,

Not Porcia, but her diviner guest?

Cel. Oh, I remember; is it then to be
The speciality of your Highness' love,
That, whereas other men's dies off by absence,
Yours quickens—if it can be love at all
Caught from one transitory glance?

Prince.   Nay, Celio;
Because a cloud may cover up the sun
At his first step into the firmament,
Are we to say he never rose at all?
Are we to say the lightning did not flash
Because it did but flash, or that the fountain
Never ran fresh because it ran so fast
Into its briny cradle and its grave?
My love, if 'twere but of one moment born,
And but a moment living, yet was love;
And love it *is*, now living with my life. (*A harp heard.*)

Cel. O fine comparisons! but hark, I hear
The widow'd turtle in the leaves away
Calling her faithless mate.

Prince.   Yes, Celio, 'tis
Porcia—if she sings to me of *love*,
I am to approach the window; but if *jealousy*,
I am to keep aloof. Listen!

Porcia (*singing within*).

> Of all the shafts to Cupid's bow,
>   The first is tipt with fire;
> All bare their bosoms to the blow,
>   And call the wound Desire.

(*She appears at the window.*)

Prince. Ah! I was waiting, lovely Porcia,
Till your voice drew me by the notes of love,

Or distanc'd me by those of jealousy.

Por. Which needs not music, prince, to signify,
Being love's plain, prose history.

Prince.   Not always ;
For instance, I know one,
Who, to refute your theory, Porcia,
Attracts men by her jealousy as much
As she repels them by her love.

Por.   Nay, then
Men must be stranger beings than I thought.

Prince. I know not how that is, I only know
That in love's empire, as in other empires,
Rebellion sometimes prospers.

Por.   That the night
Would give us leave to argue out their point!
Which yet I fear it will not.

Prince.   Why ?

Por.   My father,
Who frets about my brother's sudden absence,
Sits up enditing letters after him ;
And therefore I have brought my harp, that while
We talk together I may touch the strings,
So as he, hearing me so occupied,
May not suspect or ask for me.   Besides,
We can talk under cover of the music.

Prince. Not the first time that love has found himself
Fretted, Porcia.

Por.   Oh, the wretched jest !
But listen—
The music is for him, the words for you,
For I have much to tell you underneath
This mask of music.   (*Plays on the harp.*)
You know my father has been long resolv'd

To quit this government, and to return
To his own country place—which resolution,
First taken on my brother's suppos'd death,
My brother's sudden absence has revived;
And brought to a head—so much so, that to-morrow,
To-morrow, he has settled to depart
To Bellaflor—I scarce can say the words—
But let my tears—
    Prince.   'Tis well that you should mask
Ill news under sweet music: though, indeed,
A treason to make sweet the poison'd cup.
    Por. Who more than I—

Enter JULIA *within, hurried.*

Julia.   Madam, madam, your father
Is gone into the garden—I hear his steps.
    Por. Nay then—(*Sings*)

        Love's second is a poison'd dart,
           And Jealousy is nam'd:
        Which carries poison to the heart
           Desire had first inflam'd.

    Prince. She sings of jealousy—we must retire;
Hist, Celio!   [CELIO *and* PRINCE *retreat.*

Enter LUIS.

Julia.   Who's there?
Por.   Speak!
Luis.   Oh, I, Porcia,
Who writing in my study, and much troubled
About your brother, was seduc'd away
By your harp's pleasant sound and the cool night,
To take a turn in the garden.

F.   8

Por. Yes, sir, here
I sit, enjoying the cool air that blows
Up from the shore among the whispering leaves.

Luis. What better? but, Porcia, it grows late,
And chilly, I think: and though I'd have you here
Singing like a nightingale the whole night through,
It must not be. Will you come in? [*Exit.*

Por. Directly—
I've but a moment.

Prince (*entering*). And you shall not need
Repeat the love call, for I heard—

Por. (*playing as she speaks*). Nay, listen,
And that attentively. To-morrow, then,
We go to Bellaflor, (you know the place,)—
There in the hill-top, hid among the trees,
Is an old castle; ours, but scarcely us'd,
And kept by an old man who loves me well,
And can be secret. And if you should come
That way by chance, as hunting it may be,
I think we yet may meet.

Luis (*within*). Porcia!

Por. Sir!

Luis (*within*). It's time, indeed, to shut your window.

Por. Hark,
I dare no longer.

Prince. Then farewell!

Por. Farewell!
Remember Bellaflor: while you retreat
Among the trees, I still shall sing to you
Of love; not that dark shape of jealousy,
But in the weeds of absence.

Prince. A descant
That suits us both,—(*aside*) but on a different theme.

Por. (*singing*).

> The last of Cupid's arrows all
>   With heavy lead is set;
> That vainly weeping lovers call
>   Repentance or Regret.

[*As she retires still singing from the window within, the* PRINCE *and* CELIO *retire back into the garden.*

SCENE III. *A street before* DON DIEGO'S *house in Barcelona.* —*Enter* ALVARO *and* FABIO, *masked: other Masks pass across, and into* DIEGO'S *house.*

Alv. This is the place; here will I wait till she comes by. I know her dress, but I dared not follow her till myself disguised.

Fab. And no doubt, sir, you will find good opportunity of talking to her. 'Tis the old and acknowledged usage of this season, that any one may accost any one so long as both are masked, and so neither supposed to know the other.

Alv. Oh, a brave usage, and a brave invention that of the Carnival! One may accost whom one pleases, and whisper what one will, under the very ears of husband, father, or duenna!

Fab. So received a custom, that even among this hot-headed jealous people of Spain, no mortal quarrel has yet arisen on these occasions, though plenty to provoke it.

Alv. Look! the Masks are coming; I hear the music within. She must soon be here. Let us withdraw round this corner till she come.   [*Exeunt.*

SCENE IV. *A garden leading down to the sea; on one side a*
Portico.—Masks singing and dancing: in the course of
which enter and mix with them, JUAN, SERAFINA,
LEONELO, *and* FLORA, *and afterwards* ALVARO; *all*
masked.

CHORUS.

Tantara, tantara, come follow me all,
Carnival, Carnival, Carnivāl.
Follow me, follow me, nobody ask;
Crazy is Carnival under the mask.
Follow me, follow me, nobody knows;
Under the mask is under the rose.
Tantara, tantara, &c.

Juan. How like you all this uproar?
Ser.   O quite well.
Juan (aside).   And so should I,
Did not a shadow from that darken'd room
Trail after me.   But why torment myself!
Leon. My lord, the dancers wait.
Juan (to the musicians). Pardon me.   Strike up!
Voices. Strike up! strike up!
A Voice. The castanets!
Voices. The castanets! the castanets!
Musician. What will you have?
Voices. The Tarazana! the Tarazana!
  [*A dance, during which* ALVARO *observes* SERAFINA.
Fab. You recognise her?
Alv.   Yes, Fabio, my heart
Would recognise her under any dress,
And under any mask.
  Fab.   Now is your time.
  Alv. (to SERAFINA). Mask, will you dance with me?

Ser.   No, Cavalier;
You come too late.

    Alv.   Too late?

    Ser.   I am engag'd.

    Alv. Nevertheless—

    Ser.   Nay, sir, I am not apt
To change my mind.

    Alv.   I hop'd that in my favour
You might perhaps.

    Ser.   'Twas a delusion.

    Alv.   But,
Fair Mask, didst never change thy mind before?

    Ser. Perhaps once—to such purpose that that *once*
Forbids all other.

    Juan.   Serafina, the Mask
Has askt your hand to dance. On these occasions
You must permit him, whether known or not.
Unknown, the usage of the time allows;
If known, 'twere more discourteous to refuse.

    Ser. My lord, 'twas chiefly upon your account
That I refus'd to dance with him; if you
Desire it, I am ready.

    Juan.   How, my love,
On my account?

    Ser.   Liking your company
Much better.

    Juan.   Nay, take the humour of the time,
And dance with him. (*Aside.*) I marvel who it is
That follows Serafina, and to whom,
The very indisposition that she shows,
Argues a kind of secret inclination.

    Alv. Well, do you still reject me?—

    Ser.   I am bidden

To dance with you; what measure will you call?

Alv. Play "Love lies bleeding!"

Ser.   But why that?—

Alv.   Because
The spirit of the tune and of the words
Moves with my heart, and gives me leave beside
Amid its soft and slow divisions
To gaze on you and whisper in your ear.

(*A minuet by the Masks: during which* ALVARO *constantly
    whispers* SERAFINA, *who seems distrest; after some time,
    they return in the figure to the front of the Stage.*)

Ser. I've heard enough, sir; save for courtesy
Too much. No more.

Alv.   Brief as the happiness
That once was mine! But—

Ser.   Stay, sir, I will hear
No more. I had not danc'd with you at all,
But that I wish'd to tell you once for all
How hopeless is your passion—the great danger
Your coming hither put and puts me to,
And that not my honour only, but my life,
Depends upon your quitting me at once,
Now and for ever.

Alv.   Serafina!

Ser. (*aloud*).   I am tired;
Pardon me, friends, I cannot dance.

Juan.   My love,
What is't? Unwell?

Ser.   I know not.

A Woman.   Stop the ball!

Another. All in her honour too!

Another.   What is the matter?

Juan. You are but tir'd with dancing.

Ser.   No, no, no,
Let us go home.

Juan.   Pardon us, friends,
Continue you your revels; we will go
Into the house awhile, and rest; I think
The heat and dancing have distrest her much,
But she'll be better. To your dance again.
Come, Serafina. (*Aside.*) Leonelo! hither!
Find out the Mask that with your lady danc'd.

Leon. I'll watch him to the world's end—or beyond,
If need be.

Juan.   Good—Come, Serafina.

[*Exeunt* JUAN *and* SERAFINA.

Alv. So end my hopes for ever. Fool! who seeking
For what once lost could never more be found,
Like to a child after a rainbow running—
Leaving my father, who had only just
Recover'd me to his old heart again,
Without adieu—equipp'd this Brigantine
(Down to the bottom may she go with me!)
In chase of this—not Serafina—no—
But this false Siren,
Who draws me with the music of her beauty,
To leave me in destruction.

Leon. (*watching him*). This must be some monk, who
knows of some better entertainment elsewhere.

Alv. And after all,
Not one kind word of welcome or of thanks,
But that her life depended on my leaving her,
Who would for her have sacrificed my own
In any way but that. But it is done!
Henceforward I renounce all hope; henceforth—
And why not all despair?—the world is wide,

Eh, Fabio? and the good old saw says well
That fortune at the worst must surely mend.
Let us to sea, the ship is ready; come,
Away with all this foolery. (*Throws off mask, &c.*)
   Leon. Here is a harlequin sailor!
   Fabio.   Well resolv'd.
   Alv. Wear them what other fool may list,
I'll straight aboard, and if the wind and sea
Can rise as they were wont, I'll stretch all sail
Toward the perdition she consigns me to.
Halloa there! (*Whistles.*)

Enter SAILORS.

   Sail.   Captain?
   Alv.   How is't for a cruise?
   Sail. Oh, never better; just a breeze to keep
The ship from looking in her glass too long.
   Alv. Aboard, aboard then! Farewell all my hopes;
My love, farewell for ever!
   Voices (*within*).   Fire! fire! fire!
   All. What's this?
   Voices. Fire! fire! in Don Diego's palace!
Help! help!
   Alv.   She there! my life shall save the life
She said it jeopardied.

As he is going out, enter JUAN *with* SERAFINA *fainted in*
his arms.

   Juan. Friends! Gentlemen! if you would help in this
calamity, take charge for a moment of this most precious
thing of all, till I return.
   Alv. (*taking* SERAFINA *in his arms*). Trust me, sir.
                     [JUAN *rushes off.*

Leon. Stop, my lord, stop a moment—he is gone, and this man—

Alv. Serafina in my arms! my ship at hand!
O love, O destiny!—aboard, aboard—
O 'tis the merriest proverb of them all,
How one man rises by his neighbour's fall.

> [*Exit, carrying off* SERAFINA.

Leon. Halloa! stop him! stop him! it is my mistress; Don Juan! my lord! my lord! the rascal has carried her off! my lord! my lord!   [*Runs after* ALVARO.

1st Voice in the crowd. The fire is getting under.

2nd Voice. No lives lost?

3rd Voice. Only, they say, one poor girl of the lady Serafina's.

Enter DON JUAN *hurriedly.*

Juan. I thought I heard Leonelo calling me—But where is Serafina? This is the place—yes—Serafina! I left them here—taken her perhaps fainting as she was for help. Gentlemen, have you seen any here with a lady, fainted, in their charge—a sailor, I think?

1st Man. Not I, sir.

2nd Man. Nor I.

3rd Man. Stay, I think there were some sailors with a lady in their arms.

Juan. And where—

Enter LEONELO *breathless.*

Leon. Oh, my lord, my lord!

Juan. Speak!

Leon. The Mask who danced with my lady—

Juan. Where is she?

Leon. Was the sailor you gave her in charge to—He has carried her off.

Juan. The Mask! the sailor!

Leon. I saw him throw off his disguise, and now he has carried her off—to the shore—to sea—to the ship there now spreading her sails in the harbour.

Juan. Man! beware lest I blast thee!

Leon. As if I were the sailor! I tell you I ran after them, shouted, struggled, but was pushed aside, knocked down—

Juan. To the shore, to the shore! follow me!

Voices. What is the matter?

Juan. What I dare not name till it be avenged; Pirate! —Ruffian! Oh fool, I might have guessed—but I will find them through water and fire too. To the shore!

[*Exit* JUAN, LEONELO *after him ; confusion, &c.*

ACT III.

SCENE I. *A room in* DON LUIS' *country-house near Naples. Enter* DON LUIS *reading a letter.*

Luis. "You bid me tell you why it is Don Juan Roca has not written to you so long : and though it be pain to do so, I dare no longer defer answering you. At a carnival dance here, the palace of Don Diego de Cordona, in which the festival was held, took fire so suddenly, as people had much ado to escape with their lives. Don Juan's wife fainting from terror, he carried her out, and gave her in charge to a sailor standing near, while he himself returned to help at the fire. No doubt this sailor was a pirate : for he carried her off to his ship and set sail immediately. Don Juan re-

turning and finding her gone rushes madly after; casts him-
self into the sea in his rage and desperation; is rescued half
drowned, and taken to his house, from which he was missed
—he and his servant Leonelo—some days ago, taking scarce
any thing with him, and leaving no hint of whither he is
gone.   And since that hour we have heard nothing of him,
or of Serafina."

My heart prevents my eyes from reading more.
O heavens! to what chance and danger is   .
The fortune of the happiest, and still more
The honour of the noblest, liable!
Ill fortune we may bear, and, if we choose,
Sit folded in despair with dignity;
But honour needs must wince before a straw,
And never rest until it be avenged.
To know where Juan is, and by his side
To put myself, and run all risk with him
Till he were righted, and the offender too,
I'd give my life and all I'm worth; no corner
In the wide earth but we would ferret it,
Until—Porcia!

Enter PORCIA.

Por.   Pray, sir, pardon me,
But I would know what vexes you, you stand
Angrily talking to yourself alone:
This letter in your hand—What is it, sir?
   Luis. Nothing, nothing, Porcia; (for Juan's sake
I must dissemble)—Nay, I have received
A letter upon business that annoys me.
   Por. I'm sorry, sir, for that, for I had come
To ask a favour of you.
   Luis.   Well, why not?

Por. They say that those who ask unseasonably
Must be content with a refusal.

Luis.   Nay,
Between us two no season's out of season.

Por. So? then I'll ask. Alvaro—

Luis.   All but that!
Ask me not that way.

Por.   Then 'tis *not* the season.

Luis. The season for all else but that which never
Can be in season. How often have I told you
Never to speak to me again of him!

Por. What has my brother done, sir, after all,
To make you so inveterate?

Luis.   What done!
To leave my house, to which I only just
Had welcom'd him as only a father can,
Without adieu, or word of when or where,
And then as suddenly come back, forsooth,
Knock at my door, as if he had but made
A morning call, and think to find it open—
It and my heart—open to him as ever.

Por. But may not, sir, the thoughtlessness of youth
Be some excuse? Pray you remember, sir,
How on a sudden you yourself determin'd
To leave the cheerful city and come here,
Among dull woods and fields, and savage people;
And surely 'twas no wonder that my brother
Should, ill advis'd, no doubt, but naturally,
Slip for a month back to the busy world
To which his very dangers had endear'd him.
And now to prove
How much he feels your anger and his fault,
Since his return he has lived quietly,

I might say almost *eremitically*,
Up in the mountain, yet more solitary
And still than this is, doing penance there.
Let me plead for him, sir; let him come down,
To kiss your hand and see you once again.

   Luis. He should be grateful to you, Porcia—
Well, let him come.

   Por.   Bless you for saying so!
I'll go myself to him this evening,
And tell him this good news.

   Luis.   Do so. Ah me!
That all were settled thus! Did I but know
Where Juan is, and where his enemy!   [*Exit.*

   Julia (entering). Well, madam, you have gain'd your point.

   Por.   Yes, Julia,
Two points; for, first, my brother will come back;
And, secondly, so doing, leave the old castle
At my disposal, where the Prince and I
May meet together in security.
I'll write to Alvaro now, and do you tell
The messenger who brought his letter hither,
I'll go this evening up the mountain. So
Belardo, the old porter,
Who knows and loves me well, will look for me,
And understand the purpose of my going.

   Julia. Ah, now I see, beside his bow and arrows,
Love arms himself with trick and stratagem.

   Por. And something else; give me my Arquebuss;
So, Love and I perchance, as says the song,
May hit a hart, as we shall go along.

SCENE II. *A room in* DON LUIS' *castle in the hills.*—*Enter*
ALVARO *and* FABIO.

Alv. How is't with Serafina?
Fab.   Nay, you know.
Ever the same.
Alv. You mean still weeping?
Fab.   Ay.
Alv. Yes, from the hour when, fainting in my arms,
She pass'd from raging flame to the wild seas,
And opening those heavenly eyes again,
Still with the hue of death upon her cheek,
She saw herself in my ship—in my power,—
She has not ceas'd to weep; all my caresses
Unable to console her.
I fondly hoped that she—

Enter SERAFINA.

Ser.   Good Fabio,   [*Exit* FABIO.
Leave us awhile. "You fondly hoped," Alvaro—
So much I heard, connected with my name;
And I perhaps have something on that text
Would clear the matter up to both of us.
"You fondly hoped"—was't not that I might be
So frail, so lost to shame, and so inconstant,
That for the loss of husband, home, and honour,
Lost in one day, I might console myself
With being in his arms, who robb'd me of all!
Was't this you hoped?
Alv.   No, Serafina, but—
Ser. But what?
Alv.   And yet perhaps 'twas that I hop'd—

The very desperation of my act
Bringing its pardon with it, soon or late,
Seeing, the very element of love
Is rashness, that he finds his best excuse
In having none at all. Ah, Serafina,
How greatly must he love, who all for love
Perils the hope of being loved at all!

Ser. Poor argument! I rather draw that he
Who ventures on such desperate acts can haye
No true respect for her he outrages,
And therefore no true love. No, daring traitor—
But I'll not strive to break the heart of flint,
But wear it with my tears. Hear me, Alvaro,
In pity—in mercy—hear me.
This thing is done, there is no remedy,
Let us not waste the time in arguing
What better had been done; the stars so rul'd it—
Yea, providence that rules the stars. Well then,
What next? Alvaro, I would speak of this;
And if't be right I owe you any thing,
Be it for this one boon, a patient hearing.
Listen to me—
I never draw a breath but 'tis on fire
With Juan's vengeance; never move a step
But think I see his fierce eyes glaring at me
From some dark corner of this desolate house
In which my youth is buried. And what gain *you*
By all this crime and misery? My body,
But not my soul; without possessing which,
Beauty itself is but a breathing corpse,
But a cold marble statue, unsuffus'd
With the responsive hue of sympathy,
Possess'd, but not enjoy'd.

Oh, ill betide that villain love, not love,
That all its object and affection finds
In the mere contact of encircling arms!
But if this move you not—consider, Alvaro—
Don Juan is a nobleman—as such
Bound to avenge his honour; he must know
'Twas you who did this monstrous act, for Flora
Would tell him all.   There is one remedy:
'Tis this, that you, despairing of my love,
Which you can never gain—forego me quite,
And give me up to some cold convent's cloister,
Where buried I may wear away—
   Alv.   No more,
Rather than give you up again, Serafina,
Pray heaven's thunder—   (*Shot within.*)
   Ser.   Again, this dreadful omen!
'Tis for my death!
   Alv.   Fear not—Belardo! ho!
What shot was that?

Enter BELARDO.

   Bel.   Your sister Porcia
Is coming up the mountain; nay, is now
At the very gate.
   Ser.   O, whither must I go!
   Alv. Belardo, lead her hence.
   Bel.   Not that way, sir,
By which your sister enters.
   Alv.   In here then.
I'll go and meet Porcia.
   Ser.   Mercy, heaven!
     [*She goes in at one door, as* PORCIA *enters by another.*
   Alv. How now, Porcia, you look pleased to-day!

Por. And well I may—for two reasons, Alvaro.

Alv. Well, what are they?

Por. First, I have got my father to relax in his humour against you.

Alv. My good sister!

Por. So as he will see you at Bellaflor this very evening.

Alv. Good! and your second reason?

Por. That coming up the pass, I made the crowning shot of my life with this arquebuss—a hare at full speed—flying, I might say.

Alv. Give you joy of both your hits, Porcia.

Por. I am so proud of the last (though glad of the first, Alvaro) that I shall try my luck and skill a little longer about the castle this evening.

Alv. So—

Por. You will not wait for me, but go down at once to Bellaflor, and show my father you value his forgiveness by your haste to acknowledge it.

Alv. You say well; but you will go with me?

Por. Fear not, I shall soon be after you.

Alv. Well, if so, then—(*apart to* BELARDO,) Belardo, remember you get the lady to her room directly my sister is gone out.

Por. Our roads lie together as far as the gate at least. (*Aside to* BELARDO.)   If the Prince happen to come hither, tell him to wait for me, Belardo ; I shall be back directly. Come, brother.   [*Exeunt* ALVARO *and* PORCIA.

Bel. They say a Pander is a good business ; and yet here am I ministering both to brother and sister with very little profit at the year's end.

Ser. (*entering cautiously*).   Porcia's gone?

Bel. Yes, she is gone.

Ser. Had she resolved on going into the room where I

was she could have done it; there was neither key nor bolt within. But she is gone and I can get to my own.

Bel. No.

Ser. Belardo! why?

Bel. Some one coming.

Ser. Again!   [*She hides as before.*

Enter PRINCE.

Prince. How now, Belardo, where is your mistress? she advised me her brother would be away, and she here this evening.

Bel. Your Highness comes in good time. She went with him, but will be back directly. She is here.

Enter PORCIA.

Por. Not far behind, you see. Scarce had he taken the turn to Bellaflor, when I turn'd back.

Prince. How shall I thank you for this favour?

Por. My brother's living here has been the reason of our not meeting before : but that is remedied for the future.

Prince. And how?

Por. He is at last reconciled to my father, and is even now gone home, to Bellaflor.

Prince (aside). My heart thanks you but little, being away with another; but if I cannot avenge memory, I will thus try and deceive or amuse it. My lovely Porcia!

Bel. (aside). She hears every word they say!

Por. Ah, you flatter still.

Prince. Flatter!

Por. Do I not know there is a Siren at Naples—

Prince. Porcia, to prove to you how unfounded that suspicion is, I have these many days wholly quitted Naples, and, out of a melancholy that has taken hold of me, now

live retired in a little Villa hard by this : you may imagine
at least one reason for my doing so.   And so enchanted am
I with my solitude, that till this evening (when you broke
it as I could wish) I have not once stirred abroad ; my only
occupation being to watch some pictures that I am having
done, by the best masters of Italy and of Spain too ; one of
which country I have happened on, who might compete
with Apelles.   As I told you, I have spent whole days in
watching them at work.

Por. My jealousy whispered—

Enter BELARDO.

Bel. Unlucky to be sure.

Por. What now?

Bel. What can make your brother return so suddenly?

Por. My brother !

Bel. He is now at the gate.

Por. He must suspect the Prince !   O, my lord, hide
yourself.

Prince. Where?

Por. Any where !—quick ! here.

> [*She puts him where* SERAFINA *is.*

Prince. For your sake, Porcia.

Enter ALVARO.

Alv. I cannot be easy till I am assured that Serafina——
Porcia here?

Por. Alvaro !

Alv. You left me on a sudden?

Por. I was tired, and came back for rest.

Alv. So—

Por. But you?

Alv. I bethought me that, considering my father's late indisposition toward me, it were better you were at my side when I went to him.

Por. So—

Alv. So that if he should relapse into ill-humour, you know how to direct him.

Por. Well, shall we start again together?

Alv. Is not that best?

Por. As you please.

Alv. (aside). She will not then stumble on Serafina.

Por. (aside). I shall so get him out of the Prince's way.

[*Exeunt* PORCIA *and* ALVARO.

Bel. Now then the two imprison'd ones get out.

Enter the PRINCE, *and* SERAFINA, *her hand before her face.*

Ser. In vain—you shall not know me.

Prince.   Nay, in vain
You try to be unknown.

Ser.   Consider—

Prince.   Nay,
Down with that little hand, too small a cloud
To hide the heaven of your beauty from me.
Lady, I know you—but one such.   And know
That love himself has wrought a miracle,
To this unlikeliest place, by means unlikeliest,
Bringing us here together.

Bel. Only this was wanting to the plot! The sister's gallant in love with the brother's mistress!

Ser. Generous Orsino! if I try in vain
To hide me from you—wretched that I am
To have to hide at all—but the less wretched
Being unmaskt by your nobility—
I ask this mercy at your feet; betray not

The secret chance has now betray'd to you.
I am a wretched woman, you a Prince.
Grant me this boon; and yet one more, to leave me
To weep my miseries in solitude.

Prince. Madam, your prayer is not in vain.   Your name,
Upon the word and honour of a Prince,
Shall never pass my lips.
And for that second wish, hardest of all,
I yet will pay for one delicious glance
The greatest price I can, by leaving you.
Farewell—you owe me more anxiety
Than you believe.

Ser.   I shall not be asham'd
To own the debt, though hopeless to repay it.
But heav'n shall do that for me.   Farewell, my lord.

Prince. Farewell.   [*Exeunt* PRINCE *and* SERAFINA.

Bel. I wonder if they know the ancient line,
"I'll keep your secret, only you keep mine."   [*Exit.*

SCENE III.   *The* PRINCE'S *Villa.—Enter* DON JUAN *in
poor apparel; and* CELIO.

Cel. Your business with the Prince, sir?
Juan.   Only to speak
About a picture I have finish'd for him.

Cel. He is not here at present; not, I think,
Return'd from hunting.

Juan.   Will he soon be home?

Cel. I cannot speak to that, sir.   [*Exit* CELIO.

Juan. Why, what a fate is mine!
All of a sudden—but I dare not say it;
Scarce could I of myself believe it, if

I told it to myself; so with some things
'Tis easier to bear, than hear of them;
And how much happens daily in this strange world,
Far easier to be done than be believed.
Who could have thought that I, being what I was
A few days back, am what I am; to this
Reduc'd by that name *Honour;* whose nice laws,
Accurst be he who framed!
Little he knew the essence of the thing
He legislated for, who put my honour
Into another's hand; made my free right
Another's slave, for others to abuse,
And then myself before the world arraign'd,
To answer for a crime against myself!
And one being vain enough to make the law,
How came the silly world to follow it,
Like sheep to their own slaughter! And in all
This silly world is there a greater victim
To its accursed custom than myself!

Enter LEONELO, *poorly drest.*

Leon. Yes, one,
Who follows your misfortunes, and picks up
The crumbs of misery that fall from you;
My chief subsistence now.
 Juan.   And I have left
Country and home to chase this enemy,
Of whom as yet no vestige—
 Leon.   And no wonder,
Seeing he travels with you.
 Juan.   In these rags—
 Leon. And very hungry; and so we come at last
To Naples; for what purpose?

Juan.   Why, if't be
Some former lover; would he not return
To his own country, and hers?
    Leon.   In which meanwhile
We starve, without a stiver in our pockets,
While friends swarm round us, if you would, my lord,
Reveal yourself.
    Juan.   Shorn of my honour? No!
    Leon. And I, not being shorn of appetite,
Would publish my disgraceful want of food
To all the world. There is Don Luis now,
Your ancient friend.
    Juan.   What friend but, if he be
True to himself and me, must be my enemy,
And either wholly turn his face away,
Or look at me with pity and contempt?
I will reveal myself to no one, nay,
Reveal *myself* I cannot,—not myself
Until I be aveng'd.
    Leon.   And so you make
The painter's trade your stalking-horse,
To track your enemy, and in these rags
Come to the Prince.
    Juan.   Oh let me die in rags,
Rather than he should recognise me! Once
He saw me—
    Leon.   O my lord, fear not for that;
Hunger, and rags, and sleeplessness, and anguish,
Have chang'd you so your oldest friend would pass you.
    Juan. They have that merit then. But see—the Prince.

Enter PRINCE.

I kiss your Highness' hand.

Prince.   Well, Spaniard,
What would you with me?
Juan.   I waited on your Highness,
To tell you of a picture I had finisht.
Thinking your Grace might like—
Prince.   I thank you, sir.
What is the subject?
Juan.   Hercules, my lord;
Wherein (unless I do deceive myself)
I think the fair and terrible are join'd
With some success. .
Prince.   As how?
Juan.   As thus, my lord.
The point I have chosen in that history
Is where the faithless Centaur carries off
Deijanira, while beyond the river
Stands Hercules with such a face and gesture
As not a man, I think, who looks on it,
But would exclaim, "Jealousy and Revenge!"
Prince. I long to see it.
Juan.   That is the main group;
But far away, among the tangled thicks
Of a dark mountain gap, this Hercules
Fires his own funeral pile to the smoky clouds.
And I would have this motto for the whole,
"So Jealousy in its own flames expires."
Prince. Not only do I like the subject well,
But now especially, being deeply scorcht,
Not with the flame that burn'd up Hercules,
But that for which the unlucky Centaur died.
Juan. Indeed, my lord.
Prince.   Indeed—and, having done
This picture for me, you shall set about

One other.

Juan.   At your pleasure.

Prince.   You shall know then,
That of a certain lady whom but once
I saw, and for a moment, I became
Infatuated so, her memory
Every where and for ever, day and night,
Pursues me. Hopeless of obtaining her,
And ev'n of ever seeing her again,
Chance has discover'd to me where she lives
Conceal'd—I know not why, but so it is—
And 'twould at least console my hopeless love,
To have her picture. You are a foreigner
Who know not nor are known by any here,
So I can better trust you with a secret
I dare not even to herself reveal.

Juan. I'll do my best to serve you; but I fear,
If she be such a creature as you say,
That I shall fail to satisfy myself
Or you.

Prince. Why so?

Juan.   I tried at such a face
Once.

Prince. Nay, I know that beauty's subtlest essence
Is most impossible to seize. But yet
I shall commit this business to your hands
Most confidently.

Juan.   I'll do my best.

Prince.   Come then,
Remembering this business must be done
With all despatch and secrecy. Yourself
Must not be seen by her, nor I, who know not
(I told you) how or why she should be there;

But my authority, and a little gold,
(At least, I hope,) shall set the door ajar,
That you may catch a sight of her.   Myself
Will be at hand, and ready to protect you
Against all danger.

    Juan.   I will trust your Highness,
And also (let me say so) trust myself,
Although but a poor painter.

    Prince.   I believe it;
And each of us shall play his part, I think,
That neither shall depart unsatisfied.   [*Exit* PRINCE.

    Juan. Perhaps, but not as you suppose.   Leonelo,
Put up my brushes and my colours, and—
My pistols with them.

    Leon.   Pistols! Is't to paint
In body colour?

    Juan.   Put them up.

    Leon.   And whither
Are we to carry them?

    Juan.   I do not know.
Whither the Prince shall carry me, I go.   [*Exeunt.*

SCENE IV.   *A room in* DON LUIS' *Villa.—Enter* LUIS *and*
ALVARO.

    Alv. Now, sir, that (thanks to Porcia) you have open'd
Your arms to me once more, I cannot rest
(So favour ever calls for favour) till
You tell me what the inward trouble is
That mars your outward feature.   I was cause
Of so much trouble to you, that I dread
Lest of this also, which with troubled looks

You still keep speaking to yourself apart,
Like people in a play.
  Luis.   Alvaro, no.
Thank God, this trouble lies not at your door.
Let that suffice.
  Alv.   You will not trust me, sir?
  Luis. Why will you press me? since you must be told,
It is about my friend—Don Juan Roca.
  Alv. Don Juan!
  Luis.   Yes, Don Juan.
  Alv.   What of him?
(I'll drink the cup at once!) (*aside*).
  Luis.   What evil star
Made him my friend!
  Alv.   Too true! (*aside*). But what has happen'd?
  Luis. Why will you know? and should I dare to tell
My friend's dishonour? Well, no more than this—
Some wretch—some villain—some accursed—but
Be there bad name enough to brand him by,
I have not breath for it—nor is it well
For you or for myself—has ravisht from him
His wife, his Serafina.
And I, O God! not able to avenge him!
  Alv. (*aside*). Does he know all? and knowing whose
   the crime,
Cannot, he says, avenge it on his son?
Shall I then tell, and gain at least the grace
Of a confession? Hear me, sir.
  Luis.   Nay, nay,
I know what you would say, how vain it is
To vex myself who cannot help my friend—
We neither knowing who the villain is,
Nor whither both are fled: heaven! if we did,
I should not now be idly moaning here.

Alv. All's safe ! (*aside*).   Nor I, sir ; give me but a clue,
(Not only for Don Juan's sake, but yours,)
I'll track the villain through the world.

Luis.   Alvaro,
Your words are music to me.

Alv.   Still, my father,
I will say what to say you said was vain.
Until some clue be found, let not this grief
Consume you so.

Luis.   Such wounds are hard to heal.
Yet, quicken'd by your courage, and to show
How well I like your counsel—come, Alvaro,
I will with you to your hill castle there ;
That which has been your banishment so long,
Shall witness now our reconciliation.
We'll go this evening—now—together.

Alv.   Good, sir.
But pardon me, let me go on before
To apprize Belardo of your going thither—
And also Serafina ! (*apart*).   [*Exit.*

Luis.   Be it so !

Julia (*entering*).   My lord, Don Pedro is without,
and fain
Would speak to you.

Luis.   Admit him, Julia.
The wound re-opens—Serafina's father !
No doubt upon what errand.

Enter DON PEDRO.

Ped.   Ah, Don Luis,
Your arms ! (*They embrace.*)

Luis.   Don Pedro, I must surely thank
The cause to which my poor retirement owes
This honour.

Ped.   Yet a thankless cause, Don Luis.
These many days I have heard nothing of
Don Juan and my daughter; they neither write
Themselves, nor any one to whom I write
To ask about them answers to the purpose.
What may this mean? I have come hither thinking
That you, who are the model of all friends,
May deal more clearly with me. You may think
What I endure from this suspense. In mercy
Relieve me from it quickly.
    Luis (*aside*).   Poor old man;
What shall I say? tell his grey hairs at once
The ruin of his honour and his love?
    Ped. You pause, my lord!
    Luis. And yet I need not wonder,
I nothing hear of them if you do not.
    Ped. And you know nothing of them?

Enter PORCIA *hurriedly.*

Por.   Sir, I hear
You are going (are you not?) this evening
To the castle, with my brother.
But who is this?
    Ped.   Ever your slave, sweet lady.
    Por. Oh, pardon me, my lord.
    Luis.   Nay, pardon *me*
That I cut short your compliments, Porcia.
(This interruption, come so opportune,
Shall carry what ill news I have to tell
Into the open air at least.) Don Pedro,
I am going to the mountain, as she says;
You to the city; for some way at least
Our roads are one, and I would talk with you
About this business without interruption.

Will't please you come?

Ped.   Your pleasure's mine.   Adieu,
Fair lady.

Por.   Farewell, sir.

Luis.   Porcia, you
Will follow in the carriage.   [*Exeunt* LUIS *and* PEDRO.

Por.   And should go
More gladly, were my lover there to meet me.   [*Exit.*

SCENE V.   *The garden under* ALVARO'S *castle.—A large
grated door in the centre.—Enter* PRINCE, JUAN,
LEONELO, *and* BELARDO.

Prince (*to* BELARDO).   You know your office; take this
diamond by way of thanks.

Bel.   I know little of diamonds but that they sell for less
than you give for them.   But this [*to* JUAN] is to be your
post.

Juan.   I am ready.

Prince.   Remember, Spaniard, it is for *me* you run this
hazard, if there be any; I shall be close at hand to protect
you.   Be not frightened.

Juan.   Your Highness does not know me: were it other-
wise, danger cannot well appal him whom sorrows like mine
have left alive.

Bel.   And, another time—doubloons, not diamonds.
                    [*Exeunt* PRINCE *and* LEONELO.
Here she mostly comes of an evening, poor lady, to soothe
herself, walking and sitting here by the hour together.   This
is where you are to be.   Go in; and mind you make no
noise.   [*Puts* JUAN *into the grated door, and locks it.*

Juan (*through the grated window*).   But what are you
about?

Bel.   Locking the door to make all sure.

Juan. But had it not better be unlockt in case—
Bel. Hush! she comes.
Juan. My palette then.

Enter SERAFINA.

Ser. How often and how often do I draw
My resolution out upon one side,
And all my armed sorrows on the other,
To fight the self-same battle o'er again!
 Juan. He stands in the way; I cannot see her face.
 Bel. Still weeping, madam?
 Ser.   Wonder not, Belardo:
The only balm I have. You pity me:
Leave me alone then for a while, Belardo;
The breeze that creeps along the whispering trees
Makes me feel drowsy.
 Juan (*to* BELARDO, *whispering*). She turns her head away,
I cannot see her still.
 Ser.   What noise was that?
 Bel. Madam?
 Ser.   I thought I heard a whisper.
 Bel.   Only
The breeze, I think. If you would turn this way,
I think 'twould blow upon you cooler.
 Ser.   Perhaps it will.
Thank you. I am very miserable and very weary.
 Bel. She sleeps: that is the lady.
Make most of time.   [*Exit.*
 Juan.   Yes. Now then for my pencil.
Serafina! found at last! Whose place is this?
The Prince? no! But the stray'd lamb being here,
The wolf is not far off. She sleeps! I thought
The guilty never slept: and look some tears
Still lingering on the white rose of her cheek.

Be those the drops, I wonder,
Of guilty anguish, or of chaste despair?
This death-like image is the sculptor's task,
Not mine.
Or is it I who sleep, and dream all this,
And dream beside, that once before I tried
To paint that face—the daylight drawing in
As now—and when somehow the lamp was out,
A man—I fail'd : and what love fail'd to do,
Shall hate accomplish? She said then, if ever
She suffer'd me to draw her face again,
Might she die for it. Into its inmost depth
Heav'n drew that idle word, and it returns
In thunder.
    Ser. (dreaming). Juan! Husband! on my knees.
Oh Juan—slay me not!

       Enter ALVARO ; *she wakes and rushes to him.*

              Alvaro,
Save me, oh save me from him!
    Alv.   So the wretch
Thrives by another's wretchedness. My love!
    Juan. Alvaro, by the heavens!
    Alv.   Calm yourself;
You must withdraw awhile. Come in with me.
    Juan. Villain !
    Ser. (clinging to ALVARO). What's that?
    Juan (shaking at the door).   The door is fast;
Open it, I say !—
Then die, thou and thy paramour !
    [*Shoots a pistol at each through the grating.—Both fall:*
      SERAFINA *into the arms of* BELARDO, *who has come in*
      during the noise.—Then directly enter DON LUIS, PEDRO,
      PORCIA.

Luis. What noise is this?

Ser.   My father!—in your arms
To die;—not by your hand—Forgive me—Oh!   [*Dies.*

Ped. (taking her in his arms). My Serafina!

Luis.   And Alvaro!

Alv.   Ay,
But do not curse me now!   [*Dies.*

Enter the PRINCE *and* LEONELO.

Leon. They must have found him out.

Prince.   Whoever dares
Molest him, answers it to me. Open the door.
But what is this?   [BELARDO *unlocks the door.*

Juan (coming out). A picture—
Done by the Painter of his own Dishonour
In blood.
I am Don Juan Roca. Such revenge
As each would have of me, now let him take,
As far as one life holds. Don Pedro, who
Gave me that lovely creature for a bride,
And I return to him a bloody corpse;
Don Luis, who beholds his bosom's son
Slain by his bosom friend; and you, my lord,
Who, for your favours, might expect a piece
In some far other style of art than this:
Deal with me as you list; 'twill be a mercy
To swell this complement of death with mine;
For all I had to do is done, and life
Is worse than nothing now.

Prince.   Get you to horse,
And leave the wind behind you.

Luis.   Nay, my lord,
Whom should he fly from? not from me at least,

F.   10

Who lov'd his honour as my own, and would
Myself have help'd him in a just revenge,
Ev'n on an only son.

Ped.   I cannot speak,
But I bow down these miserable gray hairs
To other arbitration than the sword;
Ev'n to your Highness' justice.

Prince.   Be it so.
Meanwhile—

Juan.   Meanwhile, my lord, let me depart;
Free, if you will, or not. But let me go,
Nor wound these fathers with the sight of one,
Who has cut off the blossom of their age:
Yea, and his own, more miserable than all.
They know me; that I am a gentleman,
Not cruel, nor without what seem'd due cause
Put on this bloody business of my honour;
Which having done, I will be answerable
Here and elsewhere, to all for all.

Prince.   Depart
In peace.

Juan.   In peace ! Come, Leonelo.
   [*He goes out slowly, followed by* LEONELO : *and the
                  curtain falls.*

Some alterations of this play were made with a view to the English
stage, where, spite of the slightness of many parts, I still think it might
be tried.

Its companion play, the *Medico de su Honra*, is far more famous;
has some more terrible, perhaps some finer, situations; but inferior, I
think, in variety of scene, character, and incident.

It may add a little to the reader's interest, as it did to mine, to learn
from Mr Ticknor, that Calderon wrote a "*Tratado defendiendo la nobleza
de la Pintura.*"

KEEP YOUR OWN SECRET.

10—2

DRAMATIS PERSONÆ.

ALEXANDER,   *Prince of Parma.*

NISIDA,   *his Sister.*

DON CESAR,   *his Secretary.*

DON ARIAS, }
DON FELIX, }   *Gentlemen of the Court.*

DONNA ANNA,   *Sister to Don Felix.*

ELVIRA,   *her Maid.*

LAZARO,   *Don Cesar's Servant.*

KEEP YOUR OWN SECRET.

ACT I.

SCENE I. *A Room in the Palace.—Enter the* PRINCE
ALEXANDER, *and* DON ARIAS.

Prince. I saw her from her carriage, Arias,
As from her East, alight, another sun
New ris'n, or doubling him whose envious ray
Seem'd as I watch'd her down the corridor,
To swoon about her as she mov'd along;
Until, descending tow'rd my sister's room,
She set, and left me hesitating like
Some traveller who with the setting sun
Doth fear to lose his way; her image still,
Lost from without, dazzling my inner eye—
Can this be love, Don Arias? if not,
What is it? something much akin to love.

Ar. But had you not, my lord, often before
Seen Donna Anna?

Prince. Often.

Ar.   Yet till now
Never thus smitten! how comes that, my lord?
Prince. Well askt—though ignorantly. Know you not
That not an atom in the universe
Moves without some particular impulse
Of heaven? What yesterday I might abhor,
To-day I may delight in: what to-day
Delight in, may as much to-morrow hate.
All changes; 'tis the element the world,
And we who live there, move in. Thus with me;
This lady I have often seen before,
And, as you say, was ne'er a sigh the worse,
Until to-day; when, whether she more fair,
Or I less blind, I know not—only know
That she has slain me; though to you alone
Of all my friends I would my passion own.
Ar. Much thanks; yet I must wonder, good my lord,
First, that in all your commerce with Don Cupid
You never, I think, dealt seriously till now.
Prince. Perhaps: but if Don Cupid, Arias,
Never yet tempted me with such an offer?
Besides, men alter; princes who are born
To greater things than love, nevertheless
May at his feet their sovereignty lay down
Once in their lives; as said the ancient sage—
" He were a fool who had not done so once,
Though he who does so twice is twice a fool."
Ar. So much for that. My second wonder is,
That you commit this secret to *my* keeping;
An honour that, surpassing my desert,
Yea, and ambition, frights me. Good my lord,
Your secretary, Don Cesar,—
To whom you almost trust the government

Of your dominions,—whom you wholly love,
I also love, and would not steal from him
A confidence that is by right his own;
Call him, my lord: into his trusty heart
Pour out your own; let not my loyalty
To you endanger what I owe to him;
For if you lay't on me—
   Prince.   Don Arias,
I love Don Cesar with as whole a heart
As ever. He and I from infancy
Have grown together; as one single soul
Our joys and sorrows shar'd; till finding him
So wise and true, as to another self
Myself, and my dominion to boot,
I did intrust: you are his friend, and surely
In honouring you I honour him as well.
Besides, Arias, I know not how it is,
For some while past a change has come on him;
I know not what the cause: he is grown sad,
Neglects his business—if I call to him,
He hears me not, or answers from the purpose,
Or in mid answer stops. And, by the way,
We being on this subject, I would fain,
Being so much his friend, for both our sakes,
You would find out what ails and occupies him;
Tell him from me to use my power as ever,
Absolute still: that, loving him so well,
I'd know what makes him so unlike himself;
That, knowing what it is, I may at least,
If not relieve his sorrow, share with him.
   Ar. Oh, not unjustly do you bear the name
Of Alexander, greater than the great
In true deserts!

Enter LAZARO (*with a letter*).

Laz. Not here? my usual luck; had I bad news to tell
my master, such as would earn me a broken head, I should
find him fast enough; but now when I have such a letter
for him as must bring me a handsome largess, oh, to be
sure he's no where to be found. But I'll find him if I
go to—

Prince. How now? Who's there?

Laz. The Prince!—Mum! (*hides the letter and turns to go*).

Prince. Who is it, I say?

Ar. A servant, my lord, of Don Cesar's, looking for his
master, I suppose.

Prince. Call him back; perhaps he can tell us something
of his master's melancholy.

Ar. True, my lord. Lazaro!

Laz. Eh?

Ar. His Highness would speak with you.

Prince. Come hither, sir.

Laz. Oh, my lord, I do well enough here: if I were once
to kiss your Highness' feet, I could not endure common
shoe-leather for a month to come.

Ar. His humour must excuse him.

Prince. You are Don Cesar's servant, are you?

Laz. Yes, one of your trinity; so please you.

Prince. Of my trinity, how so?

Laz. As thus; your Highness is one with Don Cesar; I
am one with him; ergo—

Prince. Well, you are a droll knave. But stop, stop:
whither away so fast?

Laz. Oh, my lord, I am sure you will have none of so
poor an article as myself, who am already the property of
another too.

Prince. Nay, I like your humour, so it be in season. But there is a time for all things. I want you now to answer me seriously and not in jest : and tell me the secret of your master's melancholy, which I feel as my own. But perhaps he is foolish who looks for truth in the well of a jester's mouth.

Laz. But not so foolish as he who should throw it there. And therefore since my master is no fool, it is unlikely he should have committed his mystery to me. However, in my capacity of *Criado*, whose first commandment it is, "Thou shalt reveal thy master's weakness as thy own," I will tell you what I have gathered from stray sighs and interjections of his on the subject. There has lately come over from Spain a certain game of great fashion and credit called Ombre. This game Don Cesar learned ; and, playing at it one day, and happening to hold Basto, Malilla, Spadille, and Ace of Trumps in his hand, stood for the game ; and lost. On which he calls out "foul play," leaves the party, and goes home. Well, at night, I being fast asleep in my room, comes he to me in his shirt, wakes me up, and, dealing cards as it were with his hands, says, "If I let this trick go, I am embeasted for that, and besides put the lead into the enemy's hand ; therefore I trump with one of my matadores, and then I have four hearts, of which the ten-ace *must* make, or else let them give me back my nine cards as I had them before discarding." And this I take it is the cause of his dejection *.

* I will not answer for the accuracy of my version of this dilemma at Ombre: neither perhaps could Lazaro for his : which, together with the indifference (I presume) of all present readers on the subject, has made me indifferent about it. Cesar, I see, starts with almost the same fine hand Belinda had, who also was
> "*Just in the jaws of ruin and Codille,*"
as he was, but, unlike him, saved by that unseen king of hearts that
> "*Lurk'd in her hand and mourn'd his captive queen.*"

Prince. The folly of asking you has been properly chastised by the folly of your answer. You are right; Don Cesar would never have intrusted with a grave secret one only fit for idle jest.

Laz. Ah, they are always importing some nonsense or other from Spain. God keep your Highness; I will take warning not to intrude my folly upon you any more (until you try again to worm some truth out of me). [*Aside and exit.*

Prince. A droll fellow! Were one in the humour, he might amuse.

Ar. Oh, you will always find him in the same, whenever you are in the mood. (He cannot be sad.

Prince. He cannot be very wise then.

Ar. He is as God made him. | Did you never hear any of his stories?

Prince. I think not.

Ar. He will hardly tell you one of himself that yet might amuse you. He was one day playing at dice with me; lost all his money; and at last pawned his very sword, which I would not return him, wishing to see how he got on without. What does he but finds him up an old hilt, and clapping on a piece of lath to that, sticks it in the scabbard. And so wears it now.

Prince. We will have some amusement of him by and by.
Alas! in vain I hope with idle jest
To cool the flame that rages in my breast.
Go to Don Cesar: get him to reveal
The sorrows that he feeling I too feel.
I'll to my sister; since, whether away,
Or present, Donna Anna needs must slay,
I will not starve with absence, but e'en die
Burn'd in the sovereign splendour of her eye.

[*Exeunt severally.*

SCENE II. *A Room in* DON CESAR'S *House.—Enter* DON CESAR *and* LAZARO *meeting.*

Laz. A letter, sir, Elvira just gave me.

Ces. A letter! Give it me. How long have you had it?

Laz. I looked for you first at the Prince's.

Ces. Where I was not?

Laz. You know it! I am always looking for what cannot be found in time. But if you like the letter I shall claim my largess for all that.

Ces. Ah! what does she say?

Laz. The folly, now, of a man with his watch in his hand asking other people for the time of day!

Ces. My heart fails me. Even if your news be good it comes late.   [*He reads the letter.*

Laz. So let my reward then—only let it come at last.

Ces. O Lazaro, half drunk with my success,
I lose my wits when most I've need of them.
She writes to me, my lady writes to me
So sweetly, yea, so lovingly;
Methinks I want to tear my bosom open,
And lay this darling letter on my heart.
Where shall I shrine it?

Laz.   Oh, if that be all,
Keep it to patch your shoe with; I did so once
When some such loving lady writ to me,
And it did excellently; keeping tight
Her reputation, and my shoe together.

Ces. O Lazaro! good Lazaro! take for this
The dress I wore at Florence.

Laz.   Bless you, sir.

Ces. My letter! oh my lady!

Laz.   I bethink me
Upon remembrance, sir, as I may say,
The pockets of that dress were very large
And empty.
  Ces.   They shall be well lined.   Don Arias!

Enter DON ARIAS.

  Ar. Ay, Cesar, Arias coming to complain
On his own score, and that of one far greater.
  Ces. A solemn preamble.   But for the charge,
And him who heads it.
  Ar.   The Prince, our common Lord,
Who much perplext and troubled too, Don Cesar,
About the melancholy that of late
(No need say more of that which best you know)
Has clouded over you, has askt of me
Whom he will have to be your bosom friend,
The cause of it.—Alas, 'tis very plain
I am not what he thinks.—Well, I am come,
Say not as friend, but simple messenger,
To ask it of yourself.
  Ces.   You do yourself
And me wrong, Arias; perchance the Prince—
But yet say on.
  Ar.   His Highness bids me say
That if your sadness rise from any sense
Of straiten'd power, whatever residue
Of princely rule he hitherto reserved,
He gives into your hands; as sov'reign lord
To govern his dominions as your own.
Thus far his Highness.   For myself, Don Cesar,
Having no other realm to lord you of

Than a true heart, I'd have you think betimes,
That, deep as you are rooted in his love,
Nay, may be all the more for that, he feels
Your distaste to his service, and himself:
I'd have you think that all a subject's merits,
However highly heap'd, however long,
Still are but heaps of sand, that some new tide
Of royal favour may wash clean away,
One little error cancelling perhaps
The whole account of life-long services.
Be warn'd by me; clear up your heavy brow,
And meet his kind looks with a look as kind,
Whatever cloud be on the heart within:
If not your friend, Don Cesar, as your servant
Let me implore you.

   Ces.   Oh, Don Arias,
I kiss his Highness' feet, and your kind hands
That bring his favours to me: and to each
Will answer separately.   First, to him;—
Tell him I daily pray that Heav'n so keep
His life, that Time, on which his years are strung,
Forget the running count; and, secondly,
Assure him, Arias, the melancholy
He speaks of not a jot abates my love
Of him, nor my alacrity in his service;
Nay, that 'tis nothing but a little cloud
In which my books have wrapt me so of late
That, duty done, I scarce had time or spirit
Left to enjoy his gracious company:
Perhaps too, lest he surfeit of my love,
I might desire by timely abstinence
To whet his liking to a newer edge.
Thus much for him.   For you, Don Arias,

Whose equal friendship claims to be repaid
In other coin, I will reveal to you
A secret scarcely to myself confest,
Which yet scarce needs your thanks, come at a moment
When my brimm'd heart had overflow'd in words,
Whether I would or no.   Oh, Arias,
Wonder not then to see me in a moment
Flying from melancholy to mere joy,
Between whose poles he ever oscillates,
Whose heart is set in the same sphere with mine :
Which saying, all is said.   I love, my friend;
How deeply, let this very reticence,
That dare not tell what most I feel, declare.
Yes, I have fixt my eyes upon a star;
Toward which to spread my wings ev'n against hope,
Argues a kind of honour.   I aspir'd,
And (let not such a boast offend the ears,
That of themselves have open'd to my story,)
Not hopelessly: the heav'n to which I pray'd
Answer'd in only listening to my vows;
Such daring not defeated not disdain'd.
Two years I worshipp'd at a shrine of beauty,
That modesty's cold hand kept stainless still;
Till wearied, if not mov'd by endless prayers,
She grants them; yea, on this most blessed day,
With this thrice blessed letter.   You must see it,
That your felicitations by rebound
Double my own; the first victorious trophy
That proud ambition has so humbly won.
Oh Arias, 'tis much I have to tell,
And tell you too at once; being none of those
Who overmuch entreaty make the price
Of their unbosoming; who would, if they knew

In what the honour of their lady lies,
Name her at once, or seal their lips for ever.
But you are trusty and discreet: to you
I may commit my heart; beseeching you
To keep this love-song to yourself alone,
Assigning to the Prince, remember this,
My books sole cause of my abstraction.
Donna Anna de Castelvi—
(I can go on more freely now the name
Of her I worship bars my lips no more,)
Is she who so divides me from myself,
That what I say I scarcely know, although
I say but what I feel: the melancholy
You ask about, no gloomy sequestration
Out of the common world into a darker,
But into one a thousand times more bright;
And let no man believe he truly loves,
Who lives, or moves, or thinks, or hath his being
In any other atmosphere than Love's,
Who is our absolute master; to recount
The endless bead-roll of whose smiles and tears
I'd have each sleepless night a century,
Much have I said—have much more yet to say!
But read her letter, Arias, the first seal
Of my success, the final one, I think,
Of my sure trust in you; come, share with me
My joy, my glory, my anxiety;
And above all things, once more, Arias,
Down to your secret'st heart this secret slip;
   For every secret hangs in greater fear
   Between the speaker's mouth and hearer's ear
Than any peril between cup and lip.
   Ar. You have good cause for joy.

Ces.   You will say so
When you have read the letter.
    Ar.   You desire it. (*Reads.*)
" To confess that one is loved is to confess that one loves
too; for there is no woman but loves to be loved. But
alas, there is yet more. If to cover my love I have pretended
disdain, let the shame of now confessing it excuse me. Come
to me this evening and I will tell you what I can scarce
understand myself. Adieu, my love, adieu !"
Your hands are full indeed of happy business.
    Ces. Enough : you know what you shall tell the Prince
In my behalf : if he be satisfied
I'll wait on him directly.
    Ar.   Trust to me.
    Ces. Let my sighs help thee forward, O thou sun
What of thy race in heaven remains to run :
Oh do but think that Dafne in the west
Awaits thee, and anticipate thy rest !
                            [*Exeunt* CESAR *and* LAZARO.
    Ar. Charg'd with two secrets,
One from my Prince the other from my friend,
Each binding equally to silence, each
Equally the other's revelation needing,
How shall I act, luckless embosomer
Of other's bosoms ! how decide between
Loyalty and love with least expense to both !
The Prince's love is but this morning's flower,
As yet unsunn'd on by his lady's favour ;
Cesar's of two years' growth, expanded now
Into full blossom by her smiles and tears ;
The Prince too loves him whom his lady loves,
And were he told, might uncontested leave
The prize that one he loves already owns ;

And so both reap the fruit, and make the excuse
Of broken silence, if it needs must break.
And yet I grope about, afraid to fall
Where ill-advised good-will may ruin all.   [*Exit.*

SCENE III.   *A Corridor in the Palace.—Enter* PRINCE, DON
FELIX, DONNA ANNA, *and train.*

Prince. I must show you the way.

Anna. Your Highness must not do yourself so great
indignity.

Prince. To the bounds at least of my sister's territory.

Anna. Nay, my lord, that were undue courtesy.

Prince. What courtesy, madam, can be undue from any
man to any lady?

Anna. When that lady is your subject, whom your very
condescension dazzles to her own discomfiture.

Prince. What, as the morning star dazzles the sun whom
he precedes as petty harbinger? If I obey you 'tis that I
fear my own extinction in your rays. Adieu.

Anna. God keep your Highness.   [*Exit.*

Prince. Don Felix, will you attend your sister?

Felix. I only stay to thank your Highness, (both as sub-
ject and as servant,) for all the honour that you do us; may
Heaven so prolong your life that even oblivion herself—

Prince. Nay, truce to compliment: your sister will not of
my company, unless under your proxy. So farewell. [*Exit*
FELIX.] Is there a greater nuisance than to have such
windy nonsense stuff'd into one's ears, when delight is
vanished from the eyes!

Enter ARIAS.

But, Don Arias! You have seen Cesar?

Ar. Yes, my lord; but ere I tell you about him, would

F.   II

know how far this last interview with Donna Anna has
advanced your love.

Prince. Oh Arias, Arias, my love for her
So blends with my solicitude for him,
I scarce can hold me clear between the two.
Yet let me tell you. In my sister's room,
Whither I went, you know, upon our parting,
I saw my lady like a sovereign rose
Among the common flowers; or, if you will,
A star among the roses; or the star
Of stars, the morning star: yea, say at once
The sun himself among the host of heaven!
My eyes and ears were rapt with her; her lips
Not fairer than the words that came from them.
At length she rose to go: like the ev'ning star
Went with the ev'ning; which, how short, say love
Who 'd spin each golden moment to a year,
Which year would then seem than a moment less.

Ar. Is then, my lord, this passion so deep fixt?

Prince. Nay, but of one day's growth—

Ar.   I come in time then,
My lord, in one word, if you love Don Cesar,
Cease to love Donna Anna.

Prince.   Arias,
He who begins to hint at any danger
Is bound to tell it out—nothing, or all.
Why do you hesitate?

Ar.   Because, my lord,
But hinting this to you, I break the seal
Of secrecy to him.

Prince.   But it is broken;
And so—

Ar.   Oh, Cesar, pardon him who fails

His pledge to you to serve his Prince! My lord,
The cloud you long have seen on Cesar's brow,
Is not, as he would have you think it, born
Of bookish studies only, but a cloud,
All bright within, though dark to all without,
Of love for one he has for two long years
Silently worshipt.

 Prince. Donna Anna!

 Ar.   Ay.

 Prince. Cesar loves Donna Anna! be it so—
I love him, as you say, and would forego
Much for his sake. But tell me, Arias,
Knows Anna of his passion?

 Ar.   Yes, my lord,
And answers it with hers.

 Prince.   Oh wretched fate!
Desperate ere jealous—jealous ere in love!
If Cesar but lov'd her, I could, methinks,
Have pardon'd, even have advanc'd his suit
By yielding up my own. But that *she* loves,
Blows rivalry into full blaze again.
And yet I will not be so poor a thing
To whine for what is now beyond my reach,
Nor must the princely blood of Parma
Run jealous of a subject's happiness.
They love each other then?

 Ar.   I even now
Have seen a letter—

 Prince. Well?

 Ar.   That Donna Anna
Has written him, and in such honey'd words—

 Prince. Why, is it not enough to know she loves him?
You told me so: my mind made up to that,

Why should a foolish letter fright it back?
And yet—yet, what last spark of mortal love
But must flame up before it dies for ever
To learn but what that foolish letter said!
Know you?

   Ar.   I saw it.

   Prince.   You saw it! and what said it?

   Ar. After a chaste confession of her love,
Bidding him be to-night under her lattice.

   Prince. Under her lattice, while his Prince is left
Abroad; they two to whisper love together,
While he gnaws hopeless jealousy alone.
But why, forsooth, am I to be the victim?
If I can quench my love for Cesar's sake,
Why not he his for me? Tell me, Don Arias,
Does Cesar know my passion?

   Ar.   How should he,
You having told the secret but to me?

   Prince. By the same means that I know his.

   Ar.   My lord,
My loyalty might well be spar'd that taunt.

   Prince. Ah, Arias, pardon me, I am put out,
But not with you, into whose faithful charge
I vest my love and honour confidently.
Enough, in what I am about to do
I mean no malice or ill play to Cesar:
'Tis but an idle curiosity:
And surely 'tis but fair, that if his Prince
Leave him the lists to triumph in at leisure,
I may at least look on the game he wins.
You shall keep close to him, and tell me all
That passes between him and her I love.

   Ar. But having taunted me with my first step

In your behalf, my lord—
   Prince.   Nay, sir, my will
At once absolves and authorizes you,
For what is told and what remains to tell.
   Ar. But, sir—
   Prince.   No more—
   Ar.   I must obey your bidding,
But yet—
   Prince. I may divert my jealousy,
If not avenge it.
   Ar.   Ah! what straits do those
Who cannot keep their counsel fall into!
   Prince. All say so, and all blab, like me and you!
Look where he comes; let us retire awhile.
                  [PRINCE *and* ARIAS *retire.*

     Enter CESAR *and* LAZARO.

  Ces. O Phœbus, swift across the skies
      Thy blazing carriage post away;
      Oh, drag with thee benighted day,
    And let the dawning night arise!
    Another sun shall mount the throne
      When thou art sunk beneath the sea;
    From whose effulgence, as thine own,
      The affrighted host of stars shall flee.
  Laz. A pretty deal about your cares
      Does that same Phœbus care or know;
    He has to mind his own affairs,
      Whether you shake your head or no.
    You talk of hastening on the day?
      Why heaven's coachman is the Sun,
    Who can't be put out of his way
      For you, sir, or for any one.

Ces. The Prince! and something in my bosom tells me
All is not well. My lord, though my repentance
Does not, I trust, lag far behind my fault,
I scarce had dar'd to approach your Highness' feet,
Had not my friend, Don Arias, been before
As harbinger of my apology.

   Prince. Cesar, indeed Don Arias has told me
The story of your sadness : and so well,
I feel it, and excuse it, as my own ;
From like experience. I do not resent,
But would divert you from it. Books, my friend,
Truly are so seductive company,
We are apt to sit too long and late with them,
And drowse our minds in their society ;
This must not be ; the cause of the disease
Once known, the cure is easy ; if 'tis books
Have hurt you, lay them by awhile, and try
Other society—less learn'd perhaps,
But cheerfuller—exchange the pent-up air
Of a close study for the breathing world.
Come, we'll begin to-night ;
Visit in disguise (as I have wish'd to do)
The city, its taverns, theatres, and streets,
Where music, masque, and dancing may divert
Your melancholy : what say you to this ?

   Ces. Oh, my kind lord, whose single word of pardon
Has turn'd all leaden grief to golden joy,
Made me another man, or, if you will,
The better self I was—

   Prince.   Why this is well ;
To-night together then—

   Ces.   Yet pardon me.

   Prince. How now ?

Ces.   It almost would revive my·pain
That you should spend yourself upon a cure
Your mere forgiveness has already wrought.
Let this day's happiness suffice the day,
And its night also: 'twill be doubly sweet,
Unbought by your annoyance.
Prince.   Nay, my Cesar,
Fear not for that: after so long estrangement,
My pain would be the losing sight of you
On this first night of your recovery.
Lazaro!
Laz. My lord?
Prince.   You too shall go with us.
Laz. And not a trustier shall your Highness find
To guard your steps.
Prince.   What! you are valiant?
Laz. As ever girded sword.
Prince.   Your weapon good too?
Laz. He touches on the quick (*aside*). Yes, good enough,
My lord, for all my poor occasions.
Although when waiting on your Grace, indeed,
A sword like yours were better.
Prince.   You depreciate
Your own to enhance its value. Sharp is't?
Laz.   Ay,
Not a steel buckler but at the first blow
'Twould splinter it in two. (The sword I mean.) *Aside.*
Prince. Well temper'd?
Laz.   As you bid it.
Prince.   And the device
Inscrib'd upon it?
Laz.   "Thou shalt do no murder"—
Having no love for homicide, *per se,*

Save on occasion.

Prince.   Your description
Makes me desire to see that sword.

Laz.   My lord!

Prince. Indeed it does. Show it me.

Laz.   Oh, my lord,
I have a vow.

Ces. (aside). Oh weariness!

Prince.   A vow?

Laz. Ay, register'd in heaven!
Never to draw this weapon from her sheath
Except on mortal quarrel. If in such
Your Highness' service challenge her, why, then
She shall declare herself.

Ces.   I'm desperate!
But yet one effort more. My lord, you see
(You cannot fail) how your mere word of grace
Has of itself brighten'd me up again;
I do beseech you—

Prince.   Pardon me, my Cesar,
Rather I see the cloud that 'gins to break
Is not entirely gone; nay, will return
If you be left alone—which must not be:
If not for your sake, Cesar, yet for mine,
Who feel for your disquiet as my own;
And since our hearts are knit so close together,
Yours cannot suffer but mine straightway feels
A common pain; seek we a common cure.
To-night I shall expect you. Until then,
Farewell.   [*Exit.*

Ces.   Fortune! to see a fair occasion
So patiently pursued, so fairly won,
Lost at the very moment of success!

O Lazaro—what will my lady say?

Laz. That I can't guess.

Ces.   What will she do?

Laz.   Oh that
Is answer'd far more easily. She'll stand
All night beside the window to no purpose.

Ces. Why she must say my love was all pretence,
And her offended dignity vindicate,
Rejecting me for ever! Misery!

Laz. Dear me, sir, what is now become of all
About, "Thou dawning night, benighted day."
"Thou coachman sun!" etceteretera?

Ces. Wilt thou be ever fool?

Laz.   If thou be not,
Listen—fool's bolts, they say, are quickly shot—
Who secrets have and cannot hold 'em,
Shall surely rue the day they told 'em.

ACT II.

SCENE I.   *A Public Square in Parma.—Night.—Enter*
PRINCE, CESAR, FELIX, ARIAS, *and* LAZARO, *disguised.*

Ar. A lovely night!

Prince.   As Night we choose to call,
When Day's whole sun is but distributed
Into ten thousand stars.

Fel.   Beside the moon,
Who lightly muffled like ourselves reveals
Her trembling silver.

Laz.   What! by way, you mean,
Of making up the account?

Ces. (aside).   To think, alas !
The first sweet vintage of my love thus lost,
And, as my lady must too surely think,
By my forgetfulness. (*Aloud.*) My lord, indeed
The night wears on.   May not the chiller air
That blows from the returning tide of day
Affect you ?
   Prince.   Nay, my state forbidding me
Much to be seen about the streets by day,
The night must serve my purpose.
   Ces. (aside).   Patience then !
And I must try and draw my thoughts from her
I cannot reach. (*Aloud.*) How does the lady Flora
Please you, my lord?
   Prince.   The lady Flora ?   Oh,
What she of Milan ?   Too far off, I think,
For one's regards to reach.
   Laz.   Ah true, my lord ;
What is the use of a mistress in the moon,
Unless one were the man there ?
   Ar.   Signora Laura
Has a fair figure.
   Laz.   Yes, and asks a high one.
   Felix. A handsome hand.
   Laz.   At scolding, yes.
   Ar.   I think
She lives close by.
   Laz.   But don't you bid for her
Without fair trial first, my lord.   Your women
Are like new plays, which self-complacent authors
Offer at some eight hundred royals each,
But which, when once they're tried, you purchase dear
Eight hundred for a royal.

Ces. (aside).　　　　　　Now, methinks,
Ev'n now my lady at the lattice stands
Looking for me in vain, and murmuring
"Why comes he not? I doubted I was late,
But he comes not at all!" And then—Ah me,
✗ I have forgotten to forget!—
(*Aloud*) Celia sings well, my lord?
　　Laz.　　　　　　　　　A pretty woman
Can no more sing amiss than a good horse
Be a bad colour.
　　`Ces.*　　　　　The old Roman law
To all the ugly women us'd to assign
The fortunes of the handsome, thinking those
Sufficiently endow'd with their good looks.
　　Laz. Ah! and there Laura lives, the lass who said
She'd sell her house and buy a coach withal;
And when they ask'd her, where she'd live, quoth she,
"Why, *in* my coach!" "But when night comes," say they,
"Where then?"—"Why in the coach-house to be sure!"*
　　Ces. Indeed, indeed, my lord, the night wears on,
And sure your sister lies awake foreboding
Some danger to your person.
Consider her anxiety!
　　Prince (aside).　　Nay, *yours*
Lies nearer to my heart.
　　Ces.　　　　　　My lord?
　　Prince.　　　　　　　I said
No matter for my sister, that was all;
She knows not I'm abroad.

---

* The ambition for a coach so frequently laughed at by Calderon,
is said to be in full force now; not for the novelty of the invention,
then, nor perhaps the dignity, so much as for the real comfort of
easy and sheltered carriage in such a climate.

Ces.   My hope is gone!

Laz. There, yonder in that little house, there lives
A girl with whom it were impossible
To deal straightforwardly.

Prince.   But why?

Laz.   She's crooked.

Ar. And there a pretty girl enough, but guarded
By an old dragon aunt.

Laz.   O Lord, defend me
From all old women!

Prince.   How so, Lazaro?

Laz. Oh, ever since the day I had to rue
The conjurer's old woman.

Prince.   Who was she?

Laz. Why, my lord, once upon a time
I fell in love with one who would not have me
Either for love or money: so at last
I go to a certain witch—tell him my story:
Whereon he bids me do this; cut a lock
From my love's head and bring it to him. Well,
I watch'd my opportunity, and one day,
When she was fast asleep, adroitly lopp'd
A lovely forelock from what seem'd her hair,
But was an hair-loom rather from her wig
Descended from a head that once was young
As I thought her. For, giving it the witch,
To work his charm with, in the dead of night,
When I was waiting for my love to come,
Into my bed-room the dead woman stalk'd
To whom the lock of hair had once belong'd,
And claim'd me for her own. O Lord, how soon
"Sweetheart" and "Deary" chang'd to "Apage!"
And flesh and blood to ice.

Ces. (*aside*).   Alas! what boots it trying to forget
That which the very effort makes remember?
Ev'n now, ev'n now, methinks once more I see her
Turn to the window, not expecting me,
But to abjure all expectation,
And, as she moves away, saying, (methinks
I hear her,) "Cesar, come when come you may,
You shall not find me here." "Nay, but my love,
Anna! my lady! hear me!" Oh confusion,_
Did they observe?
      Prince (*aside to Arias*).   How ill, Don Arias,
Poor Cesar hides his heart—
      Ar.   Ev'n now he tries
The mask again.
      Prince.   Indeed I pity him,
Losing one golden opportunity;
But may not I be pitied too, who never
Shall have so much as one to lose?
      Ar.   Speak low;
You know her brother's by.
      Prince.   No matter; true
Nobility is slowest to suspect.
      Musician (*sings within*).

> Ah happy bird, who can fly with the wind,
> Leaving all anguish of absence behind;
>   Like thee could I fly,
>   Leaving others to sigh,
> The lover I sigh for how soon would I find!*

Ces. Not an ill voice!
Fel.   Nay, very good.
Prince.   How sweetly

* This little song is from the *Desdicha de la Voz.*

Sweet words, sweet air, sweet voice, atone together!
Arias, might we not on this sweet singer
Try Lazaro's metal and mettle? you shall see.
Lazaro!

Laz. My lord!

Prince.   I never go abroad
But this musician dogs me.

Laz.   Shall I tell him
Upon your Highness's request, politely,
To move away?

Prince.   I doubt me, Lazaro,
He will not go for that, he's obstinate.

Laz. How then, my lord?

Prince. Go up and strike him with your sword.

Laz. But were it brave in me, back'd as I am,
To draw my sword on one poor piping bird?
If I must do it, let me challenge him
Alone to-morrow.
But let me warn him first.

Prince.   Do as I bid you,
Or I shall call you coward.

Ces.   Lazaro,
Obey his Highness.

Laz.   O good providence, ·
Temper the wind to a shorn lamb!

Musician (within).

> Ah happy bird, whom the wind and the rain,
> And snare of the fowler, beset but in vain;
>   Oh, had I thy wing,
>   Leaving others to sing,
> How soon would I be with my lover again!

Laz. (aloud within). Pray God, poor man, if thou be
    innocent

Of any ill intention in thy chirping,
The blade I draw upon thee turn to wood!
A miracle! A miracle! (*Rushing in.*)

   Prince.   How now?

   Laz. The sword I lifted on an innocent man,
Has turn'd to wood at his assailant's prayer!
Take it, my lord, lay't in your armoury
Among the chiefest relics of our time.
I freely give it you, upon condition
You give me any plain but solid weapon
To wear instead.

   Prince.   You are well out of it.
It shall be so.

   Ces.   My lord, indeed the dawn
Is almost breaking.

   Prince.   Let it find us here.
But, my dear Cesar, tell me, are you the better
For this diversion!

   Ces.   Oh, far cheerfuller.
Though with some little effort.

   Prince.   And I too.
So love is like all other evils known;
With others' sorrow we beguile our own.   [*Exeunt.*

SCENE II.—*The Garden of* DONNA ANNA's *House;* DONNA
    ANNA *and* ELVIRA *at a window.*—*Dawn.*

   Elv. Yet once more to the window?

   Anna.   Oh Elvira,
For the last time! now undeceiv'd to know
How much deceiv'd I was!
Alas, until I find myself despis'd,
Methought I was desir'd, till hated, lov'd;

Was't not enough to know himself belov'd,
Without insulting her who told him so?
Was't not enough—
Oh wonder not, Elvira, at my passion;
Of all these men's enchantments, none more potent
Than what might seem unlikeliest—their disdain.

 Elv. Indeed you have good cause for anger, madam:
But yet one trial more.
 Anna.   And to what end?
I'll not play Tantalus again for him.
Oh shameful insult! had I dream'd of it,
Would I have written him so tenderly?
Told my whole heart?—But, once in love, what woman
Can trust herself, alas, with pen and ink?

 Elv. Were he to come now after all, how then?
Would you reproach, or turn your back on him,
Or—

 Anna. Nay, I know not. Is't not possible,
He is detain'd, Elvira, by the Prince
Upon state business?

 Elv.   You excuse him then!

 Anna. Oh, any thing to soothe me!

 Elv.   Who excuses
Will quickly pardon.

 Anna.   Ay, if he came now,
Now, as you say, Elvira,
And made excuses which I knew were false,
I *would* believe them still. Would he were come
Only to try. Could I be so deceiv'd!

Enter CESAR *and* LAZARO, *below.*

 Laz. See you not day has dawn'd, sir?

 Ces.   Mine, I doubt,

Is set for ever.   Yet, in sheer despair,
I come to gaze upon the empty east!
But look!
   Laz.   Well, sir?
   Ces.   See you not through the twilight?
   Laz. Yes, sir; a woman: and when I say a woman,
I mean two women.
   Ces.   Oh see if it be she.
   Laz. 'Twould make Elvira jealous, sir.
   Ces.   Oh‾ lady,
Is it you?
   Anna. Yes I, Don Cesar: who all night
Have waited on your pleasure, unsuspecting
What now too well I know.
My foolish passion, sir, is well reveng'd
By shamed repentance.   Oh, you come at last,
Thinking belike, sir, with the morning star
Retrieve the waste of night; oh, you lov'd me, sir,
Or seem'd to do, till having won from me
Confession of a love I feel no more,
You turn it to disdain.   Oh think not, sir,
That by one little deed in love, like law,
You gain the full possession of my heart
For ever; and for this idle interview,
Do you so profit by it as to learn
Courtesy to a lady; which when learn'd
Come and repeat to me.   [*Retires from window.*
   Ces.   And having now
Arraign'd me of the crime, why do you leave me
To plead my exculpation to the winds?
O Donna Anna, I call Heav'n to witness
'Twas not my negligence, but my ill star
That envied me such ill-deserv'd delight.

   F.   12

If it be otherwise,
Or even you *suspect* it otherwise,
Spurn me, not only now, but ever, from you.
Since better were it with a conscience clear
Rejected, than suspiciously receiv'd.
The Prince has kept me all the night with him
About the city streets : your brother, who
Was with us, can bear witness. Yet if still
You think me guilty, but come back to say so,
And let me plead once more, and you once more
Condemn, and yet once more, and all in vain,
If you will only but come back again !
　　Anna (returning to the window). And this is true ?
　　Ces. So help me Heav'n, it is !
Why, could you, Anna, in your heart believe
I could forget you ?
　　Anna.　　　　　And, Don Cesar, you
That, were it so, I could forget my love ?
But see, the sun above the mountain-tops
Begins to peep, and morn to welcome him
With all her smiles and tears. We must begone.
I shall another quick occasion find,
When I shall call, and you—not lag behind ?
　　Ces. Oh once more taken to your heart again,
My shame turns glory, and delight my pain.
Yet tell me—
　.*Anna.*　　　Well ?
　　Ces.　　　　　　Of your suspicions *one*
Lingers within you ?
　　Anna.　　　　　Ay, a legion,
That at your presence to their mistress' pride
Turn traitors, and all fight on Cesar's side !
　　Ces. Farewell then, my divine implacable !

Anna. Victim and idol of my eyes, farewell!

[*Exeunt severally.*

Laz. Well, and what has *my* mistress to say to me?
Does she also play the scornful lady?

Elv. I? why?

Laz. Because my mistress' mistress does so to my master
whose love I follow in shadow.

Elv. Oh, I did not understand.

Laz. When he's happy then I'm jolly;
When he's sad I'm melancholy:
When he's love-infected, I
   With the self-same fever fretted,
Either am bound like him to fry,
   Or if he chooses to forget it,
I must even take his cue,
And, Elvira, forget you.
Do you enact your lady. Now,
Begin. Be angry first—

Elv.   But how?

Laz. Hide up, no matter how or why,
Behind the window-blind, while I
   Underneath it caterwaul;—

Elv. What are the odds I don't reply?

Laz. Just the odds that I don't call.

SCENE III. *A Room in the Palace.*—*The* PRINCE *and* DON
   FELIX, *discovered at the back of the stage.*

Fel. Why is your Highness sad?

Prince.   Not sad, Don Felix:
Oh would it were some certain shape of sorrow
That I might grapple with, not a vague host

Of undefin'd emotions! Oh how oft
The patching up of but a single seam,
Opens a hundred others! Lucky he
Who can to disenchantment bare his eyes
Once and for all, and in oblivion
Shut up vain hope for ever!

Enter CESAR, ARIAS, *and* LAZARO, *in front.*

Ces. (*to* ARIAS *as they enter*). And so at last was satisfied.

Ar. His Highness and Don Felix.

Ces. I am sure that he who profits not by opportunity scarce covets it enough. Taking advantage of the cleared heaven, I have here written my lady, asking her when she will give me the meeting she promised; Lazaro, take the letter : Don Felix here, you can easily deliver it.

Laz. I'll feign an errand, and so get into the house. [*Exit.*

Fel. (*to* PRINCE). Cesar and Arias, my lord.

Prince. I know their business. Oh what a tempest does every breeze from that quarter raise in my bosom! Well, gentlemen?

Ar. Cesar, my lord, was telling me—

Prince. About his melancholy studies still? Pray tell me.

Ces. Nay, my lord, all melancholy flies from the sunshine of your presence.

Prince. What then?

Ces. I still distrust myself; Don Arias must, my lord, answer for me.

Prince. Don Arias, then?

Ar. (*aside*). Fresh confidence should bind me his anew. But comes too late.

Ces. (*aside to* ARIAS). Be careful what you say.

Ar. Trust me. (CESAR *retires.*)

Prince (*to* ARIAS *apart*). Well now, Don Arias.

Ar. At first much enraged against him, at last she yielded to his amorous excuses; and, finding Don Felix here, he has sent her a letter beseeching another meeting.

Prince. When?

Ar. This moment.

Prince. Who can doubt the upshot! I must contrive to thwart them. (*Aloud.*) But ere I hear your story, Arias, I must tell Don Felix what I was about to do as these gentlemen came in and interrupted me: that his sister was ill—had fainted—from some vexation or fright, as I think.

Fel. Anna?

Prince. So my sister told me. Had you not better see to her?

Fel. With your leave, my lord.   [*Exit.*

Prince (*aside*). And so, as I wished, prevent her answering, if not getting, the letter. (*Aloud.*) I will ask Nisida how it was.   [*Exit.*

Ces. What did you tell the Prince to draw this new trouble on me?

Ar. Ay, even so. Blame him who has been even lying in your service. Look you now, the Prince told me he had overheard the names "Don Felix" and "Donna Anna" between us as we came in talking; and, tethered to that, I was obliged to drag this fainting fit into the service.

Ces. Oh, if Felix find Lazaro at his house!

Ar. Fear not, anxiety will carry him home faster than a letter Lazaro.

Ces. Alas that the revival of my joy
Is the revival of a fresh annoy;
And that the remedy I long'd to seize
Must slay me faster than the old disease.   [*Exeunt.*

SCENE IV. *An Apartment in* DON FELIX'S *House.*—DONNA
ANNA *and* ELVIRA.

Elv. Well, have you finisht writing?
Anna.   I have written,
Not finisht writing. That could never be;
Each sentence, yea, each letter, as I write it,
Suggesting others still. I had hop'd, Elvira,
To sum my story up in a few words;
Took pen and paper, both at the wrong end:—
Tried to begin, my mind so full I knew not
What to begin with; till, as one has seen
The fullest vessel hardly run, until
Some inner air should loose the lingering liquid,
So my charg'd heart waited till one long sigh
Set it a flowing. I wrote, eras'd, re-wrote,
Then, pregnant love still doubling thought on thought,
Doubled the page too hastily, and blotted
All that was writ before; until my letter,
Blotted, eras'd, re-written, and perplext,
At least is a fair transcript of my heart.
Well, the sum is, he is to come, Elvira,
To-night, when Felix, as I heard him say,
Goes to our country house on business;
And all will be more quiet. But here, read it.
Elv. My lord! my lord!—the letter!

Enter FELIX.

Anna (hiding the letter).   Heavens!
Fel.   Too well
The traitorous colour flying from your cheeks

Betrays your illness and my cause of sorrow.
What is the matter?

Anna.   Nothing, brother.

Fel.   Nothing!
Your changing face and your solicitude
To assure me there is nothing, but assure me
How much there is.   I have been told in fact,
And hurried home thus suddenly,
To hear it all.

Anna (*aside*).   Alas! he knows my secret!
Felix, indeed, indeed, my love
Shall not dishonour you.

Fel.   Your love?
I'm more at loss than ever.   But perhaps
You feign this to divert me from the truth.
What is the matter, truly?

Anna.   Be assur'd
I never will disgrace you.

Fel.   Ah, she rambles,
Quite unrecover'd yet.

Anna (*apart to* ELVIRA).   What shall I do?

Elv. (*apart*).   Deny it all, there's many a step between
Suspicion and assurance.

Fel.   You, Elvira,
(My sister cannot) tell me what has happen'd.

Elv. Oh, nothing but a swoon, sir:
My mistress fainted: that is all: accounts
For all her paleness and discomfiture.

Fel. 'Twas that I heard.

Elv.   I do assure you, sir,
We thought her dead—however she dissemble
Out of her love for you.

Fel.   'Twas kind of her:

But yet not kindness, Anna, to delude me
Into a selfish ignorance of your pain.
Enough, you are better now?
   Anna.   Indeed.
   Fel.   That's well.
But, by the way, what meant you by *"your love,"*
And *"not dishonouring me?"*
   Anna.   *"My love,"* and *"not*
Dishonouring!" did I say so? I must mean,
My senses still half-drown'd, my love for you
That would not have you pain'd. A true love, Felix,
Though a mistaken, may be, as you say,
Yet no dishonour.
   Fel.   Still I have not heard
What caus'd this illness.
   Anna (aside).   He presses hard upon me,
But I'll out-double him. (*Aloud.*) The cause of it?
Why—sitting in this room,
I heard a noise in the street there: went to the window,
And saw a crowd of people, their swords out, fighting
Before the door; and (what will foolish fear
Not conjure up?) methought that one of them
Was you—and suddenly a mortal chill
Came over me, and—you must ask Elvira
For all the rest.
   Elv. (aside). Why ever have the trouble
Of coining lies when truth will pass as well!

             Enter LAZARO.

   Laz. So far so good.
   Fel. Lazaro?
   Laz. (seeing FELIX). Is't his ghost? for certainly I left
his body at the palace.

Anna. My evil stars bear hard upon me!

Laz. I'm done for, unless a good lie—(*Aloud.*) Ruffian,
rascal, scamp!

Fel. How now?

Laz. Murderer! villain!

Fel. Softly, softly, breathe awhile! what's the matter?

Laz. Nothing, nothing, yet had I not exploded incident-
ally, or as it were superficially, I had altogether burst.
Oh the rascal! the slave!

Fel. But tell me the matter.

Laz. Oh the matter—indeed the matter—you may well
ask it—indeed you may—Oh the murderer!

Fel. Come, come, tell us.

Laz. Ay, well, look here, my lords and ladies, lend me
your ears; I was at cards: yes: for you must know, my lord,
I sometimes like a bout as my betters do: you understand
this?

Fel. Yes—well?

Laz. Well, being at cards, as I say: ay, and playing pretty
high too: for I must confess that sometimes, like my betters
—you understand?

Fel. Go on—go on.

Laz. Well, being, as I said, at cards,
And playing pretty high too—mark me that—
I get into discussion or dispute,
(Whichever you will call it) with a man,
If man he may be call'd who man was none—
Ye gods! to prostitute the name of man
On such as that!—call him a manikin,
A mandarin, a mandrake,
Rather than man—I mean in *soul*, mark you;
For in his outward man he was a man,
Ay, and a man of might. Nay, more than man,

A giant, one may say. Well, as I said,
This wretch and I got to high words, and then
(Whither high words so often lead) to blows;
Out came our swords. The rascal having seen
What a desperate fellow at my tool I was,
Takes him eleven others of his kidney,
Worse than himself, and all twelve set on me.
I seeing them come on, ejaculate,
"From all such rascals, single or in league,
Good Lord, deliver us," set upon all twelve
With that same sword, mark me, our gracious Prince
Gave me but yesternight, and, God be praised,
Disgrac'd not in the giving—
Beat the whole twelve of them back to a porch,
Where, after bandying a blow with each,
Each getting something to remember me by,
Back in a phalanx all came down on me,
And then dividing, sir, into two parties,
Twelve upon this side—do you see? and nine
On this—and three in front—
 Fel.   But, Lazaro,
Why, twelve and nine are twenty-one—and three—
Why, your twelve men are grown to twenty-four!
How's this?
 Laz. How's this? why, counting in the shadows—
You see I count the shadows—twenty-four,
Shadows and all—you see!*
 Fel.   I see.
 Laz.   Well, sir,
Had not that good sword which our gracious Prince

---

* One cannot fail to be reminded of the multiplication of Falstaff's
men in buckram, not the only odd coincidence between the two poets.
Lazaro's solution of the difficulty seems to me quite worthy of Falstaff.

Gave me but yesterday broke in my hand,
I should have had to pay for mass, I promise you,
For every mother's son of them!

Fel.   Indeed!
But, Lazaro, I see your sword's entire:
How's that?

Laz.   The most extraordinary part
Of all—   .   .

Fel. Well, tell us.

Laz.   Why, I had first us'd
My dagger upon one: and when my sword
Snapt, with its stump, sir, daggerwise I fought,
As thus; and that with such tremendous fury,
That, smiting a steel buckler, I struck out
Such sparks from it, that, by the light of them,
Snatching up the fallen fragment of my sword,
I pieced the two together.

Fel.   But the dagger
You fought with first, and lost, you say—why, Lazaro,
'Tis in your girdle.

Laz.   I account for that
Easily. Look, sir, I drew it, as I said,
And struck amain. The man I drew it on,
Seeing the coming blow, caught hold of it,
And struck it back on me; I, yet more skilful,
With God's good help did so present myself
That, when he struck at me, my own dagger's point
Return'd into its sheath, as here you see it.
Enough, I heard the cry of "Alguazils!"
Ran off, and, entering the first open door,
Now ask for sanctuary at your feet.

Fel. I think it is your trepidation
Makes you talk nonsense.

Anna. Surely, my brother, this was the riot that so frighted me.

Fel. And was I then the man, "if man it could be called who man was none," that Lazaro fought with?

Anna. I know not, I only know 'twas some one of a handsome presence like yours.

Fel. (aside). Perhaps his master—I much suspect it was Cesar that was dicing, and afterward fighting; and his servant, to cover him, invents this foolish story—(*Aloud.*) I will look into the street and see if it be clear.   [*Exit.*

Elv. Now say your say.

Anna (giving LAZARO *her letter).* And quickly, Lazaro; taking this letter—

Laz. (giving CESAR'S). And you this premium upon it.

Anna. Bid him be sure to come to me this evening; I have much to say. And thus much to you, Lazaro; your quarrel came in the nick of time to account for a swoon I had occasion to feign.

Elv. Quick! quick! he's coming back.

Laz. Madam, farewell.

Anna.   And if my plot succeed,
Feign'd quarrel shall to true love-making lead.   [*Exeunt.*

SCENE V. *A Room in the Palace;* CESAR *and* ARIAS
talking: to whom after a time enter LAZARO.

Laz. Oh, I have had rare work.

Ces. The letter! (*takes it from* LAZARO.)

Ar. And how did all end?

Laz. Well—as I am home at last safe and sound.

Ces. Arias, you share my heart; even read my letter with me. (*They read.*)

Laz. (*aside*). That my master should trust that babbler who let out about my wooden sword to the Prince! my life upon't, he'll do the same to him; for he who sucks in gossip is the first to leak it.

Ar. Sweetly she writes!

Ces.   How should it be but sweet,
Where modesty and wit and true love meet?

Ar. And expects you this evening!

Ces. Till which each minute is an hour, each hour
A day, a year, a century!

Laz.   .   And then
In sæcula sæculorum. Amen.

Ar. The Prince!

Ces.   I dread his seeing me.

Ar.   But how?

Ces. Lest, as already twice, he thwart me now.

Enter PRINCE.

Prince. Cesar here, when I am on fire to know the upshot of my plot upon his letter! I must get quit of him.

Ces. Good day, my lord.

Prince. Well, any news abroad?

Ar. Not that I know of, my lord.

Prince. Cesar, there are despatches in my closet, have been lying there since yesterday, should they not be seen to at once?

Ces. My lord! (*Aside.*) I foresaw it!

Prince. Yes! I would have you look to them and report them to me directly.

Ces. (*aside*). Ah, this is better! (*Aloud.*) I'll see to them. (*Aside.*) And then, I trust, day's work with daylight o'er,
Man, nor malicious star, shall cross me more.

[*Exeunt* CESAR *and* LAZARO.

Prince. And now about the letter?

Ar. I only know, my lord, that though Felix got home first, Lazaro got there somehow, somehow gave her the letter, and somehow got an answer.

Prince. Hast seen it?

Ar. Yes, my lord.

Prince. And—

Ar. She appoints another meeting this evening.

Prince. And I must myself despatch his work, so as to leave him free to-night! Oh Arias, what can I do more?

Ar. Cannot your Highness go there yourself, and so at least stop further advancement?

Prince. True, true; and yet I know not; it might be too suspicious. I must consider what shall be done;

And what more subtle engine I may try

Against these lovers' ingenuity.   [*Exeunt.*

ACT III.

SCENE I. *A Room in the Palace.*—PRINCE *and* DON ARIAS.

Ar. How well the night went off! did not the music,
The lights, the dances, and the ladies' eyes,
Divert your Grace's sadness?

Prince.   Rather, Arias,
Doubled it.
Whithersoever Donna Anna móv'd,
My eyes, that ever followed hers along,
Saw them pursue Don Cesar through the crowd
And only rest on him; I curs'd him then,

And then excus'd him, as the judge should do
Whose heart is yearning with the guilt he damns.
   Ar. Where will this passion end?
   Prince.   I think in death,
Led by the fatal secret you have told me.
   Ar. I err'd, my lord; but all shall yet be well.
But hush! Don Cesar comes.
   Prince.   Make out of him
How sits the wind of love. Behind this screen
I'll listen. (*Hides.*)

Enter CESAR.

  · *Ar.* Well, Don Cesar?
   Ces.   Nay, *ill*, Don Cesar!
Misfortune on misfortune! ev'n good fortune
Forswears her nature but to scowl on me!
Led by her letter, as the shades of night
Were drawing in, I went—not now to stand
Under her lattice with the cold, cold moon
For company, but in the very room
My lady warms and lightens with her presence!
There when we two had just begun to whisper
The first sweet words of love, upon a sudden
As by some evil spirit prompted, her brother
Comes in, and on some frivolous pretext
Carries her to the palace. I suspect
He knows my purpose.
   Ar.   Nay—
   Prince (*listening*).   He little thinks
His evil spirit is so near him now.
   Ces. Ay, and dead weary of these sicken'd hopes
And lost occasions, I have resolv'd to break
Through disappointment and impediment,

And turning secret love to open suit,
Secure at once her honour, and her brother's,
And my own everlasting happiness,
By asking her fair hand, fore all the world!   [*Exit.*
   Ar. You heard, my lord?
   Prince (advancing).   And if he ask her hand,
Felix will grant it as assuredly
As I would my own sister's! Oh, Don Arias,
What now?
   Ar.   Don Felix comes.
   Prince.   There's yet one way,
He comes in time—Felix!

Enter FELIX.

   Fel.   My lord!
   Prince.   Come hither.
You came in time—were present in my thoughts
Before your coming. Hark you. I have long
Long'd to requite your many services,
By more substantial meed than empty breath,
Too oft, they say, the end of princes' favour.
Much I design for you; but in mean time,
As some foretaste and earnest of my love,
A kinsman, a near kinsman of my own,
Has set his heart upon the lady Anna,
Your sister; fain would have her hand in marriage:
And I, with your good liking,
Have promis'd it to him.
   Fel.   Oh, my good lord,
Your favour overpowers me!
   Prince.   Much content
Both for his sake, so near of my own blood,

(His letters show how deep his passion is,)
And yours, if you approve it.
 Fel.   Did I not,
Your will would be my law.
 Prince.   Why this is well then.
We'll talk it over at our leisure; meanwhile,
For certain reasons, let this contract be
Between ourselves alone—you taking care
To pledge your sister's hand no other way.
 Fel. Oh, trust to me, my lord—Heav'n watch above
Your Highness!
 Prince (aside). Oh mad end of foolish love! [*Exit.*
 Fel. I'll straight away,
And tell my sister of the happiness
Awaits her. And may be shall learn of her
How my own suit prospers with Nisida,
The Prince's sister, which his present favour
Now blows upon so fairly. Cesar!

Enter CESAR.

 Ces. Well found at last. Oh, Felix!
 Fel.   What is't now?
Your heart seems labouring.
 Ces.   Yours must lighten it.
You know, Don Felix, how by blood and birth
I am a gentleman—not less, I trust,
In breeding and attainment; my estate
Sufficient for my birth—nurst by the Prince
In his own palace from my earliest years,
Until, howe'er unworthy of such honour,
Receiv'd into his inmost heart and council:
So far at least fitted for state affairs,
As ever given from my earliest youth

F.   13

Rather to letters than to arms.   Enough:
You know all this, and know, or ought to know,
How much I am your friend?
 Fel.   I do believe it.
 Ces. Yea, Felix, and would fain that friendship knit
By one still closer tie—Have you not guess'd,
By many a sign more unmistakeable
Than formal declaration, that I love—
Presumptuously perhaps—but that I love
One of your house.   Which saying all is said:
For she is all your house who calls you "Brother."
 Fel. Cesar, Heav'n knows how faithfully my heart
Answers to yours in all; how much I prize
The honour you would do me.   Would to God
That I had seen the signs of love you talk of,
Pointing this way; there is, I do assure you,
No man in all the world to whom more gladly
I would ally my sister and myself;
But I did not.   I grieve that it is so,
But dare not cancel what is now, too late,
Irrevocably agreed on with another.
 Ces. By this "too late," I think you only mean
To tantalize my too late declaration.
If that be your intent, I am well punisht
Already; be content with my contrition.
You say you love me; and would well desire
To see me wed your sister; seal at once
My happiness, nor chill the opening day,
Nor my love's blossom, by a lingering "*Yea.*"
 Fel. Indeed, indeed, my Cesar, not to revenge
Delay of speech, or insufficient token,
But with repeated sorrow I repeat,
My sister's hand is pledg'd beyond recall,

And to another; whom, for certain reasons,
I dare not name, not even to herself,
As yet—
   Ces.   If I survive, 'tis that fate knows
How much more terrible is life than death!
Don Felix, you have well reveng'd yourself
Upon my vain ambition, speech delay'd,
And signs that you would not articulate;
But let my fate be as it will, may hers,
Hers, yea, and his whose life you link to hers,
Be so indissolubly prosperous,
That only death forget to envy them!
Farewell.
   Fel.   Farewell then: and remember, Cesar,
Let not this luckless business interrupt
Our long and loving intimacy.
   Ces.   Nay,
It shall not, cannot, Felix, come what may.
                         [Exeunt severally.

Enter PRINCE.

   Prince.   When in my love's confusion and excess
   I fancy many a fond unlikely chance,
Desire grows stronger, resolution less,
   I linger more the more I would advance.
False to my nobler self, I madly seize
   Upon a medicine alien to my ill;
And feeding still with that should cure disease,
   At once my peace and reputation kill
By turns; as the conflicting passions fire,
   And chase each other madly through my breast,
I worship and despise, blame and admire,
   Weep and rejoice, and covet and detest.

                        13—2

Alas! a bitter bargain he must choose,
Who love with life, or life with love, must lose!

Enter LAZARO.

Laz. Where can my master be? I shall go crazy, I think, running from room to room, and house to house, after him and his distracted wits.

Prince. Lazaro! Well, what news abroad?

Laz. Ah, my lord, there has been little of that under the sun this long while, they say. For instance, the slasht doublets just come into fashion, and which they call new; why 'twas I invented them years ago.

Prince. You! how?

Laz. Why, look you; once on a time when I was not so well off as now, and my coat was out at elbows, the shirt came through: many saw and admired—and so it has grown into a fashion.

Prince. Who listens to you but carries away food for reflection!   [*Exit.*

Laz. Aha! you are somewhat surfeited with that already, I take it.

So while the world her wonted journey keeps,
Lazarus chuckles while poor Dives weeps.

Enter CESAR.

Ces. Lazaro, I waited till the Prince was gone.
Listen to me. Don Felix has betroth'd
His sister to another, not to me;
He will not tell me whom, nor does it matter:
All ill alike. But out of this despair
I'll pluck the crown that hope could never reach.
There is no time to lose; this very night
I'll carry her away.

Laz.   Only beware
Telling Don Arias what you mean to do.
Is't possible you see not all along
Your secret playing on his faithless lips?
Here's one last chance.
    Ces.   True, true.
    Laz.   You cannot lose
By secrecy—what gain by telling him?
    Ces. You may be right: and to clear up the cause
Of past mischance, and make the future safe,
I'll take your counsel.
    Laz.   Then hey for victory!
Meanwhile, sir, talk with all and trust in none,
And least of all in him is coming hither.
And then in ocean when the weary sun
Washes his swollen face, "there shall be done
A deed of dreadful note."

Enter ARIAS.

    Ar. How now, Don Cesar?
    Laz. (aside).   Here are you, be sure,
When aught is stirring.
    Ar.   How speeds Love with you?
    Laz. (aside). The lighter, sir, now you are left behind.
    Ces. Arias, my friend! All's lost!
The love I grew deep in my heart of hearts
Is wither'd at the moment of its blossom.
I went to Felix, ask'd his sister's hand:
It was betroth'd, he told me, to another:
I was too late. All's lost! It were in vain
Weeping for that I never can attain:
I will forget what I must needs forego,
And turn to other—

Laz. (*to* ARIAS).   Pray, sir, pardon me;
But pri'thee say no more to him just now;
It brings on such a giddiness.
    Ar.   Alas!
But can I be of service?
    Laz.   Only, sir,
By saying nothing more.
    Ar.   I am truly sorry.   [*Exit.*
Laz. That you can lie no longer in the matter.
Oh, the Lord speed you!
    Ces. O Love, if mortal anguish ever move thee,
At this last hour requite me with one smile
For all thy sorrows! let what I have suffer'd
Appease thy jealous godhead!   I complain not
That you condemn my merits as too poor
For the great glory they aspire unto;
Yet who could brook to see a rival bear
The wreath that neither can deserve to wear!

Enter PRINCE *and* ARIAS.

Prince (*to* ARIAS).   Even so?
Good.   That he may not think 'twas out of malice,
I made my business trench upon his love,
Now that his love's but Love-in-idleness,
I'll occupy him still.   Cesar!
    Ces.   My lord!
Prince. I had like to have forgot.   'Tis Monday, is't not?
I have despatches both for Rome and Naples.
We must see to them to-night.
    Ces.   My lord!
    Prince.   Bring hither
Your writing.
    Ces. (*apart*).   Oh! the cup-full at my lips,

And dasht down, and for ever!

[*To* LAZARO.]   Villain, the victory you told me of!

Laz. What fault of mine, sir?

Ces.   What fault! said you not

All now was well?

Laz.   Is't I who make it wrong?

Ces. You meddled.

Prince.   Are you ready?

Ces.   Immediately.

Alas, alas! how shall my pen run clear

Of the thick fountain that is welling here!

Prince (aside).   And I shall learn from you how that
   dark pair

Contrive to smile, Jealousy and Despair.

[*Desk and papers brought in: exeunt* ARIAS *and* LAZARO.

Now, are you ready?   (CESAR *sits at the desk.*)

Ces.   Ay, my lord.

Prince.   Begin then.

"I am secretly"—

Ces. "Secretly"—driven to madness!

Prince. "About the marriage"—

Ces. "Marriage"—that never shall take place!

Prince. "All is fair for you"—

Ces. "For you"—though perdition to me!

Prince. "Believe me"—

Ces. I shall not survive it!

Prince. "That Donna Anna of Castelvi"—

Ces. "That Donna Anna"—I can write no more!

Prince. "Is such in birth, beauty, and wit"—

Ces. Oh, my lord, pardon me; but may I know

This letter's destination?

Prince.   Eh? to Flanders.

Why do you ask?

Ces.   To Flanders! But, my lord,
Surely no Flemish courier leaves to-day.
Might not to-morrow—
Prince (*aside*).   At the name of Anna
His colour chang'd. (*Aloud.*) No matter. 'Tis begun,
And we'll ev'n finish it. Where left I off?
Ces. (*reading*). "Can write no more"—
Prince.   Eh? "Write no more?" Did I
Say that?
Ces.   My lord!
Prince.   The letter. Give me it.
. *Ces.* (*aside*).   Come what come may then, what is writ is
     writ!
Prince (*reading*).   "I am secretly driven to madness
about the marriage that never shall take place. All is fair
for you, though perdition to me. Believe me I shall not
survive it, that Donna Anna—I can write no more."
Was this what I dictated?
Ces. (*throwing himself at the* PRINCE's *feet*). O my lord,
O noble Alexander! if the service
You have so often prais'd beyond desert
Deserve of you at all, snatch not from me
The only crown I ever ask'd for it,
To gild a less familiar brow withal.
This lady, Donna Anna,
Whom you are now devoting to another,
Is mine, my lord; mine, if a two years' suit
Of unremitted love not unreturn'd
Should make her mine; which mine beyond dispute
Would long ere this have made her, had not I
How many a golden opportunity
Lost from my love to spend it on my Prince!
And this is my reward! Oh, knew I not

How the ill star that rules my destiny
Might of itself dispose the gracious Prince,
Who call'd me for his friend from infancy,
To act my bitterest enemy unawares,
I might believe some babbler—
    Prince.   Nay, Don Cesar,
If in all these cross purposes of love
You recognise the secret hand of fate,
Accuse no mortal tongue, which could not reach
The stars that rule us all, wag as it would.
Enough. I am aggriev'd, and not, I think,
Unjustly, that without my pleasure, nay,
Without my knowledge even, you, my subject,
And servant, (leaving the dear name of friend,)
Dispos'd so of yourself, and of a lady
Whose grace my court considers as its own.
Give me the pen: and, as you write so laxly,
I must myself report—
    Ces.   My lord!
    Prince.   The pen. (*He writes.*)
    Ces. If in misfortune's quiver there be left
One arrow, let it come!
    Prince.   You could not write,
Don Cesar; but perhaps can seal this letter:
'Tis for Don Felix; send it to him straight.
Or stay—I'd have it go by a sure hand:
Take it yourself directly.
    Ces.   At one blow
My love and friendship laid for ever low!   [*Exit.*

Enter FELIX *and* ARIAS.

    Ar. The letter must be written.
    Prince.   Oh, Don Felix,

I have this moment sent to you.   No matter :
'Twas but to say I have this instant heard
Your sister's bridegroom is in Parma ; nay,
Perhaps already at your house.
 Fel.   Oh, my lord,
How shall I thank you for this gracious news ?
 Prince. Nay, we will hear them from your sister's lips.
To her at once.   [*Exit* FELIX.
      And now, Don Arias,
You have to swear upon the holy cross
That hilts this sword, that neither Donna Anna
Know that I ever lov'd her, nor Don Cesar
I ever cross'd his love.
 Ar.   Upon this cross
I swear it ; and beseech you in return
Never, my lord, to tell Don Cesar who
Reveal'd his secret.
 Prince.   Be it so.   I promise.
And now to see whether indeed I dare
Compete with him whose lofty name I wear.   [*Exeunt.*

SCENE II. *A Room in* FELIX'S *House.*—ANNA *and* ELVIRA.

 Anna. · Beside the charge of my own love, Elvira,
Whose crosses, I believe, will slay me soon,
My brother has confided to me at last,
His passion for the Princess Nisida ;
And, for he knows that I am near her heart,
Would have me whisper it into her ears ;
Which, were it such a passion as *I* feel,
His eyes would have reveal'd her long ago.
However, I have told her, and have got
An answer such—But look ! he comes.

Enter FELIX.

Fel.   Oh, sister,
Might but your news be half as good as mine!
A largess for it, come.   You are betroth'd,
By me, and by the Prince himself, to one
In all ways worthy of you, and who long
Has silently ador'd.

Anna (aside).   Is it possible?
Cesar!   (*Aloud*). Well, ask the largess that you will.

Fel. The Princess—

Anna.   Well?

Fel.   What says she?

Anna.   ·.   All she could
At the first blush—nothing—and that means all:
Go to her, and press out the lingering Yes
That lives, they say, in silence.

Fel.   Oh, my sister!
But who comes here?

Enter CESAR *and* LAZARO.

Ces. (*giving the letter*). I, Felix.   This must be
My warrant—from the Prince.   Oh misery!

Fel. I thank you, Cesar.   (*Reads.*)
"Because happiness is the less welcome when anticipated,
I have hitherto withheld from you, that he to whòm I have
engaged your sister's hand, is—Don Cesar! in whom unites
all that man or woman can desire.   If the man lives who
can deserve such glory, it is he.   Farewell."

Ces. Great Heav'n!

Fel.   Nay, read the letter.

Enter PRINCE, NISIDA, ARIAS, *and Train.*

Prince.   He shall not need,
Myself am here to speak it.

Ces. (kneeling).   Oh, my lord!

Prince. Rise, Cesar. If your service, as it did,
Ask'd for reward, I think you have it now;
Such as not my dominion alone,
But all the world beside, could not supply.
Madam, your hand; Don Cesar, yours. I come
To give away the bride:
And after must immediately away
To Flanders, where by Philip's trumpet led,
I will wear Maestricht's laurel round my brows;
Leaving meanwhile Don Felix Governor
Till my return—by this sign manual.

                    (*Puts* NISIDA'S *hand in* FELIX'S.)

Fel. My lord, my lord!

Laz.   Elvira!

Elv.   Lazaro!

Laz. I must be off. Our betters if we ape,
And they ape marriage, how shall we escape?

Ar. And learn this moral. None commend
A secret ev'n to trustiest friend:
Which secret still in peril lies
Even in the breast of the most wise;
And at his blabbing who should groan
Who could not even keep his own?

There are three other plays by Calderon, on this subject of keeping
one's love secret; a policy, whose neglect is punisht by a policy charac-
teristically Spanish. 1. *Amigo, Amante, y Leal:* which has the same
Prince and Arias, only the Prince confides his love to his rival. 2. *El
Secreto a Voces:* where it is the ladies who shuffle the secret about the
men. And 3. *Basta Callar*, a more complicated intrigue than any.

GIL PEREZ, THE GALLICIAN.

DRAMATIS PERSONÆ.

GIL PEREZ.

ISABEL,   *his Sister.*

DON ALONSO,   } *his two Friends.*
MANUEL MENDEZ,

PEDRO,   }
CASILDA,   *Servants in his house.*

DONNA JUANA,   *a Portuguese Lady.*

JUAN BAPTISTA,   *a Lover of Isabel.*

THE LORD HIGH ADMIRAL OF PORTUGAL.
DONNA LEONOR,   *his Cousin.*

A SHERIFF.
A JUDGE.
LEONARDO,   *a Traveller.*

ALGUAZILS, OFFICERS, ATTENDANTS, FARMERS, &c.

GIL PEREZ, THE GALLICIAN.

ACT I.

SCENE I. *·Outside* GIL PEREZ'S *House.—Enter* PEDRO *running;* GIL PEREZ *after him with a drawn dagger; and* ISABEL *and* CASILDA *interceding.*

Isab. FLY, Pedro, fly!

Gil.   And what the use his flying
If I be after him?

Ped.   Hold him! hold him back,
Both of you!

Gil.   By the Lord, I'll do for him.

Isab. But why so savage with him?

Gil.   He must pay
The long arrear of mischief you've run up.

Isab. I understand you not.

Gil.   I'll kill him first,
And then explain.

Isab. I, who dread not bodily violence,
Dread your injurious words. What have I done
That you should use me thus?—my enemy,
And not my brother.

Gil.   You say well your enemy,
Who, if you do as you have done so long,
Will one day bathe his sword in your heart's blood,
And after in his own, and so wipe out
One scandal from the world.
    Ped.   As the good soul
Who meddles to make peace between two brawlers
Oft gets the bloody nose, I'll take the hint.
Farewell, fair Spain! for evermore farewell!
    Gil. Here! hark you, sir;
Before you go; you have escap'd this time
By luck, not by desert. I give you warning,
Keep from my sight: for if I see your face
Fifty years hence, among the antipodes,
I'll pay you off.
    Ped.   Pray don't disturb yourself;
I'll take you at your word, and straight be off
To some old friends of mine—indeed relations—
In central Africa—the Ourang Outangs:
A colony so distant as I trust
Will satisfy us both. And so, good bye.
                    [*Exit;* CASILDA *after him.*
    Isab. He's gone, poor fellow.
And now perhaps, sir, as we are alone,
You'll tell me why you do affront me thus.
    Gil. Sister—oh, would to God that I had none
To call by such a name at such expense!
And can you think that I have been so blind,
As well as dumb, not to be ware the tricks
Of the sly gentleman who follows you
So constantly, and who, if this goes on,
Will one day filch away, not your own only,
But the long garner'd honour of our house?

Why, I have seen it all from first to last,
But would not show my teeth till I could bite;
Because, in points like this, a man of honour
Speaks once, and once for all.
This once is now.   I'll speak my mind to you;
Which, if you cannot understand, to-morrow
I must repeat in quite another language.
I know your man—Juan Baptista—one
Not man enough for me, and so, I tell you,
Not for my sister.   This should be enough,
Without his being, as he is, a Jew.
To get you from his reach I brought you here
To Salvatierra, deep amid the mountains,
And safe enough I thought; but even here
His cursed letters reach you through the hands
Of that fine rascal I have just pack'd off.
There; I have told my story; take't to heart;
Dismiss your man at once, or, by the Lord,
If you and he persist, I'll fire his house,
And save the Inquisition that much trouble.

Isab. Your anger makes you blind—accusing me
Of things I never did.

Gil.   You never did!

Isab. But so it is, poor women must submit
To such insinuations.

Gil.   Pray, was't I
Insinuated that letter then?

Isab.   Peace, peace!
I can explain it all, and shall, when fit.
What would you have of me? You are my brother,
And not my husband, sir; consider that:
And therefore, in fraternal kindness bound,
Should even take my word without ado.

F.   14

You talk of honour: is not honour then
Slow to suspect—would rather be deceived
Itself than prematurely to accuse?
I am your sister, Perez, and I know
My duty towards you and myself. Enough—
Which, if you cannot understand, to-morrow
I must repeat in quite another language.   [*Exit.*

Gil. She says not ill; it better were indeed
Had I kept on the mask a little longer,
Till they had dropt theirs beyond all denial.
She's right, and I was wrong; but from this time
I'll steer another course.

Enter CASILDA.

Cas.   A gentleman
(Of Portugal, he says,) is at the door,
And asks for you.
Gil.   Bid him come in. Away,
My troubles, for a while!   [*Exit* CASILDA.

Enter MANUEL MENDEZ.

Man.   'Twas well, Gil Perez,
You sent so quickly, or my impetuosity
Had overrun your leave.
Gil.   What, Manuel Mendez!
Come to my arms. What! you in Salvatierra?
Man. And, I assure you, at no small expense
Of risk and heart-ache.
Gil.   That's unwelcome news.
Man. Not when 'tis all forgotten in the joy
Of seeing you again.
Gil.   I shall not rest

Till I have heard; ill-manner'd though it be
To tax a man scarce winded from a journey
With such expense of breath.
   Man.   Then listen, Gil.
You, I am sure, remember (time and absence
Cannot have washt so much from memory)
The pleasant time when you were last at Lisbon,
And grac'd my house by making it your home.
I need not tell of all we did and talk'd,
Save what concerns me now; of the fair lady
You knew me then enamour'd of, (how deeply
I need not say—being a Portuguese,
Which saying, all is said)—Donna Juana,
At whose mere name I tremble, as some seer
Smit with the sudden presence of his God.
Two years we lived in the security
Of mutual love, with so much jealousy
(Without which love is scarcely love at all)   `
As serv'd to freshen up its sleeping surface,
But not to stir its depths. Ah, dangerous
To warm the viper, or, for idle sport,
Trust to the treacherous sea—sooner or later
They turn upon us; so these jealousies
I lik'd to toy with first turn'd upon me;
When suddenly a rich young cavalier,
Well grac'd with all that does and ought to please,
(For I would not revenge me with my tongue
Upon his name, but with my sword in 's blood,)
Demanded her in marriage of her father;
Who being poor, and bargains quickly made
'Twixt avarice and wealth, quickly agreed.
The wedding day drew nigh that was to be
The day of funeral too—mixt dance and dirge,

And grave and bridal chamber both in one.
The guests were met; already night began
Loose the full tide of noisy merriment,
When I strode in; straight through the wedding throng
Up to the bride and bridegroom where they were,
And, seizing her with one hand, with the other
Struck him a corpse; and daring all, to die
Fighting, or fighting carry off my prize,
Carried her off; lifted her on a horse
I had outside; struck spur; and lightning-like
Away, until we reach'd the boundary
Of Portugal, and, safe on Spanish ground,
At last drew breath and bridle. Then on hither,
Where I was sure of refuge in the arms
Of my old friend Gil Perez; whom I pray
Not so much on the score of an old friendship,
So long and warm, but as a fugitive
Asking protection at his generous hands—
A plea the noble never hear in vain.
Nor for myself alone, but for my lady
Who comes with me, and whom I just have left
Under the poplars by the river-side,
Till I had told my news, and heard your answer.
A servant whom we met with on the way,
Pointed your house out—whither, travel-tir'd,
Press'd for my life, and deep in love with her
I bring, as curst by those I left behind,
And trusting him I come to—
   Gil.   Tut, tut, tut!
Go on so, I'll not answer you at all;
All this fine talk to me! from Manuel Mendez!
As if 'twere not enough to say "Friend Gil,
I've left a gentleman I slew behind,

And got a living lady with me, so
Am come to visit you." Why go about
With phrases and fine speeches? I shall answer
Quite unpolitely thus, " Friend Manuel,
This house of mine is yours—for months, for years,
For all your life, with all the service in 't
That I or mine can do for you." So back,
And bring your lady, telling her from me
I stay behind because I am unapt
At such fine speeches as her lover makes.

    Man. Oh, let me thank you—

    Gil.   Nay, 'twere better far
Go to your lady; who may be ill at ease
Alone in a strange place.   [*Exit* MANUEL.
                What, Isabel!   (*She enters.*)
Isabel, if my former love and care
Deserve of you at all, forget awhile
All difference, (for there's a time for all,)
And help me now to honour an old friend
To whom I owe great hospitalities ;
Manuel Mendez, who with his bride is come
To be my guest.

    Isab.   I'll do my best for you.
But hark! what noise?   (*Shouts and fighting within.*)

    Gil.   A quarrel's up somewhere.

    Voice within. Take him alive or dead.

    Another voice.   He'll slip us yet!

    Isab. Some one on horseback flying at full speed
From his pursuers.

    Voices within.   Fire upon him! fire!   (*Shots within.*)

    Isab. Mercy, he's dead!

    Gil.   Not he; only his horse;
And see he's up again, and gallantly

Flashing his sword around on his pursuers
Keeps them at bay, and fighting, fighting, still
Retreats—
    Isab.   And to our house too—

Enter DON ALONSO.

    Alon.   Shelter! shelter!
In pity to a wretched man at last
Foredone!
    Gil.   What, Don Alonso!
    Alon.   But a moment,
To ask you cover my retreat, Gil Perez;
My life depends on reaching Portugal.
    Gil. Away then to the bridge you see below there.
God speed you.
    Alon.   And keep you!   [*Exit.*
    Voices without.   This way! this way!
    Gil. But just in time!

Enter SHERIFF *with Officers.*

    Officer.   I'm sure he pass'd by here.
    Gil. Well, gentlemen, your business?
    Sher.   Don Alonso—
Came he this way?
    Gil.   He did, and he went that,
And must almost, unless I much mistake,
Be got to Portugal. For, by the Lord, sir,
His feet seem'd feather'd with the wind!
    Sher.   Away then!
After him!
    Gil.   Stop a moment!
    Sher.   Stop! what mean you?

Gil. Just what I say.   Come, Mr Sheriff, come,
You've done your duty; be content with that;
And don't hunt gentlemen like wolves to death;
Justice is one thing, and fair play's another,
All the world over.
  Sher.   When I've got my man
I'll answer you.
  Gil.   Perhaps before.
  Sher.   Why, sir,
Would you detain me?
  Gil.   Why, if logic fails,
I must try other argument.
  Sher.   As what, sir?
  Gil. Why, mathematical.   As how?   Look here.
You see me draw this line.   Well then, 'fore God,
The man who passes it—dies.   Q. E. D.
  Sher. Down with him !
  Gil.   Back, I advise you.
  Voices.   Down with him !
  Gil. Chicken-hearts ! Curs ! Oh, you will down with me,
Will you indeed? and this the way you do it?
        (*He fights with them.*)
  One. Oh, I am slain.
  Sher.   I'm wounded.
  Gil.   Back with you !
      [*Exit, driving them in.*

SCENE II. *The River-side.—Enter* JUANA *and* MANUEL.

Jua. Oh never did I owe more to your love,
Than for this quick return.
  Man.   O my Juana,
The love such beauty as your own inspires,

Surmounts impossibilities. However,
I needed not go on to Salvatierra,
Lighting on what I look'd for by the way,
Among the mountains; where my friend Gil Perez
(Whose honour I insult if I declare it)
Has pitcht his tent, with hospitality
Prophetic of our coming;
So peaceably our love may fold its wings
Under the shadow of my friend's.

Jua.   Oh, Manuel,
She who has left home, country, friends, and fame,
And would contentedly leave life, for you,
Desires no other temple of her love
Than a bleak rock, whose unchang'd stedfastness
Shall not out-wear her own.

Alon. (within).   I can no more!

Jua. Listen! What noise is that?

Man.   A cavalier
Still with his sword in his exhausted hand.
He falls!

Enter ALONSO, *who falls at the side.*

Alon. They e'en must have me.

Man.   Courage, sir.
Wounded? (*Voices within.*)

Alon.   Hark! the bloodhounds are close by;
And worse, they must have slain Gil Perez first.
Who else—

Enter GIL.

Gil. Confound the rogues, they've got the bridge
And the way to 't, and heav'n itself, I think,
To fight upon their side.

Man.   Gil, what is this?

Gil. Trying to help a friend out of a ditch,
I've tumbled in myself.

Man.   Come, we are two
In hand, and one in heart; at least can fight
And die together.

Alon.   Nay, add me;
The cause—

Gil.   There's but a moment. Manuel,
I charge you by your friendship,
Draw not your sword to-day.

Man.   Not I my sword
When theirs are on you?

Jua. (*clinging to* MANUEL). Heav'ns!

Voices, within.   This way! this way!

Man. They're coming.

Gil. (*to* ALONSO).   Listen! you can swim?

Alon.   Alas—

Gil. I mean upon my shoulders. Manuel,
We two shall cross to Portugal,
Where follow us they may, but cannot seize us.
Meanwhile I leave you master of my house
And honour, centred (no time to say more)
In Isabel, my sister. Swear to me
That you will see to this.

Man.   I swear it, Gil.

Gil. Enough, your hand! Adieu! Now, courage, sir!
(*Takes* ALONSO *on his shoulders and plunges into the river.*)

Jua. The man swims like a dolphin.

Gil. (*within*).   Manuel,
Remember!

Man.   How he wrestles with the flood!
And now is half-way over.

Gil. (within).   Manuel,
Remember! I have trusted all to you.
    Man. Waste not your breath.   I'll do 't.
    Gil. (within).   Adieu!
    Man.   Adieu!
                        [*Exit* MANUEL *with* JUANA.

SCENE III.   *The Portuguese bank of the River.—Enter the*
    ADMIRAL *of Portugal and* DONNA LEONOR *as from
    hunting.*

    Adm. Since summer's fiery Sirius, fair cousin,
Neither from place nor power in heaven declines,
Will you not rest?
    Leonor.   Ah, what a noble sport
Is hunting! who so abject-spirited
As not to love its generous cruelty?
    Adm. It is indeed a noble imitation
Of noblest war.   As when a white-tuskt boar
Holds out alone against the yelling pack,
Gores one, o'erthrows another, all the while
Bristling his back like to some ridge of spears:
While many a gallant hound, foil'd in his onset,
Tears his own flesh in disappointed rage,
Then to the charge again—he and his foe,
Each with redoubled fury firing up:
A chivalry that nature has implanted
Ev'n in the heart of beasts.
    Leonor.   .   So in falconry,
That I love even better; when the heron
Mounts to the wandering spheres of air and fire,
Pois'd between which alternately she burns

And freezes, while two falcons, wheeling round,
Strive to out-mount her, tilting all along
The fair blue field of heaven for their lists ;
Until out-ris'n and stricken, drencht in blood,
Plumb down she falls like to some crimson star ;
A rivalry that nature has implanted
Ev'n in the breast of birds.

Enter PEDRO.

Ped. Which is the way, I wonder? What with fright and
weariness, I must rest awhile. Well, this is Portugal, where
to be sure a poor Spanish pimp may hope to escape ferocious
honour. That I should lose a post where others make their
thousands at my first function ! But who are these? Fine
folks too ! Pray Heaven they be in want of an officer.

Adm. A horse will soon carry you to the villa. Hark
you, sir ! (*To* PEDRO.)

Ped. My lord !

Adm. Who are you ?

Ped. Nay, how should I know ?

Adm. But are you one of my people ?

Ped. Yes, if you like it. As said Lord Somebody, who
neither serv'd king, man, or God, but who entering the
palace one day at supper-time, and seeing all the chamber-
lains at work without their coats, whips off his, and begins
carrying up dishes. Suddenly in comes the major-domo,
who perceiving a stranger, asks if he be sworn of the service.
"Not yet," says he, "but if swearing is all that's wanted, I'll
swear to what you please." So 'tis with me. Make me your
servant, and I'll swear and forswear anything.

Adm. You are liberal of your humour.

Ped. 'Tis all I have to be liberal of; and it would not be
right to spare that.

Gil. (within).   Hold on, hold on !

Leonor. Who's that ?

Adm. ˙Look, some one with erect head and vigorous arms, buffeting the wave before him.

Leonor. With another on his shoulders too.

Adm. (to PEDRO).   Now, would you win an earnest of future favour, plunge in to his assistance.

Ped. I would, sir, but I'm a wretched swimmer.

Leonor. They have reacht the shore at last.

Enter GIL PEREZ *and* ALONSO, *drencht..*

Alon. Thank Heaven for our escape !

Gil. Ah, we're well quit of it.

Ped. Now, sir, if I can help.   But Lord ha' mercy ! (*Sees* GIL.)

Adm. What ! going just when you are wanted ?

Ped. I was born, my lord, with a tender heart ; that see- ing these poor fellows so drencht, bleeds for them.   That he should pursue me even to Portugal !   (*Is creeping away.*)

Adm. What ! only just come, and going?

Ped. Oh, my lord, a sudden call.   Excuse me.   [*Exit.*

Adm. 'Tis an idiot.   But let me help you.

Alon. My life is in your hand.

Adm. In my hand?   How is that?

Alon. You shall hear, if I may first know to whom I tell my story.   Misfortune forces me to be cautious.

Adm. You are right ; but need fear nothing from the Lord High Admiral of Portugal, who now speaks to you, and pledges himself to protect you so long as you stand on his estate.

Alon. Enough, my lord.
My name is Don Alonso de Tordoya,

Not un-illustrious in Spain. I love
A noble lady; whom going to visit,
When this same westering sun was young in heav'n,
I found a rival with her. I rush'd out,
Bidding him follow with his sword; he follow'd;
We fought, and with two passes in his side
I left him dead: the cry was after us;
The officers of justice at my heels.
No time to lose; I leap'd upon a horse,   _
And rode, until a shot, aim'd at his rider,
Kill'd him; then, taking to my feet, fled on,
Till, coming to a country house, I saw,
To my great joy, my friend—
     Gil.   Here enter I;
Who, seeing Don Alonso so hard set,
Offer'd my services to keep them back
Till he was safe in Portugal.
That country house of mine—a pleasure house
Some call it, though I've found but little there—
Stands in a narrow mountain gorge, through which
He and the bloodhounds after him must pass
To reach the river; as he says, he came,
And saw, and fled; had scarce got fifty yards,
Up comes the Sheriff with his yelling pack
Panting and blowing. First most courteously
I begg'd them spare themselves as well as him
Further pursuit, but all in vain; push on
They would; whereon I was oblig'd to draw;
Disabled four or five, Heav'n help their souls!
Till, having done as much as he to figure
In justice's black book, like him I fled
After him to the river; where on finding
The bridge occupied by the enemy,

Catching my sword between my teeth, and him
Upon my shoulders, I so dash'd in,
And, at last, over; where now, thanks to Heav'n,
We meet your Excellency, who vouschafes
Your shelter and protection.

Adm.   ·   'Twas my word,
And I'll abide by't.

Alon.   I have need
Of all assurance, for the man I slew
Was of great note.

Adm.   His name?

Alon. Prefacing that he was a cavalier
Of wholly noble parts and estimation,
And that 'tis no disparagement to valour
To be unfortunate, I may repeat it,—
Don Diego d'Alvarado.

Adm.   Wretched man!
My cousin! you have slain him!

Leonor.   You have slain
My brother, traitor!

Gil.   Oh, I see my sword
Must e'en be out again.

Alon.   Your Excellency
Will pause before he draws his sword on one
Surrender'd at his feet. My lord, remember
I slew Don Diego in the face of day,
In fair and open duel. And, beside,
Is not your Excellency's honour pledg'd
To my security?

Gil.   Beside all which,
I say that if all Portugal, and all
Within it, admiralty and army too,
Combine, you shall not touch him while I live.

Adm. I know not what to do; upon one side
My promise, on the other the just call
Of retribution for my kinsman's death.
I must adjudge between them. Don Alonso,
The word of Honour is inviolable,
But not less so her universal law.
So long as you stand upon ground of mine
I hold your person sacred: for so far
My promise holds; but set your foot beyond
E'en but an inch—remember, death awaits you.
And so farewell.

  Leonor. Nay, hold! though you have pledged
Your promise—

  Adm. What I pledge is pledg'd for you,
As for myself; content you.

        [*Exeunt* ADMIRAL *and* LEONOR.

  Alon.   Well, friend Gil,
What say you to all this?

  Gil.   Why then, I say,
At least 'tis better than it was. To-day
The mouse, shut in the cupboard, there must stay:
But will jump out to-morrow—if she may.

ACT II.

SCENE I. *A Wood near San Lucar in Andalusia.—Enter*
  MANUEL *and* JUANA *as travelling.*

  Man. Misfortune on misfortune!

  Jua.   Ay, they call
One to another.

Man.   Ah, my love!
That you should wander thus about with me
And find no home! Gallicia, that I thought
Should be our port, unkindly storm'd us out
To Salvatierra, whence before the gale
We drive to Andalusia.
      Jua.   Manuel,
My home is ever where you are.
      Man.   Oh how
Requite such love! but you shall rest awhile
Till I and the poor fellow we pick'd up
Have found fit resting-place in San Lucar.
Pedro!

Enter PEDRO.

      Ped. Sir!
      Man.   Come you with me;
While you, Juana, underneath those trees—
      Jua. Weep your departure.   [*Exit* JUANA.
      Man.   It shall not be long.
Although her grief blindly anticipates
A longer separation than she knows!
      Ped. Alas, and how is that? and how can you
Foredoom such pain to one who loves you so?
Pardon me who am but your servant, sir,
And that but these two days, for saying it.
      Man. Ah, Pedro, 'tis not I who wills all this,
But fate; that, stronger than all human will,
Drove me from Portugal to Gallicia,
Thence hither; where my fate still urging on,
I must to sea, joining the armament
That sails to plant the banner of the church
Over the golden turrets of the north:

Leaving my lady—not, as you surmise,
Deserted and dishonour'd here behind,
But in some holy house at San Lucar,
With all the little substance I possess,
Till I return.   For to a soldier
His sword is property enough.   (*Drums within.*)
 Ped.   And hark
The drum that answers you—
 Man.   No doubt a troop
Recruiting for this war.
 Ped.   See, they are coming.
 Man. I'll take occasion by the forelock then.
Pedro, go, tell the Ensign of the troop
Two men would join his ranks. I'll to Juana.   [*Exit.*

   Enter GIL PEREZ *with soldiers.*

 Ped. This one looks affable. Pray, sir, can you court-
eously inform me which is the Ensign?
 Soldier. There—he with the red sash.
 Ped. What, he with the lofty presence and broad should-
ers?
 Soldier. Ay!
 Gil (*to the soldiers*). Well then, my lads, we shall agree
together very well, eh?
 Soldiers. Long live our noble Ensign!   [*Exeunt soldiers.*
 Ped. Now's the time!
 Gil (*to himself*). 'Fore heaven, this soldiering would be
pleasant enough did not that trouble follow and plague
me.
 Ped. Sir!
 Gil. Leaving Isabel at such a risk—
 Ped. Sir Ensign! •

F.   15

Gil. That as fast as I gain honour here I run the chance of losing more at home.

Ped. Noble Sir Ensign!

Gil. One good thing, however, my good Manuel keeps guard for me.

Ped. He must surely be deaf this side—I'll try the other. Noble Ensign!

Gil (turning round). Who is that?

Ped. (recognising him gradually). A soldier—no, I only mean one who would be—no soldier. If I said I wish'd to be a soldier, sir, I lied.

Gil. Rascal! you here? did I not warn you whenever and wherever—

Ped. Oh yes, yes, but how should I ever expect to find you here a soldiering?

Gil (setting upon him). I'll teach you I *am* here, scoundrel, to whom I owe half my trouble.

Ped. Help! murder! help!

Enter MANUEL.

Man. A soldier set upon my servant! stop, sir! how do you dare—Gil Perez!

Gil. Manuel!

Man. Why, did I not leave you in Portugal?

Gil. And I you at Salvatierra, engaged to me by solemn promise and old love to guard my honour there?

Man. We both have cause for wonder. I will tell you all; but first we must be alone.

Gil. Ay, another wonder; this fellow yours?

Man. In travelling hither we found him by the way, and took him.

Gil. Well, this saves your life for this time, sir: but, remember, you will not always have a friend at hand to do so much for you.

Ped. I know that; I only wish you would be so gracious as to tell me where you are next bound, that I may take good care not to go thither. But I know one place at least to which you cannot follow me—my own estate—and thither I set off immediately.   [*Exit.*

Gil. We are alone. Come, I will tell you first
My story. As you say you saw us last,
Alonso and myself, in Portugal;
Such an escape as (so the wise men say)
Is from the frying-pan into the fire.
We landing from the river on the estate
Of that great potentate the High Admiral,
Whose cousin, it turn'd out, was the very man
Alonso slew; whereat the Admiral,
Who had, before he knew this, promis'd us
Protection, gave us truly such protection
As the cat gives the mouse that she thinks safe
Under her paw. But we escap'd from her,
And after much adventures came at last
To San Lucar here, where the Duke, who now
Is general of the war that our good king
Wages with England, courteously receiv'd us;
Gave Don Alonso a regiment; made me
An Ensign in it as you see; enough—
I know you will not wish a longer story
From one whose heart, until you tell him yours,
Hangs from a hair.

Man.   To take the story up then
Where you did, Perez—scarcely had you plung'd
Into the river, than the sheriff's rout

Came after you ; but, seeing all was lost,
Went angry to their homes, and I to yours ;
Where I receiv'd such hospitality
As our old friendship—But I falter here,
Scarce knowing how to tell—
Nay, almost doubting if to tell at all,
Or to conceal, what to conceal and tell
At once were best. You made me promise, Gil,
At parting—yea, with those last words hard wrung
Out of your breathless struggle with the flood—
That I would watch the honour of your house.
I did so: and it is because I did so
That I was forc'd to leave it.
   Gil.   Manuel,
Your words are slaying me by syllables.
But tell me all—How was't?
   Man.   One Juan Baptista
Courted your sister.
   Gil.   Well?
   Man.   And came at last
To such a boldness, that one night he stole
Into the house.   .
   Gil.   Manuel !
   Man.   I, who was watching,
Ran from my chamber, found a muffled man ;
Threw myself on him ; he, alerter yet,
Leap'd from the window, and I after him
Into the street, where two he'd posted there
Came to his rescue ; one of them I slew,
The other wounded, while the rogue himself
Fled and escap'd. What could I do, my friend,
A foreigner, charg'd with a homicide
In a strange country, with Juana too

Involv'd with me? If I were wrong to fly,
I did so thinking how yourself would act
In a like case.

 Gil.   'Tis true, I cannot blame you.
Ah! he said truer may be than he meant,
Who liken'd a true friend to a true mirror,
That shows one all oneself indeed, but all
Revers'd; that when I look into your breast
To see my honour, I but see disgrace   -
Reflected there. I must begone at once
To Salvatierra; for to leave my name
In danger is to let it run to shame.

Enter ALONSO.

Oh, Don Alonso, you are come in time.
If aught that I have ever done for you
Deserve return, requite me, I beseech you,
By giving Manuel here the Ensigncy
I must throw up.

 Alon.   But why?
 Gil.   I must at once
To Salvatierra, where my honour lies
In the utmost peril.

 Alon.   But—
 Gil.   I am resolv'd.

 Alon. I fain might try dissuade you, but I know
Your honour will not call in vain. Enough:
Be't as you will—on one condition.

 Gil.   Well?

 Alon. That I may go with you, and share your risk,
Who more than shar'd, and conquer'd mine.

Man.   Nay, sir,
If any one do that it must be I,
His older friend, who bringing this ill news
Must see him safely through it.
    Alon.   But 'twas I
Who drew him from his home, where, till I came,
He liv'd in peace and quiet, but where now
This outrage has grown up in his forc'd absence.
And surely, the world over, 'tis ill manners
For one who, having drawn a friend from home,
Lets him return alone.
    Man.   Well, be you courteous,
I'll not be cowardly.
    Gil.   Oh, this rivalry
Proves the nobility of both ! But, friends,
Neither must go with me ; you both are here
Fled in like peril of your lives from home,
And how could I avail me of your love
At such a price ? Nay, I may want you both
In greater risks hereafter ; and whom look to,
If you be lost?
    Alon.   True, but if one of us
Went with you now, the other—
    Man.   And that one
Must be myself.
    Alon.   You see, sir, one *will* go.
Do you choose which.
    Man.   Content.
    Gil.   How shall I choose,
When to choose one must needs the other hurt?
But if it needs must be—
I say that Don Alonso, so engag'd
In high and even holy business here,

Must not forego't for mine.   If one will come,
Let it be Manuel.

Alon.   I live to hear
This insult from your lips !   But I'll have vengeance ;
Neither shall go unless you take with you
Thus much at least to compensate
For what you leave.   These jewels may assist you
Where my sword cannot.   (*Giving jewels.*)

Gil.   I accept them, sir,
As freely as they're given.   Come, embrace me.
And now to punish an unworthy sister,
And that ill traitor, from whose heart I swear
My bleeding honour with this sword to tear.

SCENE II.   *Outside* GIL PEREZ'S *House at Salvatierra ; as in*
ACT I. SCENE I.—*Enter* ISABEL *and* CASILDA.

Isab. What !   Donna Leonor ·d'Alvarado, come to Sal-
vatierra ?

Cas. Yes.

Isab. And for what purpose ?

Cas. They say, to avenge her brother's death.   I myself
have seen her conferring with Juan Baptista.

Isab. And what do you infer from that ?

Cas. He is, they say, chief witness against Don Alonso
and your brother, for this murder.

Isab. Against my brother too !   O Casilda, is it not
shameful that Juan Baptista should revenge with slanders
behind my brother's back whom he dares not meet face to
face !   Nay, that a traitor be revenged at all on him he has
betrayed ! thriving here at home while my brother is banisht !

Cas. But there's something else.   He charges your brother's friend Manuel with murdering his men.

Isab. In proving which, my honour must be publicly canvassed and compromised !

Enter PEDRO.

Ped. Oh, what a long way it has seemed ; as it will when fear fetters one's legs.   Oh, permit me, madam, since fate has sent me back to your feet, to kiss but the little toe, the pink, the pearl, the petty Benjamin of those ten toes.   But above all, tell me, for Heaven's sake, is my master here ?

Isab. No, Pedro, you at least are safe.   He, alas, is far away.

Ped. So one might think ; but yet on the other hand I'd swear he must be here.

Isab. Pedro !

Ped. Oh yes, his sole vocation now is to dodge my steps like some avenging ghost of *Capa and Espada.*

Enter JUAN BAPTISTA.

Bapt. (*speaking to himself*).   If they condemn him
To death, as, on my evidence alone,
They must, he'll not return to plague me more
At Salvatierra.   But, fair Isabel,
How blest am I on whom the star of beauty,
Bright rival of the sun,
Beams out such rays of love !

Isab.   Stand off !   Away !
Not rays of love, whatever heretofore
I and my beauty may have beam'd, Baptista,
But now, if rays at all, lightnings of rage

And indignation from my heart and eyes.
Approach them at your peril! What, false traitor,
You come to court me with my brother's blood
Upon you, shed too in no manly duel,
Face to face, hand to hand, in the open field,
But like a murderer,
Behind his back stabbing him dead with slander—
Never!   [*Exit.*

Bapt. But, Isabel!
Cas.   Your day is over.   -   [*Exit.*
Bapt. And that I should lose her by the very means I
hoped to win her with!
Ped. Let not this prevent your memory acknowledging
one who has suffered banishment, and lives in terror of his
life, on your account.
Bapt. Pedro!
Ped. And at your service.
Bapt. Ah, would you were!
Ped. Try me.
Bapt. But are you still Isabel's servant?
Ped. I trust so.
Bapt. Oh, good Pedro, I would fain explain to her, and
wipe out (as I easily can) the offence she has taken against
me; and if you will but be my friend, and leave the door
ajar to-night, that I may tell her the whole story, I'll pay
you well for it.
Ped. Well, I think there can be no danger in that. Why,
if you should happen to call loudly outside the door to-night,
and I let you in, forgetting to ask who it is—surely I shall
not be to blame?
Bapt. 'Tis well; the sun is already setting; go you to
your post, and I shall be at mine immediately.
                                      [*Exeunt severally.*

SCENE III. *A Room in* GIL PEREZ'S *House.—Enter*
ISABEL *and* CASILDA.

Isab. Casilda, now the flaming sun has set,
See to the doors ; and you and Ines there
Sing to me—'twill beguile my melancholy.
No merry song, however ; something sad
As my own fancies.   (*They sing within.*)
                              Hark ! what noise is that ?
One calling at the door at such an hour !—
Again !—Bid Pedro see—
Why, what is it that makes me tremble so ?
From head to foot-—   .

Enter PEDRO *hurriedly.·*

Ped.   O madam !
Isab.   Well ?
Ped.   ·   O madam—
Opening the door—only to ask—a man
All muffled up ran by me—(*Aside.*) 'Tis all right.

Enter GIL PEREZ, *cloakt.*

Isab. Who's this ?
Gil (*discovering himself*). I, Isabel.
Isab.   Oh heavens !
Gil.   Well, sister,
What troubles you ?
    Ped.   Oh Lord, oh Lord, oh Lord ! (*Hides.*)
    Isab. O Gil, how have you dared to venture here,
Your very life at stake !

Gil.   Small risk to one
Whom your ill doings have half kill'd already.
    Isab. I do not understand you—
    Gil.   You need not:
I come not to explain, but to avenge;
And, mark my words, what I have come to do,
I'll do.
    Isab. Alas! is it my fault then, brother,
That traitors of their gold can make them wings
To fly into my house?
    Gil.   Be not afraid;
I shall not judge of you or any one
Unheard, as others seem to judge of me.
What is the matter?
    Isab.   Nay, I only know
You are accus'd of aiding, how I know not,
In Don Diego's death—on evidence,
As 'tis believ'd, the Judge (who now is here,
Inflam'd by Donna Leonor) declares
Sufficient to convict you of your life
And property—Alas, alas, my brother!
    Gil. You shall away with me; for 'tis not well
To leave you here alone and unprotected.
But I must see first what this Judge has got
To say against me.
    Isab.   But how get at it?
    Gil. Why from the fountain-head. But, by the Lord,
If I must fly or die for't,
I'll not do so for nothing, I'll begin
My vengeance on this rascal.   (*Pulling out* PEDRO.)
    Ped.   Oh begin
On some one else and sum up all on me!
    Gil. How come you here?

Ped.   Oh, I will tell the truth
And nothing but the truth.
Gil.   Well !
Ped.   Being assur'd
That you were coming hither—
Gil.   Well ?
Ped.   I came
Before.
Gil. And why, when—
Ped.   That by doing so
You should not see my face, (which you declar'd,
Seeing again, you'd kill me,) but my back,
Which as you never swore at—
Gil (*striking him*).   Villain, die !
Ped. (*falling as dead*). Oh ! I am slain !
Gil.   Come, Isabel, 'tis I
Must bear you on my shoulders through the flames
That rise all round.   [*Exeunt* GIL *and* ISABEL.
Ped. (*rising*).   Oh, angel of sham death,
How much I owe your out-spread wings to-day,
Under whose shadow—Yo escaparè.   [*Exit.*

SCENE IV.   *An open Gallery in the Judge's House at Salva-
    tierra.—Enter Judge, and attendants, with lights, &c.*

Judge. Here in this gallery where the air is cool
Set out my desk and papers.
I must examine all these depositions.
    1*st Attendant.* 'Tis done, my lord.
    2*nd Attendant.*   My lord, a stranger asks
Admittance—upon something, as he says,
Important to the matter now in hand.

Judge. Admit him, then.

Gil (without).　　　Manuel, keep the door;
And, till my lord and I have had our talk,
Let no one enter.

Man. (without). Trust me.

Enter GIL.

Gil.　　　　　First permit me
To kiss your lordship's hand.   And secondly,
Having important matter to disclose
About this business, I would tell it you
Alone—

Judge (to attendants). Retire !　　*[Exeunt attendants.*

Gil.　　　　And with your lordship's leave
Will take a chair.

Judge.　　Sit, sir.

Gil.　　　　May I presume
To ask your lordship how Gallicia
Agrees with you ?

Judge.　　I thank you, very well.

Gil. I'm very glad of that.   Humph—as I take it,
Your lordship is come down into these parts
On a great trial ?

Judge.　　Yes, the case is this ;
A certain Don Alonso de Tordoya,
And one Gil Perez of this place, are charg'd
With slaying Don Diego d'Alvarado.

Gil. Slaying ?

Judge.　　In duel, sir.

Gil.　　　　I marvel much
They should have dragg'd your lordship from the city
And from the court that you so much adorn,

Into this beggarly place, to try a cause
That happens almost every day in Spain.
   Judge. True, sir, but this is not by any means
The whole, or kernel, of the case. These men,
Beside, and after, the said homicide,
Resisted the king's officers; this Perez
Especially—a notable ruffian
Who lives among these hills a lawless life
Of violence and murder—struck the Sheriff,
And—but I'm scarce entitled to say more
To one whose very name I know not.
   Gil.   Oh !
My name is quickly told, if that be all.
   Judge. What is it then ?
   Gil.   Gil Perez.
   Judge.   Ho ! without !
   Man. (appearing at the door). My lord !
   Judge.   And who are you ?
   Gil.   A friend of mine.
   Man. Who will take care that no one else comes in,
Till you have done.   [*Exit.*
   Gil.   Your lordship sees how 'tis—
Be not alarm'd—pray take your chair again—
I've much to say to you.
   Judge (aside).   Better submit.
This desperate man may have a score beside—
Well, sir, your business with me ?
   Gil.   Why, my lord,
I for these many days have been, so please you,
Away from home; suddenly coming back,
My friends here tell me of a mortal suit
Your lordship has against me; when I ask
For the particulars, some say one thing,

And some another.   I, who naturally
Am somewhat interested in the truth,
Think it the wisest course to come at once
Straight to head-quarters.

    Judge.   This is strange proceeding.

    Gil. Oh, if your lordship scruple telling me,
These papers will not.   I'd not for the world
Annoy your lordship.   (*Takes the papers.*)

    Judge.   What are you about, sir?

    Gil. Conning my brief.

    Judge.   But, sir—

    Gil.   Now pray, my lord,
Resume your seat; let me not ask you. this
So very often. (*Reading.*) Ah—the bare indictment
I know in a rough way, no need read that:
But for the evidence.   Ah, here it is.
Humph; the first witness called, Andrew Ximenes:
"Andrew Ximenes, being duly sworn,
"Deposeth thus: that he was cutting wood,
"When the two gentlemen came out to fight;
"And stood to watch them; that, after some passes,
"Don Diego fell; and the officers of justice
"Then coming up, the other leap'd on horse,
"And fled: but being brought to ground by a shot
"That kill'd his horse, then ran, until he reach'd
"Gil Perez's house,"—here enter I,—"who first
"Courteously ask'd the Sheriff to desist
"Hunting the gentleman; but when the Sheriff
"Persisted, drew on him and on his people,
"And fought them back; but how and when exactly
"The wound was given, deponent cannot say.
"And all this he deposeth upon oath,
"Andrew Ximenes—"   And he says the truth;

Andrew is a good, honourable fellow.
Now for the second, Gil Parrado; humph.
"Parrado, duly sworn, deposeth thus;
"That, hearing a commotion, he ran out
"And got in time to see"—here enter I—
"Gil Perez fighting with the officers,
"Then on a sudden running to the river
"Plunge in. And that is all he knows of it."
How short and sweet!
"Next and third witness, Juan Baptista,"—ay,
Now for this exemplary Christian—
"Juan Baptista sworn, deposeth thus:
"That, as luck fell, he was behind a tree
"When the two gentlemen came out to fight;
"That they fought fairly hand to hand, until"—
Here enter I—"Gil Perez suddenly
"Rush'd from a thicket by, and join'd himself
"With Don Alonso, and the two together
"Maliciously and treacherously slew
"Don Diego." Pray, my lord, what is the worth
Of such a witness, who himself admits
He stood behind a tree watching two men
Set on a third, and slay him, and yet never
Ran to his help? Well—humph—"And after this,
"Saw Don Alonso jump upon a horse
"And fly, while Perez drew his sword upon
"The officers of justice, and slew one,
"And maim'd another." Give me leave, my lord,
To take this leaf. (*Tears it out.*)
         I'll bring it back to you
When I have made this rascal Jew confess
(If ever Jews confess) what he *did* see,
If any thing; but fair that if a judge

Decide on evidence, that evidence
At least be true; that he should hear moreover
Both sides, accus'd as well as his accuser.
As to that Sheriff's wounds—the only count
To which I own—I never sought the fray;
The fray sought me, as I stood innocently
At my own door; and pray what man of honour—
What would your lordship's sober self have done
In such a case?

    Judge.   Within! within there! ho!
Perez himself is here! the culprit! Seize him!

    Man. (appearing). Ay, do, if you can catch him.

    Gil.   Manuel,
Let them come up; I have no more to say.
And you and I, who walk'd in by the door,
Can jump out of the window.

    Voices (within).   Seize him! Seize him!

    Judge. One word, Gil Perez; if you yield at once,
I'll be your friend.

    Gil.   I make no friends of lawyers,
And never trust their promises.

    Judge.   If not,
As sure as Heav'n, I'll bring you to the scaffold.

    Gil. If you can catch me.

    Judge.   Cannot I?

    Gil.   Well, try.

    Judge. Ho there! upon him; and if he resist,
Cut him down!

    Man.   Now then, Gil!

    Gil.   Now, Manuel!
Out with the lights! or wanting them, we two
Will strike them, knaves, in plenty out of you.

    (*Confusion and Melée, in which* GIL *and* MANUEL *escape*.)

F.   15

ACT III.

SCENE I. *On a Mountain by Salvatierra.—Enter* GIL
PEREZ, MANUEL, ISABEL, *and* JUANA.

Gil. This mountain then, upon whose wrinkled edge
The weary moon reclines, must be our fort;
Where, in some green and shady spot of it,
(Hung round with savage, inaccessible rocks,)
While Isabel and your Juana rest,
You and I, Manuel, will steal into
The little village nestled there below,
And of such travellers as come this way,
Demand (our own all gone) a scanty living,
By fair entreaty, not by violence;
Until, pursuit giv'n up, we may retreat
Elsewhere, to live upon what little means
Injustice leaves us.
    Man.   Gil, 'tis nothing new
For criminals to hide
Ev'n where they did the crime, where vengeance least
Expects to find them, and hunts round in vain.
And even should they light upon the place,
Surely we two, back'd by these friendly rocks,
Can keep at bay the rabble that we foil'd
On level ground.
    Isab.   I have listen'd to you both,
And take it ill you reckon on yourselves
Alone; when I, who though a woman, having yet

Your blood, Gil Perez, running in my veins,
And something of your spirit in my heart,
Am at your side.
 Jua.   And I, who, like a coward,
Chime in the last; yet, if with little power,
With right good will indeed.
 Gil.   Well spoken both!
But I maintain it as a golden law,
Women be women ever : keep you quiet,
And comforting yourselves as best you may,
While Manuel and I, as becomes men,
Provide for you in all.
 Isab.   Well, we at least,
If fit for nothing else, can pray for you.
         [*Exeunt* ISABEL *and* JUANA.
 Gil. Now they are gone, I want to talk with you
On a grave matter, Manuel. 'Tis this.
Among those depositions at the Judge's,
One rascal, and a rascal too whose gold
Makes weigh his witness against honesty,
Declar'd on oath he saw me, me, Gil Perez,
Abetting Don Alonso treacherously
To slay Don Diego.
 Man.   Who was this?
 Gil.   Why one
Who has not this alone to answer for,
As you will know when I name—Juan Baptista.
 Man. A coward, who, as all such villains do,
Flies to the tongue for vengeance, not the sword;
Behind one's back too—
Why, let us go at once, and in broad day
Before all eyes, before the very Judge's
He lied to, drag the rascal from his house,

And make him eat his words in the very place
He spit them forth in.
  Gil.   All this we will do,
But at some better opportunity,
And fitter place. I've heard my grandsire say,
   "If you begin the fray, why then
    You must abide the how and when;
    But who's drawn into it, I trow,
    May suit himself with when and how."
But footsteps! Hark!—
Now to commence our calling, as new members
Of the most courteous cut-purse company.

Enter LEONARDO, *travelling.*

  Leon. (*speaking as he enters*). Lead on the horses, Mendo,
  'tis so pleasant
Under the shadow of these wooded rocks,
I'll walk some way alone.
  Gil.   Your servant, sir.
  Leon. Sir, God be with you?
  Gil.   Travelling all alone?
And whither, may I ask?
  Leon.   To Lisbon, sir.
  Gil. And whence?
  Leon.   I started at the break of day
From Salvatierra.
  Gil.   Ay? Then you can tell
What news is stirring there.
  Leon.   Oh nothing, sir.
Unless perhaps the exploits of a fellow
The terror of that country; one Gil Perez,

I think; who, when justice was at his heels
After some crime or other I forget,
Wounded the Sheriff, kill'd his officer,
And then was impudent enough to walk
Into the very Judge's house, and there,
Before his very eyes, snatch up and read
The depositions drawn up against him.

 Gil. A very curious story, that!

 Leon.   And then,
Though half the place was up in arms on him,
He, and another who is, as I hear,
Much such another rascal as himself,
Broke through them all and got away scot free!
But they are after him.

 Gil.   This is the news?

 Leon. All that I know of.

 Gil.   Well—before you go,
I'll ask you, sir, who by your speech and bearing
Seem a good fellow. If a friend of yours,
Came flying for his life, the Philistines
Close on his heels, and fell before your feet,
At your own door, exhausted, and beseeching
Help and protection of you—let me ask
What would you do?

 Leon.   What do? why, give it him.

 Gil. You would? and would you, in so doing,
Deserve the name of rascal for your pains?

 Leon. No, certainly.

 Gil.   And when a writ was out
Against you for so doing, charging you
With murder, threatening death and confiscation,
Would you be more a rascal for demanding
Such needful information of the Judge

As he alone could give of evidence
Which you suspected, and found false?
 Leon.   No, truly.
 Gil. One question more. If, damn'd by such false
  witness,
You were found guilty, all your property
Confiscated, yourself condemn'd to die,
Might not you fly the misdirected sword
Of justice, and of those who well could spare
Beg a poor tithe of what she robb'd you wholly,
And be no rascal still?
 Leon.   Oh clearly, clearly.
 Gil. This granted then, look to the inference.
I am Gil Perez; I who struck the Sheriff,
And kill'd his man, and read the Judge's papers,
And flying hither, shorn of house and home,
Ask you for that of which the law robs me;
Which, having plenty, if you will not give,
By your own free admission I may take,
And be no rascal still.
 Leon.   You need not use
My argument against me; I respect
And pity you, Gil Perez; take this chain;
If it be not enough, I pledge my word
I'll bring you more hereafter.
 Gil.   All you say
Tells of a generous heart. But ere I take
Your present, tell me—do you give it me
For fear, alone, and in my power, may be,
Or of good will?
 Leon.   Good will! I swear to you,
Gil Perez, I would even do the same
Had I a squadron at my side.

Gil.   As such
I take it, then.   For when my life must pay,
As soon or late it must, the penalty
Of hungry vengeance, I shall lay it down
Contented in my conscience, and report
That I but took from those who had to give,
And freely gave; the only retribution
My evil star allow'd me.
   Leon.   True enough.
Is there aught else that I can do for you?
   Gil. Nothing.
   Leon.   Farewell—and may a better fate
Await you.
   Gil.   Farewell—shall I see you safe
Over the mountain?
   Leon.   Not a step—adieu.   [*Exit.*
   Man. Sure never robbery was known to wear
So fair a face.
   Gil.   Tut, tut, you're not to call it
Robbery, but preferment, Manuel.
But who are these?

Enter two Farmers.

   1*st Farm.* I tell you I have bought the stock of vines
Upon his farm.
   2*nd Farm.*   What, Gil's?
   1*st Farm.*   Yes; sold, you know,
To pay the costs of prosecution,
Judges and Alguazīls and such; and I
Am carrying them the money.
   Man.   Fair game this.

Gil. I know him, a near neighbour. Well, friend Antony,
How goes it with you?

1st Farm.   What! Gil Perez! you!
When the whole country's after you?

Gil. And if they catch me nobody's the worse
Except myself. But till they catch and kill me,
(When I shall want, you know, no more to live on,)
I've not a stiver; clipt of the estate
Whose price you carry in your pocket there.
Now, I'd not starve; but, on the other hand,
Would not wrong any one to keep me from't:
How shall we settle that?

1st Farm.   Oh easily—
Take this—and this (*offers money*)—I had better give it up
At once, for fear. (*Aside.*)

Gil.   But do you give me this
Of free good will?

1st Farm.   Why as to that, Gil Perez,
My will is good to serve you; but, you see,
I am not very rich.

Gil.   You mean by that
You would not give this money could you help it?

1st Farm. Why certainly.

Gil.   Then keep it and begone
In peace.

1st Farm. Gil Perez!

Gil.   I'll not have it said
I robb'd—not shamed to beg in my distress.

2nd Farm. And I pray, Gil, and he who likes may
        hear me,
God keep you from your enemies. I have here
Six pieces that my wife knows nothing of;
You're welcome.

Gil.   Not a penny; go your ways,
Or night will reach you ere you reach your homes.
                              [*Exeunt Farmers.*
    Man. Gil, while you talk'd with them, I've heard a
        sound
As of pursuit—listen!—and many too.
    Gil. Let us up higher then !
    Man.   Beware, the trees
Will whisper of our whereabout.
    Gil.   Then here
Behind the rocks that tell no tales.
    Man.   Quick, quick ! (*They hide.*)

        Enter DONNA LEONOR, JUAN BAPTISTA, *Judge,*
                Alguazils, &*c.*

    Bapt. Here, madam, till the scorching sun be sunk,
Tarry awhile.
    Leonor.   My cousin's grievous sickness
Calls me with all speed homeward.
    Judge.   And as yet
No vestige of these ruffians, whom to find
And bring to justice, madam, in your cause,
I'll peril my own life.
    Gil.   Hist, Manuel !
    Man. Ay, but speak lower.
    Gil.   When better than now
Can I avenge Alonso and myself,
When judge, accus'd, accuser, and false witness,
Are all together?
    Man.   Wait awhile.
    Gil.   But—

Man.   See,
Fresh comers.
Gil.   I shall lose the golden moment.

Enter some, dragging along PEDRO.

Judge. A prisoner?

1*st Man.* One of Gil Perez's knaves, my lord, whom
we have just now caught creeping over to Portugal. The
very day Perez swam over there this fellow was missed
from Salvatierra, and returned on the very evening of his
return.

Judge. Very suspicious indeed.

Pedro. Very, my lord, I grant it. Yes, wherever I go, to
Portugal, Flanders, Germany, China, Japan, 'tis all the same.
I am sure to find him there.

Judge. You know then where he is now?

Ped. Oh, doubtless close at hand : he must be, I being
here ; he is such a constant master, that if you put me in
prison he'll soon surrender only to follow me there.

Judge. Point out the place, then.

Ped. Would to Heav'n I could, for were he clapt up safe
I'd not follow *him*, I promise you. Indeed, my lord, I live
in terror of my life from him.
Flying from him it was I fled from home
To Portugal ; where the first man I saw
Was he I thought I'd left at Salvatierra :
Flying to Andalusia, the first face
I saw was his I left in Portugal :
Till, rushing homeward in despair, the man
I thought I'd left behind in Andalusia,
Met me at once, and having knockt me down,
Left me for dead. Well, I got up at last,

And fled again : but, scarcely got a mile,
Your people seize me on suspicion
Of knowing where he hides, and so far justly,
That carrying me by way of a decoy,
I'll lay my life he soon were in the trap.

Judge. Your folly, or your cunning, sir, shall not mislead
us ; tell me where your master is at once, or the wooden
horse—

Ped. Alas, I'm a bad rider.

Judge. Take him to the village and keep him close. By
his looks I doubt not, spite of this affected simplicity, he's a
desperate ruffian.

Ped. I seem such a desperate fellow to him ! Dear me,
of the four men here let one depart, and leave three, and
one of the three leave two, and one of the two one ; and
that one leave half himself ; and that half his half ; and that
quarter his half, till it comes to *nil:* it would still be nilly
willy with me.   [*Exit, guarded by Alguazils.*

Gil.   Manuel,
The Alguazils are gone.

Man.   Now for it then.

Gil (appearing). God save this noble company !

All.   Gil Perez !

Gil. Be not alarm'd ; I have but a few words
To say to one of you, this Juan Baptista.

Judge. Holloa ! my guards !

Man.   Judge, never strain your throat,
Unless you would be answer'd by such guards
As waited on you yesterday.

Judge. Is this the way that I, and, in my person,
That justice is insulted ?

Gil.   Nay, my lord,
You least of all should tax a criminal

Who so punctiliously respects yourself,
And the realm's Justice in your belly lodg'd,
That not to waste you in a vain pursuit,
He waits on you himself.

    Judge.   Impudent man!
And this before that most illustrious lady
Your treachery has render'd brotherless;
And who with daily prayers—

    Gil.   And 'tis for this—
That she may hear my vindication
Ev'n from the very lips that made the charge,
And cease an unjust persecution,
Unworthy of her noble name and blood,
That I am here. For, madam, if I prove
That Don Alonso in fair duel slew
Your brother, and without my treacherous help,
Or any man's, would you pursue us still?

    Leonor. No, sir; for though the laws of duel are
For men alone, I know enough of them
To pardon all that was in honour done,
Ev'n to my cost. Prove what you say you will,
And Don Alonso may take sanctuary
In my own house against myself and all.

    Gil. 'Tis nobly said. On this I take my stand:
And since 'tis general and accepted law
That what a witness first shall swear, and then
Forswear, stand for no evidence at all,
Stand forth, Juan Baptista;
Here is your deposition; I will read it
Before the very Judge you swore it' to,
And before this great lady, and do you
Substantiate or deny it point by point.

    Judge. Audacity!

Gil (*reading*).   In the first place you swear,
That, "As luck fell, you were behind a tree
"When the two gentlemen came out to fight."
Say, is this true?
   Bapt.   It is.
   Gil.   "And that they fought
"Hand to hand fairly, until suddenly
"Gil Perez, rushing from a thicket, sided
"With Don Alonso." Now, bethink you well;
Is this the truth, Baptista?
   Bapt.   Yes. I swear it.
   Gil. Infamous liar! (*Shoots him with a pistol.*)
   Bapt. (*falling*). Heav'n have mercy on me!
   Gil. My lord, you must another murder add
To my black catalogue. Come, Manuel,
We must away while we have time. Farewell.
                   [*Exeunt* GIL *and* MANUEL.
   Judge. By the most sacred person of my king,
I swear to punish this audacity,
If it should cost my life.
   Bapt.   Oh, listen, lady;
While I have breath to speak. I'm justly slain.
I tried to swear Gil Perez's life away
To gain his sister; he has told you true:
In fair and open duel, hand to hand,
Was Don Diego slain. Oh let my death
Atone for this, and my last dying words
Attest it. (*Dies.*)

     Enter the Alguazils with PEDRO.

   Alg. We heard a pistol, and returned, my lord, to see.
   Judge. It was Gil Perez; that is his work. (*Pointing to*
BAPTISTA.)

Ped. There, said I not the truth?

Judge. He must not escape; after him! As to this fellow here, who is plainly in his secrets, let two Alguazils keep guard upon him here, lest he do further mischief; the rest come with me.

Ped. What crime have I committed? Did I not tell you, my lord, he would come, and did he not come?

Judge. Peace, traitor! Come, madam.   [*Exeunt.*

SCENE II. *Another Pass in the same Mountain—firing and shouting heard; after which, enter* ISABEL *and* JUANA *on a platform of rock above the stage.*

Isab. That arquebuss! of which only the thunder
Has reach'd us of perhaps some deadly bolt
On one of those we love!
Why tarry they so long? What think you, Juana?
Jua. Oh what, but share your fears!
Isab.   Let us descend,
And learn the truth at once; better at once
To die, than by this torture.

(*As they are about to descend, enter to them suddenly* GIL
PEREZ *and* MANUEL.)

Gil.   Wait!
Isab.   My brother!
Jua. Manuel!
Gil.   They are coming; hide we here;
There is no time—

Enter Judge, LEONOR, *Alguazils, &c.*

Judge. After them! after them!
By Heav'n, this mountain-top shall be the scaffold
On which the wretch shall expiate his crimes.
Two thousand scudi for the man who brings,
Dead or alive, Gil Perez!
    Gil (appearing above).   By the Lord,
You rate me cheap, my lord; I'll set you higher—
I say four thousand scudi for the Judge,
Alive or stuff'd!
    Judge. There he is!   Fire!   (*Alguazil fires and wounds*
        GIL.)
    Gil (falling).   God help me!
    Judge. Yield.
    Gil (struggling). I've an arm left yet.
    Alg.   He'll fight when dead.
    Judge. Away with him!   (*Judge and Alguazils carry off*
        GIL.)
    Man. (struggling with JUANA). Leave hold of me, I say.
    Jua. Oh! Manuel!
    Isab.   Oh! my brother!
    Man.   Let me go,
Or I will dash you headlong with myself.   (*He rushes down,*
        ISABEL *and* JUANA *after him.*)

SCENE III.   *Same as* SCENE I.—PEDRO *discovered guarded*
            by two Alguazils.

Ped. Shots and shouting!   They must be at work.   Per-
haps you gentlemen will wait, while I go and see.
    Alg. Be quiet, or two bullets—

Ped. Oh, one would be enough, thank you. Well, if I mustn't go, will you two gentlemen? and leave me to wait for you? I'm quite indifferent.

Alg. We leave you not an instant or an inch.

Ped. Were ever guards half so polite! Sure, I must be a holiday to be so strictly kept.

Alg. Hark! They are coming.

Enter Judge and Alguazils with GIL, *a cloak thrown over him.*

Judge. Where is the other prisoner?

Alg. Here, my lord.

Judge. March on with us.

Alg. 2. My lord, this man will faint with loss of blood and weariness.

Judge. Halt then, and let him breathe awhile.

(*They uncover* GIL, *and* PEDRO *sees him.*)

Ped. I might have guessed it! Let me be in the bilboes, on the very scaffold, he must be with me: he will die on purpose to lie in the same grave with me, I think!

Gil. Whose voice is that?

Ped. Nobody's.

Gil. Pedro? Courage, my poor boy. My day is over. Oh, vanity of mortal strength!

Judge. But who are these?

Enter DONNA LEONOR, *with* ISABEL, JUANA, *and Servants.*

Leonor. I, Donna Leonor, who, falling in
With these sad ladies, do repent me much,
That, mis-directed by a lying tongue,
I have pursued this gentleman—I doubt

To death—if not, I charge you from this moment
Leave him at liberty.
 Isab.   Or else—

Enter suddenly MANUEL *and* DON ALONSO, *and Followers.*

 Alon.   Or else,
Look to it.
 Gil. Don Alonso! whom I thought
Far off upon the seas?
 Alon.   And should have been,
But when my foot was on the very plank
That rock'd upon the foam along the beach,
I, who could never get you from my heart,
And knew that you had come to peril hither,
Could but return once more to him who sav'd
My life, though he had wav'd me from his side.
Enough; I am in time. I tell you, sir,
Give up this man at once. (*To the Judge.*)
 Judge.   Not for you all!
 Alon. Then at him and his people!

(ALONSO, MANUEL, *and their people rush on the Judge,*
 Alguazils, &c., disarm them, and beat them out.)

 Alon. (*embracing* GIL). My friend is free.
 Gil. And what first use shall make
Of freedom?
 Ped. Why, turn Friar; you can then
Be free and easy too, and leave me so.
Oh, sir, have I not had enough of terror,
Exile, and hunger, to deserve your pardon?
Plead for me, Don Alonso.
 Alon.   Gil—

Gil.   Nay, nay,
What could you seem about to ask of me
But granted ere 'twas said?   Go.   I forgive you.
With which magnanimous forbearance now
Gil Perez, the Gallician, makes his bow.

"Thus ends," says Calderon, "the first part of the *hazanas notables* of Luis Perez," whose name I have, for sundry reasons, (and without offence to the hero, I hope,) changed to *Gil*.   He was "a notorious robber," says Mr Ticknor, a kind of Spanish Rob Roy perhaps; at all events, one whose historical reality is intimated by greater distinctness of character than is usual in these plays.   Of such gentry examples are never wanting in Spain, where so little alters to this day; witness the career of the famous José Maria, quite lately ended; and who, I read in a book of Travels, was, like Gil, a farmer, for his first calling; a most merciful robber when he took to his second; and who performed Gil's feat of confronting, if not a Judge, a Prime Minister in his own den.

Gil perhaps had better have "played his pranks" (as Fuller says of Robin Hood) in prose; but he was a lawless fellow, and blank verse lay in his way.   Those who think his style altogether too heroic for a country robber, will at least find my version more than excused by the original.

THREE JUDGMENTS AT A BLOW.

17—2

DRAMATIS PERSONÆ.

PEDRO IV.,   *King of Arragon.*
DON MENDO TORELLAS, *his Minister.*
DONNA VIOLANTE,   *Mendo's Daughter.*
ELVIRA,   *her Maid.*

DON LOPE DE URREA.
DONNA BLANCA,   *his Wife.*
DON LOPE,   *their Son.*
BEATRICE,   *their Servant.*

DON GUILLEN,   *a Friend of Don Lope's.*
VICENTE,   *Young Lope's Servant.*

ROBBERS, OFFICERS, ROYAL SUITE, &c.

THREE JUDGMENTS AT A BLOW.

ACT I.

SCENE I. *A Mountain Pass near Saragossa. Shot within. Then enter* DON MENDO *and* VIOLANTE *pursued by Robbers, among whom is* VICENTE.

Men. Villains, let steel or bullet do their worst,
I'll die ere yield.
    Viol.   Heav'n help us !
    Robber I.   Fool, to strive
Against such odds—upon their own ground too,
Red with the blood of hundreds like yourselves.
    Vic. Come, sir, no more ado ;
But quietly give my young madam up,
Nice picking for our captain.
    Men. Not while a drop of blood is in my body.
    Robbers. Here's at you then !
    Viol.   My father !

(*As the Robbers attack* MENDO, *enter* DON LOPE.)

    Lope. How now? whom have you here?
    Vic.   Oh, noble captain,

We found this lady resting from the sun
Under the trees, with a small retinue,
Who of course fled.
All but this ancient gentleman, who still
Holds out against us.
    Lope (*to* MENDO). What can you expect
Against such numbers?
    Men.   Not my life, but death.
You come in time—
Upon my knees I do beseech of you (*kneels*)
No other mercy save of instant death
To *both* of us.
    Lope.   Arise! you are the first
Has mov'd me to the mercy you decline.
This lady is—your wife?
    Men.   My only daughter!
    Viol. In spirit as in blood. If by his death
You think to make you masters of my life,
Default of other weapon, with these hands
I'll cease the breath of life, or down these rocks
Dash myself headlong.
    Lope.   Lady, calm yourself;
Your beauty has subdued an angry devil
One like yourself first rais'd within my soul.
Your road lies whither, sir?
    Men.   To Saragossa.
Where if I could requite—
    Lope.   Your name?
    Men.   Don Mendo
Torellas, after a long embassage
To Paris, Rome, and Naples, summon'd back
By Pedro, king of Arragon—with whom
If't be (as oft) some youthful petulance,

Calling for justice or revenge at home,
Drives you abroad to these unlawful courses,
I pledge my word—

Lope.   Alas, sir, I might hail
Your offer could I hope that your deserts,
However great, might cancel my account
Of ill-deserving. But indeed my crimes
Have gather'd so in number, and in weight,
And condemnation—committed, some of them,
To stave away the very punishment
They must increase at last; others, again,
In the sheer desperation of forgiveness
That all had heap'd upon me—

Men.   Nay, nay, nay;
Despair not; trust to my good offices;
In pledge of which here, now, before we part,
I swear to make your pardon the first boon
I'll ask for or accept at the king's hand.
Your name?

Lope.   However desperate, and asham'd
To tell it, you shall hear it—and my story.
Retire !   (*To the Robbers, who exeunt.*)
        Don Mendo, I am Lope, son
Of Lope de Urrea, of some desert,
At least in virtue of my blood.

Men.   Indeed !
Urrea and myself were, I assure you,
Intimate friends of old,—another tie,
If wanting one, to bind me to your service.

Lope. I scarce can hope it, sir; if I, his son,
Have so disgrac'd him with my evil ways,
And so impoverisht him with my expenses,
Were you his friend, you scarcely can be mine.

And yet, were I to tell you all, perhaps
I were not all to blame.
   Men.   Come, tell me all;
'Tis fit that I should hear it.
   Viol.   I begin
To breathe again.
   Lope. Then listen, sir. My father in his youth,
As you perhaps may know, but *why* I know not,
Held off from marriage; till, bethinking him,
Or warn'd by others, what a shame it were
So proud a name should die for want of wearer,
In his late years he took to wife a lady
Of blameless reputation, and descent
As noble as his own, but so unequal
In years, that she had scarcely told fifteen ·
When age his head had whiten'd with such snows
As froze his better judgment.
   Men.   Ay, I know
Too well—too well! (*Aside.*)
   Lope. Long she repell'd his suit,
Feeling how ill ill-sorted years agree;
But, at the last, before her father's will ·
She sacrific'd her own. Oh sacrifice
That little lacks of slaughter! So, my father
Averse from wedlock's self, and she from him,
Think what a wedlock this must be, and what
The issue that was like to come of it!
While other sons cement their parents' love,
My birth made but a wider breach in mine.
Just in proportion as my mother lov'd
Her boy, my father hated him—yes, hated,
Even when I was lisping at his knees
That little language charms all fathers' hearts.

Neglecting me, himself, as I grew up
He neither taught, nor got me taught, to curb
A violent nature, which by love or lash
May even be corrected in a wolf:
Till, as I grew, and found myself at large,
Spoilt both by mother's love and father's hate,
I took to evil company, gave rein
To every passion as it rose within,
Wine, dice, and women—what a precipice
To build the fabric of a life upon !
Which, when my father
Saw tottering to its fall, he strove to train
The tree that he had suffer'd to take root
In vice, and grow up crooked—all too late !
Though not revolting to be ruled by him,
I could not rule myself. And so we liv'd
Both in one house, but wholly apart in soul,
Only alike in being equally
My mother's misery. Alas, my mother !
My heart is with her still ! Why, think, Don Mendo,
That, would she see me, I must creep at night
Muffled, a tip-toe, like a thief, to her,
Lest he should know of it ! why, what a thing
That such a holy face as filial love
Must wear the mask of theft ! But to sum up
The story of my sorrows and my sins
That have made me a criminal, and him
Almost a beggar ;—
In the full hey-day of my wilfulness
There liv'd a lady near, in whom methought
Those ancient enemies, wit, modesty,
And beauty, all were reconcil'd ; to her,
Casting my coarser pleasures in the rear,

I did devote myself—first with mute signs,
Which by and by began to breathe in sighs,
And by and by in passionate words that love
Toss'd up all shapeless, but all glowing hot,
Up from my burning bosom, and which first
Upon her willing ears fell unreprov'd,
Then on her heart, which by degrees they wore
More than I us'd to say her senseless threshold
Wore by the nightly pressure of my feet.
She heard my story, pitied me
With her sweet eyes; and my unruly passion,
Flusht with the promise of first victory,
Push'd headlong to the last; not knowing, fool!
How in love's world the shadow of disappointment
Exactly dogs the substance of success.
In fine, one night I stole into her house,
Into her chamber; and with every vow
. Of marriage on my tongue; as easy then
To utter, as thereafter to forswear,
When in the very jewel I coveted
Very compliance seem'd to make a flaw
That made me careless of it when possess'd.
From day to day I put our marriage off
With false pretence, which she at last suspecting,
Falsely continued seeming to believe,
Till she had got a brother to her side,
(A desperate man then out-law'd, like myself,
For homicide,) who, to avenge her shame,
With other two waylaid me on a night
When as before I unsuspectingly
Crept to her house; and set upon me so,
All three at once, I just had time to parry
Their thrusts, and draw a pistol, which till then

They had not seen, when——
Voices (*within*). Fly! Away! Away!

Enter VICENTE.

Lope. What is the matter now?
Vic.   Captain!
Lope.   Well, speak.
Vic. We must be off; the lady's retinue
Who fled have rous'd the soldiery, and with them
Are close upon our heels. We've not a moment.
Lope. Then up the mountain!
Men.   Whither I will see
They shall not follow you; and take my word
I'll not forget my promise.
Lope.   I accept it.
Men. Only, before we part, give me some token,
The messenger I send may travel with
Safe through your people's hands.
Lope (*giving a dagger*).   This then.
Men.   A dagger?
An evil-omen'd pass-word.
Lope.   Ah, Don Mendo,
What has a wretched robber got to give
Unless some implement of death! And see,
The wicked weapon cannot reach your hand,
But it must bite its master's. (*His hand bleeding.*)
Ill-omen'd as you say!
Voices (*within*). Away! Away!
Vic.   They're close upon us!
Viol. O quick! begone! My life hangs on a thread
While yours is in this peril.
Lope.   That alone

Should make me fly to save it.   Farewell, lady.
Farewell, Don Mendo.
 Men. and Viol. Farewell!
 Lope.   What strange things
One sun between his rise and setting brings! [*Exit.*
 Men. Let us anticipate, and so detain
The soldiers.   That one turn of Fortune's wheel
Years of half-buried memory should reveal!
 Viol. Could I believe that crime should ever be
So amiable!   How fancy with us plays,
And with one touch colours our future days!
         [*Exeunt severally.*

SCENE II. *An Audience Hall in the Palace of* PEDRO, *King
 of Arragon.—Enter* DON LOPE DE URREA, *and* DON
 GUILLEN.

 Guil. Such bosom friends, sir, as from infancy
Your son and I have been, I were asham'd,
You being in such trouble, not to offer
My help and consolation.   Tell me aught
That I can serve you in.
 Urr.   Believe me, sir,
My heart most deeply thanks your courtesy.
When came you to the city?
 Guil.   Yesterday,
From Naples.
 Urr. Naples?
 Guil.   To advance a suit
I have in Arragon.
 Urr.   I too am here
For some such purpose; to beseech the king

A boon I doubt that he will never grant.
   Guil. Ev'n now his Highness comes.

                 Enter King PEDRO *and Train.*

   Urr. So please your Majesty, listen to one,
Of whom already you have largely heard—
Don Lope de Urrea.
   King.   Oh! Don Lope!
   Urr. I come not hither to repeat in words⁻
The purport of so many past petitions,
My sorrows now put on a better face ·
Before your Highness' presence. I beseech you
To hear me patiently.
   King.   Speak, Urrea, speak!
   Urr. Speak if I can, whose sorrow rising still
Clouds its own utterance. My liege, my son,
Don Lope, lov'd a lady here; seduc'd her
By no feign'd vows of marriage, but compell'd
By me, who would not listen to a suit
Without my leave contracted, put it off
From day to day, until the lady, tired
Of a delay that argued treachery,
Engag'd her brother in the quarrel; who
With two companions set upon my son
One night to murder him. The lad, whose metal
Would never brook affront, nor car'd for odds,
Drew on all three; slew one—a homicide
That nature's common law of self-defence
Permits. The others fled, and set on him
The officers of justice, one of whom
In his escape he struck—
A self-defence against your laws I own

Not so to be excus'd—then fled himself
Up to the mountains. I must needs confess
He better had deserv'd an after-pardon
By lawful service in your camp abroad
Than aggravating old offence at home,
By lawless plunder; but your Highness knows
It is an ancient law of honour here
In Arragon, that none of noble blood
In mortal quarrel quit his native ground.
But to return. The woman, twice aggriev'd,
Her honour and her brother lost at once,
(For him it was my son slew of the three,)
Now seeks to bring her sorrows into port:
And pitying my grey hairs and misery,
Consents to acquit my son on either count,
Providing I supply her wherewithal
To hide her shame within some holy house;
Which, straiten'd as I am, (that, by my troth,
I scarce, my liege, can find my daily bread,)
I have engag'd to do; not only this,
But, in addition to the sum in hand,
A yearly income—which to do, I now
Am crept into my house's poorest rooms,
And, (to such straits may come nobility!)
Have let for hire what should become my rank
And dignity to an old friend, Don Mendo
Torellas, who I hear returns to-day.
To Saragossa. It remains, my liege,
That, being by the plaintiff's self absolv'd,
My son your royal pardon only needs;
Which if not he nor I merit ourselves,
Yet let the merits of a long ancestry,
Who swell your glorious annals with their names

Writ in their blood, plead for us not in vain;
Pity the snows of age that misery
Now thaws in torrents from my eyes; yet more,
Pity a noble lady—my wife—his mother—
Who sits bow'd down with sorrow and disgrace
In her starv'd house.

King.   This is a case, Don Lope,
For my Chief Justice, not for me.

Urr.   Alas!
How little hope has he who, looking up
To dove-ey'd mercy, sees but in her place
Severely-sworded justice!

King.   Is't not fit
That the tribunal which arraign'd the crime
Pronounce the pardon also?

Urr.   Were it so,
I know not where to look for that tribunal,
Or only find it speechless, since the death
Of Don Alfonso.

King.   His successor's name
This day will be announc'd to Arragon.

Urr. Yet let a father's tears—

King.   They might indeed
The marble heart of justice make to bleed.

          ·[*Exeunt* KING, DON GUILLEN, *and Train.*

Urr. And thus to satisfy the exigence
Of public estimation, one is forc'd
To sacrifice entreaty and estate
For an ill son.
Yet had but this petition been inflam'd
With love, that love of his had lit in me,
My prayer had surely prosper'd. But tis done,
Fruitless or not: *well* done, for Blanca's sake;

Poor Blanca, though indeed she knows it not,
And scarcely would believe it—
But who comes here?—the friend of better days,
Don Mendo! I would hide me from his eye,
But, oh indignity, his ancient friend,
Equal in birth and honour to himself,
Must now, reduc'd to't by a shameless son,
Become his tavern-keeper! For the present
I may hold back—the King too! come to meet
And do him honour.

Enter, meeting, KING, *with Train, and* DON MENDO.

Men. My royal master, let me at your feet
Now and for ever—
King.   Rise, Don Mendo, rise,
Chief Justice of all Arragon.
Men.   My liege,
How shall I rise with such a weight of honour
And solemnest responsibility,
As you have laid upon my neck!
King.   'Tis long
Since we have met. How fare you?
Men.   How but well,
On whom your royal favour shines so fair!
King. Enough. You must be weary. For to-day
Go rest yourself, Chief Justice. And to-morrow
We'll talk together. I have much to tell,
And much to ask of you.
Men.   Your Highness knows
How all my powers are at your sole command,
And only well employ'd in doing it.
                    [*Exit* KING *with Train.*

Urr. If it be true that true nobility
Slowly forgets what once it has esteem'd,
I think Don Mendo will not turn away
From Lope de Urrea.
 Men.   My old friend!
I must forget myself, as well as honour,
When I forget the debt I owe your love.
 Urr. For old acquaintance then I kiss your hand;
And on two other counts. First, as your host,
You know, on your arrival; be assur'd
That I shall do my best to entertain you:
And, secondly, congratulating you
On your new dignity, which you hardly don
Before I am your suitor.
 Men.   Oh, Don Lope,
How gladly shall I serve you!
 Urr.   This memorial
I had presented to the king, and he
Referr'd to his Chief Justice.
 Men.   Oh trust to me,
And to my loyal friendship in the cause.
 Urr. A son of mine, Don Mendo,—
 Men.   Nay, no more—
I am appriz'd of all.
 Urr.   I know that men
Think my heart harden'd toward my only son.
It might have been so; not, though, till my son's
Was flint to me. O Mendo, by his means
My peace of mind, estate, and good repute
Are gone for ever!
 Men.   Nay, be comforted:
I fill a post where friendship well can grant
What friendship fairly asks. Think from this hour

F.   18

That all is ended. Not for your sake only,
But for your son's; to whom (you soon shall hear
The whole strange history) I owe my life,
And sure shall not be slack to save his own.
All will be well. Come, let us to your house,
Whither, on coming to salute the king,
I sent my daughter forward.

   Urr.   I rejoice
To think how my poor Blanca will rejoice
To do her honour. You remember Blanca?

   Men. Remember her indeed, and shall delight
To see her once again. (*Aside.*) O lying tongue,
To say so, when the heart beneath would fain
We had not met, or might not meet again!

SCENE III. *A Room in* URREA'S *House.—Enter* BLANCA
   and VIOLANTE *in travelling dress, meeting.*

   Blan. How happy am I that so fair a guest
Honours my house by making it her own,
And me her servant!
To welcome and to wait on Violante
I have thus far intruded.

   Viol.   Nay, Donna Blanca,
Mine is the honour and the happiness,
Who, coming thus to Arragon a stranger,
Find such a home and hostess. Pardon me
That I detain you in this ante-room,
My own not ready yet.

   Blan.   You come indeed

Before your people look'd for you.
Viol.   But not
Before my wishes, lady, I assure you :
Not minding on the mountains to encounter
Another such a risk.
    Blan.   There was a first then ?
    Viol. So great that I assure you—and too truly, (*aside*)—
My heart yet beats with it.
    Blan.   How was't ?
    Viol.   Why, thus :
In wishing to escape the noon-day sun,
That seem'd to make both air and land breathe fire,
I lighted from my litter in a spot
That one might almost think the flowers had chosen
To tourney in, so green and smooth the sward
On which they did oppose their varied crests,
So fortified above with closing leaves,
And all encompass'd by a babbling stream.
There we sat down to rest ; when suddenly
A company of robbers broke upon us,
And would have done their worst, had not as suddenly
A young and gallant gentleman, their captain,
Arrested them, and kindly—but how now ?
Why weep you, Donna Blanca ?
    Blan.   Weeping, yes,
My sorrows with your own—But to your tale.
    Viol. Nay, why should I pursue it if my trouble
Awake the memory of yours ?
    Blan.   Your father,
Saw he this youth, this robber cavalier
Who grac'd disgrace so handsomely ?
    Viol.   Indeed,
And owes his life and honour to him.

Blan.   Oh !
He had aton'd for many a foregone crime
By adding that one more ! But I talk wild ;
Pardon me, Violante.
I have an anguish ever in my breast
At times will rise, and sting me into madness ;
Perhaps you will not wonder when you hear
This robber was my son, my only son,
Whose wicked ways have driv'n him where he is,
From home, and law, and love !
   Viol.   Forgive me, lady,
I mind me now—he told us—
But I was too confus'd and terrified
To heed to names. Else credit me—

Enter URREA *and* MENDO.

   Urr. Largess ! a largess, wife ! for bringing you
Joy and good fortune to our house, from which
They have so long been banisht.
   Blan.   Long indeed !
   Urr. So long, methinks, that coming all at once
They make me lose my manners. (*To* VIOLANTE.) This
    fair hand
Must, as I think it will, my pardon sign ;
Inheriting such faculty. Oh, Blanca,
I must not let one ignorant moment slip—
You know not half our joy.
Don Mendo, my old friend, and our now guest,
Grac'd at the very threshold by the King
With the Chief-Justiceship of Arragon,
Points his stern office with an act of mercy,

By pardoning your Lope—whom we now
Shall have once more with us, I trust, for ever.
Oh join with me in thanking him!
 Blan.   I am glad,
Don Mendo, that we meet under a roof
Where I can do you honour.   For my son,
I must suppose from what your daughter says,
You would, without our further prayer or thanks,
Have done as you have done.
 Mend.   Too true—I know—
And you still better, lady—that, all done,
I am your debtor still.

     Enter ELVIRA.

 Elv. Madam, your room is ready.
 Viol.   May I then
Retire?
 Blan. If I may wait upon you thither.
 Urr. Nay, nay, 'tis I that as a grey-hair'd page
Must do that office.
 Mend.   Granted, on condition
That I may do as much for Donna Blanca.
 Viol. As master of the house, I must submit
Without condition. [*Exeunt* VIOLANTE *and* URREA.
 Blan.   You were going, sir?—
 Mend. To wait upon you, Blanca.
 Blan.   Nay, Don Mendo,
Least need of that.
 Mend.   Oh, Blanca, Heaven knows
How much I have desir'd to talk with you!
 Blan. And to what purpose, sir?
No longer in your power—perhaps, nor will—

To do as well as talk.

Mend.   If but to say
How to my heart it goes seeing you still
As sad as when I left you years ago.

Blan. "As sad?—as when you left me years ago"—
I understand you not—am not aware
I ever saw you till to-day.

Mend.   Ah, Blanca,
Have pity!

Blan.   Nay, Don Mendo, let us cease
A conversation, uselessly begun,
To end in nothing. If your memory,
Out of some dreamt-of fragments of the past,
Attach to me, the past is dead in time;
Let it be buried in oblivion.

Mend. Oh, with what courage, Blanca, do you wield
Your ready woman's wit!

Blan.   I know not why
You should say that.

Mend.   But *I* know.

Blan.   If't be so,
Agree with me to say no more of it.

Mend. But how?

Blan.   By simple silence.

Mend.   How be silent
Under such pain?

Blan.   By simple suffering.

Mend. Oh, Blanca, how learn that?

Blan.   Of me—and thus.
Beatrice!

Enter BEATRICE.

Beat. Madam?

Blan.   Light Don Mendo to
His chamber.   Thus be further trouble sped.
Mend. Nay, rather coals of fire heap'd on my head!
                                    [*Exeunt severally.*

ACT II.

SCENE I.   *A Room in Urrea's House.—Enter* URREA *and*
BLANCA *on one side, and* LOPE *and* VICENTE *on the other.*

Lope. Thrice blessed be the day, that brings me back
In all humility and love, my father,
To kiss your feet once more.
Urr.   Rise up, my son,
As welcome to your parents as long lookt for.
Rise and embrace me.
Lope.   Till I have your hand
I scarcely dare.
Urr.   Then take it, Lope—there—
And may God make thee virtuous as thy father
Can pray for thee.   Thy mother too—
Lope.   O madam,
I scarcely dare with anguish and repentance
Lift up my eyes to those I have made weep
So many bitter tears—
Blan.   You see, my son,
You keep them weeping still—not bitter tears,
But tears of joy—Oh, welcome home again!
Vic. Where is there any room for a poor devil
Who has done penance upon rock and water

This many a day, and much repents him of
His former sins?
    Urr.   What you alive too?
    Vic.   Yes, sir,
This saddle's pad, (*showing* LOPE,) or, if you like, the beast
That bears the saddle—or, by another rule,—
That where the cat jumps also goes her tail.
    Lope (*to his father*). You see, sir, in such godly company
I must repent.
    Vic.   Why, devil take't—
    Urr.   What, swearing?
    Vic. But some poor relic of our former life
That yet will stick.   Madam, permit me,
If not to kiss your hand, nor ev'n your feet,
At least the happy ground on which they walk.
    Blan. Rise, rise.   How can I less than welcome one
Who has so loyally stood by my son,
Through evil and through good.
    Vic.   A monument
As one might say, madam, *ad perpetuam
Fidelis Amicitiæ Memoriam.*

Enter BEATRICE.

    Beat. What ! is my master home?   Then, by the saints,
Saving your presence, and before your faces,
I must embrace him.
    Lope.   Thanks, good Beatrice.
    Urr. You see how all rejoice to see you, Lope,
But none so more than I ; believe 't.   But now
'Tis time you wait on Mendo, and acknowledge
The kindness he has done us.   See, Beatrice,
If he be in his room, or busy there.   [*Exit* BEATRICE.

Meanwhile, my son, I crave one patient hearing
To what I have to say.

  Vic.   Now for a lecture.

  Lope. Silence, sir! Coming here, we must expect
And bear such things. Pray speak, sir.

  Urr.   You see, Lope,
(And doubtless must have heard of it before,)
In what a plight we are: my property,
What yet remains of it, embroil'd and hamper'd,
And all so little, that this last expense,
Of getting (as I have) your Estifania,
Who has already cost us all so much,
Into a convent; to do this, I say,
I have been forc'd to let my house for hire
To my old friend; yea, almost, I assure you,
To beg from door to door. Enough of that.
'Tis done; and you are now at last restor'd
To home, and station—wealth I cannot say—
But all is well that ends well. All I ask,
(And 'tis with tears and with a broken voice
I ask it: I would ask it on my knees
If these white hairs forbade not such descent,)
That from this day, in pity to us all—
Perhaps in gratitude—you would repent
Your past excess; yea, surfeited with that,
Would henceforth tame your headlong passions down
Into a quiet current. Help me, son,
Restore the shaken credit of our house,
And show—let us *both* show—that misery
Has taught us not in vain. Let us be friends
Henceforth; no rivalry of love or hate
Between us; each doing what in him lies
To make what may remain of life to each

Happy and honourable. On my part
I stake a father's love and tenderness;
And will not you as freely on your side
Wager your filial obedience?
Your father asks, implores you. Oh, consider
You may not always have a friend in need
To rescue you as now: nay, disappoint
His mercy and again provoke the laws
He now remits, that friend may turn to foe
And sacrifice the life he vainly spar'd.

 Vic. There only wants, "in sæcula sæculorum,"
To finish off with.

 Lope.   Sir, I promise you
Amendment, that shall make the past a foil
To set the future off.

Enter MENDO.

 Men.   I come in time
To vouch fulfilment of so fair a vow.

 Lope. Oh, sir—

 Men.   I knew you on your road to me;
Your errand too; and thus much have forestall'd
Of needless courtesy.

 Lope.   Pray God, reward you
With such advancement in your prince's love
As envy, the court Hydra, shall not hiss,
But general love and acclamation
Write in gold letters in our history,
For ages and for ages. Sir, your hand!

 Men. My heart, my heart, you shame me by your thanks,
For service that the veriest churl had paid
For what you did me, Lope.

Why, I'm your debtor still. But now, enough !
I cannot steal more time from business ;
The king expects me.

Urr.   I too must abroad.

Lope. Would I could wait on both—but, as it is,
I think my father's self would waive his right,
In favour of our common benefactor.

Urr. Indeed, indeed, I do rejoice you should.

                              [*Exit with* BLANCA.

Men. And I, not knowing if your choice be right,
Know that I would not lose you for a moment,
So glad your presence makes me.   [*Exit with* LOPE.

*Vic.** Beatrice ! Beatrice !

Beat. Well?

Vic. Think you not, now that our principals are fairly
out of the way, you owe me a kiss on my arrival ?

Beat. Ay, hot from the oven.

Vic. Ah Beatrice ! if you only knew what heart-aches
you've cost me.

Beat. You indeed, robbing and murdering, and I don't
know what beside, up in the mountains ! and then my new
madam that's come with you, Donna Violante ; with her
fine Elvira,—I know, sir, when your master was courting his
mistress, you—

Vic. Now, my own Beatrice, if you could only know what
you are talking of as well as I, how little jealousy could such
a creature as that give you !

Beat. Well—but why ?

Vic. Not a woman at all, neither maid nor mermaid—
Why, didn't I catch her with all those fine locks of hers
clean off her head ?

---

* Vicente's flirtation with the two Criadas, and its upshot, is familiar
to English play-goers in the comedy of "The Wonder."

Beat. Clean off her head?

Vic. The woman's bald.

Beat. Bald?

Vic. As my hand! besides, all that fine white *chevaux-de-frise* that ornaments her gums.

Beat. Well?

Vic. All sham.

Beat. What, my fine madam there false teeth?

Vic. Oh, and half a dozen villainous things I could tell you, did it become a gentleman to tell tales of ladies. But see, here is master coming back.

Beat. Good bye then, for the present, Vicente. False teeth and a wig!   [*Exit.*

Enter DON LOPE.

Lope. Vicente, have you by any chance seen Violante?

Vic. Not that I know of, sir; she may however have passed without my knowing her.

Lope. Vicente still! As if it were possible one who had once seen such beauty could ever forget it.

Vic. Why, sir, if her maid Elvira happened to be by her side--

Lope. Fool!

Vic. Pray is it impossible in the system of things that the maid should be handsomer than the mistress?

Lope. Oh could I but see her!

Vic. Take càre, take care, sir. Beware of raising the old devil—and now we are but just out of the frying-pan—

Lope. Beware *you*, sir! I tell you I ill liked my father's lecture; do not you read me another. It were best that no one crossed me, or by heaven!—But who comes here?

Vic. Don Guillen de Azagra.

Enter DON GUILLEN.

Lope.   What?
Ask what reward you will of me, Vicente.
Don Guillen de Azagra back again!
    Guil. And could not wait a moment, hearing you
Were also back, Don Lope, till I found you,
As well to give you welcome as receive it.
    Lope. Our old affection asks for nothing less
On both sides.   Oh, you are welcome!   ⁻
    Guil. Well can he come, who comes half dead between
Dead hope and ·quickening passion!
    Lope.   How is that?
    Guil. Why, you remember how three years ago
I went to Naples—to the wars there?
    Lope.   Yes,
We parted, I remember, sadly enough
On both sides, in the Plaza del Aseo ;
Unconsciously divining the sad days
That were about to dawn on one of us.
    Guil. Nay, upon both.   I am no stranger, Lope,
To your misfortunes; and Heav'n knows I felt them!
But they are over, Heav'n be thankt! mine yet
Are sadly acting.   You can help me now,
If not to conquer, to relieve them.
    Lope.   Ay,
And will strain every nerve for you.   But first
Must hear your story.
    Guil.   Well—I went to Naples,
Where, as you know, our King by force of arms
Was eager to revenge the shameful death
Of Norandino, whom the king of Naples
Had on the scaffold treacherously murder'd.

Of which, and Naples too, I say no more
Than this; that, entering the city,
I saw a lady in whom the universe
Of beauty seem'd to centre; as it might be
The sun's whole light into a single beam,
The heavenly dawn into one drop of dew,
Or the whole breathing spring into one rose.
You will believe I lov'd not without cause,
When you have heard the lady that I speak of
Is—

 Vic. Donna Violante!

 Lope.   Knave and fool!

 Vic. Why so, sir! only for telling you I saw the lady coming this way; but, I suppose seeing people here, she has turned back.

 Lope. Will you retire awhile, Don Guillen? this lady is my father's guest.

 Guil. (*aside*). Beside, she might be angry finding me here.   [*Exit.*

 Lope. 'Fore Heaven, my mind misgave me it was she he spoke of!

 Vic. Well, you have got the weather-gage. Tackle her now.

Enter VIOLANTE *and* ELVIRA.

 Lope. Nay, lady, turn not back. What you, the sun
I see by, to abridge my little day
By enviously returning to the west
As soon as ris'n, and prematurely drawing
The veil of night over the blush of dawn!
Oh, let me not believe I fright you now,
As yesterday I did, fair Violante,
Arm'd among savage rocks with savage men,

From whose rude company your eyes alone
Have charm'd me, and subdued for the first time
A fierce, unbridled will.

  Viol.   It were not strange,
Don Lope, if my bosom trembled still
With that first apparition.   But in truth
I had not hesitated,
Had I not seen, or fancied, at your side
Another stranger.

  Lope.   Oh, a friend; and one
Who spoke with me of *you ;* nay, who retir'd
Only for fear of drawing new disdain
Upon old love; and left me here indeed,
To speak in his behalf.

  Viol.   Alas, Elvira,
Was't not Don Guillen?

  Elv.   Yes.

  Viol.   Don Lope plead
Another's, and Don Guillen's love !   (*She is going.*)

  Lope.   At least
Let me attend you to my mother's door.

  Viol. Nay, stay, sir.

  Lope.   Stay ! and lose my life in losing
This happy opportunity !

  Viol.   Are life
And opportunity the same?

  Lope.   So far,
That neither lost ever returns again.

  Viol. If you have aught to tell me, tell it here
Before I go.

  Lope. Only to ask if you
Confess yourself no debtor to a heart
That long has sigh'd for you?

Viol.   You, sir, are then
Pleading another's cause?
Lope.   . I might be shy
To plead in my own person—a reserve
That love oft feels—and pardons.
Viol.   'Tis in vain.
I will not own to an account of sighs
Drawn up against me without my consent;
So. tell your friend; and tell him he mistakes
The way to payment making you, of all,
His agent in the cause.
Lope.   Nay, nay, but wait.
Viol. No more—Adieu!   [*Exit.*
Lope.   She thought I only us'd
Another's suit as cover to my own,
And cunningly my seeming cunning turns
Against myself. But I will after her;
If Don Guillen come back, tell him, Vicente,
I'll wait upon him straight.   [*Exit.*
Vic. Madam Elvira!
Elv. Well, Monsieur Cut-throat?
Vic. Well, you are not scared at my face now?
Elv. I don't know that—your face remains as it was.
Vic. Come, come, my queen, do me a little favour.
Elv. Well, what is that?
Vic. Just only die for love of me; I always make a
point of never asking impossibilities of any woman.
Elv. Love is out of the question! I perhaps might *like*
you, did I not know the lengths you go with that monkey
Beatrice.
Vic. With whom?
Elv. I say with Beatrice. Bystanders see as much, sir,
as players.

Vic. I with Beatrice! Lord! lord! if you only knew half what I know, Elvira, you'd not be jealous of her.

Elv. Why, what do you know of her?

Vic. A woman who, could she breed at all, would breed foxes and stoats—a tolerable outside, but only, only go near her—Foh! such a breath! beside other peculiarities I don't mention out of respect to the sex. But this I tell you, one of those sparkling eyes of hers is glass, and her right leg a wooden one.

Elv. Nonsense!

Vic. Only you look, and see if she don't limp on one side, and squint on the other.

Don Guillen (entering at one side). I can wait no longer.

Don Lope (entering at the other). It is no use; she is shut up with my mother. Now for Don Guillen.

Elv. They are back.

Vic. We'll settle our little matter by and by.

Elv. Glass eyes and wooden legs!   [*Exit.*

Lope (To DON GUILLEN). Forgive my leaving you so
    long; I have been
Waiting on one who is my father's guest,
The lady Violante.

Guil.   So sweet duty
Needs no excuse.

Lope.   Now to pursue your story—

Guil. Ah—where did I leave off?

Lope.   About the truce
Making at Naples, when you saw a lady—

Guil. Ay, but I must remember one thing, Lope,
Most memorable of all. The ambassador
Empower'd to treat on our good king's behalf
Was Mendo de Torellas, whose great wisdom
And justice, both grown grey in state affairs,

F.   19

Well fitted him for such authority;
Which telling you, and telling you beside,
That when the treaty made, and he left Naples,
I left it too, still following in his wake
The track of a fair star who went with him
To Saragossa, to this very house—
Telling you this, I tell you all—tell who
My lady is—his daughter—Violante,
Before whose shrine my life and soul together
Are but poor offerings to consecrate.

    Vic. (*aside*).   A pretty market we have brought our
       pigs to !
Who'll bet upon the winner?

    Lope (*aside*).   Oh confusion !
But let us drain the cup at once.   Don Guillen,
Your admiration and devotedness
Needed the addition of no name to point
Their object out.   But tell me,
Ere I advise with you, how far your prayer
Is answer'd by your deity?

    Guil.   Alas !
Two words will tell—

    Lope.   And those?

    Guil.   Love unreturn'd !
Or worse, return'd with hate.

    Vic. (*aside*).   Come, that looks better.

    Guil. My love for her has now no hope, Don Lope,
But in your love for me.   She is your guest,
And I as such, beside my joy in you,
May catch a ray of her—may win you even
To plead for me in such another strain
As has not yet wearied her ears in vain;
Or might you not ev'n now, as she returns,

Give her a letter from me; lest if first
She see, or hear from others of my coming,
She may condemn my zeal for persecution,
And make it matter of renew'd disdain.
I'll write the letter now, and bring it you
Ere she be back.   [*Exit.*

   Vic. (*to* LOPE). Good bye, sir.
   Lope.   Whither now,
Vicente?
   Vic.   To the mountains—I am sure
You'll soon be after me.
   Lope.   I understand—
But stay awhile.
True, I love Violante, and resent
Don Guillen's rivalry: but he's my friend—
Confides to me a passion myself own,
And cannot blame.
Wait we awhile, Vicente, and perhaps
A way will open through the labyrinth
Without our breaking through.
   Vic.   How glad I am
To see you take't so patiently! Now, sir,
Would you be rul'd—
   Lope.   What then?
   Vic.   Why simply, sir,
Forget the lady—but a few days' flame,
And then—
   Lope.   Impossible!
   Vic.   What's to be done then?
   Lope. I know not—But she comes.

Enter VIOLANTE.

   Viol.   Still here, Don Lope!

19—2

Lope. Ah, what in nature will its centre leave,
Or, forc'd away, recoils not faster still?
So rivers yearn along their murmuring beds
Until they reach the sea; the pebble thrown
Ever so high, still faster falls to earth;
Wind follows wind, and not a flame struck out
Of heavy wood or flint, but it aspires
Upward at once and to its proper sphere.

Viol. All good philosophy, could I but see
How to apply it here.

Lope.   And yet, how easy!
Your beauty being that to which my soul
Ever flies fastest, and most slowly leaves.

Viol. Surely this sudden rapture scarce agrees
With what I heard before.

Lope.   How, Violante?

Viol. Have you not haply chang'd parts in the farce,
And ris'n from second character to first?

Lope. My second did not please you—come what will,
Casting feign'd speech and character aside,
I'll e'en speak for myself in my own person.
Listen to me—Don Guillen—

Guil. (*listening at the side*).   Just a moment
To hear him plead my cause.

Lope. Following your beauty, as a flower the sun,
Has come from Italy to Arragon,
And, as my friend, by me entreats of you
To let him plead his suit.

Guil.   Would I could stay
To hear the noble Lope plead my cause,
But summon'd hence—   [*Exit.*

Viol.   Ill does your second part
Excuse your ill performance of the first;

One failure might be pardon'd, but two such
Are scarce to be excus'd.

Lope.   Oh, tell me then
Which chiefly needs apology!

Viol.   I will.
First for your friend Don Guillen; bid him cease
All compliment and courtship, knowing well
How all has been rejected hitherto,
And will hereafter, to the ruthless winds.

Lope. And on the second count—my own?

Viol.   How easily
Out of his answer you may draw your own!

Lope. Alas!

Viol.   For when the judge has to pronounce
Sentence on two defendants, like yourselves,
Whose charge is both alike, and bids the one
Report his condemnation to the other;
'Tis plain—

Lope.   That both must suffer?

Viol.   Nay, if so
The judge had made one sentence serve for both.

Lope. Great heavens!

Guil. (listening at the side). The man dismiss'd, I'll hear
    the rest.

Viol. Oh, let it be enough to tell you now
The heart that once indeed was adamant,
Resisting all impression—but at last
Ev'n adamant you know—

Guil.   Oh, she relents!

Lope. Oh, let me kiss those white hands for those
    words!

Guil. Excellent friend! he could not plead more warmly
Were 't for himself.

Lope.   Oh for some little token
To vouch, when you have vanisht from my eyes,
That all was not a dream !
    Viol. (giving him a rose).   This rose, whose hue
Is of the same that should my cheek imbue !   [*Exit.*

Enter GUILLEN.

Guil. Oh how thrice welcome is my lady's favour,
Sent to me by the hand of such a friend !
How but in such an attitude as this
Dare I receive it ? (*Kneels*).
    Lope.   Rise, Don Guillen, rise :
Flowers are but fading favours that a breath
Can change and wither.
    Guil.   What mean you by this?
    Lope. Only that though the flower in my hands
Is fresh from Violante's, I must tell you
It must not pass to yours.
    Guil.   Did not I hear you
Pleading my cause?
    Lope.   You might—
    Guil.   And afterwards,
When I came back again, herself confess
That, marble as she had been to my vows,
She now relented tow'rd me !
    Lope.   If you did,
'Twould much disprove the listener's adage.
    Guil.   How ?
    Lope. You set your ears to such a lucky tune,
As took in all the words that made for you,
But not the rest that did complete the measure.
    Guil. But did not Violante, when you urg'd her
In my behalf, say she relented ?

Lope.   Yes.

Guil. To whom then?

Lope.   To myself.

Vic.   The cat's unbagg'd!

Guil. To you!

Lope.   To me.

Guil.   Don Lope, you must see
That ev'n my friendship for you scarce can stomach
Such words—or credit them.

Lope.   Let him beware
Who doubts my words, stomach them as he can.

Guil. But 'tis a jest :
Bearing my happy fortune in your hands,
You only, as old love has leave to do,
Tantalize ere you give it me.   Enough,
Give me the rose.

Lope.   I cannot, being just
Given to me, and for me.

Guil.   His it is
Whose right it is, and that is mine ; and I
Will have it.

Lope.   If you can.

Guil.   Then follow me,
Where (not in your own house) I may chastise
The friendship that must needs have play'd me false
One way or other.   ·   [*Exit.*

Lope.   Lead the way then, sir.

Enter hurriedly DONNA BLANCA *and* VIOLANTE *from
opposite sides.*

Viol. Don Lope, what is this?

Lope.   Nothing, Violante.

Viol. I heard your angry voices in my room,
And could not help—
Blan.   And I too. O my son,
Scarce home with us, and all undone already!
Where are you going?
Lope.   No where; nothing; leave me.
Viol. Tell me the quarrel—Oh! I dread to hear.
Lope. What quarrel, lady? let me go: your fears
Deceive you.
Blan.   Lope, not an hour of peace
When you are here!
Lope.   Nay, madam, why accuse me,
Before you know the cause?

Enter URREA.

Urr.   How now?—disputing?
Blanca and Violante too? What is it?
Blan. Oh, nothing! (I must keep it from his father.)
Nothing—he quarrell'd with Vicente here,
And would have beat him—and we interposed;
Indeed, no more.
Vic.   The blame is sure to fall
Upon my shoulders.
Urr.   Is't not very strange,
Your disposition, Lope? never at peace
With others or yourself.
Lope.   'Tis nothing, sir.
Vic. He quarrell'd with me, sir, about some money
He thought he ought to have, and couldn't find
In his breeches' pocket.
Urr.   Go, go—get you gone, knave.
Vic. Always fair words from you at any rate. (*Aside.*)

Urr. And for such trifles, Lope, you disturb
My house, affright your mother and her guest
With your mad passion.
 Lope.   I can only, sir,
Answer such charge by silence, and retire.
Now for Don Guillen.   [*Exit.*
 Blan.   Oh let him not go!
 Urr. Why not? 'tis a good riddance.   Violante,
You must excuse this most unseemly riot
Close to your chamber.   My unruly son,
When his mad passion's rous'd, neither respects
Person or place.
 Viol. Nay, sir, I pardon him.
And should, for I'm the cause! (*Aside.*)
 Blan.   Ah, wretched I,
Who by the very means I would prevent
His going forth, have op'd the door to him.
(*Noise within of swords, and the voices of* LOPE *and* GUILLEN
fighting.)
 Urr. What noise is that again?

     Enter ELVIRA.

Elv.   'Tis in the street.

     Enter BEATRICE.

Beat. Oh, my young master fighting—run, sir, run!
Urr. And 'tis for this I've sacrific'd myself!

Enter fighting LOPE *and* GUILLEN ; *Gentlemen and others
trying to part them.*

 Urr. (*going between them*).   Hold, Lope! Hold, Don
 Guillen!

Voices.   Part them! part them!

Guil. Traitor!

Lope.   Traitor!—I say that he's the traitor
Whoever—

Urr.   Madman, can you not forbear
When your grey-headed father holds your sword!

Lope. And in so doing robs me of the honour
I never got from him.

Urr.   Oh! ruffian!
But if this graceless son will not respect
His father, my white hairs appeal to you,
Don Guillen.

Guil.   And shall not appeal in vain—
Out of respect, sir, for your age and name,
And for these gentlemen who interpose,
I shall refer the issue of this quarrel
To other time and place.

Lope.   A good excuse
For fear to hide in.

Guil.   Fear!

Urr.   Madman! again!
That the respect his rival shows to me
Should make my son despise him.   By these heav'ns
This staff shall teach you better.

Lope.   Strike me not!
Beware—beware!

Urr.   Why, art thou not asham'd—

Lope. Yes, of respect for you that's fear of me.

Guil. Whoever says or thinks what I have done
Is out of fear of you, I say—

Urr.   He lies!
I'll top your sentence for you.

Lope.   Then take thou
The answer !   (*Strikes* URREA, *who falls: confusion.*)
A voice.   What have you done ?
Another.   Help, help !
Voices. After him, after him !—the parricide !
                    (LOPE *rushes out and the people after him.*)
Guil. I know not how to leave the poor old man—
Come, let me help you, sir.
Urr.   Parricide !
May outrag'd Heaven that has seen thy crime,
Witness my curse, and blast thee ! Every sword
That every pious hand against thee draws,
Caught up into the glittering elements,
Turn thunderbolt, (as every weapon shall
Drawn in God's cause,) and smite thee to the centre !
That sacrilegious hand which thou hast rais'd
Against this snow-white head—how shall it show
Before Heaven's judgment bar ; yea, how can Heav'n
Ev'n now behold this deed, nor quench its sun,
Veil its pure infinite blue with awful cloud,
And with a terrified eclipse of things
Confound the air you breathe, the light you see,
The ground you walk on !
Guil.   Pray sir, compose yourself—
Your cloak—your staff—
Urr.   My staff ! what use is that,
When it is steel that must avenge my wrong ?
Yet give it me—fit instrument
Wherewith to chastise a rebellious child—
Ay, and he did not use his sword on me,
Mark that, nor I on him—give me my staff.
Alas, alas ! and I with no strength left
To wield it, only as I halt along,

Feeling about with it to find a grave,
And knocking at deaf earth to let me in.*
   Guil. Nay, calm yourself,
The population of the place is up
After the criminal.
   Urr.   And to what purpose?
They cannot wipe away my shame by that.
Let the whole city turn its myriad eyes
Upon me, and behold a man disgrac'd—
Disgrac'd by him to whom he gave a being.
I say, behold me all—the wretched man
By his own flesh and blood insulted, and
On his own flesh and blood crying Revenge!
Revenge! revenge! revenge!
Not to the heavens only, nor to Him
Who sits in judgment there, do I appeal,
But to the powers of earth. Give me my hat,
I'll to the king forthwith.
   Vic.   Consider, sir;
You would not enter into the palace gates
So suddenly, and in this plight?

---

* Como me podre vengar
  Si aquel, que me ha de ayudar
  A sustentarme, me advierte
  Que armado en la terra dura
  Solo ha de irme aprovechando
  De aldaba, con que ir llamando
  A mi misma sepultura?

Ne deth, alas! ne will not han my lif.
Thus walke I like a resteles caitif,
And on the ground, which is my modres gate,
I knocke with my staf erlich and late,
And say to hire, "Leve mother, let me yn."
              Chaucer's Pardoner's Tale.

Urr.   Why not,
Whose voice should over-leap the firmament,
And without any preparation enter
The palace-doors of God—
King Pedro! king of Arragon! Christian king!
Whom fools the Cruel call, and Just the wise,
I call on you, King Pedro*—
    King (entering with MENDO *and Train).*   Who calls the
        king?
Urr. A wretch who, falling at your feet, implores
Your royal justice.
    King.   I remember you;
Don Lope de Urrea, whose son I pardon'd.
What would you of me?
    Urr.   That you would, my king,
Unpardon him you pardon'd; draw on him
The disappointed sword of justice down.
That son—*my* son—if he indeed be mine—
(Oh, Blanca, pure as the first blush of day,
Pardon me such a word!) has, after all
My pain and sacrifice in his behalf;
Has, in defiance of the laws of man
And God, and of that great commandment, which,
Though fourth on the two tables, yet comes first
After God's jealous honour is secur'd,
Has struck me—struck his father—in a fray

---

* The Biographie Universelle says it was Don Pedro of *Castile*
about whose cognomen there was some difference of opinion; a defence
of him being written in 1648 by Count de Roca, ambassador from Spain
to Venice, entitled, "El Rey Don Pedro, llamado el Cruel, el Justiciero,
y el Necessitado, defendido." It is he, I suppose, figures in the "Medico
de su Honra." He flourished at the same time, however, with his
namesake of Arragon.

Wherein that father tried to save his life.
I have no vindication ; *will* have none,
But at your hands and by your laws ; unless,
If you deny me that, I do appeal
Unto the King of kings to do me justice ;
Which I will have, that heav'n and earth may know
How a bad son begets a ruthless sire !

    King. Mendo!

    Men.   My liege.

    King.   I must again refer
This cause to you. (*To* URREA.) Where is your son?

    Urr.   Fled ! fled !

    King (*to* MENDO). After him then, use all the powers
    I own
To bring the wretch to justice. See me not
Till that be done.

    Men.   I'll do my best, my liege.

    King. I have it most at heart. In all the rolls .
Of history, I know of no like quarrel :
And the first judgment on it shall be done
By the Fourth Pedro, king of Arragon.

                         [*Exeunt severally.*

ACT III.

SCENE I.   *A Wild Place.—Enter* MENDO *and Officers of
Justice armed.*

    1*st Officer.* Here, my lord, where the Ebro, swollen with
her mountain streams, runs swiftest, he will try to escape.

    Men. Hunt for him then, leaving neither rock nor thicket
unexplored. (*They disperse.*)

Oh, what a fate is mine,
Having to seek what most I dread to find,
Once thought the curse of jealousy alone!
The iron king will see my face no more
Unless I bring Don Lope to his feet:
Whom, on the other hand, the gratitude
And love I bear him fain would save from justice.
Oh, how——

Enter some, fighting with DON LOPE.

Lope.   I know I cannot save my life,
But I will sell it dear.
Men.   Hold off! the king
Will have him taken, but not slain.   And I,
If I can save him now, shall· find a mean
To do it afterwards—
Don Lope!
Lope.   I should know that voice, the face
I cannot, blind with fury, dust, and blood.
Or was't the echo of some inner voice,
Some far off thunder of the memory,   .
That moves me more than all these fellows' swords?
Is it Don Mendo?
Men.   Who demands of you
Your sword, and that you yield in the king's name.
Lope. I yield?
Men.   Ay, sir, what can you do beside?
Lope. Slaying be slain.   And yet my heart relents
Before your voice; and now I see your face
My eyes dissolve in tears.   Why, how is this?
What charm is on my sword?
Men.   'Tis but the effect
And countenance of justice that inspires

Involuntary awe in the offender.

Lope. Not that. Delinquent as I am, I could,
With no more awe of justice than a mad dog,
Bite right and left among her officers ;
But 'tis yourself alone : to you alone
Do I submit myself; yield up my sword
Already running with your people's blood,
And at your feet—

Men.   Rise, Lope. Heaven knows
How gladly would your judge change place with you
The criminal ; far happier to endure
Your peril than my own anxiety.
But do not you despair, however stern
Tow'rds you I carry me before the world.
The king is so enrag'd—

Lope.   What, he has heard !

Men. Your father cried for vengeance at his feet.

Lope. Where is my sword ?

Men.   In vain. 'Tis in my hand.

Lope. Where somehow it affrights me—as before
When giving you my dagger, it turn'd on me
With my own blood.

Mendo.   Ho there !
Cover Don Lope's face, and carry him
To prison after me. (*Aside*). Hark, in your ear,
Conduct him swiftly, and with all secrecy,
To my own house—in by the private door,
Without his knowing whither,
And bid my people watch and wait on him.
I'll to the king—Alas, what agony,
I know not what, grows on me more and more !

                              [*Exeunt.*

SCENE II.   *A Room in the Palace.—Enter* KING.

King. Don Mendo comes not back, and must not come,
Till he have done his errand.   I myself
Can have no rest till justice have her due.
A son to strike his father in my realm
Unaw'd, and then unpunisht!
But by great Heav'n the law shall be aveng'd
So long as I shall reign in Arragon.
Don Mendo!

Enter MENDO.

Mendo.   Let me kiss your Highness' hand.
King. Welcome, thou other Atlas of my realm,
Who shar'st the weight with me.   For I doubt not,
Coming thus readily into my presence,
You bring Don Lope with you.
Men.   Yes, my liege;
Fast prisoner in my house, that none may see
Or talk with him.
King.   Among your services
You have not done a better.
The crime is strange, 'tis fit the sentence on it
Be memorably just.
Men.   Most true, my liege,
Who I am sure will not be warp'd away
By the side current of a first report,
But on the whole broad stream of evidence
Move to conclusion.   I do *know* this charge
Is not so grave as was at first reported.
King. But is not thus much·clear—that a son smote
His father?
Men.   Yes, my liege.
King.   And can a charge

F.   20

Be weightier?

Men.   I confess the naked fact,
But 'tis the special cause and circumstance
That give the special colour to the crime.

King. I shall be glad to have my kingdom freed
From the dishonour of so foul a deed
By any extenuation.

Men.   Then I think
Your Majesty shall find it here.   'Tis thus:
Don Lope, on what ground I do not know,
Fights with Don Guillen—in the midst o' the fray,
Comes old Urrea, at the very point
When Guillen was about to give the lie
To his opponent—which the old man, enrag'd
At such unseemly riot in his house,
Gives for him; calls his son a fouler name
Than gentleman can bear, and in the scuffle
Receives a blow that in his son's blind rage
Was aim'd abroad—in the first heat of passion
Throws himself at your feet, and calls for vengeance,
Which, as I hear, he now repents him of.
He's old and testy—age's common fault—
And, were not this enough to lame swift justice,
There's an old law in Arragon, my liege,
That in our courts father and son shall not
Be heard in evidence against each other;
In which provision I would fain persuade you
Bury this quarrel.

King.   And this seems just to you?

Men. It does, my liege.

King.   Then not to me, Don Mendo,
Who will examine, sentence, and record,
Whether in such a scandal to the realm

The son be guilty of impiety,
Or the sire idle to accuse him of 't.
Therefore I charge you have Urrea too
From home to-night, and guarded close alone;
It much imports the business.

Men.   I will, my liege.

                    [*Exeunt severally.*

SCENE III.   *A Corridor in* URREA'S *House, with three
doors in front.—Enter from a side door* VIOLANTE
and ELVIRA.

Viol. Ask me no more, Elvira; I cannot answer when
my thoughts are all locked up where Lope lies.

Elv. And know you where that is?   Nearer than you
think; there, in my lord your father's room.

Viol. There!   Oh, could I but save him!

Elv. You can at least comfort him.

Viol. Something must be done.   Either I will save his
life, Elvira, or die with him.   Have you the key?

Elv. I have one; my lord has the master-key.

Viol. Yours will do, give it me.   I am desperate, Elvira,
and in his danger drown my maiden shame; see him I will
at least.   Do you rest here and give me a warning if a foot-
step come.   (*She enters centre door.*)

SCENE IV.   *An inner Chamber in* URREA'S *House.*—LOPE
discovered.

Lope. Whither then have they brought me?   Ah, Violante,
Your beauty costs me dear!   And even now
I count the little I have yet to live
Minute by minute, like one last sweet draught,
But for your sake.   Nay, 'tis not life I care for,
But only Violante.

                    20—2

Violante (entering unseen). Oh, his face
Is bathed in his own blood; he has been wounded.
Don Lope!

Lope.   Who is it calls on a name
I thought all tongues had buried in its shame?

Viol. One who yet—pities you.

Lope (turning and seeing her).   Am I then dead,
And thou some living spirit come to meet me
Upon the threshold of another world;
Or some dead image that my living brain
Draws from remembrance on the viewless air,
And gives the voice I love to? Oh, being here,
Whatever thou may'st be, torment me not
By vanishing at once.

Viol.   No spirit, Lope,
And no delusive image of the brain;
But one who, wretched in your wretchedness,
And partner of the crime you suffer for,
All risk of shame and danger cast away,
Has come—but hark!—I may have but a moment—
The door I came by will be left unlockt
To-night, and you must fly.

Lope.   Oh, I have heard
Of a fair flower of such strange quality,
It makes a wound where there was none before,
And heals what wound there was. Oh, Violante,
You who first made an unscath'd heart to bleed,
Now save a desperate life!

Viol.   And I have heard
Of two yet stranger flowers that, severally,
Each in its heart a deadly poison holds,
Which, if they join, turns to a sovereign balm.
And so with us, who in our bosoms bear

A passion which destroys us when apart,
But when together—

Elvira (calling within). Madam! madam! your father!

Viol. Farewell!

Lope. But you return?

Viol. To set you free.

Lope. That as it may; only return to me.

[*Exit* VIOLANTE, *leaving* LOPE.

SCENE V. *Same as* SCENE III. ELVIRA *waiting.—Enter*
VIOLANTE *from centre door.*

Viol. Quick! lock the door, Elvira, and away with me on wings. My father must not find me here.

Elv. Nay, you need not be frightened, he has gone to my lady Blanca's room by the way.

Viol. No matter, he must not find me; I would learn too what is stirring in the business.

Oh, would I ever drag my purpose through,
I must be desperate and cautious too. [*Exit.*

Elv. (locking the door). Well, that's all safe, and now myself to hear what news is stirring.

Vicente (talking as he enters). In the devil's name was there ever such a clutter made about a blow? People all up in arms, and running here and there, and up and down, and every where, as if the great Tom of Velilla was a ringing.

Elv. Vicente! what's the matter?

Vic. Oh, a very great matter, Elvira. I am very much put out indeed.

Elv. What about, and with whom?

Vic. With all the world, and my two masters, the young and old one, especially.

Elv. But about what?

Vic. With the young one for being so ready with his fists, and the old one bawling out upon it to heaven and earth, and then Madam Blanca, she must join in the chorus too; and then your grand Don Mendo there, with whom seizing's so much in season, he has seized my master, and my master's father, and Don Guillen, and clapt them all up in prison. Then I've a quarrel with the king!

Elv. With the king! You must be drunk, Vicente.

Vic. I only wish I was.

Elv. But what has the king done?

Vic. Why let me be beaten at least fifty thousand times, without caring a jot: and now forsooth because an old fellow gets a little push, his eyes flash axe and gibbet. Then, Elvira, I'm very angry with you.

Elv. And why with me?

Vic. Because, desperately in love with me as you are, you never serenade me, nor write me a billet-doux, nor ask me for a kiss of my fair hand.

Elv. Have I not told you, sir, I leave that all to Beatrice?

Vic. And have I not told you, Beatrice may go hang for me?

Elv. Oh, Vicente, could I believe you!

Vic. Come, give me a kiss on credit of it; in case I lie, I'll pay you back.

Elv. Well, for this once.

Enter BEATRICE.

Beat. The saints be praised, I've found you at last!

Vic. Beatrice!

Elv. Well, what's the matter?

Vic. You'll soon see.

Beat. Oh, pray proceed, proceed, good folks.   Never mind me: you've business—don't interrupt it—I've seen quite enough, besides being quite indifferent who wears my cast-off shoes.

Elv. I beg to say, madam, I wear no shoes except my own, and if I *were* reduced to other people's, certainly should not choose those that are made for a wooden leg.

Beat. A wooden leg?   Pray, madam, what has a wooden leg to do with me?

Elv. Oh, madam, I must refer you to your own feelings.

Beat. I tell you, madam, these hands should tear your hair up by the roots, if it had roots to tear.

Vic. Now for her turn.

Elv. Why, does she mean to insinuate my hair is as false as that left eye of hers?

Beat. Do you mean to insinuate my left eye is false?

Elv. Ay; and say it to your teeth.

Beat. More, madam, than I ever could say to yours, unless, indeed, you've *paid*, madam, for the set you wear.

Elv. Have you the face to say my teeth are false?

Beat. Have *you* the face to say my eye's of glass?

Elv. I'll teach you to say I wear a wig.

Beat. Would that my leg *were* wood just for the occasion.

Vic. Ladies, ladies, first consider where we are.

Beat. Oh ho! I think I begin to understand.

Elv. Oh, and so methinks do I.

Beat. It is this wretch—

Elv. This knave—

Beat. This rascal—

Elv. This vagabond—

Beat. Has told all these lies.

Elv. Has done all this mischief.

Spoken together.

(*They set upon and pinch him, &c.*)

Vic. Ladies, ladies—Mercy! oh! ladies! just listen!

Elv. Listen indeed! If it were not that I hear people coming—

Vic. Heaven be praised for it!

Beat. We will defer the execution then—And in the mean while shall we two sign a treaty of peace?

Elv. My hand to it—Agreed!

Beat.   Adieu!

Elv.   Adieu! [*Exeunt* BEATRICE *and* ELVIRA.

Vic. The devil that seiz'd the swine sure has seiz'd you,
And all your pinches make me tenfold writhe
Because you never gave the king his tithe.   [*Exit.*

SCENE VI. DONNA BLANCA'S *Apartment: it is dark.—
Enter the* KING *disguised, and* BLANCA *following him.*

Blan. Who is this man,
That in the gathering dusk enters our house,
Enmaskt and muffled thus? what is't you want?
To croak new evil in my ears? for none
But ravens now come near us—Such a silence
Is not the less ill-omen'd.   Beatrice!
A light! my blood runs cold—Answer me, man,
What want you with me?
King.   Let us be alone,
And I will tell you.
Blan.   Leave us, Beatrice—
I'll dare the worst—And now reveal yourself.
King. Not till the door be lockt.
Blan.   Help, help!
King.   Be still.
Blan. What would you? and who are you then?
King (discovering himself).   The king.

Blan. The king!

King.   Do you not know me?

Blan.   Yea, my liege
Now the black cloud has fallen from the sun.
But cannot guess why, at an hour like this,
And thus disguis'd—Oh, let me know at once
Whether in mercy or new wrath you come
To this most wretched house!

King.   In neither, Blanca;
But in the execution of the trust
That Heav'n has given to kings.

Blan.   And how, my liege,
Fall I beneath your royal vigilance?

King. You soon shall hear: but, Blanca, first take breath,
And still your heart to its accustom'd tune,
For I must have you all yourself to answer
What I must ask of you.   Listen to me.
Your son, in the full eye of God and man,
Has struck his father—who as publicly
Has cried to me for vengeance—such a feud
Coming at length to such unnatural close,
Men 'gin to turn suspicious eyes on you,—
You, Blanca, so mixt up in such a cause
As in the annals of all human crime
Is not recorded.   Men begin to ask
Can these indeed be truly son and sire?
This is the question, and to sift it home,
I am myself come hither to sift you
By my own mouth.   Open your heart to me,
Relying on the honour of a king
That nothing you reveal to me to-night
Shall ever turn against your good repute.
We are alone, none to way-lay the words

That travel from your lips; speak out at once;
Or, by the heavens, Blanca,—

Blan.   Oh, my liege,
Not in one breath
Turn royal mercy into needless threat;
Though it be true my bosom has so long
This secret kept close prisoner, and hop'd
To have it buried with me in my grave,
Yet if I peril my own name and theirs
By such a silence, I'll not leave to rumour
Another hour's suspicion; but reveal
To you, my liege, yea, and to heav'n and earth,
My most disastrous story.

King.   I attend.

Blan. My father, though of lineage high and clear
As the sun's self, was poor; and knowing well
How in this world honour fares ill alone,
Betroth'd the beauty of my earliest years
(The only dowry that I brought with me)
To Lope de Urrea, whose estate
Was to supply the much he miss'd of youth.
We married—like December wed to May,
Or flower of earliest summer set in snow;
Yet heaven witness that I honour'd, ay,
And lov'd him; though with little cause of love,
And ever cold returns; but I went on
Doing my duty toward him, hoping still
To have a son to fill the gaping void
That lay between us—yea, I pray'd for one
So earnestly, that God, who has ordain'd
That we should ask at once for all and nothing
Of Him who best knows what is best for us,
Denied me what I wrongly coveted.

Well, let me turn the leaf on which are written
The troubles of those ill-assorted years,
And to my tale. I had a younger sister,
Whom to console me in my wretched home,
I took to live with me—of whose fair youth
A gentleman enamour'd—Oh, my liege,
Ask not his name—yet why should I conceal it,
Whose honour may not leave a single chink
For doubt to nestle in?—Sir, 'twas Don Mendo,
Your minister; who, when his idle suit
Prosper'd not in my sister's ear, found means,
Feeing one of the household to his purpose,
To get admittance to her room by night;
Where, swearing marriage soon should sanction love,
He went away the victor of an honour
That like a villain he had come to steal;
Then, but a few weeks after, (so men quit
All obligation save of their desire,)
Married another, and growing great at court,
Went on your father's bidding into France
Ambassador, and from that hour to this
Knows not the tragic issue of his crime.
I, who perceiv'd my sister's alter'd looks,
And how in mind and body she far'd ill,
With menace and persuasion wrung from her
The secret I have told you, and of which
She bore within her bosom such a witness
As doubly prey'd upon her life. Enough;
She was my sister, why reproach her then,
And to no purpose now the deed was done?
Only I wonder'd at mysterious Heav'n,
Which her misfortune made to double mine,
Who had been pining for the very boon

That was her shame and sorrow; till at last,
Out of the tangle of this double grief
I drew a thread to extricate us both,
By giving forth myself about to bear
The child whose birth my sister should conceal.
'Twas done—the day came on—I feign'd the pain
She felt, and on my bosom as my own
Cherish'd the crying infant she had borne,
And died in bearing—for even so it was;
I and another matron (who alone
Was partner in the plot)
Assigning other illness for her death.
This is my story, sir—this is the crime,
Of which the guilt being wholly mine, be mine
The punishment; I pleading on my knees
My love both to my husband and my sister
As some excuse.   Pedro of Arragon,
Whom people call the Just, be just to me:
I do not ask for mercy, but for justice,
And that, whatever be my punishment,
It may be told of me, and put on record,
That, howsoever and with what design
I might deceive my husband and the world,
At least I have not sham'd my birth and honour.
  King (apart). Thus much at least is well; the blackest
     part
Of this unnatural feud is washt away
By this confession, though it swell the list
Of knotted doubts that Justice must resolve;
As thus:—Don Lope has revil'd and struck
One whom himself and all the world believe
His father—a belief that I am pledg'd
Not to disprove.   Don Mendo has traduc'd

A noble lady to her death; and Blanca
Contriv'd an ill imposture on her lord:
Two secret and one public misdemeanour,
To which I must adjudge due punishment.—
Blanca, enough at present, you have done
Your duty; Fare you well.

Blan.　　　　　　　　Heav'n keep your Highness!

Don Mendo (knocking within). Open the door.

King.　　　　　　　· Who calls?

Blan.　　　　　　　　I know not, sir.

King. Open it, then, but on your life reveal not ·
That I am here.　　(KING *hides,* BLANCA *opens the door.*)

· *Blan.*　　　　Who is it calls?

Enter MENDO.

Men.　　　　　　　　I, Blanca.

Blan. Your errand?

Men.　　　　　　Only, Blanca, to beseech you
Fear not, whatever you may hear or see
Against your son. His cause is in· my hands,
His person in my keeping; being so,
Who shall arraign my dealings with him?

King (coming forth).　　　　　　I.

Men. My liege, if you—

King.　　　　　　Enough; give me the key
Of Lope's prison.

Men.　　　This it is, my liege:
Only—

King. I know enough. Blanca, retire.
Mendo, abide you here. To-night shall show
If I be worthy of my name or no.　　　*[Exit.*

Men. What is the matter, Blanca?

Blan.　　　　　　　Your misdeeds,

And mine, Don Mendo, which just Heaven now
Revenges with one blow on both of us.
After the King! nor leave him till he swear
To spare my Lope, who, I swear to you,
Is not my son, but yours, and my poor Laura's!

Men. Merciful Heav'ns! But I will save his life
Come what come may to me.

Blan.   Away, away, then!

                            [*Exeunt severally.*

SCENE VII. *Same as* SCENE III.—*Enter* VIOLANTE *and*
ELVIRA *at a side door.*

Elv. Consider, madam.

Viol. No!

Elv. But think—

Viol. I tell you it must be done.

Elv. They will accuse your father.

Viol. Let them; I tell you it must be done, and *now;* I
ask'd you not for advice, but to obey me. Unlock the door.

Elv. Oh how I tremble! Hark!

Viol. A moment! They must not find him passing out—
the attempt and not the deed confounding us.* Listen!

Elv. (*listening at a side door*). I can hear nothing distinct,
only a confused murmur of voices.

Viol. Let me—hush!—Hark! they are approaching!

Enter MENDO.

Men. Anguish, oh! anguish!

Viol.   My father!

Men.   Ay, indeed,

* Y se queda su intencion
  Sin su efecto descubierta.

And a most wretched one.
Viol.   What is it, sir?
Tell me at once.
Men.   I know not. Oh, 'tis false!
I know too well, and you must know it too.
My daughter, the poor prisoner who lies there
Is my own son, not Blanca's, not Urrea's,
But my own son, your brother, Violante!
Viol. My brother!
Men.   Ay, your brother, my own son,
Whom we must save!
Viol.   Alas, sir, I was here
On the same errand, ere I knew—but hark!
All's quiet now.   (*A groan within.*)
Men.   Listen! What groan was that?
Viol. My hand shakes so, I cannot—
Lope (*within*).   Mercy, O God!
Men. The key, the key!—but hark! they call again
At either door; we must unlock.

(*They unlock the side doors.—Enter through one* BLANCA *and* `
    BEATRICE, *through the other* URREA *and* VICENTE.)

Urr.   Don Mendo,
The king desires me from your mouth to learn
His sentence on my son.
Blan.   Oh, Violante!
Men. From me! from me! to whom the king as yet
Has not deliver'd it.—
But what is this? Oh, God!

(*The centre door opens and* DON LOPE *is discovered, garrotted,
    with a paper in his hand, and lights at each side.*)

Urr.   A sight to turn

Rancour into remorse.

Men.   :   In his cold hand
He holds a scroll, the sentence, it may be,
The king referr'd you to. Read it, Urrea ;
I cannot. Oh, my son, the chastisement
That I alone have merited has come
Upon us both, and doubled the remorse
That I must feel—and stifle !

    Urr. (*reading*). "He that reviles and strikes whom he
      believes
His father, let him die for't ; and let those
Who have disgrac'd a noble name, or join'd
An ill imposture, see his doom ; and show
Three judgments summ'd up in a single blow."

MAYOR OF ZALAMEA.

21

DRAMATIS PERSONÆ.

KING PHILIP II.
DON LOPE DE FIGUEROA.
DON ALVARO DE ATAIDE.

PEDRO CRESPO, *a Farmer of Zalamea.*
JUAN, *his Son.*
ISABEL, *his Daughter.*
INES, *his Niece.*

DON MENDO, *a poor Hidalgo.*
NUÑO, *his Servant.*

REBOLLEDO, *a Soldier.*
CHISPA, *his Mistress.*

*A Sergeant, a Notary, Soldiers, Labourers, Constables,
Royal Suite, &c.*

THE MAYOR OF ZALAMEA.

ACT I.

SCENE I. *Country near Zalamea.*—*Enter* REBOLLEDO, CHISPA, *and Soldiers.*

Reb. Confound, say I, these forced marches from place to place, without halt or bait; what say you, friends?

All. Amen!

Reb. To be trailed over the country like a pack of gipsies, after a little scrap of flag upon a pole, eh?

1st Soldier. Rebolledo's off!

Reb. And that infernal drum which has at last been good enough to stop a moment stunning us.

2nd Sold. Come, come, Rebolledo, don't storm: we shall soon be at Zalamea.

Reb. And where will be the good of that if I'm dead before I get there? And if not, 'twill only be from bad to worse: for if we all reach the place alive, as sure as death up comes Mr Mayor to persuade the Commissary we had better march on to the next town. At first Mr Commissary replies very virtuously, "Impossible! the men are fagged to death." But after a little pocket persuasion, then it's all "Gentlemen, I'm very sorry: but orders have come for us

21—2

to march forward, and immediately "—and away we have to trot, foot weary, dust bedraggled, and starved as we are. Well, I swear if I do get alive to Zalamea to-day, I'll not leave it on this side o' sun-rise for love, lash, or money. It won't be the first time in my life I've given 'em the slip.

1st Sold. Nor the first time a poor fellow has had the slip given him for doing so. And more likely than ever now that Don Lope de Figueroa has taken the command, a fine brave fellow they say, but a devil of a Tartar, who'll have every inch of duty done, or take the change out of his own son, without waiting for trial either*.

Reb. Listen to this now, gentlemen! By Heaven, I'll be beforehand with him.

2nd Sold. Come, come, a soldier shouldn't talk so.

Reb. I tell you it isn't for myself I care so much, as for this poor little thing that follows me.

Chis. Signor Rebolledo, don't you fret about me; you know I was born with a beard on my heart if not on my chin, if ever girl was; and your fearing for me is as bad as if I was afeard myself. Why, when I came along with you I made up my mind to hardship and danger for honour's sake; else if I'd wanted to live in clover, I never should have left the Alderman who kept such a table as all Aldermen don't, I promise you. Well, what's the odds? I chose to leave him and follow the drum, and here I am, and if I don't flinch, why should you?

Reb. 'Fore Heaven, you're the crown of womankind!

---

* Don Lope de Figueroa, who figures also in the *Amar despues de la Muerte*, was (says Mr Ticknor) "the commander under whom Cervantes served in Italy, and probably in Portugal, when he was in the *Tercio de Flándes*,—the Flanders Regiment,—one of the best bodies of troops in the armies of Philip II.," and the very one now advancing, with perhaps Cervantes in it, to Zalamea.

Soldiers. So she is, so she is, Viva la Chispa !

Reb. And so she is, and one cheer more for her, hurrah ! especially if she'll give us a song to lighten the way.

Chis. The castanet shall answer for me.

Reb. I'll join in—and do you, comrades, bear a hand in the chorus.

Soldiers. Fire away !

Chispa sings.

I.

Titiri tiri, marching is weary,
    Weary, weary, and long is the way :
Titiri tiri, hither, my deary,
    What meat have you got for the soldier to-day?
"Meat have I none, my merry men,"
Titiri tiri, then kill the old hen.
    "Alas and a day! the old hen is dead!"
Then give us a cake from the oven instead.
    Titiri titiri titiri tiri,
Give us a cake from the oven instead.

II.

Admiral, admiral, where have you been-a?
    "I've been fighting where the waves roar."
Ensign, ensign, what have you seen-a?
    "Glory and honour and gunshot galore ;
Fighting the Moors in column and line,
Poor fellows, they never hurt me or mine—
    Titiri titiri titiri tina"—

1st Sold. Look, look, comrades—what between singing and grumbling we never noticed yonder church among the trees.

Reb. Is that Zalamea?

Chis. Yes, that it is, I know the steeple. Hurrah ! we'll finish the song when we get into quarters, or have another as good ; for you know I have 'em of all sorts and sizes.

Reb. Halt a moment, here's the sergeant.

2nd Sold. And the captain too.

Enter Captain and Sergeant.

Capt. Good news, gentlemen, no more marching for to-day at least; we halt at Zalamea till Don Lope joins with the rest of the regiment from Llerena. So who knows but you may have a several days' rest here?

Reb. and Solds. Huzzah for our captain!

Capt. Your quarters are ready, and the Commissary will give every one his billet on marching in.

Chis. (singing). Now then for

> Titiri tiri, hither, my deary,
> Heat the oven and kill the old hen.

[Exit with Soldiers.

Capt. Well, Mr Sergeant, have you my billet?

Serg. Yes, sir.

Capt. And where am I to put up?

Serg. With the richest man in Zalamea, a farmer, as proud as Lucifer's heir-apparent.

Capt. Ah, the old story of an upstart.

Serg. However, sir, you have the best quarters in the place, including his daughter, who is, they say, the prettiest woman in Zalamea.

Capt. Pooh! a pretty peasant! splay hands and feet.

Serg. Shame! shame!

Capt. Isn't it true, puppy?

Serg. What would a man on march have better than a pretty country lass to toy with?

Capt. Well, I never saw one I cared for, even on march. I can't call a woman a woman unless she's clean about the hands and fetlocks, and otherwise well appointed—a lady in short.

Serg. Well, any one for me who'll let me kiss her. Come, sir, let us be going, for if you won't be at her, I will.

Capt. Look, look, yonder!

Serg. Why, it must be Don Quixote himself with his very Rosinante too, that Michel Cervantes writes of.

Capt. And his Sancho at his side. Well, carry you my kit on before to quarters, and then come and tell me when all's ready.   [*Exeunt.*

SCENE II. *Zalamea, before* CRESPO'S *House.—Enter* DON MENDO *and* NUÑO.

Men. How's the gray horse?

Nun. You may as well call him the *Dun;* so screw'd he can't move a leg.

Men. Did you have him walk'd gently about?

Nun. Walk'd about! when it's corn he wants, poor devil!

Men. And the dogs?

Nun. Ah, now, they might do if you'd give them the horse to eat.

Men. Enough, enough—it has struck three. My gloves and tooth-pick.

Nun. That sinecure tooth-pick!

Men. I tell you I would brain anybody who insinuated to me I had not dined—and on game too. But tell me, Nuño, haven't the soldiers come into Zalamea this afternoon?

Nun. Yes, sir.

Men. What a nuisance for the commonalty who have to quarter them!

Nun. But worse for those who haven't.

Men. What do you mean, sir?

Nun. I mean the squires. ˙Ah, sir; if the soldiers aren't billeted on them, do you know why?

Men. Well, why?

Nun. For fear of being starved—which would be a bad job for the king's service.

Men. God rest my father's soul, says I, who left me a pedigree and patent all blazon'd in gold and azure, that exempts me from such impositions.

Nun. I wish he'd left you the gold in a more available shape, however.

Men. Though indeed when I come to think of it, I don't know if I owe him any thanks; considering that unless he had consented to beget me an Hidalgo at once, I wouldn't have been born at all, for him or any one.

Nun. Humph! Could you have help'd it?

Men. Easily.

Nun. How, sir?

Men. You must know that every one that is born is the essence of the food his parents eat.

Nun. Oh! Your parents did eat then, sir? You have not inherited *that* of them, at all events.

Men. Which forthwith converts itself into proper flesh and blood—ergo, if my father had been an eater of onions, for instance, he would have begotten me with a strong breath; on which I should have said to him, "Hold, I must come of no such nastiness as that, I promise you."

Nun. Ah, now I see the old saying is true.

Men. What is that?

Nun. That hunger sharpens wit.

Men. Knave, do you insinuate—

Nun. I only know it is now three o'clock, and we have neither of us yet had any thing but our own spittle to chew.

Men. Perhaps so, but there are distinctions of rank.   An Hidalgo, sir, has no belly.

Nun. Oh Lord! that I were an Hidalgo!

Men. Possibly; servants 'must learn moderation in all things.   But let me hear no more of the matter; we are under Isabel's window.

Nun. There again—If you are so devoted an admirer, why on earth, sir, don't you ask her in marriage of her father? by doing which you would kill two birds with one stone; get yourself something to eat, and his grandchildren squires.

Men. Hold your tongue, sir, it is impious.   Am I, an Hidalgo with such a pedigree, to demean myself with a plebeian connexion just for money's sake?

Nun. Well, I've always heard say a mean father-in-law is best; better stumble on a pebble than run your head against a post.   But, however, if you don't mean marriage, sir, what do you mean?

Men. And pray, sir, can't I dispose of her in a convent in case I get tired of her?   But go directly, and tell me if you can get a sight of her.

Nun. I'm afraid lest her father should get a sight of me.

Men. And what if he do, being my man?   Go and do as I bid you.

Nun. (*after going to look*).   Come, sir, you owe one meal at least now—she's at the window with her cousin.

Men. Go again, and tell her something about her window being another East, and she a second Sun dawning from it in the afternoon.   (ISABEL *and* INES *come to the window.*)

Ines. For heaven's sake, cousin, let's stand here and see the soldiers march in.

Isab. Not I, while that man is in the way, Ines; you know how I hate the sight of him.

Ines. With all his devotion to you !

Isab. I wish he would spare himself and me the trouble.

Ines. I think you are wrong to take it as an affront.

Isab. How would you have me take it ?

Ines. Why, as a compliment.

Isab. What, when I hate the man ?

Men. Ah ! 'pon the honour of an Hidalgo, (which is a sacred oath,) I could have sworn that till this moment the sun had not risen. But why should I wonder ? when indeed a second Aurora—

Isab. Signor Don Mendo, how often have I told you not to waste your time playing these fool's antics before my window day after day ?

Men. If a pretty woman only knew, la ! how anger improved its beauty ! her complexion needs no other paint than indignation. Go on, go on, lovely one, grow angrier, and lovelier still.

Isab. You sha'n't have even that consolation ; come, Ines.   [*Exit.*

Ines. Beware of the portcullis, sir knight.

(*Shuts down the blind in his face.*)

Men. Ines, beauty must be ever victorious, whether advancing or in retreat.

Enter CRESPO.

Cres. That I can never go in or out of my house without that squireen haunting it !

Nun. Pedro Crespo, sir !

Men. Oh—ah—let us turn another way ; 'tis an ill-conditioned fellow.

As he turns, enter JUAN.

Juan. That I never can come home but this ghost of an Hidalgo is there to spoil my appetite.

Nun. His son, sir!

Men. He's worse. (*Turning back.*) Oh, Pedro Crespo, good day, Crespo, good man, good day. [*Exit with* Nuño.

Cres. Good day indeed; I'll make it bad day one of these days with you, if you don't take care. But how now, Juanito, my boy?

Juan. I was looking for you, sir, but could not find you; where have you been?

Cres. To the barn, where high and dry,
The jolly sheaves of corn do lie, -
Which the sun, arch-chemist old,
Turn'd from black earth into gold,
And the swinging flail one day
On the barn-floor shall assay,
Separating the pure ore
From the drossy chaff away.
This I've been about—And now,
Juanito, what hast thou?

Juan. Alas, sir, I can't answer in so good rhyme or reason.   I have been playing at fives, and lost every bout.

Cres. What signifies if you paid?

Juan. But I could not, and have come to you for the money.

Cres. Before I give it you, listen to me.
There are things two
Thou never must do;
Swear to more than thou knowest,
Play for more than thou owest;
And never mind cost,
So credit's not lost.

Juan. Good advice, sir, no doubt, that I shall lay by for its own sake as well as for yours. Meanwhile, I have also heard say,

Preach not to a beggar till
The beggar's empty hide you fill.

Cres. 'Fore Heaven, thou pay'st me in my own coin. But—

Enter Sergeant.

Serg. Pray, does one Pedro Crespo live hereabout?

Cres. Have you any commands for him, if he does?

Serg. Yes, to tell him of the arrival of Don Alvaro de Ataide, captain of the troop that has just marcht into Zalamea, and quartered upon him.

Cres. Say no more; my house and all I have is ever at the service of the king, and of all who have authority under him. If you will leave his things here, I will see his room is got ready directly; and do you tell his Honour that, come when he will, he shall find me and mine at his service.

Serg. Good—he will be here directly.   [*Exit.*

Juan. I wonder, father, that, rich as you are, you still submit yourself to these nuisances.

Cres. Why, boy, how could I help them?

Juan. You know; by buying a patent of Gentility.

Cres. A patent of Gentility! upon thy life now dost think there's a soul who doesn't know that I'm no gentleman at all, but just a plain farmer? What's the use of my buying a patent of Gentility, if I can't buy the gentle blood along with it! will any one think me a bit more of a gentleman for buying fifty patents? Not a whit; I should only prove I was worth so many thousand royals, not that I had gentle blood in my veins, which can't be bought at any price. If a fellow's been bald ever so long, and buys him a fine wig, and claps it on; will his neighbours think it is his own hair a bit the more? No, they will say, "So and so has a fine wig; and, what's more, he must have paid handsomely for it too." But they know his bald pate is safe under it all the while. That's all he gets by it.

Juan. Nay, sir, he gets to look younger and handsomer, and keeps off sun and cold.

Cres. Tut! I'll have none of your wig honour at any price. My grandfather was a farmer, so was my father, so is yours, and so shall you be after him. Go, call your sister.

Enter ISABEL *and* INES.

Oh, here she is. Daughter, our gracious king (whose life God save these thousand years!) is on his way to be crowned at Lisbon; thither the troops are marching from all quarters, and among others that fine veteran Flanders regiment, commanded by the famous Don Lope de Figueroa, will march into Zalamea, and be quartered here to-day; some of the soldiers in my house. Is it not as well you should be out of the way?

Isab. Sir, 'twas upon this very errand I came to you, knowing what nonsense I shall have to hear if I stay below. My cousin and I can go up to the garret, and there keep so close, the very sun shall not know of our whereabout.

Cres. That's my good girl. Juanito, you wait here to receive them in case they come while I am out looking after their entertainment.

Isab. Come, Ines.

Ines. Very well—
Though I've heard in a song what folly 'twould be
To try keep in a loft what won't keep on the tree.

[*Exeunt.*

Enter Captain and Sergeant.

Serg. This is the house, sir.

Capt. Is my kit come?

Serg. Yes, sir, and (*aside*) I'll be the first to take an inventory of the pretty daughter.   [*Exit.*

Juan. Welcome, sir, to our house ; we count it a great honour to have such a cavalier as yourself for a guest, I assure you. (*Aside.*) What a fine fellow ! what an air ! I long to try the uniform, somehow.

Capt. Thank you, my lad.

Juan. You must forgive our poor house, which we devoutly wish was a palace for your sake. My father is gone after your supper, sir; may I go and see that your chamber is got ready for you ?

Capt. Thank you, thank you.

Juan. Your servant, sir.   [*Exit.*

Enter Sergeant.

Capt. Well, sergeant, where's the Dulcinea you told me of ?

Serg. Deuce take me, sir, if I havn't been looking everywhere in parlour, bed-room, kitchen, and scullery, up-stairs and down-stairs, and can't find her out.

Capt. Oh, no doubt the old fellow has hid her away for fear of us.

Serg. Yes, I ask'd a serving wench, and she confess'd her master had lock'd the girl up in the attic, with strict orders not even to look out so long as we were in the place.

Capt. Ah ! these clodpoles are all so jealous of the service. And what is the upshot ? Why, I, who didn't care a pin to see her before, shall never rest till I get at her now.

Serg. But how, without a blow-up ?

Capt. Let me see ; how shall we manage it ?

Serg. The more difficult the enterprise, the more glory in success, you know, in love as in war.

Capt. I have it!

Serg. Well, sir? ·

Capt. You shall pretend—but no, here comes one will serve my turn better.

Enter REBOLLEDO *and* CHISPA.

Reb. (*to* CHISPA). There he is; now if I can get him into a good humour—

Chis. Speak up then, like a man.

Reb. I wish I'd some of your courage; but don't you leave me while I tackle him.   Please your Honour—

Capt. (*to Sergeant*). I tell you I've my eye on Rebolledo to do him a good turn; I like his spirit.

Serg. Ah, he's one of a thousand.

Reb. (*aside*). Here's luck!   Please your Honour—

Capt. Oh, Rebolledo—Well, Rebolledo, what is it?

Reb. You may know I am a gentleman who has, by ill luck, lost all his estate; all that ever I had, have, shall have, may have, or can have, through all the conjugation of the verb "*to have.*"   And I want your Honour—

Capt. Well?

· *Reb.* To desire the ensign to appoint me roulette-master to the regiment, so I may pay my liabilities like a man of honour.

Capt. Quite right, quite right; I will see it done.

Chis. Oh, brave captain!   Oh, if I only live to hear them all call me Madam Roulette!

Reb. Shall I go at once and tell him?

Capt. Wait.   I want you first to help me in a little plan I have.

Reb. Out with it, noble captain.   Slow said slow sped, you know.

Capt. You are a good fellow; listen. I want to get into that attic there, for a particular purpose.

Reb. And why doesn't your Honour go up at once?

Capt. I don't like to do it in a strange house without an excuse. Now look here; you and I will pretend to quarrel; I get angry and draw my sword, and you run away up stairs, and I after you, to the attic, that's all; I'll manage the rest.

Chis. Ah, we get on famously.

Reb. I understand. When are we to begin?

Capt. Now directly.

Reb. Very good. (*In a loud voice*) This is the reward of my services—a rascal, a pitiful scoundrel, is preferred, when a man of honour—a man who has seen service—

Chis. Halloa! Rebolledo up! All is not so well.

Reb. Who has led you to victory—

Capt. This language to me, sir?

Reb. Yes, to you, who have so grossly insulted and de-frauded—

Capt. Silence! and think yourself lucky if I take no further notice of your insolence.

Reb. If I restrain myself, it is only because you are my captain, and as such—but 'fore God, if my cane were in my hand—

Chis. (*advancing*). Hold! Hold!

Capt. I'll show you, sir, how to talk to me in this way.

(*Draws his sword.*)

Reb. It is before your commission, not you, I retreat.

Capt. That sha'n't save you, rascal!

(*Pursues* REBOLLEDO *out.*)

Chis. Oh, I sha'n't be Madam Roulette after all. Murder! murder!　　　　　　　　　　　　[*Exit, calling.*

SCENE III.   ISABEL'S *Garret*.   ISABEL *and* INES.

Isab. What noise is that on the stairs?

Enter REBOLLEDO.

Reb. Sanctuary! Sanctuary!

Isab. Who are you, sir?

Enter Captain.

Capt. Where is the rascal?

Isab. A moment, sir! This poor man has flown to our feet for protection; I appeal to you for it; and no man, and least of all an officer, will refuse that to any woman.

Capt. I swear no other arm than that of beauty, and beauty such as yours, could have withheld me. (*To* REBOLLEDO.) You may thank the deity that has saved you, rascal.

Isab. And I thank you, sir.

Capt. And yet ungratefully slay me with your eyes in return for sparing him with my sword.

Isab. Oh, sir, do not mar the grace of a good deed by poor compliment, and so make me less mindful of the real thanks I owe you.

Capt. Wit and modesty kiss each other, as well they may, in that lovely face. (*Kneels.*)

Isab. Heavens! my father!

Enter CRESPO *and* JUAN *with swords.*

Cres. How is this, sir? I am alarmed by cries of murder in my house—am told you have pursued a poor man up to my daughter's room; and, when I get here expecting to find you killing a man, I find you courting a woman.

Capt. We are all born subjects to some dominion— soldiers especially to beauty. My sword, though justly rais'd against this man, as justly fell at this lady's bidding.

F.   22

Cres. No lady, sir, if you please; but a plain peasant girl—my daughter.

Juan (*aside*). All a trick to get at her. My blood boils. (*Aloud to Captain.*) I think, sir, you might have seen enough of my father's desire to serve you to prevent your requiting him by such an affront as this.

Cres. And, pray, who bid thee meddle, boy? Affront! what affront? The soldier affronted his captain; and if the captain has spared him for thy sister's sake, pray what hast thou to say against it?

Capt. I think, young man, you had best consider before you impute ill intention to an officer.

Juan. I know what I know.

Cres. What! you will go on, will you?

Capt. It is out of regard for you I do not chastise him.

Cres. Wait a bit; if that were wanting, 'twould be from his father, not from you.

Juan. And, what's more, I wouldn't endure it from any one but my father.

Capt. You would not?

Juan. No! death rather than such dishonour!

Capt. What, pray, is a clodpole's idea of honour?

Juan. The same as a captain's—no clodpole no captain, I can tell you.

Capt. 'Fore Heaven, I must punish this insolence.

(*About to strike him.*)

Cres. You must do it through me, then.

Reb. Eyes right!—Don Lope!

Capt. Don Lope!

Enter DON LOPE.

Lope. How now? A riot the very first thing I find on joining the regiment? What is it all about?

Capt. (*aside*). Awkward enough !

Cres. (*aside*). By the lord, the boy would have held his own with the best of 'em.

Lope. Well ! No one answer me ? 'Fore God, I'll pitch the whole house, men, women, and children, out of windows, if you don't tell me at once. Here have I had to trail up your accursed stairs, and then no one will tell me what for.

Cres. Nothing, nothing at all, sir.

Lope. Nothing ? that would be the worst. excuse of all : but swords aren't drawn for nothing ; come, the truth ?

Capt. Well, the simple fact is this, Don Lope ; I am quartered upon this house ; and one of my soldiers—

Lope. Well, sir, go on.

Capt. Insulted me so grossly I was obliged to draw my sword on him. He ran up here where it seems these two girls live ; and I, not knowing there was any harm, after him ; at which these men, their father or brother, or some such thing, take affront. This is the whole business.

Lope. I am just come in time then to settle it. First, who is the soldier that began it with an act of insubordination ?

Reb. What, am I to pay the piper ?

Isab. (*pointing to Reb.*). This, sir, was the man who ran up first.

Lope. This ? handcuff him !

Reb. Me ! my lord ?

Capt. (*aside to Reb.*) Don't blab, I'll bear you harmless.

Reb. Oh, I dare say, after being marcht off with my hands behind me like a coward. Noble commander, 'twas the captain's own doing ; he made me pretend a quarrel, that he might get up here to see the women.

Cres. I *had* some cause for quarrel, you see.

Lope. Not enough to peril the peace of the town for.

Halloa there ! beat all to quarters on pain of death.   And, to prevent further ill blood here, do you (*to the Captain*) quarter yourself elsewhere till we march.   I'll stop here.

Capt. I shall of course obey you, sir.

Cres. (*to* ISABEL). Get you in. (*Exeunt* ISAB. *and* INES.) I really ought to thank you heartily for coming just as you did, sir ; else, I'd done for myself.

Lope. How so ?

Cres. I should have killed this popinjay.

Lope. What, sir, a captain in his Majesty's service ?

Cres. Ay, a general, if he insulted me.

Lope. I tell you, whoever lays his little finger on the humblest private in the regiment, I'll hang him.

Cres. And I tell you, whoever points his little finger at my honour, I'll cut him down before hanging.

Lope. Know you not, you are bound by your allegiance to submit ?

Cres. To all cost of property, yes ; but of honour, no, no, no !   My goods and chattels, ay, and my life—are the king's ; but my honour is my own soul's, and that is—God Almighty's !

Lope. 'Fore God, there's some truth in what you say.

Cres. 'Fore God, there ought to be, for I've been some years saying it.

Lope. Well, well.   I've come a long way, and this leg of mine (which I wish the devil who gave it would carry away with him !) cries for rest.

Cres. And who prevents its taking some ? the same devil I suppose, who gave you your leg, gave me a bed (which I don't want him to take away again, however) on which your leg may lie if it like.

Lope. But did the devil, when he was about it, make your bed as well as give it ?

Cres. To be sure he did.

Lope. Then I'll unmake it—Heaven knows I'm weary enough.

Cres. Heaven rest you then.

Lope (*aside*). Devil or saint alike he echoes me.

Cres. (*aside*). I and Don Lope never shall agree.

ACT II.

SCENE I.   *In Zalamea.—Enter* DON MENDO *and* NUÑO.

Men. Who told you all this?

Nuñ. Ginesa, her wench.

Men. That, whether that riot in the house were by accident or design, the captain has ended by being really in love with Isabel?

Nuñ. So as he has as little of comfort in his quarters as we of eatable in ours—ever under her window, sending her messages and tokens by a nasty little soldier of his.

Men. Enough, enough of your poisoned news.

Nuñ. Especially on an empty stomach.

Men. Be serious, Nuño. And how does Isabel answer him?

Nuñ. As she does you. Bless you, she's meat for your masters.

Men. Rascal! This to me! (*Strikes him.*)

Nuñ. There! two of my teeth you've knockt out, I believe: to be sure they weren't of much use in your service.

Men. By Heaven, I'll do so to that captain, if—

Nuñ. Take care, he's coming, sir.

Men. (*aside to* NUÑO). This duel shall be *now*—though

night be advancing on—before discretion come to counsel milder means.   Come, and help me arm.

Nuñ. Lord bless me, sir, what arms have you got except the coat over the door?

Men. In my armoury I doubt not are some pieces of my ancestors that will fit their descendant.   [*Exeunt.*

Enter Captain, Sergeant, and REBOLLEDO.

Capt. I tell you my love is not a fancy; but a passion, a tempest, a volcano.

Serg. What a pity it is you ever set eyes on the girl!

Capt. What answer did the servant give you?

Serg. Nay, sir, I have told you.

Capt. That a country wench should stand upon her virtue as if she were a lady!

Serg. This sort of girls, captain, don't understand gentlemen's ways.   If a strapping lout in their own line of life courted them in their own way, they'd hear and answer quick enough.   Besides, you really expect too much, that a decent woman should listen after one day's courtship to a lover who is perhaps to leave her to-morrow.

Capt. And to-day's sun-setting!

Serg. Your own love too, but from one glance—

Capt. Is not one spark enough for gunpowder?

Serg. You too, who would have it no country girl could be worth a day's courtship!

Capt. Alas, 'twas that was my ruin—running unawares upon a rock.   I thought only to see a splay-footed gawky, and found a goddess.   Ah, Rebolledo, could you but get me one more sight of her!

Reb. Well, captain, you have done me one good turn, and though you had like to run me into danger, I don't mind venturing again for you.

Capt. But how? how?

Reb. Well, now, look here. We've a man in the regiment with a fair voice, and my little Chispa—no one like her for a flash song. Let's serenade at the girl's window; she must, in courtesy or curiosity, look out; and then—

Capt. But Don Lope is there, and we mustn't wake him.

Reb. Don Lope? When does he ever get asleep with that leg of his, poor fellow? Besides, you can mix along with us in disguise, so as at least *you* won't come into question.

Capt. Well, there is but this chance, if it be but a faint one; for if we should march to-morrow!—come, let us set about it; it being, as you say, between ourselves that I have any thing to do with it.

[*Exeunt Captain and Sergeant.*

Enter CHISPA.

Chis. He's got it, at any rate.

Reb. What's the matter now, Chispa?

Chis. Oh, I mark'd his face for him.

Reb. What, a row?

Chis. A fellow there who began to ask questions as to my fair play at roulette—when I was all as fair as day too— I answered him with this. (*Showing a knife.*) Well, he's gone to the barber's to get it dressed.

Reb. You still stand kicking when I want to get to the fair. I wanted you with your castanets, not your knife.

Chis. Pooh! one's as handy as the other. What's up now?

Reb. Come with me to quarters; I'll tell you as we go along.   [*Exeunt.*

SCENE II. *A trellis of Vines in* CRESPO'S *garden.—Enter*
CRESPO *and* DON LOPE.

Cres. Lay the table here. (*To* LOPE.) You'll relish your
supper here in the cool, sir. These hot August days at
least bring their cool nights by way of excuse.

Lope. A mighty pleasant parlour this !

Cres. Oh, a little strip my daughter amuses herself with ;
sit down, sir. In place of the fine voices and instruments
you are us'd to, you must put up with only the breeze play-
ing on the vine leaves in concert with the little fountain
yonder. Even the birds (our only musicians) are gone to
bed, and wouldn't sing any the more if I were to wake them.
Come sit down, sir, and try to ease that poor leg of yours.

Lope. I wish to heaven I could.

Cres. Amen !

Lope. Well, I can at least bear it. Sit down, Crespo.

Cres. Thank you, sir. (*Hesitating.*) ·

Lope. Sit down, sit down, pray.

Cres. Since you bid me then, you must excuse my ill
manners. (*Sits.*)

Lope. Humph ! Do you know, I am thinking, Crespo,
that yesterday's riot rather overset your good ones ?

Cres. Ay ?

Lope. Why how else is it that you, whom I can scarce
get to sit down at all to-day, yesterday plump'd yourself
down at once, and in the big chair too ?

Cres. Simply because yesterday you *didn't* ask me. To-day
you are courteous, and I am shy.

Lope. Yesterday you were all thistle and hedgehog ; to-
day as soft as silk.

Cres. It is only because you yourself were so. I always
answer in the key I'm spoken to : yesterday you were all

out of tune, and so was I.   It is my principle to swear with
the swearer, and pray with the saint; all things to all men.
So much so as I declare to you your bad leg kept me awake
all night.   And, by the by, I wish, now we are about it,
you would tell me which of your legs it is that ails you:
for, not knowing, I was obliged to make sure by swearing
at both of mine: and one at a time is quite enough.

Lope.   Well, Pedro, you will perhaps think I have some
reason for my tetchiness, when I tell you that for thirty
years during which I have served in the Flemish wars
through summer's sun, and winter's frost, and enemy's bul-
lets, I have never known what it is to be an hour without
pain.

Cres.   God give you patience to bear it!

Lope.   Pish! can't I give it myself?

Cres.   Well, let him leave you alone then!

Lope.   Devil take patience!

Cres.   Ah, let him! he wants it; only it's too good a job
for him.

Enter JUAN *with Table, &c.*

Juan.   Supper, sir!

Lope.   But what are my people about, not to see to all
this?

Cres.   Pardon my having been so bold to tell them I and
my family would wait upon you, so, as I hope, you shall
want for nothing.

Lope.   On one condition then, that as you have no fear of
your company now, your daughter may join us at supper.

Cres.   Juan, bid your sister come directly.   [*Exit* JUAN.

Lope.   My poor health may quiet all suspicion on that
score, I think.

Cres.   Sir, if you were as lusty as I wish you, I should

have no fear. I bid my daughter keep above while the re-
giment was here because of the nonsense soldiers usually
talk to girls. If all were gentlemen like you, I should be
the first to make her wait on them.

Lope (*aside*). The cautious old fellow !

Enter JUAN, ISABEL, *and* INES.

Isab. (*to* CRESPO). Your pleasure, sir ?

Cres. It is Don Lope's, who honours you by bidding you
to sup with him.

Lope (*aside*). What a fair creature ! Nay, 'tis I that
honour myself by the invitation.

Isab. Let me wait upon you.

Lope. Indeed no, unless waiting upon me mean supping
with me.

Cres. Sit·down, sit down, girl, as Don Lope desires you.

[*They sit at table.   Guitar heard within.*

Lope. Music too !

Cres. None of ours. It must be some of your soldiers,
Don Lope.

Lope. Ah, Crespo, the troubles and dangers of war must
have a little· to sweeten them betimes. The uniform sits
very tight, and must be let out every now and then.

Juan. Yet 'tis a fine life, sir.

Lope. Do you think you would like to follow it ?

Juan. If I might at your Excellency's side.

SONG (*within*).

Ah for the red spring rose,
   Down in the garden growing,
Fading as fast as it blows,
   Who shall arrest its going?
Peep from thy window and tell,
Fairest of flowers, Isabel.

Lope (*aside*). Pebbles thrown up at the window too!
But I'll say nothing, for all sakes. (*Aloud.*) What foolery!

Cres. Boys! Boys! (*Aside.*) To call her very name too!
If it weren't for Don Lope—

Juan (*going*). I'll teach them—

Cres. Holloa, lad, whither away?

Juan. To see for a dish—

Cres. They'll see after that.   Sit still where thou art.

SONG (*within*).

Wither it would, but the bee
Over the blossom hovers,
And the sweet life ere it flee
With as sweet art recovers,
Sweetest at night in his cell,
Fairest of flowers, Isabel.

Isab. (*aside*). How have I deserved this?

Lope (*knocking over his chair*). This is not to be
borne!

Cres. (*upsetting the table*). No more it is!

Lope. I meant my leg.

Cres. And I mine.

Lope. I can eat no more, and will to bed.

Cres. Very good : so will I.

Lope. Good night, good night, to you all.

All. Good night, sir.

Lope (*aside*). I'll see to them.   [*Exit.*

Cres. (*aside*). I'll shut the girls up, and then look after
'em. (*Aloud.*) Come, to bed. (*To* JUAN.) Holloa, lad,
again!   This is the way to thy room, is it not?

[*Exeunt severally.*

SCENE III. *Outside* CRESPO'S *House.—The Captain, Sergeant,* REBOLLEDO, CHISPA, *&c., with guitars.—At one corner,* MENDO *in old armour, with* NUÑO, *observing them.—It is dark.*

Men. (*aside to* NUÑO). You see this?

Nuñ. And hear it.

Men. I am bloodily minded to charge into them at once, and disperse them into chaos; but I will see if she is guilty of answering them by a sign.

Capt. No glance from the window yet!

Reb. Who'd stir for a sentimental love song? Come, Chispa, you can give us one that would make her look out of the grave.

Chis. Here am I on my pedestal. Now for it. (*She sings.*)

> There once was a certain Sampayo
>   Of Andalusia the fair;
> A Major he was in the service,
>   And a very fine coat did he wear.
> And one night, as to-night it might happen,
>   That as he was going his round,
> With the Garlo half drunk in a tavern—

Reb. *Asonante* to "*happen*," you know.

Chis. Don't put me out, Rebolledo—(*Sings.*)

> With the Garlo half drunk in a tavern
>   His lovely Chillona he found.

CHORUS.

> With the Garlo half drunk in a tavern
>   His lovely Chillona he found.

SECOND STANZA.

> Now this Garlo, as chronicles tell us,
>   Although rather giv'n to strong drinks,

Was one of those terrible fellows
Is down on a man ere he winks.
And so while the Major all weeping
Upbraided his lady unkind,
The Garlo behind him came creeping
And laid on the Major behind.

CHORUS.

The Garlo, &c.

(*During Chorus*, DON LOPE *and* CRESPO *have entered at different sides with swords, and begin to lay about them.*)

Cres. What something in this way, perhaps! ⎱
Lope. After this fashion, may-be! ⎰ *Together.*

(*The Soldiers are driven off.*)

Lope. Well, we're quit of them, except one. But I'll soon settle him.

Cres. One still hanging about. Off with you!

Lope. Off with *you*, rascal! (*They fight.*) By Heaven, he fights well!

Cres. By Heaven, a handy chap at his tool!

Enter JUAN *with sword and torch.*

Juan. Where is Don Lope?

Lope. Crespo!

Cres. Don Lope!

Lope. To be sure, didn't you say you were going to bed?

Cres. And didn't you?

Lope. This was my quarrel, not yours.

Cres. Very well, and I come out to help you in it.

Re-enter Captain and Soldiers with swords.

1st Sold. We'll soon settle them.

Capt. Don Lope!

Lope. Yes, Don Lope. What is all this, sir?

Capt. The soldiers were singing and playing in the street, sir, doing no offence to any one, but were set upon by some of the town's people, and I came to stop the riot.

Lope. You have done well, Don Alvaro, I know your prudence; however, as there is a grudge on both sides, I shall not visit the town's people this time with further severity; but, for the sake of all parties, order the regiment to march from Zalamea to-morrow—nay, to-day, for it is now dawn. See to it, sir: and let me hear of no such disgraceful riots hereafter.

Capt. I shall obey your orders, sir.

[Exit with soldiers, &c.

Cres. (*aside*). Don Lope is a fine fellow! we shall cog together after all.

Lope (*to* CRESPO *and* JUAN). You two keep with me, and don't be found alone.   *[Exeunt.*

Re-enter MENDO, *and* NUÑO *wounded.*

Men. 'Tis only a scratch.

Nuñ. A scratch? Well, I could well have spared that.

Men. Ah, what is it compared to the wound in my heart!

Nuñ. I would gladly exchange for all that.

Men. Well, he did lay upon your head handsomely, didn't he?

Nuñ. Ah, and on my tail too; while you, under that great shield of yours,—   (*Drum.*)

Men. Hark! what's that?

Nuñ. The soldiers' reveille. I heard say they were to leave Zalamea to-day.

Men. I am glad of it, since they'll carry that detestable captain off with them at all events.   *[Exeunt.*

SCENE IV.   *Outside Zalamea.—Enter Captain, Sergeant,*
REBOLLEDO, *and* CHISPA.

Capt. March you on, Sergeant, with the troop. I shall
lie here till sun-down, and then steal back to Zalamea for
one last chance.

Serg. If you are resolved on this, sir, you had better do
it well attended, for these bumpkins are dangerous, once
affronted.

Reb. Where, however, (and you ought to tip me for my
news,) you have one worst enemy the less.

Capt. Who's that?

Reb. Isabel's brother. Don Lope and the lad took a
fancy to each other and have persuaded the old father to
let him go for a soldier; and I have only just met him as
proud as a peacock, with all the sinew of the swain and the
spirit of the soldier already about him.

Capt. All works well; there is now only the old father
at home, who can easily be disposed of. It only needs that
he who brought me this good news help me to use it.

Reb. Me do you mean, sir? So I will, to the best of my
power.

Capt. Good; you shall go with me.

Serg. But if Don Lope should happen on you?

Capt. He is himself obliged to set off to Guadalupe this
evening, as the king is already on the road. This I heard
from himself when I went to take his orders. Come with
me, Sergeant, and settle about the troops marching, and then
for my own campaign.   [*Exeunt Captain and Sergeant.*

Chis. And what am I to do, Rebolledo, meanwhile? I
shan't be safe alone with that fellow whose face I sent to be
stitcht by the barber.

Reb. Ah, how to manage about that? You wouldn't dare go with us?

Chis. Not in petticoats; but in the clothes of that runaway stable boy? I can step into them free of expense.

Reb. That's a brave girl.

Chis. (*singing*).

And now who shall say
The love of a soldier's wife lasts but a day?

[*Exeunt.*

SCENE V. CRESPO'S *Garden Porch.* DON LÒPE, CRESPO,
JUAN.

Lope. I have much to thank you for, Crespo, but for nothing so much as for giving me your son for a soldier. I do thank you for that with all my heart.

Cres. I am proud he should be your servant.

Lope. The king's! the king's!—*my* friend. I took a fancy to him from the first for his spirit and affection to the service.

Juan. And I will follow you to the world's end, sir.

Cres. Though you must make allowance for his awkwardness at first, sir, remembering he has only had ploughmen for teachers, and plough and pitch-forks for books.

Lope. He needs no apology. And now the sun's heat abates towards his setting, I will be off.

Juan. I will see for the litter.   [*Exit.*

Enter ISABEL *and* INES.

Isab. You must not go, sir, without our adieu.

Lope. I would not have done so; nor without asking pardon for much that is past, and even for what I am now about to do.   But remember, fair Isabel, 'tis not the price of the gift, but the good will of the giver makes its value. This brooch, though of diamond, becomes poor in your hands, and yet I would fain have you wear it in memory of Don Lope.

Isab. I take it ill you should wish to repay us for an entertainment—

Lope. No, no, no repayment; that were impossible if I wished it.   A free keepsake of regard.

Isab. As such I receive it then, sir.   Ah, may I make bold to commit my brother to your kindness?

Lope. Indeed, indeed, you may rely on me.

Enter JUAN.

Juan. The litter is ready.

Lope. Adieu, then, all.

All. Adieu, adieu, sir.

Lope. Ha, Peter! who, judging from our first meeting, could have prophesied we should part such good friends?

Cres. I could, sir, had I but known—

Lope (going). Well?

Cres. That you were at once as good as crazy.   (*Exit* LOPE.)   And now, Juan, before going, let me give thee a word of advice in presence of thy sister and cousin; thou and thy horse will easily overtake Don Lope, advice and all. By God's grace, boy, thou com'st of honourable if of humble stock; bear both in mind, so as neither to be daunted from trying to rise, nor puffed up so as to be sure to fall.   How many have done away the memory of a defect by carrying themselves modestly; while others again have gotten a blemish only by being too proud of being born without one. There is a just humility that will maintain thine own dignity, and yet make thee insensible to many a rub that galls the

F.   23

proud spirit. Be courteous in thy manner, and liberal of
thy purse ; for 'tis the hand to the bonnet and in the pocket
that makes friends in this world; of which to gain one good,
all the gold the sun breeds in India, or the universal sea
sucks down, were a cheap purchase. Speak no evil of
women ; I tell thee the meanest of them deserves our
respect ; for of women do we not all come? Quarrel with
no one but with good cause; by the Lord, over and over
again, when I see masters and schools of arms among us, I
say to myself, "This is not the thing we want at all, *How to
fight*, but *Why to fight?* that is the lesson we want to learn."
And I verily believe if but one master of the *Why to fight*
advertised among us he would carry off all the scholars.
Well—enough—You have not (as you once said to me) my
advice this time on an empty stomach—a fair outfit of
clothes and money—a good horse—and a good sword—
these, together with Don Lope's countenance, and my
blessing—I trust in God to live to see thee home again
with honour and advancement on thy back. My son, God
bless thee ! There—And now go—for I am beginning to
play the woman.

Juan. Your words will live in my heart, sir, so long as it
lives. (*He kisses his father's hand.*) · Sister ! (*He embraces
her.*)

Isab. Would I could hold you back in my arms !

Juan. Adieu, cousin !

Ines. I can't speak.

Cres. Be off, else I shall never let thee go—and my word
is given !

Juan. God bless you all !   [*Exit.*

Isab. Oh, you never should have let him go, sir.

Cres. (*aside*). I shall do better now. (*Aloud.*) Pooh,
why, what the deuce could I have done with him at home

here all his life—a lout—a scape-grace perhaps.   Let him go serve his king. .

Isab. Leaving us by night too!

Cres. Better than by day, child, at this season—Pooh!— (*Aside.*)   I must hold up before them.

Isab. Come, sir, let us in.

Ines. No, no, cousin, e'en let us have a little fresh air now the soldiers are gone.

Cres. True—and here I may watch my Juan along the white, white road.   Let us sit.   (*They sit.*)

Isab. Is not this the day, sir, when the Town Council elects its officers?

Cres. Ay, indeed, in August—so it is.   And indeed this very day.

(*As they talk together, the Captain, Sergeant,* REBOLLEDO, *and* CHISPA *steal in.*)

Capt. (*whispering*). 'Tis she! you know our plan; I seize her, and you look to the others.

Isab. What noise is that?

Ines. Who are these?

(*The Captain seizes and carries off* ISABEL—*the Sergeant and* REBOLLEDO *seize* CRESPO.)

Isab. (*within*). My father!   My father!

Cres. Villains!   A sword!   A sword!

Reb. Kill him at once.

Serg. No, no.

Reb. We must carry him off with us then, or his cries will rouse the town.   [*Exeunt, carrying* CRESPO.

ACT III.   .

SCENE I.   *A Wood near Zalamea.   It is dark.—Enter*
ISABEL.

Isab. Oh never, never might the light of day arise and
show me to myself in my shame! Oh, fleeting morning
star, mightest thou never yield to the dawn that even now
presses on thy azure skirts! And thou, great Orb of all,
do thou stay down in the cold ocean foam; let night for
once advance her trembling empire into thine! For once
assert thy voluntary power to hear and pity human misery
and prayer, nor hasten up to proclaim the vilest deed that
Heaven, in revenge on man, has written on his guilty
annals! Alas! even as I speak, thou liftest thy bright,
inexorable face above the hills! Oh! horror! What shall
I do? whither turn my tottering feet? Back to my own
home? and to my aged father, whose only joy it was to see
his own spotless honour spotlessly reflected in mine, which
now—And yet if I return not, I leave calumny to make my
innocence accomplice in my own shame! Oh that I had
stayed to be slain by Juan over my slaughter'd honour!
But I dared not meet his eyes even to die by his hand.
Alas!—Hark! What is that noise?

Crespo (within). Oh in pity slay me at once!
Isab. One calling for death like myself?
Cres. Whoever thou art—
Isab. That voice!   [*Exit.*

SCENE II.   *Another place in the Wood.* CRESPO *tied to a
tree.—Enter to him* ISABEL.

Isab. My father! ·
Cres. Isabel! Unbind these cords, my child.

Isab. I dare not—I dare not yet, lest you kill before you hear my story—and you must hear that.

Cres. No more, no more! Misery needs no remembrancer.

Isab. It must be.

Cres. Alas! Alas!

Isab. Listen for the last time. You know how, sitting last night under the shelter of those white hairs in which my maiden youth had grown, those wretches, whose only law is force, stole upon us. He who had feign'd that quarrel in our house, seizing and tearing me from your bosom as a lamb from the fold, carried me off; my own cries stifled, yours dying away behind me, and yet ringing in my ears like the sound of a trumpet that has ceas'd!—till here, where out of reach of pursuit,—all dark—the very moon lost from heaven—the wretch began with passionate lies to excuse his violence by his love—his love!—I implored, wept, threatened, all in vain—the villain—But my tongue will not utter what I must weep in silence and ashes for ever! Yet let these quivering hands and heaving bosom, yea, the very tongue that cannot speak, speak loudliest! Amid my shrieks, entreaties, imprecations, the night began to wear away and dawn to creep into the forest. I heard a rustling in the leaves; it was my brother—who in the twilight understood all without a word—drew the sword you had but just given him—they fought—and I, blind with terror, shame, and anguish, fled till—till at last I fell before your feet, my father, to tell you my story before I die! And now I undo the cords that keep your hands from my wretched life. So—it is done! and I kneel before you—your daughter—your disgrace and my own. Avenge us both; and revive your dead honour in the blood of her you gave life to!

Cres. Rise, Isabel; rise, my child. God has chosen thus to temper the cup that prosperity might else have made too sweet. It is thus he writes instruction in our hearts: let us bow down in all humility to receive it. Come, we will home, my Isabel, lean on me. (*Aside.*) 'Fore Heaven, an' I catch that captain! (*Aloud.*) Come, my girl! Courage! so.

Voice (*within*). Crespo! Peter Crespo!

Cres. Hark!

Voice. Peter! Peter Crespo!

Cres. Who calls?

Enter Notary.

Not. Peter Crespo! Oh, here you are at last!

Cres. Well?

Not. Oh, I've had a rare chase. Come—a largess for my news. The corporation have elected you Mayor!

Cres. Me!

Not. Indeed. And already you are wanted in your office. The king is expected almost directly through the town; and, beside that, the captain who disturbed us all so yesterday has been brought back wounded—mortally, it is thought— but no one knows by whom.

Cres. (*to himself*). And so when I was meditating revenge, God himself puts the rod of justice into my hands! How shall I dare myself outrage the law when I am made its keeper? (*Aloud.*) Well, sir, I am very grateful to my fellow-townsmen for their confidence.

Not. They are even now assembled at the town-hall, to commit the wand to your hands; and indeed, as I said, want you instantly.

Cres. Come then.

Isab. Oh, my father!

Cres. Ay, who can now see that justice is done you. Courage! Come.   [*Exeunt.*

SCENE III.   *A Room in Zalamea.—Enter the Captain*
wounded, and Sergeant.

Capt. It was but a scratch after all.   Why on earth bring
me back to this confounded place ?

Serg. Who could have known it was but a scratch till
'twas cured ?   Would you have liked to be left to bleed to
death in the wood ?

Capt. Well, it is cured however : and now to get clear
away before the affair gets wind.   Are the others here ?

Serg. Yes, sir.

Capt. Let us be off then before these fellows know ; else
we shall have to fight for it.

Enter REBOLLEDO.

Reb. Oh, sir, the magistrates are coming !

Capt. Well, what's that to me ?

Reb. I only say they are at the door.

Capt. All the better.   It will be their duty to prevent
any riot the people might make if they knew of our being
here.

Reb. They know, and are humming about it through the
town.

Capt. I thought so.   The magistrates must interfere, and
then refer the cause to a court martial, where, though the
affair is awkward, I shall manage to come off.

Cres. (*within*). Shut the doors ; any soldier trying to
pass, cut him down !

Enter CRESPO, *with the wand of office in his hand, Constables,*
Notary, &c.

Capt. Who is it dares give such an order ?

Cres. And why not?

Capt. Crespo! Well, sir. The stick you are so proud of has no jurisdiction over a soldier.

Cres. For the love of Heaven don't discompose yourself, captain; I am only come to have a few words with you, and, if you please, alone.

Capt. Well then, (*to soldiers, &c.*) retire awhile.

Cres. (*to his people*). And you—but hark ye; remember my orders. [*Exeunt Notary, Constables, &c.*

Cres. And now, sir, that I have used my authority to make you listen, I will lay it by, and talk to you as man to man. (*He lays down the wand.*) We are alone, Don Alvaro, and can each of us vent what is swelling in his bosom; in mine at least, till it is like to burst!

Capt. Well, sir?

Cres. Till last night (let me say it without offence) I knew not, except perhaps my humble birth, a single thing fortune had left me to desire. Of such estate as no other farmer in the district; honoured and esteemed (as now appears) by my fellow-townsmen, who neither envied me my wealth, nor taunted me as an upstart; and this even in a little community, whose usual, if not worst, fault it is to canvass each other's weaknesses. I had a daughter too— virtuously and modestly brought up, thanks to her whom heaven now holds! Whether fair, let what has passed— But I will leave what I may to silence—would to God I could leave all, and I should not now be coming on this errand to you! But it may not be :—you must help time to redress a wound so great, as, in spite of myself, makes cry a heart not used to overflow. I must have redress. And how? The injury is done—by you : I might easily revenge myself for so public and shameful an outrage, but I would have retribution, not revenge. And so, looking about, and considering the matter on all sides, I see but one way which perhaps will not be amiss for either of us. It is this. You shall forthwith take all my substance, without reserve of a single farthing for myself or my son, only what you choose to allow us; you shall even brand us on back or forehead, and sell us like slaves or mules by way of adding to the fortune I offer you—all this, and what you will beside, if only you will with it take my daughter to wife, and restore the honour you have robbed. You will not surely eclipse your own in so doing; your children will still be your children if my grandchildren; and 'tis an old saying in Castile, you know, that, "'Tis the horse redeems the saddle." This is what I have to propose. Behold, (*he kneels,*) upon my knees I ask it—upon my knees, and weeping such tears as only a father's anguish melts from his frozen locks! And what is my demand? But that you should restore what you have robbed: so fatal for us to lose, so easy for you to restore; which I could myself now wrest from you by the hand of the law, but which I rather implore of you as a mercy on my knees!

Capt. You have done at last? Tiresome old man! You may think yourself lucky I do not add your death, and that of your son, to what you call your dishonour. 'Tis your daughter saves you both; let that be enough for all. As to the wrong you talk of, if you would avenge it by force, I have little to fear. As to your magistrate's stick there, it does not reach my profession at all.

Cres. Once more I implore you—

Capt. Have done—have done!

Cres. Will not these tears—

Capt. Who cares for the tears of a woman, a child, or an old man?

Cres. No pity?

Capt. I tell you I spare your life, and your son's : pity enough.

Cres. Upon my knees, asking back my own at your hands that robbed me?

Capt. Nonsense !

Cres. Who could extort it if I chose ?

Capt. I tell you you could not.

Cres. There is no remedy then ?

Capt. Except silence, which I recommend you as the best.

Cres. You are resolved ?

Capt. I am.

Cres. (*rising, and resuming his wand*). Then, by God, you shall pay for it ! Ho there !

Enter Constables, &c.

Capt. What are these fellows about ?

Cres. Take this captain to prison.

Capt. To prison ! you can't do it.

Cres. We'll see.

Capt. Am I a bonâ fide officer or not ?

Cres. And am I a straw magistrate or not ? Away with him !

Capt. The king shall hear of this.

Cres. He shall—doubt it not—perhaps to-day ; and shall judge between us. By the by, you had best deliver up your sword before you go.

Capt. My sword !

Cres. Under arrest, you know.

Capt. Well—take it with due respect then.

Cres. Oh yes, and you too. Hark ye, (*to Constable, &c.*) carry the captain with due respect to Bridewell ; and there with due respect clap on him a chain and hand-cuffs; and not only him, but all that were with him, (all with due respect,) respectfully taking care they communicate not together.   For I mean with all due respect to examine them on the business, and if I get sufficient evidence, with the most infinite respect of all, I'll wring you by the neck till you're dead, by God!

Capt. Set a beggar on horseback!   [*They carry him off.*

Enter Notary and others with REBOLLEDO, *and* CHISPA *in boy's dress.*

Not. This fellow and the page are all we could get hold of.   The other got off.

Cres. Ah, this is the rascal who sung.   I'll make him sing on t'other side of his mouth.

Reb. Why, is singing a crime, sir?

Cres. So little that I've an instrument shall make you do it as you never did before.   Will you confess?

Reb. What am I to confess?

Cres. What pass'd last night?

Reb. Your daughter can tell you that better than I.

Cres. Villain, you shall die for it!   [*Exit.*

Chis. Deny all, Rebolledo, and you shall be the hero of a ballad I'll sing.

Not. And you too were of the singing party?

Chis. Ah, ah, and if I was, you can't put me to the question.

Not. And why not, pray?

Chis. The law forbids you.

Not. Oh, indeed, the law?   How so, pray?

Chis. Because I'm in the way ladies like to be who love Rebolledo.   [*Exeunt, carried off, &c.*

SCENE IV. *A Room in* CRESPO'S *House.—Enter* JUAN
pursuing ISABEL *with a dagger.*

Isab. Help, help, help!   [*Exit.*
Juan. You must not live!

Enter CRESPO, *who arrests him.*

Cres. Hold! What is this?
Juan. My father! To avenge our shame—
Cres. Which is to be avenged by other means, and not
by you. How come you here?
Juan. Sent back by Don Lope last night, to see after
some missing soldiers, on approaching the town I heard
some cries—
Cres. And drew your sword on your officer, whom you
wounded, and are now under arrest from me for doing it.
Juan. Father!
Cres. And Mayor of Zalamea. Within there!

Enter Constables.

Take him to prison.
Juan. Your own son, sir?
Cres. Ay, sir, my own father, if he transgressed the law I
am made guardian of. Off with him! (*They carry off* JUAN.)
So I shall keep him out of harm's way at least. And now
for a little rest. (*He lays by his wand.*)
Lope (*calling within*). Stop! Stop!
Cres. Who's that calling without? Don Lope!

Enter LOPE.

Lope. Ay, Peter, and on a very confounded business too.
But at least I would not put up any where but at your
friendly house.

Cres. You are too good.   But, indeed, what makes you back, sir, so suddenly?

Lope. A most disgraceful affair; the greatest insult to the service! One of my soldiers overtook me on the road, flying at full speed, and told me— Oh, the rascal!

Cres. Well, sir?

Lope. That some little pettifogging Mayor of the place had got hold of a captain in my regiment, and put him in prison! In prison! 'Fore Heaven, I never really felt this confounded leg of mine till to-day, that it prevented me jumping on horseback at once to punish this trumpery Jack-in-office as he deserves. But here I am, and, by the Lord, I'll thrash him within an inch of his life!

Cres. You will?

Lope. Will I!

Cres. But will he stand your thrashing?

Lope. Stand it or not, he shall have it.

Cres. Besides, might your captain happen to deserve what he met with?

Lope. And, if he did, *I* am his judge, not a trumpery mayor.

Cres. This mayor is an odd sort of customer to deal with, I assure you.

Lope. Some obstinate clodpole, I suppose.

Cres. So obstinate, that if he's made up his mind to hang your captain, he'll do it.

Lope. Will he? I'll see to that. And if you wish to see too, only tell me where I can find him.

Cres. Oh, close here.

Lope. You know him?

Cres. Very well, I believe.

Lope. And who is it?

Cres. Peter Crespo. (*Takes his wand.*)

Lope. By God, I suspected it.

Cres. By God, you were right.

Lope. Well, Crespo, what's said is said.

Cres. And, Don Lope, what's done is done.

Lope. I tell you, I want my captain.

Cres. And I tell you, I've got him.

Lope. Do you know he is the king's officer?

Cres. Do you know he ravished my daughter?

Lope. That you are out-stripping your authority in meddling with him?

Cres. Not more than he is in meddling with me.

Lope. Do you know my authority supersedes yours?

Cres. Do you know I tried first to get him to do me justice with no authority at all, but the offer of all my estate?

Lope. I tell you, *I'll* settle the business for you.

Cres. And I tell you I never leave to another what I can do for myself.

Lope. I tell you once more and for all, I must have my man.

Cres. And I tell you once more and for all, you shall— when you have cleared him of the depositions.

Lope. The depositions! What are they?

Cres. Oh, only a few sheets of parchment tagged together with the evidence of his own soldiers against him.

Lope. Pooh! I'll go myself, and take him from the prison.

Cres. Do, if you like an arquebuss ball through your body.

Lope. I am accustomed to that. But I'll make sure. Within there!

Enter Orderly.

Have the regiment to the market-place directly under arms, I'll see if I'm to have my prisoner or not.   [*Exit.*

Cres. And I—Hark ye! [*Exit, whispering to a Constable.*

SCENE V. *Before the Prison in Zalamea.—A Street in the centre.—Enter on one side* DON LOPE *with Troops; at the other, before the Prison, Labourers, Constables, &c. armed: and afterward,* CRESPO.

Lope. Soldiers, there is the prison where your captain lies. If he be not given up instantly at my last asking, set fire to the prison ; and, if further resistance be made, to the whole town.

Cres. Friends and fellow-townsmen, there is the prison where lies a rascal capitally convicted—

Lope. They grow stronger and stronger. Forward, men, forward ! (*As the Soldiers are about to advance, trumpets and shouts of* "*God save the King*," *within.*)

Lope. The king !

All. The king !

Enter KING PHILIP II. *through centre Street, with Train, &c. Shouting, Trumpets, &c.*

King. What is all this ?

Lope. 'Tis well your Majesty came so suddenly, or you would have had one of your whole towns by way of bonfire on your progress.

King. What has happened ?

Lope. The mayor of this place has had the impudence to seize a captain in your Majesty's service, clap him in prison, and refuses to surrender him to me, his commander.

King. Where is this mayor ?

Cres. Here, so please your Majesty.

King. Well, Mr Mayor, what have you to offer in defence?

Cres. These papers, my Liege : in which this same captain is clearly proved guilty, on the evidence of his own soldiers, of carrying off and violating a maiden in a desolate place, and refusing her the satisfaction of marriage though peaceably entreated to it by her father with the endowment of all his substance.

Lope. This same mayor, my Liege, is the girl's father.

Cres. What has that to do with it? If another man had come to me under like circumstances, should I not have done him like justice? To be sure. And therefore, why not do for my own daughter what I should do for another's? Besides, I have just done justice against my own son for striking his captain; why should I be suspected of straining it in my daughter's favour? But here is the process; let his Majesty see for himself if the case be made out. The witnesses are at hand too; and if they or any one can prove I have suborned any evidence, or any way acted with partiality to myself, or malice to the captain, let them come forward, and let my life pay for it instead of his.

King (after reading the papers). I see not but the charge is substantiated: and 'tis indeed a heavy one. Is there any one here to deny these depositions? (*Silence.*) But, be the crime proved, *you* have no authority to judge or punish it. You must let the prisoner go.

Cres. You must send for him then, please your Majesty. In little towns like this, where public officers are few, the deliberative is forced sometimes to be the executive also.

King. What do you mean?

Cres. Your Majesty will see. (*The prison gates open, and the Captain is seen within, garrotted in a chair.*)

King. And you have dared, sir!—

Cres. Your Majesty said the sentence was just; and what is well said cannot be ill done.

King. Could you not have left it for my imperial Court to execute?

Cres. All your Majesty's justice is only one great body with many hands; if a thing be to be done, what matter by which? Or what matter erring in the inch, if one be right in the ell?

King. At least you might have beheaded him, as an officer and a gentleman.

Cres. Please your Majesty, we have so few Hidalgos hereabout, that our executioner is out of practice at beheading. And this, after all, depends on the dead gentleman's taste; if he don't complain, I don't think any one else need for him.

King. Don Lope, the thing is done; and, if unusually, not unjustly—Come, order all your soldiers away with me toward Portugal; where I must be with all despatch. For you—(*to* CRESPO) what is your name?

Cres. Peter Crespo, please your Majesty.

King. Peter Crespo, then, I appoint you perpetual Mayor of Zalamea. And so farewell.   [*Exit with Train.*

Cres. (*kneeling*). God save your Highness!

Lope. Friend Peter, his Highness came just in time.

Cres. For your captain, do you mean?

Lope. Come now—confess, wouldn't it have been better to have given up the prisoner, who, at my instance, would have married your daughter, saved her reputation, and made her wife of an Hidalgo?

Cres. Thank you, Don Lope, she has chosen to enter a convent and be the bride of one who is no respecter of Hidalgos.

Lope. Well, well, you will at least give me up the other prisoners, I suppose?

Cres. Bring them out. (JUAN, REBOLLEDO, CHISPA, *brought out.*)

Lope. Your son too!

F.   24

Cres. Yes, 'twas he wounded his captain, and I must punish him.

Lope. Come, come, you have done enough—at least give *him* up to his commander.

Cres. Eh? well, perhaps so; I'll leave his punishment to you.

With which now this true story ends—
Pardon its many errors, friends.

———————

Mr Ticknor thinks Calderon took the hint of this play from Lope de Vega's "Wise Man at Home;" and he quotes (though without noticing this coincidence) a reply of Lope's hero to some one advising him to assume upon his wealth, that is much of a piece with Crespo's answer to Juan on a like score in the first act of this piece. Only that in Lope the answer *is* an answer : which, as Juan says, in Calderon it is not; so likely to happen with a borrowed answer.

This is Mr Ticknor's version from the older play:

> He that was born to live in humble state
> Makes but an awkward knight, do what you will.
> My father means to die as he has liv'd,
> The same plain collier that he always was;
> And I too must an honest ploughman die.
> 'Tis but a single step or up or down;
> For men there must be that will plough or dig,
> And when the vase has once been fill'd, be sure
> 'Twill always savour of what first it held.

I must observe of the beginning of Act III., that in this translation Isabel's speech is intentionally reduced to prose, not only in measure of words, but in some degree of idea also. It would have been far easier to make at least verse of almost the most elevated and purely beautiful piece of Calderon's poetry I know; a speech (the beginning of it) worthy of the Greek Antigone, which, after two Acts of homely talk, Calderon has put into his *Labradora's* mouth. This, admitting for all culmination of passion, and Spanish passion, must excuse my tempering it to the key in which (measure only kept) Calderon himself sets out.

BEWARE OF SMOOTH WATER.

DRAMATIS PERSONÆ.

Don Alonso.

Donna Clara,
Donna Eugenia, } *his Daughters.*

Don Torribio, *his Nephew.*

Mari Nuño,
Brigida, } *his Servants.*
Otañez,

Don Felix,
Don Juan, } *Gallants.*
Don Pedro,

Hernando, *Don Felix's Servant.*

BEWARE OF SMOOTH WATER.

ACT I.

SCENE I. *A Room in* DON ALONSO'S *House at Madrid.—*
Enter ALONSO *and* OTAÑEZ, *meeting.*

Otañ. My own dear master!
Alon.   Welcome, good Otañez,
My old and trusty servant!
Otañ.   Have I liv'd
To see what I so long have long'd to see,
My dear old master home again!
Alon.   You could not
Long for 't, Otañez, more than I myself.
What wonder, when my daughters, who, you know,
Are the two halves that make up my whole heart,
Silently call'd me home, and silently
(For maiden duty still gagg'd filial love)
Out of the country shade where both have grown,
Urg'd me to draw the blossom of their youth
Where it might ripen in its proper day.

Otañ. Indeed, indeed, sir. Oh that my dear lady
Were but alive to see this happy hour!

Alon. Nay, good Otañez, mar it not recalling
What, ever sleeping in the memory,
Needs but a word to waken into tears.
God have her in his keeping! He best knows
How I have suffer'd since the king, my master,
Despatching me with charge to Mexico,
I parted from her ne'er to see her more;
And now come back to find her gone for ever!
You know 'twas not the long and roaring seas
Frighted her for herself, but these two girls—
For them she stay'd—and full of years and honour
Died, when God will'd! and I have hasten'd home
Well as I may, to take into my hands
The charge death slipp'd from hers.

Otañ.   Your own good self!
Though were there ever father, who could well
Have left that charge to others, it was you,
Your daughters so religiously brought up
In convent with their aunt at Alcalá.
Well, you are come, and God be prais'd for it!
And, at your bidding, here are they, and I,
And good old Mari Nuño—all come up
To meet you at Madrid. I could not wait
The coach's slower pace, but must spur on
To kiss my old master's hand.

Alon.   Myself had gone
To meet them; but despatches of the king's
Prevented me. They're well?

Voices (within).   Make way there—way!

Otañ. And lovely as the dawn. And hark! are here
To answer for themselves.

Enter CLARA, EUGENIA, MARI NUÑO, *as from travel.*

Clara (kneeling). Sir, and my father—by my daily prayers
Heav'n, won at last in suffering me to kiss
These honour'd hands, leaves me no more to ask,
Than at these honour'd feet to die,
With its eternal blessing afterward.

Eug. And I, my father, grateful as I am
To Heav'n, for coming to your feet once more,
Have yet this more to ask—to live with you
For many, many happy years to come!

Alon. Oh, not in vain did nature fix the heart
In the mid bosom, like a sun to move
Each circling arm with equal love around!
Come to them—one to each—and take from me
Your lives anew.   God bless you!
Come, we are here together in Madrid,
And in the sphere where you were born to move.
This is the house that is to be your own
Until some happy lover calls you his;
Till which I must be father, lover, husband,
In one.   Brigida!

Enter BRIGIDA.

Brig.   Sir?
Alon.   My daughters' rooms
Are ready?
Brig.   Ay, sir, as the sky itself
For the sun's coming.
Alon.   Go and see them then,
And tell me how you like what I have bought,
And fitted up for your reception.
Clara. I thank you, sir, and bless this happy day,

Though leaving my lov'd convent far away.

Eug. (aside). And I twice bless it, that no longer hid
In a dull cell, I come to see Madrid.

[*Exeunt* CLARA *and* EUGENIA.

Mari Nuño. Now the young ladies, sir, have had their
    turn,
Shall not I kiss your hand?

Alon.   Oh, welcome too,
Good Mari Nuño; who have been so long
A mother to them both. And, by the by,
Good Mari Nuño, now we are alone,
I'd hear from you, who know them both so well,
Their several characters and dispositions,
And not, as 'twere, come blindfold to the charge
That Heav'n has laid upon me.

Mari.   You say well, sir.
Well, I might say at once, and truly too,
That nothing need be said in further praise
But that they are your daughters. But to pass,
Lest you should think I flatter,
From general to individual,
And to begin with the eldest, Donna Clara;
Eldest in years and in discretion too,
Indeed the very pearl of prudence, sir,
And maidenly reserve; her eyes still fixt
On earth in modesty, or heav'n in prayer;
As gentle as a lamb, almost as silent;
And never known to say an angry word:
And, such her love of holy quietude,
Unless at your desire, would never leave
Her cloister and her missal. She's, in short,
An angel upon earth, whom to be near
And wait on, one would sell oneself a slave.

So much for her. Donna Eugenia,
Though unexceptionable in heart and head,
As, God forgive me, any child of yours
Must be, is different,—not for me to say
Better or worse,—but very different :
Of a quick spirit, loving no control ;
Indeed, as forward as the other shy ;
Quick to retort, and sharply ; so to speak,
Might sometimes try the patience of a saint ;
Longing to leave a convent for the world,
To see and to be seen ; makes verses too ;
Would not object, I think, to have them made
(Or love, may be) to her—you understand ;
Not that I mean to say—
   Alon.   Enough, enough.
Thanks for your caution as your commendation :
How could I fortify against weak points
Unless I knew of them? And, to this end,
Although Eugenia be the younger sister,
I'll see her married first ; husband and children
The best specific for superfluous youth :
And to say truth, good Mari, the very day
Of my arrival hither, I despatch'd
A letter to my elder brother's son,
Who still maintains our dwindled patrimony
Up in the mountains, which I would reclaim,
Or keep it rather in its lawful line,
By an alliance with a child of mine.
All falls out luckily. Eugenia
Wedded to him shall make herself secure,
And the two stems of Cuadradillos so
Unite and once more flourish, at a blow.   [*Exeunt.*

SCENE II. *A Room in* DON FELIX'S *House;* DON FELIX,
        and HERNANDO *dressing him.*

Hern. Such fine ladies, sir, come to be our neighbours.

Fel. So they ought to be, such a noise as they made in
coming.

Hern. One of them already betroth'd, however.

Fel. So let her, and married too, if she would only let
me sleep quiet.   But what kind of folks are they ?

Hern. Oh, tip-top.   Daughters of the rich old Indian has
bought the house and gardens opposite, and who will give
them all his wealth when they marry, which they say he has
brought them to Madrid expressly to do.

Fel. But are they handsome ?

Hern. I thought so, sir, as I saw them alighting.

Fel. Rich and handsome then ?

Hern. Yes, sir.

Fel. Two good points in a woman, at all events, of which
I might profit, such opportunities as I have.

Hern. Have a care, sir, for the old servant who told me
this, told me also that the papa is a stout fiery old fellow,
who'd stick the Great Turk himself if he caught him trifling
with his daughters.

Fel. That again is not so well ; for though I'm not the
Great Turk, I've no mind to share that part of his fortune.
But of the two girls, what said your old servant? who, as
such, I suppose told you all that was amiss in them at least.

Hern. Well, you shall judge.   One, the oldest, is very
discreet.

Fel. Ah, I told you so.

Hern. The other lively.

Fel. Come, that sounds better.   One can tackle her hand

to hand, but the grave one one can only take a long shot at with the eyes.

Hern. Whichever it be, I should like to see you yourself hit one of these days, sir.

Fel. Me? The woman is not yet cast who will do that. If I meddle with these it is only because they lie so handy.

Hern. And handsome as well as handy!

Fel. Pooh! I wouldn't climb a wall to pluck the finest fruit in the world. But hark! some one's at the door. See who 'tis.

Enter DON JUAN *in travelling dress.*

Juan. I, Felix, who seeing your door open, could not but walk in without further ado.

Fel. You know that it and my heart are ever open to you. Welcome, welcome, Don Juan! all the more welcome for being unexpected: for though I had heard we might one day have you back, I did not think to see you yet.

Juan. Why, the truth is I got my pardon sooner than I expected.

Fel. Though not than I prayed for. But tell me all about it.

Juan. You know I was obliged to fly to Italy after that unlucky duel. Well, there the great duke of Terranova, who (as good luck would have it) was then going ambassador to Hungary, took a fancy to me, and carried me with him; and, pleased with what service I did him, interested himself in my fortunes, and one good day, when I was least expecting it, with his own hand put my pardon into mine.

Fel. A pardon that never should have needed asking, all of an unlucky quarrel at cards.

Juan. So you and the world suppose, Felix: but in truth there was something more behind.

Fel. Ah?

Juan. Why the truth is, I was courting a fair lady, and with fair hope of success, though she would not confess it, urging that her father being away at the time, her mother would not consent in his absence. Suddenly I found I had a rival, and took occasion of a casual dispute at cards to wipe out the score of jealousy ; which I did with a vengeance to both of us, he being killed on the spot, and I, forc'd to fly the country, must, I doubt, ere this, have died out of my lady's memory, where only I cared to live.

Fel. Ay, you know well enough that in Madrid Oblivion lies in the very lap of Remembrance, whether of love or loathing. I thank my stars I never pinn'd my faith on woman yet.

Juan. Still the same sceptic?

Fel. Ay, they are fine things, but my own heart's ease is finer still; and if one party must be deceived, I hold it right in self-defence it should not be I. But come ; that you may not infect me with your faith, nor I you with my heresy, tell me about your journey.

Juan. How could it be otherwise than a pleasant one, such pageants as I had to entertain me by the way?

Fel. Oh, you mean our royal master's nuptials?

Juan. Ay!

Fel. I must hear all about them, Juan ; even now, upon the spot.

Juan. Well then, you know at least, without my telling you, how great a debt Germany has owed us—

Enter DON PEDRO *hastily.*

Ped. My dear Don Felix!

Fel. Don Pedro! By my faith, my door must be the door of heaven, I think ; for all the good keep coming in

by't.   But how comes your University term so soon
over?

Ped.   Alas, it's *not* over, but—

Fel.   Well?

Ped.   I'll tell you.

Juan.   If I be in your way—

Ped.   No, no, sir, if you are Felix's friend you command
my confidence. My story is easily told. A lady I am
courting in Alcalá is suddenly come up to Madrid, and I
am come after her. And to escape my father's wrath at
playing truant, I must beg sanctuary in your house awhile.

Fel.   And this once will owe me thanks for your enter-
tainment, since I have Don Juan's company to offer you.

Juan.   Nay, 'tis I have to thank you for Don Pedro's.

Fel.   Only remember, both of you, that however you may
amuse one another, you are not to entertain me with your
several hearts and darts. Hernando, get us something to
eat; and till it comes you shall set off rationally at least,
Juan, with the account of the royal nuptials you were be-
ginning just as Don Pedro came in.

Juan.   On condition you afterwards recount to me your
rejoicings in Madrid meanwhile.

Fel.   Agreed.

Ped.   I come in happy time to hear you both.

Juan.   You know, as I was saying, what a debt
Germany has ow'd us since our fair Maria
Her title of the Royal Child of Spain
Set in the crown of Hungary—a debt
They only could repay us as they do,
Returning us one of the self-same stock,
So like herself in beauty and desert,
We seem but taking what we gave away.
If into Austria's royal hand we gave

Our royal rose, she now returns us one
Sprung of the self-same stem, as fair, as sweet
In maiden graces; and if double-dyed
In the imperial purple, yet so fresh,
She scarce has drunk the dawns of fourteen Aprils.
The marriage contract sign'd, the marriage self
Delay'd, too long for loyal Spain's desire,
That like the bridegroom for her coming burn'd,
(But happiness were hardly happiness
Limp'd it not late,) till her defective years
Reach'd their due blossom—Ah, happy defect,
That every uncondition'd hour amends!
At last arose the day—the day of days—
When from her royal eyrie in the North
The imperial eaglet flew. Young Ferdinand,
King of Bohemia and Hungary
Elect, who not in vain Rome's holy hand
Awaits to bind the laurel round his brow,
As proxy for our king espous'd her first,
And then, all lover-like, as far as Trent
Escorted her, with such an equipage
As when the lords and princes of three realms
Out-do each other in magnificence
Of gold and jewel, ransackt from the depths
Of earth and sea, to glitter in the eye
Of Him who sees and lights up all from heav'n.
So, like a splendid star that trails her light
Far after her, she cross'd fair Italy,
When Doria, Genoa's great Admiral,
Always so well-affected to our crown,
Took charge of her sea-conduct; which awhile,
Till winds and seas were fair, she waited for
In Milan; till, resolv'd on embarkation,

The sea, that could not daunt her with his rage,
Soon as her foot was on his yellow shore,
Call'd up his Tritons and his Nereids
Who love and make a calm, to smooth his face
And still his heaving breast; on whose blue flood
The golden galley in defiance burn'd,
Her crew in wedding pearl and silver drest;
Her silken sail and cordage, fluttering
With myriad flags and streamers of all dye,
Sway'd like a hanging garden over-head,
Amid whose blossoms stood the royal bride,
A fairer Venus than did ever float
Over the seas to her dominions
Arm'd with the arrows of diviner love.
Then to the sound of trump and clarion
The royal galley, and with her forty more
That follow'd in her wake as on their queen,
Weigh'd, shook out sail, and dipp'd all oars at once,
Making the flood clap hands in acclamation;
And so with all their streamers, as 'twere spring
Floating away to other hemispheres,
Put out to sea; and touching not the isles
That gem the midway deep—not from distrust
Of friendly France in whose crown they are set,
And who (as mighty states contend in peace
With courtesies as with hard blows in war)
Swell'd the triumphal tide with pageantries
I may not stop to tell—but borne upon,
And (as I think) bearing, fair wind and wave,
The moving city on its moving base
With sail and oar enter'd the Spanish Main,
Which, flashing emerald and diamond,
Leap'd round the golden prow that clove between,

And kiss'd the happy shore that first declin'd
To meet its mistress. Happy Denia,
That in her golden sand holds pearly-like
The first impression of that royal foot !
I will not tell—let Felix, who was here,
And has new breath—how, landed happily,
Our loyal Spain—yea, with what double welcome—
Receiv'd the niece and consort of our king,
Whom, one and both, and both in one, may Heav'n
Bless with fair issue, and all happiness,
For years and years to come !

Enter HERNANDO.

Hern. Sir, sir !

Fel. Well ?

Hern. Your two new neighbours—just come to the window.

Fel. Gentlemen, we must waive my story then, for as the proverb goes, "*My Lady first.*" (*He looks out.*) By Heaven, they are divine !

Juan. Let me see. (*Aside.*) By Heaven, 'tis she !

Ped. Come, it is my turn now. (*Aside.*) Eugenia ! I must keep it to myself.

Fel. I scarce know which is handsomest.

Juan. Humph ! both pretty girls enough.

Ped. Yes, very well.

Fel. Listen, gentlemen ; whether handsome, or pretty, or very well, or all three, you must not stare at them from my window so vehemently ; being the daughters of a friend of mine, and only just come to Madrid.

Juan (*aside*). That the first thing I should see on return-ing to Madrid, is she for whose love I left it !

Ped. (*aside*). That the first thing I see here is what I came for the very purpose of seeing !

Hernando (*entering*). Table is serv'd, sir.

Fel. To table, then. I know not how it is with you, gentlemen, but for myself, my appetite is stronger than my love.

Juan (*aside to* FELIX). You jest as usual; but I assure you it is one of those very ladies on whom my fortune turns!

[*Exit.*

Fel. Adieu to one then.

Ped. All this is fun to you, Felix; but believe me, one of those ladies is she I have followed from Alcalá. [*Exit.*

Fel. Adieu to both then—unless indeed you are both of you in love with the same. But, thank God,

> I that am in love with neither,
> Need not plague myself for either.
> The least expense of rhyme or care
> That man can upon woman spare.

But they are very handsome nevertheless. [*Exit.*

SCENE III. *An Apartment in* DON ALONSO'S *House.—
Enter* CLARA *and* EUGENIA.

Clara. Is't not a pretty house, Eugenia,
And all about it?

Eug. I dare say you think so.

Clara. But do not you then?

Eug. No—to me it seems
A sort of out-court and repository,
Fit but for old Hidalgos and Duennas,
Too stale and wither'd for the blooming world,
To wear away in.

F. 25

Clara.   I like its quietude;
This pretty garden too.
     Eug.   A pretty thing .
To come for to Madrid—a pretty garden!
I tell you were it fuller of all flowers
Than is a Dutchman's in his tulip-time,
I want the lively street whose flowers are shops,
Carriages, soldiers, ladies, cavaliers,
Plenty of dust in summer, dirt in winter,
And where a woman sitting at her blind
Sees all that passes.   Then this furniture!
     Clara. Well—surely velvet curtains, sofas, chairs,
Rich Indian carpets, beds of Damascene,
Chandeliers, gilded mirrors, pictures too—
What would you have, Eugenia?
     Eug.   All very well,
But, after all, no marvellous result
Of ten years spent in golden India.
Why, one has heard how fine a thing it is
To be my Lord Mayor's daughter; what must be,
Methought, to own a dowry from Peru!
And when you talk about the furniture,
Pictures, chairs, carpets, mirrors, and all that—
The best of all is wanting.
     Clara.   What is that?
     Eug. Why, a coach, woman!   Heav'n and earth, a
     coach !
What use is all the money-bonds and gold
He has been boasting of in all his letters,
Unless, now come at last, he plays the part
We've heard so long rehearsing?
     Clara.   Not to spare
Your father even, Eugenia!   For shame!

'Tis time to tie your roving tongue indeed.
Consider, too, we are not in the country,
Where tongue and eyes, Eugenia, may run wild
Without offence to uncensorious woods;
But in a city, with its myriad eyes
Inquisitively turn'd to watch, and tongues
As free and more malicious than yours
To tell—where honour's monument is wax,
And shame's of brass.   I know, Eugenia,
High spirits are not in themselves a crime;
But if to men they *seem* so?—that's the question.
For it is almost better to do ill
With a good outward grace than well without;
Especially a woman; most of all
One not yet married; whose reputation
One breath of scandal, like a flake of snow,
May melt away; one of those tenderest flowers
Whose leaves ev'n the warm breath of flattery
Withers as fast as envy's bitterest wind,
That surely follows short-liv'd summer praise.
Ev'n those who praise your beauty, grace, or wit,
Will be the first, if you presume on them,
To pull the idol down themselves set up,
Beginning with malicious whispers first,
Until they join the storm themselves have rais'd.
And most if one be giv'n oneself to laugh
And to make laugh : the world will doubly yearn
To turn one's idle giggle into tears.
I say this all by way of warning, sister,
Now we are launcht upon this dangerous sea.
Consider of it.
    Eug.   "Which that all may do
May Heav'n—" Come, Clara, if the sermon's done,

Pray finish it officially at once,
And let us out of church. These homilies
In favour of defunct proprieties,
Remind one of old ruff and armour worn
By 'Don Punctilio and Lady Etiquette
A hundred years ago, and past with them
And all their tedious ancestors for ever.
I am alive, young, handsome, witty, rich,
And come to town, and mean to have my fling,
Not caring what malicious people say,
If nothing true to say against my honour.
And so with all sail set, and streamers flying,
(A coach shall be my ship, and I will have it!)
I mean to glide along the glittering streets
And down the Prado, as I go along
Capturing what eyes and hearts I find by the way,
Heedless of every little breath of scandal
That such as you turn back affrighted by.
I'll know the saints' days better than the saints
Themselves; the holidays and festivals
Better than over-done apprentices.
If a true lover comes whom I can like
As he loves me, I shall not turn away:
As for the rest who flutter round in love,
Not with myself, but with my father's wealth,
Or with themselves, or any thing but me,
You shall see, Clara, how I'll play with them,
Till, having kept them on my string awhile
For my own sport, I'll e'en turn them adrift
And let them go, the laugh all on my side.
And therefore when you see—
    Clara.   How shall I dare
To see what even now I quake to hear!

Enter ALONSO.

Alon. Clara! Eugenia!

Both. Sir?

Alon. Good news, good news, my girls! What think you? My nephew, Don Torribio Cuadradillos, my elder brother's elder son, head of our family and inheritor of the estate, is coming to visit me; will be here indeed almost directly. What think you now?

Eug. (aside). One might have thought, from such a flourish of trumpets, the king was coming at least.

Alon. Mari Nuño!

Mari (entering). Sir?

Alon. Let a chamber be got ready for my nephew, Don Torribio, directly. Brigida!

Brig. (entering). Sir?

Alon. See that linen be taken up into Don Torribio's room. Otañez, have dinner ready for my nephew, Don Torribio, directly he arrives. And you two, (*to his daughters,*) I expect you will pay him all attention; as head of the family, consider. Ay, and if he *should* take a fancy to one of you—I know not he will—but if he *should*, I say, whichever it be, she will take precedence of her sister for ever. (*Aside.*) This I throw out as a bait for Eugenia.

Eug. It must be Clara, then, sir, for she is oldest you know.

Clara. Not in discretion and all wife-like qualities, Eugenia.

Eug. Clara!

Alon. Hark! in the court!

Don Torribio (speaking loud within). Hoy! good man there! Can you tell me if my uncle lives hereabout?

Alon. 'Tis my nephew, surely !

Torr. (*within*). Why, fellow, I mean of course Don Alonso—who has two daughters, by the token I'm to marry one of 'em.

Alon. 'Tis he ! I will go and receive him. [*Exit.*

Torr. (*within*). Very well then. Hold my stirrup, Lorenzo.

Eug. What a figure !

Enter ALONSO *and* TORRIBIO.

Alon. My nephew, Don Torribio, giving thanks to Heaven for your safe arrival at my house, I hasten to welcome you as its head.

Torr. Ay, uncle, and a head taller, I promise you, than almost any body in the parish.

Alon. Let me introduce your cousins to you, who are so anxious for your acquaintance.

Torr. Ah, that's proper of 'em, isn't it ?

Both. Welcome, sir.

Alon. And how are you, nephew ?

Torr. Very tired, I promise you : for the way is long and my horse a rough goer, so as I've lost leather.

Alon. Sit down, and rest till they bring dinner.

Torr. Sitting an't the way to mend it. But, however—- (*Sits.*) Nay, though I be head of the house, I an't proud—- you can all of you sit down too.

Clara (*aside*). Amiable humility !

Eug. (*aside*). No wonder the house is crazy if this be its head !

Torr. Well, now I come to look at you, cousins, I may say you are both of you handsome girls, indeed ; which'll put me to some trouble.

Clara. How so, cousin?

Torr. Why, didn't you ever hear that if you put an ass between two bundles of hay, he'll die without knowing which to begin on, eh?

Alon. His father's pleasant humour!

Clara. A courteous comparison!

Eug. (aside). Which holds as far as the ass at least.

Torr. Well, there's a remedy. I say, uncle, musn't cousins get a dispensation before they marry?

Alon. Yes, nephew.

Torr. Well then, when you're about it, you can get two dispensations, and I can marry both my cousins. Aha! Well, but, uncle, how are you? I had forgot to ask you that.

Alon. Quite well, in seeing you in my house at last, and to reap, I trust, the fruits of all my travel.

Torr. Ah, you may say that. Oh, cousins, if you could only see my pedigree and patent, in a crimson velvet case; and all my forefathers painted in a row—I have it in my saddle bags, and if you'll wait a minute—

Enter MARI NUÑO.

Mari. Dinner's ready.

Torr. (looking at MARI). Lord a' mercy, uncle, what's this? something you brought from India, belike; does it speak?

Alon. Nay, nephew, 'tis our Duenna.

Torr. A what?

Alon. A Duenna.

Torr. A tame one?

Alon. Come, come, she tells us dinner's ready.

Torr. Yes, if you believe her; but I've heard say,

Duennas always lie. However, I'll go and see for myself.
[*Exit.*

   Clara. What a cousin!

   Eug. What a lover!

   Mari. Foh! I wonder how the watch came to let the
plague into the city!   [*Exit.*

   Alon. You are silent, both of you?

   Both. Not I, sir.

   Alon. I understand you; Don Torribio
Pleases you not—Well, he's a little rough;
But wait a little; see what a town life
Will do for him; all come up so at first,
The finest diamonds, you know, the roughest—
Oh, I rejoice my ancestor's estate
Shall to my grandchildren revert again!
For this I tell you—one, I care not which,
But one of you, shall marry Don Torribio:
And let not her your cousin does not choose,
For one more courtly think herself reserv'd;
By Heaven she shall marry, if e'er marry,
One to the full as rough and country-like.
What, I to see my wealth, so hardly won,
Squander'd away by some fine town gallant,
In silks and satins! see my son-in-law
Spend an estate upon a hat and feather!
I tell you I'll not have it. One of you
Must marry Don Torribio.   [*Exit.*

   Clara.   I'll die first.

   Eug. And I'll live an old maid—which much is worst?

ACT II.

SCENE I.   *A Room in* DON FELIX'S *House.*—FELIX *and*
HERNANDO; *to whom Enter* JUAN.

Fel. Well, Juan, and how slept you?
Juan.   As one must
In your house, Felix; had not such a thought
No house can quiet woke me long ere dawn.
  Fel. Indeed! How so?
  Juan.   Felix, the strangest thing—
But now we are alone I'll tell you all.
Last night—the very moment that I saw
That angel at the window, as at Heaven's gate—
The fire that I myself had thought half dead
Under the ashes of so long an absence,
Sprung up anew into full blaze. Alas!
But one brief moment did she dawn on us,
Then set, to rise no more all the evening,
Watch as I would. But day is come again,
And as I think, Felix, the holyday
When our new Queen shall make her solemn entry
Into Madrid; and she, my other Queen,
Will needs be up—be up and out betimes;
So I forestall the sun in looking for her,
And now will to the door beneath her window
Better to watch her rising.   ·
But, as you love me, not a word of this
Breathe to Don Pedro.   [*Exit.*
  Fel.   And does he think
Because his memory of her is quick,
Hers is of him? Aha!

Hern.   Nay, if he like it,
"Oh, let him be deceiv'd!"

Fel.   'Twas wisely said
By him who self-deception us'd to call
The cheapest and the dearest thing of all.
Ha! here's the other swain! and now to see
How he has prosper'd. I begin to think
My house is turn'd into a Lazar-house
Of crazy lovers.

Enter PEDRO.

Good day, Don Pedro.

Ped.   As it needs must be
To one who hails it in your house, and opposite
My lady's! Oh, you cannot think, my Felix,
With what a blessed conscience of all this
I woke this morning! I can scarce believe 't.
Why, in your house, I shall have chance on chance,
Nay, certainty of seeing her—*to-day*
Most certainly. But I'll go post myself
Before the door; she will be out betimes
To mass.

Fel.   Well, you will find Don Juan there.

Ped. Eh? Well, so much the better, I can do 't
With less suspicion, nay, with none at all
If you will go with us. Only, Don Felix,
Breathe not a word to him about my love.

As he is going, re-enter JUAN.

Fel. Juan again?

Juan.   I only came to ask
What church we go to? (*Aside to* FELIX.) Let us keep
    at home.

Fel. Don Pedro, what say you?

Ped.   Oh, where you please.
(*Aside.*) Stir not!

Fel. (*aside*).   How easy to oblige two friends
Who ask the same, albeit with divers ends!
(*Aloud.*) What, are your worships both in love, perhaps,
As Spanish cavaliers are bound to be,
And think I've nothing else to do, forsooth,
Than follow each upon his wildgoose chase?
Forgetting I may take 't into my head
To fall in love myself—perhaps with one,
Or both, of those fair ladies chance has brought
Before my windows. Now I think upon 't,
I am, or mean to be, in love with one;
And, to decide with which, I'll e'en wait here
Till they both sally forth to church themselves.
So, gentlemen, would you my company,
I must not go with you, you stay with me.

Ped. Willingly.

Juan. Oh, most willingly! (*Aside to* FELIX.) How well
You manag'd it.

Ped. (*aside to* FELIX). 'Tis just as I could wish.

Fel. (*aside*). And just as I, if thereby I shall learn
Whether they love the same; and, if the same,
Whether the one—But come, come! 'tis too late
For wary me to wear love's cap and bells.

Juan. Since we must do your bidding on this score,
We'll e'en make you do ours upon another,
And make you tell us, as you promis'd both,
And *owe* to me—what, when our Queen was landed,
You fine folks of Madrid did in her honour.

Ped. Ay, if you needs will fetter our free time,
Help us at least to pass it by the story

You had begun.

Fel.   Well then, to pick it up
Where Juan left it for us, on the shore.
There, when our Queen was landed, as I hear,
The Countess Medellin, her Chamberlain,
Of the Cordona family, receiv'd her,
And the Lord Admiral on the King's part,
With pomp that needed no excuse of haste,
And such a retinue (for who claims not
To be the kinsman, friend, or follower,
Of such a name?) as I believe Castile
Was almost drain'd to follow in his wake.
Oh, noble house! in whom the chivalry
Of courage, blameless worth, and loyalty,
Is nature's patent of inheritance
From generation to generation!
And so through ringing Spain, town after town,
And every town a triumph, on they pass'd.
Madrid meanwhile—

   Juan.   Stop, stop! They're coming out!
   Ped. Where! Let me see.
   Juan.   The servant only.
   Fel.   Nay,
They'll follow soon.
   Juan.   Till when, on with your story.
   Fel. Madrid then, sharing in the general joy
Of her king's marriage, and with one whose mother
Herself had nurst—though, as you said, half sick
Of hope deferr'd, had, at the loyal call,
That never fails in Spain, drawn to her heart
The life-blood of the realm's nobility
To do her honour; not only when she came,
But, in anticipation of her coming,

With such prelusive pomps, as if you turn
Far up time's stream as history can go,
In hymeneals less august than these,
You shall find practis'd—torchéd troop and masque,
With solemn and preliminary dance,
Epithalamium and sacrifice,
Invoking Hymen's blessing. So Madrid,
Breathing new Christian life in Pagan pomp,
With such epithalamium as all Spain
Rais'd up to Heav'n, into sweet thunder tun'd
Beyond all science by a people's love,
Began her pageant. First, the nightly masque,
So fair as I have never seen the like,
Nor shall again; nor which, unless you draw
On your imagination for the type
Of what I tell, can I depict to you;
When, to the sound of trumpet and recorder,
The chiming poles of Spain and Germany
Beginning, drew the purple mountain down,
Glittering with veins of ore and silver trees,
All flower'd with plumes, and taper-starr'd above,
With monster and volcano breathing fire,
While to and fro torch-bearing maskers ran
Like meteors; all so illuminating night,
That the succeeding sun hid pale in cloud,
And wept with envy, till he dawn'd at length
Upon the famous Amphitheatre,
Which, in its masonry out-doing all
That Rome of a like kind in ruin shows,
This day out-did itself,
In number, rank, and glory of spectators,
Magnificence of retinue, multitude,
Size, beauty, and courage, of the noble beasts

Who came to dye its yellow dust with blood;
As each horn'd hero of the cloven hoof,
Broad-chested, and thick-neckt, and wrinkle-brow'd,
Rush'd roaring in, and tore the ground with 's foot,
As saying, "Lo! this grave is yours or mine!"
While that yet nobler beast, noblest of all,
Who knights the very knighthood that he carries,
Proud in submission to a nobler will,
Spurn'd all his threats, and, touch'd by the light spur,
His rider glittering like a god aloft,
Turn'd onset into death.   Fight follow'd fight,
Till darkness came at last, sending Madrid
Already surfeited with joy, to dream
Of greater, not unanxious that the crown
And centre of the centre of the world
Should not fall short of less renowned cities
In splendour of so great a celebration;
While too the hundreds of a hundred nations,
In wonder or in envy cramm'd her streets;
Until her darling come at last, whose spouse
Shall lay his own two empires at her feet,
And crown her thrice; as Niece, and Spouse, and Queen.
    Juan. A charming story, finisht just in time,
For look!   (*They look out.*)
    Fel.   That is the father, Don Alonso.
    Juan. Indeed!
    Ped. (*aside*).   That's he then! But that strange man
        with him,
Who's he?
    Hern.   Oh, I can tell you that;
His nephew, an Asturian gentleman,
Betroth'd to one of the daughters.
    Juan (*aside*).   Not to mine!

Ped. (aside). Not my Eugenia, or by Heav'n—
But we shall scarcely see them, Felix, here,
Wrapt in their mantles too.

Fel.   And I would pay
My compliment to Don Alonso.

Juan.   Come,
Let us go down with you into the street.
(Aside.) Oh love, that in her memory survive
One thought of me, not dead if scarce alive !

Ped. (aside). Oh, may her bosom whisper her 'tis still
Her eyes that draw me after where they will !   [*Exeunt.*

SCENE II.   *Street between the Houses of* ALONSO *and* FELIX :
ALONSO *and* TORRIBIO *waiting.*

Alon. If you really affect Eugenia, nephew,—*(aside)* as I
wished,—I will communicate with her after church, and if
all be well (as I cannot doubt) get a dispensation forthwith.
But they are coming.

Enter from ALONSO'S *door* CLARA, EUGENIA *in mantles,
the latter with a handkerchief in her hand;* MARI
NUÑO, BRIGIDA, *and* OTAÑEZ *behind; and at the
same time* FELIX, JUAN, *and* PEDRO *opposite.*

Clara. Cover your face, Eugenia.   People in the street.

Eug. Well, I'm not ashamed of it.   *(Aside.)*   Don Pedro !
and Don Juan !

Fel. (whispers). Which is it, Don Juan ?

Juan. She with the handkerchief in her hand.   I'll go
wait for her at the church.   [*Exit.*

Ped. (to JUAN). That is she with the white kerchief in
her hand.   I'll follow them.

Fel. (*aside*). The same, then!

Clara. Eugenia, lend me your handkerchief, it is hot. (*Takes the handkerchief and uncovers her face towards* FELIX.) And let us go, and do not you look behind you.

Fel. And she I most admired.

[*Exeunt* CLARA, EUGENIA, &c., PEDRO *after them.*

Torr. Uncle, what are these fellows hanging about our doors for?

Alon. Nay, 'tis the public street, you know.

Torr. What, my cousins' street?

Alon. To be sure.

Torr. I'll not suffer any one I don't like to hang about it, however, and least of all these perfumery puppies.

Alon. But if they happen to live here, nephew?

Torr. Don't let 'em live here, then.

Alon. But if they own houses?

Torr. They musn't own houses, then.

Fel. Don Alonso, permit me to kiss your hand on your arrival among us. I ought indeed first to have waited upon you in your own house; but this happy chance makes me anticipate etiquette.

Torr. Coxcomb!

Alon. Thank you, sir; had I known you intended me such a favour, I should have anticipated your anticipation by waiting upon you. Give me leave to present to you my nephew, Don Torribio de Cuadadrillos, who will also be proud of your acquaintance.

Torr. No such thing, I shan't at all.

Alon. Nephew, nephew!

Fel. I trust you are well, sir?

Torr. Oh, so, so, thank ye, for the matter of that, neither well nor ill, but mixt-like. (ALONSO *salutes* FELIX *and exit with* TORRIBIO.)

Fel. Now then, I know both face, and dress, and name,
And that my rival friends both love the same;
The same too that myself of the fair pair
Thought yester-eve the fairest of the fair:
Was 't not enough for my two friends that they
Turn enemies—must I too join the fray?
Oh, how at once to reconcile all three,
Those two with one another, and with me!

Re-enter JUAN *hastily.*

Juan. On seeing me, my friend, her colour chang'd:
She loves me still, Don Felix! I am sure
She loves me! Is not the face—we know it is,
The tell-tale index of the heart within?
Oh happiness! at once within your house,
And next my lady's! What is now to do
But catch the ball good fortune throws at us!
You know her father, you will visit him
Of course, and then—and then—what easier?
Draw me in with you, or after you—or perhaps
A letter first—ay, and then afterward—
But why so dumb?
Fel.   I scarce know how to answer.
Juan, you know I am too much your friend
To do you any spite?
Juan.   How could I dream it?

Enter PEDRO *hastily.*

Ped. Oh, Felix, if my love—
Fel. (*aside*).   The other now!
He must be stopt. A moment, gentlemen,
Before you speak, and let me tell you first
A case of conscience you must solve for me.

You both have mighty matters, I doubt not,
To tell me, such as warm young gentlemen
Are never at a loss for in Madrid;
But I may have my difficulties too.
(*Aside.*) The same will serve for both.

Ped. Well, let us hear.

Fel. Suppose some friend of yours, dear as you will,
Loving your neighbour's daughter—(such a case
Will do as well as any)—ask'd of you
To smuggle him, his letters, or himself,
Into that neighbour's house, there secretly
To ply a stolen love; what would you do?

Ped. Do it of course!

Juan.   Why not?

Fel.   Well, I would not.

Ped. But why?

Fel.   Because, however it turn'd out,
I must do ill; if one friend's love succeeded
I had play'd traitor to the other still;
If unsuccessful, not that cost alone,
But also, without counter-profiting,
Him whom I sacrific'd so much to serve.

Ped. If that be your determination,
I have no more to say.   [*Exit.*

Juan.   Nor I: farewell;
I must find other means.   [*Exit.*

Fel.   ·   Of all the plagues,
For one with no love profit of his own
Thus to be pester'd with two lovers' pains!
And yet, what, after all, between the two—
Between the *three*, perhaps, am I to do?
Fore Heav'n, I think 'twill be the only way
To get her to untie who drew the knot; ·

No woman ever at a loss
To mend or mar a matter as she wills.
Yet 'tis an awkward thing to ask a lady,
" Pray, madam, which of these two sighing swains
" Do you like best? or both? or neither, madam?"
Were not a letter best?   But then who take it?
Since to commit her letter, would so far
Commit her honour to another's hands?
By Heav'n, I think I've nothing left to do,—
But ev'n to write it, and to take it too;
A ticklish business—but may fair intent
And prudent conduct lead to good event!   [*Exit.*

SCENE III.   *An Apartment in* DON ALONSO'S *House.—*
Enter CLARA, EUGENIA, MARI NUÑO, *&c.*

Clara. Here, take my mantle, Mari.   Oh, I wish we had
a chaplain of our own in the house, not to go abroad through
the crowded streets!

Eug. And I, that church were a league of crowded street
off, and we obliged to go to it daily.

Mari. I agree with Señora Clara.

Brigida. And I with Señora Eugenia.

Mari. And why, pray?

Brig. Oh, madam, I know who it is deals most in sheep's
eyes.

Enter DON ALONSO.

Alon. (talking to himself as he enters). How lucky he
should have pitcht on the very one I wanted! (*Aloud.*) Oh,
Eugenia, I would speak with you.   Nay, retire not, Clara,
for I want you to pardon me for the very thing Eugenia is
to thank me for.

Clara. A riddle, sir. I pardon you?

Alon. Listen, both of you. Your cousin Don Torribio has declared his love for Eugenia : and though I could have wish'd to marry you, Clara, first, and to the head of our house too, yet my regret at your missing it is almost cancell'd by the joy of your sister's acceptance.

Clara. And so with me, believe me, sir. I am well content to be slighted so long as she is happy : which may she be with my cousin these thousand years to come. (*Aside.*) Oh, providential rejection !   [*Exit.*

Torribio (*peeping in*). Ah ! what a wry face she makes !

Alon. And you, Eugenia, what say you?

Eug. (*aside*). Alas ! surprise on surprise ! (*Aloud.*) Nay, sir, you know, I hope, that I am ever ready to obey you.

Alon. I look'd for nothing else of you.

Torr. Nor I.

Alon. Your cousin is waiting your answer in his chamber. I will tell him the good news, and bring him to you. [*Exit.*

Eug. Only let him come ! Alas !

Torr. (*entering*). How lightly steps a favour'd lover forth! Give you joy, cousin.

Eug. The wretch !

Torr. Being selected by the head of your house.

Eug. Sir, one word, I wouldn't marry you if it should cost me my life.

Torr. Ah, you are witty, cousin, I know.

Eug. Not to you, sir. And now especially, I mean to tell you sober truth, and abide by it, so you had better listen. I tell you once again, and once for all, I wouldn't marry you to save my life !

Torr. Cousin ! After what I 'heard you tell your father ?

Eug. What I said then was out of duty to him ; and what I now say is out of detestation of you.

Torr. I'll go and tell him this, I declare I will.

Eug. Do, and I'll deny it.   But I mean it all the same, and swear it.

Torr. Woman, am I not your cousin?

Eug. Yes.

Torr. And head of the family?

Eug. I dare say.

Torr. An Hidalgo?

Eug. Yes.

Torr. Young?

Eug. Yes.

Torr. Gallant?

Eug. Very.

Torr. And dispos'd to you?

Eug. Very possibly.

Torr. What do you mean then?

Eug. Whatever you choose, so long as you believe I mean what I say.   I'll never marry you.   You might be all you say, and fifty other things beside, but I'll never marry any man without a capacity.

Torr. Capacity! without a Capacity! I who have the family estate, and my ancestors painted in a row on the patent in my saddle-bags ! I who—

Enter ALONSO.

Alon. Well, nephew, here you are at last; I've been hunting every where to tell you the good news.

Torr. And what may that be, pray?

Alon. That your cousin Eugenia cordially accepts your offer, and—

Torr. Oh, indeed, does she so?   I tell you she 's a very odd way of doing it then.   Oh uncle, she has said that to me I wouldn't say to my gelding.

Alon. To you?

Torr. Ay, to me—here—on this very spot—just now.

Alon. But what?

Torr. What? why, that I had no Capacity! But I'll soon settle that; I either have a Capacity or not—If I have, she lies; if not, I desire you to buy me one directly, whatever it may cost.

Alon. What infatuation!

Torr. What, it costs so much, does it? I don't care, I'll not have it thrown in my teeth by her or any woman; and if you won't, I'll go and buy a Capacity, and bring it back with me, let it cost—ay, and weigh—what it will.

[*Exit.*

Alon. Nephew, nephew! Stop him there!

Enter CLARA *and* EUGENIA.

Clara. What is the matter, sir?

Alon. Oh, graceless girl, what have you been saying to your cousin?

Eug. I sir? Nothing.

Alon. Oh! if you deceive me! But I must first stop his running after a Capacity!   [*Exit.*

Eug. What can I have done?

Clara. Nay, attempt not dissimulation with me, who know how you would risk even your advancement for a sarcasm.

Eug. It was all for your sake, if I did, Clara.

Clara. For my sake! oh, indeed, you think I can have no lovers but what you reject? Poor little fool! I could have enough if I chose to lay out for them as some do; but many will pluck at an apple who will retire from a fortress.

Eug. Hark! they are coming back; I dare not face them both as yet.   [*Exit.*

Enter DON FELIX.

Fel. Permit me, madam—

Clara.   Who is this?

Fel.   One, madam,
Who dares to ask one word with you.

Clara.   With me?

Fel. Indeed with you.

Clara.   You cannot, sir, mean me.

Fel. Once more, and once for all, with you indeed;
Let me presume to say so, knowing well
I say so in respect, not in presumption.

Eug. (*peeping*). Why, whom has my staid sister got with
    her?

Clara. With me! My very silence and surprise
Bid you retire at once.

Fel.   Which I will do
When you will let this silence speak to you
With less offence perhaps than could my tongue.

                    (*Offering her a letter.*)

Eug. Oh, if he would but try if fort or apple!

Clara. A letter too!—for me!

Fel.   And, madam, one
It most imports your honour you should read.
For, that being once in question, I make light
That my friends' lives, Don Juan and Don Pedro,
Are in the balance too.

Eug.   Don Juan! Don Pedro!

Clara. What, sir, is this to me, who neither know
Don Juan, nor Don Pedro, nor yourself?

Fel. Having then done my duty to my friends,
And (once again I say 't) to yourself, madam,
Albeit in vain—I'll not offend you more

By my vain presence.   (*Going.*)
 Clara.   Nay, a moment—wait.
I must clear up this mystery. Indeed,
I would not be discourteous or ungrateful :
But ere I thank you for your courtesy,
Know you to whom you do it ?
 Fel.   To Donna Eugenia.
 Clara. Well, sir ?
 Eug.   Oh, the hypocrite !
 Fel.   You are the lady?
 Clara. Enough—give me the letter, and adieu.
 Eug. I can forbear no longer. (*Coming out.*) Sister,
  stop !
Oh ! what to do !—the letter—
 Clara.   Well ?
 Eug.   I tell you
My father and my cousin are coming up,
And if they see—
 Clara. Well, if they see ? what then !
I wish them both to see and hear it all.
(*Calling.*) Sir ! Father ! Cousin ! Otañez !
 Alon. (*within*).   Clara's voice ?
 Fel. What to do now ?
 Eug.   Alas, to tell the truth,
When I but wish'd to lie !
 Clara (*calling*). This way, sir, here !
 Eug. Will you expose us both? In here ! in here !
      [*She hides* FELIX *behind arras.*

Enter ALONSO, TORRIBIO, MARI NUÑO, OTAÑEZ, &*c.*

 Alon. What is the matter ?
 Clara. There is some one in the house, sir. A man—I
saw him stealing along the corridor, towards the garret.

Brigida. It must be a robber.

Alon. A robber?

Mari. What more likely in a rich Indian's house?

Alon. I'll search the house.

Torr. I'll lead the forlorn hope, though that garret were Maestricht itself. Now, cousin, you shall see if I've a Capacity or not. [*Exeunt* ALONSO *and the men.*

Clara. Do you two watch in the passage. (*Exeunt* MARI NUÑO *and* BRIGIDA.) And now, sir, the door is open, give me the letter and begone.

Fel. Adieu, madam, neglect not its advice.

Eug. Alas, alas, she has it!

Fel. She's all too fair! come, honour, come, and shame False love from poaching upon friendship's game! [*Exit.*

Re-enter ALONSO, *&c.*

Alon. We can see nothing of him, daughter.

Clara. Nay, sir, he probably made off when the alarm was given. Take no more trouble.

Alon. Nay, we'll search the whole house.

Torr. What do you say to my Capacity now, cousin?

[*Exeunt* ALONSO, TORRIBIO, *&c.*

Clara. You see, Eugenia, in what your enterprises end. At the first crack, you faint and surrender. I have done all this to show you the difference between talking and doing. And now go; I have got the letter, and want to read it.

Eug. And so do I! but—

Clara. Go! I am mistress now. (*Exit* EUGENIA.) May they not have written to me under cover of her name? let me see. (*Reads.*) "Let not him offend honour by the very means he takes to secure it; at least let his good intention excuse his ill seeming. Don Juan, more than ever enamoured of you, hangs about your doors; Don Pedro follows every

step you take; they are both in my house; it is impossible
but the secret must soon escape both, who must then refer
their rivalry to the sword, and all to the scandal of your
name. You can, by simply disowning both, secure their
lives, your own reputation, and my peace of mind as their
friend and host. Adieu!"
Oh what perplexing thoughts this little letter
Buzzes about my brain, both what it says,
And leaves unsaid!—oh, can it be for me?
And is the quiet nun really belov'd
Under the cover of an idle flirt?
Or is it but for her—the vain, pert thing,
Who thinks her eye slays all it looks upon?
If it be so, and she, not I, is lov'd,
I yet may be reveng'd—
    Eug. (entering).   On whom?
    Clara.   Eugenia!
This letter that has fallen to my hands,
But meant for you—
    Eug.   Oh, I know all about it.
    Clara. Know all about it! know then that two men
Are even now following your steps like dogs
To tear your reputation between them,
And then each other for that worthless sake,
And yet—
    Eug.   A moment, you shall see at once
How easily I shall secure myself,
And them, and supersede your kind intentions.
Signor Don Pedro!   (*Calls at the window.*)
    Clara.   What are you about?
    Eug. Listen and you will hear.
    Clara.   You dare not do it!
    Eug. My father's safely lockt up in his room,

(Thanks to the gout your false alarm has brought,)
My cousin gone to buy capacities,
And now's my time.   (*Calling at the window.*)
                    Don Pedro! Signor Don Pedro!
  Ped. (*coming below to the window*).
He well may wait to have his name thrice call'd
When such a goddess—
    Eug.   Listen, sir, to me.
It is because, I say, *because* this room,   _
Away from father's and duenna's ears,
Allows some harmless speech, it also bars
All nearer access than the ears and eyes
Of father or duenna both could do.
But, seeing harm of harmless trifling come,
I now entreat, implore, command you, sir,
To leave this window and my threshold clear,
Now and for ever!
    Ped.   Hear me—
    Eug.   Pardon me,
I cannot.
    Ped.   But this once—
    Eug.   If you persist
I must be rude.
    Ped.   Oh, how do worse than—
    Eug. (*shutting the blinds down*).   Thus!
  Clara. And to your other gallant?
    Eug.   Why not think
If he were here, I'd do the same to him?
Oh, Clara, be assur'd my levities
Are but the dust on youth's butterfly wing,
Though prudes and sinners too take fright at them;
Like that benighted traveller, you know,
Who, frighted by a shallow brook that jump'd

And bubbled at his right, swerv'd to the left
And tumbled into one that lay quite still,
But deep enough to drown him for his pains.   [*Exit.*
    Clara. What, did she hear what to myself I said?
Or saw my colour change from white to red?
Or only guess'd me waiting for the prey
Her idle chatter ought to fright away?
If chance have done more than all prudence could,
Prudence at least may make occasion good.
And if these lovers by mistake should woo,
Why (by mistake) should I not listen too?
And teach the teacher, to her proper cost,
Those waters are least deep that prattle most.

ACT III.

SCENE I. *Room in* ALONSO'S *House.* CLARA *and* MARI
NUÑO.

    Clara. It is so, indeed.
    Mari. You know you can always rely on my old love to
you. But indeed I cannot but wonder at your sister's
forwardness.
    Clara. Yes; to think of two cavaliers after her at once!
I look upon it as my duty to set all to right; to do this I
must once more speak to him who warned me of it; and I
want you to give him this letter—in *her* name, remember—
this will bring him here to-night, and I shall undeceive him
for ever. But hark! some one—

TORRIBIO *is about to enter.*

    Mari. 'Tis that wretch. Stay, sir, no man comes in here.

Torr. Away, troublesome duenna.

Mari. It's not decent, I tell you.

Torr. An't my cousin decent; and an't I?

Clara. What is the matter?

Torr. This old woman won't let me come in.

Clara. She is right, unless my father be with you.

Torr. Oh, I understand—

Those that are out

Still will pout.

Clara. Well, since she who is in, and may grin, is not
here, you have no business neither.   For me, what grudge
I have against you, be assur'd I can and will repay.   Mari,
remember.   [*Exit.*

Mari. Hark! some one at the door.   [*Exit.*

Torr. By heav'n and earth, I do begin suspect!
I say again I do begin suspect!—
And valour rises with suspicion—
I shall ere long be very terrible.
Ancestors!   Head of house!   Capacity!
For passing through the house—let me not say it,
Till I have told my tongue it lies to say it—
In passing through the passage, what saw I
Within Eugenia's room, behind her bed!
I saw—   (*Re-enter* MARI NUÑO *with a letter.*)

Mari. A letter, madam,—Where is she?

Torr. Woman, she was, but is not.   A letter too?
Give it me.

Mari.   You too!

Torr.   Give it me, or dread
My dreadful vengeance on your wither'd head.

Mari. Leave hold of it.—

Torr.   I'll not!   The more you pull,
The more—

Mari.   Then take that on your empty skull!

> (*Deals him a blow, and calls.*)

Help!   Help!

Torr.   You crying, when two teeth are out—

Mari.   "As   swelling   prologues   of "—Help!   murder!
murder!

Enter EUGENIA, CLARA, ALONSO, BRIGIDA, *&c.*

Alon. What is the matter now?   •

Mari. Don Torribio, sir, because I wouldn't let him have
my young lady's letter, has laid violent hands on me.

Torr. I?

All. Don Torribio!

Torr. I tell you—

Alon. Indeed, nephew, your choleric jealousy carries you
too far.   A respectable female in my house!

Torr. I tell you that it is *me* who—

Alon. I know—enough—make not the matter worse by
worse excuses.   Give me the letter has been the cause of
such unseemly conduct.

Eug. (*aside*).   If it should be from one of them!

Clara (*aside to* EUGENIA). Nothing I hope from your
gallants.

Alon. (*reads*). "My dear nieces, this being the day of the
Queen's public entry, I have engag'd a balcony, and will
send my coach for you directly to come and see it with me."
This, you see, nephew, is all your suspicions amount to!
My cousin, Donna Violante, inviting my daughters to witness
this august ceremony!   If you still suspect; here, take it,
and read it for yourself.

Torr. (*after looking at the letter*).   I tell you what, uncle,
if they wait till I've read it, they'll not see the sight at all.

Alon. Why so?

Torr. Because I can't read.

Alon. That this should be !

Torr. But that's no matter neither.   They can teach me before they go.

Alon. What, when it's to-day ? almost directly ?

Torr. Can't it be put off ?

Alon. 'Tis useless saying more.   Daughters, such a ceremony happens, perhaps, but once in a life ; you must see it.   On with your mantles, whether Don Torribio approve or not.   I am lame, you see, and must keep at home ; to hear about it all from you on your return.

Clara. At your pleasure, sir.

Eug. Shall I stay with you, sir, while Clara—

Alon. No, no.   Both of you go.

Clara (*aside to* MARI, *while putting on her mantle*).   Remember the letter !

Mari. Trust to me.

Eug. (*aside*).   I wonder if they will be there !

[*Exeunt all but* TORRIBIO.

Torr. Whether the Queen enter to-day,

To-morrow, or keep quite away,

Let those go see who have a mind ;

I am resolv'd to stay behind :

And now all gone, and coast quite clear,

Clear up the secret I suspect and fear.   [*Exit.*

SCENE II.   *A Room in* FELIX'S *House.*—FELIX *and* HERNANDO.

Hern. Not going to see the Entry, sir ?

Fel. What use going to a festival if one has no spirits for it ?

Hern. Humph, what makes you out of spirits?

Fel. Why should you ask?

Hern. Nay, then, you have already answer'd me. You are in love.

Fel. I scarce know whether you are right or wrong, Hernando. I have indeed seen a lady whose very beauty forbids all hope of my attaining it.

Hern. How so, sir?

Fel. She who has enslav'd Don Juan and Don Pedro has fetter'd me, at last! I should care little for their rivalry, had not each made me keeper of his love, so that—Hark!

Mari Nuño (within). Don Felix!

Fel. Who is that?

Hern. Some one calling you.

Mari (within). Señor Don Felix!

Fel. Well?

Mari (within). From Donna Eugenia!

[*A letter is thrown in at the window.*

Fel. From Eugenia! (*Reads.*) "Grateful to you for your advice, I have already begun to follow it; but, in order to that, I must see you once again, this evening! Adieu!" Here's a dilemma! For if—

Hern. Don Juan!

Enter JUAN.

Juan (aside).   What was that?

Fel.   Don Juan back,
When such a festival—

Juan.   And you? Oh, Felix,
I know not how to speak or hold my tongue!

Fel. A riddle! How is that?

Juan.   Why, if I speak
I needs must anger you; if not, myself.

Fel. I do not understand it yet.

Juan.   Nor I ;
Yet if you give me leave (as leave they give
To children and to fools to say their mind)
I'll say mine.

Fel.   Surely say it.

Juan.   Tell me then—
That letter I saw flying in at the window
As I came up, what was it?

Fel.   That of all
That you could ask, Juan, I cannot answer—
Must not—relying on our old regard
For fair construction.

Juan.   I believe it, Felix :
Yet seeing that you first excus'd yourself
From helping on my suit, upon the score
Of other obligation ; and that now,
Ev'n now, but a few wretched minutes back,
Eugenia herself, in the public street,
Forbad me from her carriage angrily
From following her more—What can I think
But that she loves another ? when besides,
Coming back suddenly, I hear her name
Whisper'd—oh what so loud as an ill whisper !—
By you, and see a letter too thrown in,
Which on my coming up confus'd you hide,
And will not say from whom—I say, Don Felix,
What can I think?

Fel. (aside).   And I, what can I do?
Who, even if I may excuse myself,
Must needs embroil Don Pedro !

Juan.   Answer me.

Fel. Have I not answer'd you sufficiently,

F.   27

In saying that my old and well-tried love
Should well excuse my silence?

Juan.   I confess
Your love, old and well tried as you profess;
And on that very score ask of you, Felix,
What you would do if one as true and tried
In a like case seal'd up his lips to you?

Fel. Leave them unlockt in fullest confidence.

Juan. Alas! how much, much easier to give
Than follow ev'n the counsel one implores!
Felix, in pity I entreat of you,
Show me that letter!

Fel.   Gladly should you see it
If no one but myself were implicate.

Juan. There *is* then some one else?

Fel.   There is.

Juan.   Who else?

Fel. That's what I cannot tell you.

Juan.   Dare not trust
A friend as true to you as you to him?

Fel. In anything but this.

Juan.   What can this do
But aggravate my worst suspicions?

Fel. I cannot help it.

Juan.   I must tell you then
My friendship for you, Felix, may defer,
But not forego, the reading of that letter.

Fel. I am sorry, sir, your friendship must abide
In ignorance till doomsday.

Juan.   You'll not show it?

Fel. No, never.

Juan.   Follow me, sir.

Fel.   Where you please.

As they are going out, enter PEDRO.

Ped. How now? Don Juan and Felix quarrelling?

Fel. Nay, only walking out.

Ped.   What, walking out,
With hands upon your swords and inflam'd faces?
You shall not go.

Hern.   That's right, sir, keep them back,
They were about—

Fel.   Peace, rascal!

Ped.   Friends may quarrel,
But surely not to such extremity
But that a third may piece the quarrel up
Without the sword. The cause of your dispute?

Fel. I must be silent.

Juan.   And so must not I;
Who will not have it thought
That I forgot my manners as a guest
For any idle reason. You, Don Pedro,
Though lately known to me, are a gentleman,
And you shall hear my story.

Fel.   Not a word,
Or else—

Ped. Nay, Felix—

Juan.   I will speak it out!
Don Pedro, I confided to Don Felix,
My friend and host, the love I long have borne
For one with whom he could advance my suit,
And promis'd so to do it; but instead,
Yea, under the very mask of doing it,
Has urg'd his own; has even now receiv'd
A letter through that ready window thrown,
He dares not show me; and to make all sure,

27—2

I heard him whispering as I came upstairs,
The very name of my Eugenia—
   Ped.   Hold!
This is my quarrel.
He who pretends to love Eugenia
Must answer it to me.
   Juan.   Two rivals, then!
   Fel. Two enemies grown out of two old friends
By the very means I us'd to keep them so!
   Juan. Keep them, indeed!
   Ped.   When with base treachery—
   Juan. Hypocrisy—
   Ped.   Under the name of friend—
   Juan. A pretty friend—
   Ped.   You robb'd me—
   Juan (turning to PEDRO).   You! Dare *you*
Pretend—
   Ped. (to JUAN). Dare *I!* Dare *you,* sir?
   Fel.   Peace, I say,
And hear me speak!
   Juan (to FELIX). The time is past for that.
Follow me, sir.
   Ped.   No, *me.*
   Fel. One, or the other, or together both,
I'll either lead or follow, nothing loath!
                      [*Exeunt wrangling.*

SCENE III.   ALONSO *sitting.—Enter* TORRIBIO.

   Torr. Oh, uncle!
   Alon. Well, what now?
   Torr. Oh, such a thing! I suspected it!
   Alon. Well, tell me.

Torr. Such a thing !

Alon. Speak, man.

Torr. When we were searching the house for the man cousin Clara told us of—

Alon. Well ?

Torr. Passing by cousin Eugenia's room, I saw—I have not breath to say it !

Alon. Speak, sir.

Torr. Those men in the house—those dandies about the door—I know how they get in now—when I found in my cousin's room—behind her very bed—

Alon. Don Torribio !

Torr. The very ladder they climb up by !

Alon. A ladder ?

Torr. Ah, and a very strong one too, all of iron and cord.

Alon. If this were true—

Torr. Wait till I show it you, then.   [*Exit.*

Alon. Not in vain did Mari Nuño warn me of her dangerous disposition ! If he have such a proof of her incontinence how will he marry her ?

Re-enter TORRIBIO *with a fardingale.*

Torr. There, uncle, there it is, hoops, and steps, and all !

Alon. This a ladder ?

Torr. Ah, that, if it were all let out, would scale the tower of Babel, I believe.

Alon. I can scarce control my rage. Fool! this is a fardingale, not a ladder.

Torr. A what-ingale ?

Alon. A fardingale, fool !*

* "A hoop of whalebone, used to spread out the petticoat to a wide circumference;"—Johnson; who one almost wonders did not spread

Torr. Why, that's worse than the ladder !

Alon. You will fairly drive me out of my senses ! Go, sir, directly, and put it back where you took it from, and for Heaven's sake, no more of such folly !   [*Exit.*

Torr. Well—to think of this ! and my cousin that look'd so nice too !

Voices (within). Coach there ! coach !

Enter MARI NUÑO.

Mari. They are come back. I must get lights. Who's this ?

Torr. Nobody.

Mari. What are you doing with that fardingale ; and where did you get it ?

Torr. Nothing, and nowhere.

Mari. Come, give it me at once, lest I give you the fellow of the cuff I gave you before.

Torr. For fear of which, take that upon your wrinkled chaps. (*Strikes her, and calls out.*) Help ! help ! Murder ! murder ! Help !

out into a wider circumference of definition about the "*poore verdingales*," that (according to Heywood)

————"must lie in the streete,
To have them no doore in the citye made meete."

The Spanish name is "guarda infanta," which puzzles Don Torribio, as to what his cousin had to do with infants. Our word was first (as Heywood writes) *verdingale:* which, as Johnson tells us, "much exercised the etymology of Skinner, who at last seems to determine that it is derived from *vertu garde.*" This, however, Johnson thinks does not at all get to the bottom of the etymology, which may, he says, be found in Dutch. Perhaps the old French *petenlair* was of the same kindred.

Enter ALONSO, CLARA, EUGENIA, *&c. in mantles.*

Alon. What now?

Torr. Mari Nuño there, only because I wish'd her good night, laid violent hands on me.

Mari. Oh the wretch! he wanted to make love to me—and worse—declaring he would none of any who used such a thing as this.   (*Showing fardingale.*)

Alon. Let us hear no more of such folly. There is some· thing else to-day to tell of.   Well, (*to his daughters,*) you have seen this procession?

Eug. Ay, sir; the greatest sight, I believe, that Spain has seen since she was greatest of nations.

Alon. I, who could not go myself, am to see it, you know, in your recital.

Eug. As best we can, sir.

Clara (*aside to* MARI NUÑO). Have you seen Don Felix?

Mari (*aside*). Enough, he will be here.   But when?

Clara. When the story is done, and all weary are gone to bed.

Mari. Good.   [*Exit; the rest sit down.*

Clara. Begin you then, Eugenia, I will chime in.

Eug. This being the long-expected day
When our fair Spain and fairest Mariana
Should quicken longing hope to perfect joy,
Madrid awoke, and dress'd her squares and streets
In all their glory; through all which we pass'd
Up to the Prado, where the city's self,
In white and pearl array'd, by ancient usage,
Waited in person to receive the bride
By a triumphal arch that rose heaven-high,
The first of four all nam'd and hung about
With emblems of the four parts of the world,

(Each with a separate element distinct,)
Of which our sovereign lord was now to.lay
The four crowns at his sovereign lady's feet.
    Clara. And this first arch was Europe; typified
By the wide Air, which temperatest she breathes,
And which again, for double cognizance,
Wore the imperial eagle for its crest;
With many another airy symbol more,
And living statues supplementary
Of Leon and Castile, each with its crown,
Austria, the cradle of the royal bride,
And Rome, the mistress of the faith of all.
    Eug. Here then, when done the customary rite
Of kissing hands and due obeisance,
Drum, trumpet, and artillery thundering,
With that yet lordliest salute of all,
A people's universal acclamation ;
(And never in the world were subjects yet
So proud, and bow'd, and with so good a cause ;)
Under a golden canopy she mov'd
Tow'rd San Geronimo, whose second arch,
Of no less altitude and magnificence,
Deck't with the sixty crowns of Asia,
Receiv'd her next, wearing for cognizance
Earth, of which Asia is the largest piece :
Which Earth again carried a lion's mane,
As proclamation of her noblest growth.
    Clara. Thence passing on, came to where Africa,
Her waste of arid desert embleming
By Fire, whose incarnation, the Sun,
Burn'd on this arch as in his house in heaven,
Bore record of the trophies two great Queens
Upon the torrid continent had won,

Who, one with holy policy at home,
The other in Granada by the sword,
Extirpated deadly Mahometism.

Eug. Last, to the Holy Virgin dedicate,
From whose cathedral by the holy choir
Chaunted Te Deum, rose in splendid arch
America, wearing for her device
The silver image of the Ocean,
That roll'd the holy cross to the New World.
And so all pass'd to the Escurial,
In front of which, in two triumphal cars,
Two living statues were—one Mercury,
Who, as divine ambassador, thus far
Had brought the royal bride propitiously ;
The other, Hymen, who took up the charge
Mercury left, and with unquenching torch,
While cannon, trumpet, choir, and people's voice
Thunder'd her praises, took the palfrey's rein,
Who gloried in the beauty that he bore,
And brought and left her at her palace door.

Alon. Well done, well done, both of you, in whose lively
antiphony I have seen it all as well as if I had been there.

Torr. Well, for my part I neither wanted to see it nor
hear of it.

Alon. No? why so, nephew?

Torr. Lord, I've seen twice as good as that down in my
country many a time, all the boys and girls dancing, and the
mayor, and the priest, and—

Alon. Peace, peace. Come, Brigida, light me to my
room, I am sleepy.

Eug. And I; with sight-seeing, and sight-telling, I suppose.
(*Aside.*) And with a heavy heart, alas !

[*Exeunt* ALONSO, EUGENIA, *and* BRIGIDA.

Clara. Will not you to bed too, sir?

Torr. Not till I've had my supper, I promise you. Oh, I don't care for all your sour looks, not I, nor your threats of revenge neither.

Clara. You don't?

Torr. No, I defy you.

Clara. Not if I were to prove to you that she you slighted me for loves another?

Torr. Oh, cousin Clara!

Clara. Shall I prove it to you?

Torr. Oh, if my ancestors could hear this, what would they say?

Clara. I don't know. But you may hear if you like what she says to your rival.

Torr. Ha!

Clara. Go into this balcony, and you will hear her talking to him in the street.

Torr. I knew! I guess'd! the ladder!

(*He goes into the balcony and she shuts him in.*)

Clara. There cool yourself in the night till I let you out. And now to have *you* safe too. (*Locks* EUGENIA'S *door.*) And now, all safe, for the first time in my life Love and I meet in fair field. Mari Nuño! (*Enter* MARI.) Where is the Cavalier?

Mari. Waiting in my chamber.

Clara. Bring him. You understand it is all for Eugenia's good?

Mari. I understand.   [*Exit, and returns with* FELIX.

Fel. I fly, madam, to your feet. (*Kneels.*)

Clara. Rise, sir, 'tis about your letter I sent to you.

Fel. Alas, madam, all is worse than ever!

Clara. What has happened?

Fel. Not only did my two friends fall out with each other, as I expected, but with me for the very good services I was doing them; insulted me till I could withhold my sword no longer; we went out to fight; were seen, pursued, and disperst by the alguazils. I return'd home to await them, but as yet know nothing more of them.

Clara. Alas, sir, what do I not owe you for your care on my behalf?

Fel. More perhaps than you imagine.

Clara. Tell me all at least, that I may at-least know my debt, if unable to repay it.

Fel. Alas, I dare not say what is said in not saying.

Clara. Said, and not said? I do not understand.

Fel. I, alas, too well!

Clara. Explain to me then, sir.

Fel. No, madam. If what I feel is so much on my friends' account, it is still more for their sakes that I keep it unsaid.

Clara. Hark! what noise is that? Mari Nuño, what is the matter?

Enter MARI NUÑO.

Mari. Oh, madam, some one is getting over the garden wall! Your father has heard the noise; and is got up with his sword.

Clara. If he should find you!

Fel. He need not. This balcony—

Clara. No, no!

Torribio (within). Thieves! Murder! Help!

(*He opens the balcony;* TORRIBIO *falls forward on him, push'd in by* JUAN *with his sword drawn.*)

Torr. Murder! Murder!   ⎫

Juan (to FELIX*).* Thou too here, traitor!   ⎬ *All at once.*

Fel. (drawing his sword). Who are these?   ⎭

(*Confusion,* *in which enter* ALONSO *with drawn sword,*
OTAÑEZ, BRIGIDA, *&c.*)

Alon. Two! Torribio, to my side!
Fel. Wait! wait! Let me explain.
Alon. Don Felix!
Fel. Listen to me, all of you, I say! I was sent for to
prevent, not to do, mischief, by Donna Eugenia herself—

Enter EUGENIA.

Eug. By *me,* sir!
Clara. Hold, hold, Eugenia!
Eug. I will *not* hold when my name is in question without
my— Sent for by me, sir!
Fel. Not by you, madam; by Donna Eugenia, (*pointing
to* CLARA) to prevent—
Alon. and Eug. Clara!
Torr. Ah, 'twas she put me to freeze in the balcony, too.
Clara (*to* FELIX). Sir, you come here to save another
from peril. Leave me not in it.
Fel. I leave you, madam, who would lay down my life for
you! and all the rather if you are *not* Donna Eugenia.
Alon. None but her father or her husband must do that.
Fel. Then let me claim to do it as the latter. (*Kneels to*
CLARA.)
Alon. But Clara?
Clara. Sir, I am ready to obey my father—and my
husband.
Eug. And I, sir. And to prove my duty, let me marry
my cousin at once, and retire with him to the mountains.
Torr. Marry me! No, indeed! No Capacities, and
ladders, and—what-d'ye-call-'ems—for me. I'll e'en go

back as I came, with my ancestors safe in my saddle-bags,
I will.

Juan (*to* ALONSO). Permit me, sir.   I am Don Juan de
Mendoza; a name at least not unknown to you.   I have
loved your daughter long; and might have had perchance
favourable acceptation from her mother long ago, had not
you yourself been abroad at the time.

Alon. I now remember to have heard something of the
kind.   What say you, Eugenia ?

Eug. I am ready to obey my father—and my husband.
With which at last our comedy shall close,
Asking indulgence both of friends and foes.

Clara. And ere we part our text for envoy give,—
Beware of all smooth waters while you live !

This Comedy seems an Occasional Piece, to celebrate the marriage
of Philip IV. with Anna Maria of Austria, and the pageants that
Calderon himself was summoned to devise and manage.   This marriage
was in 1649; when Calderon, as old as the century, was in his prime ;
and I think the airy lightness of the dialogue, the play of character, the
easy intrigue, and the happily introduced wedding rhapsodies, make it
one of the most agreeable of his comedies.

As I purposely reduced the swell of Isabel's speech in the last play,
I must confess that the present version of these wedding pageants,
though not unauthorized by the original, had perhaps better have been
taken in a lighter tone to chime in with so much common dialogue.
But they were done first, to see what could be made of them : and, as
little dramatic interest is concerned, are left as they were; at least not
the less like so much in Calderon, where love and loyalty are concerned ;
and to be excused by the reader as speeches *spouted* by boys on holiday
occasions.

A BIRD'S-EYE VIEW

OF

FARÍD-UDDÍN ATTAR'S

BIRD-PARLIAMENT.

I am indebted to the kindness of Professor Cowell for the following account of this translation. W. A. W. .

Fitzgerald was first interested in 'Attar's Manṭiḳ-uṭ-ṭair' by the extracts given in De Sacy's notes to his edition of that poet's Pand-nâmah, and in 1856 he began to read the original in a MS. lent to him by Mr Newton of Hertford. In 1857 Garcin de Tassy published his edition of the Persian text, of which he had previously given an analysis in his "La poésie philosophique et religieuse chez les Persans"; and Fitzgerald at once threw himself into the study of it with all his characteristic enthusiasm. De Tassy subsequently published in 1863 a French prose translation of the poem; but the previous analysis was, I believe, Fitzgerald's only help in mastering the difficulties of the original. He often wrote to me in India, describing the pleasure he found in his new discovery, and he used to mention how the more striking apologues were gradually shaping themselves into verse, as he thought them over in his lonely walks. At last, in 1862, he sent me the following translation, intending at first to offer it for publication in the Journal of the Bengal Asiatic Society; but he soon felt that it was too free a version for the pages of a scientific journal. He then talked of publishing it by itself, but the project never assumed a definite shape, though I often urged him to print the 'Bird-Parliament' as a sequel to the 'Salâmân'.

BIRD-PARLIAMENT.

Once on a time from all the Circles seven
Between the stedfast Earth and rolling Heaven
The Birds, of all Note, Plumage, and Degree,
That float in Air, and roost upon the Tree;
And they that from the Waters snatch their Meat,
And they that scour the Desert with long Feet:
Birds of all Natures, known or not to Man,
Flock'd from all Quarters into full Divan,
. On no less solemn business than to find
Or choose, a Sultan Khalif of their kind,
For whom, if never their's, or lost, they pined. }
The Snake had his, 'twas said; and so the Beast
His Lion-lord: and Man had his, at least:
And that the Birds, who nearest were the Skies,
And went apparell'd in its Angel Dyes,
Should be without—under no better Law
Than that which lost all other in the Maw—
Disperst without a Bond of Union—nay,
Or meeting to make each the other's Prey—

F.   28

This was the Grievance—this the solemn Thing
On which the scatter'd Commonwealth of Wing,
From all the four Winds, flying like to Cloud
That met and blacken'd Heav'n, and Thunder-loud
With Sound of whirring Wings and Beaks that clash'd
Down like a Torrent on the Desert dash'd :
Till by Degrees, the Hubbub and Pell-mell
Into some Order and Precedence fell,
And, Proclamation made of Silence, each
In special Accent, but in general Speech
That all should understand, as seem'd him best,
The Congregation of all Wings addrest.

And first, with Heart so full as from his Eyes
Ran weeping, up rose Tajidar* the Wise ;
The mystic Mark upon whose Bosom show'd
That He alone of all the Birds THE ROAD
Had travell'd : and the Crown upon his Head
Had reach'd the Goal ; and He stood forth and said.

"Oh Birds, by what Authority divine
I speak you know by *His* authentic Sign,
And Name, emblazon'd on my Breast and Bill :
Whose Counsel I assist at, and fulfil :
At His Behest I measured as he plann'd
The Spaces of the Air and Sea and Land ;
I gauged the secret sources of the Springs
From Cloud to Fish† : the Shadow of my Wings

---

* *Tájidár—"Crown-wearer"*—one Epithet of the *"Hudhud"*, a
beautiful kind of Lapwing, Niebuhr says, frequenting the Shores of
the Persian Gulf, and supposed to have the Gift of Speech &c.

† From Máh, the Moon, to Máhi, the Fish, on which the World
was fabled to repose. As Attair says in the Introduction : "God has

Dream'd over sleeping Deluge: piloted
The Blast* that bore Sulayman's Throne: and led
The Cloud of Birds that canopied his Head;
Whose Word I brought to Balkis†: and I shared
The Counsel that with Asaf he prepared.
And now *you* want a Khalif: and I know
Him, and his whereabout, and How to go:
And go alone I could, and plead your cause
Alone for all: but, by the eternal laws,
Yourselves by Toil and Travel of your own
Must for your old Delinquency atone.
Were you indeed not blinded by the Curse
Of Self-exile, that still grows worse and worse,
Yourselves would know that, though *you* see him not,
He *is* with you this Moment, on this Spot,
Your Lord through all Forgetfulness and Crime,
Here, There, and Everywhere, and through all Time.
But as a Father, whom some wayward Child
By sinful Self-will has unreconciled,
Waits till the sullen Reprobate at cost
Of long Repentance should regain the Lost;
Therefore, yourselves to see as you are seen,
Yourselves must bridge the Gulf you made between
By such a Search and Travel to be gone
Up to the mighty mountain Káf, whereon
Hinges the World, and round about whose Knees
Into one Ocean mingle the Sev'n Seas;

placed the Earth on the back of the Bull: and the Bull on the Fish;
but the Fish on what? On Nothing; but nothing comes of Nothing,
and therefore all this is Nothing," or, as the Sufi expounds himself in
the Poem, all the visible and material Universe merges into an Abstract
Essence of Deity.

   * The East Wind.
   † *Balkis* is Queen of Sheba; *Asaf*, Solomon's Vizier.

In whose impenetrable Forest-folds
Of Light and Dark "Symurgh"* his Presence holds;
Not to be reach'd, if to be reach'd at all
But by a Road the stoutest might apal;
Of Travel not of Days or Months, but Years—
Life-long perhaps: of Dangers, Doubts, and Fears
As yet unheard of: Sweat of Blood and Brain
Interminable—often all in vain—
And, if successful, no Return again:
A Road whose very Preparation scared
The Traveller who yet must be prepared.
Who then this Travel to Result would bring
Needs both a Lion's Heart beneath the Wing,
And even more, a Spirit purified
Of Worldly Passion, Malice, Lust, and Pride:
Yea, ev'n of Worldly *Wisdom*, which grows dim
And dark, the nearer it approaches *Him*,
Who to the Spirit's Eye alone reveal'd,
By sacrifice of Wisdom's self unseal'd;
Without which none who reach the Place could bear
To look upon the Glory dwelling there."

One Night from out the swarming City Gate
Stept holy Bajazyd, to meditate
Alone amid the breathing Fields that lay
In solitary Silence leagues away,
Beneath a Moon and Stars as bright as Day.
And the Saint wondering such a Temple were,
And so lit up, and scarce one worshipper,
A voice from Heav'n amid the stillness said;
"The Royal Road is not for all to tread,

* Sýmurgh—i.e. "Thirty-Birds"—a fabulous Creature like the Griffin
of our Middle Ages: the Arabian *Anka.*

Nor is the Royal Palace for the Rout,
Who, even if they reach it, are shut out.
The Blaze that from my Harím window breaks
With fright the Rabble of the Roadside takes;
And ev'n of those that at my Portal din,
Thousands may knock for one that enters in."

Thus spoke the Tajidar: and the wing'd Crowd,
That underneath his Word in Silence bow'd,
Clapp'd Acclamation: and their Hearts and Eyes
Were kindled by the Firebrand of the Wise.
They felt their Degradation: they believed
The word that told them how to be retrieved,
And in that glorious Consummation won
Forgot the Cost at which it must be done.
"They only *long'd* to follow: they would go
Whither he led, through Flood, or Fire, or Snow "--
So cried the Multitude. But some there were
Who listen'd with a cold disdainful air,
Content with what they were, or grudging Cost
Of Time or Travel that might all be lost;
These, one by one, came forward, and preferr'd
Unwise Objection: which the wiser Word
Shot with direct Reproof, or subtly round
With Argument and Allegory wound.

The Pheasant first would know by what pretence
The Tajidar to that pre-eminence
Was raised—a Bird, but for his lofty Crest
(And such the Pheasant had) like all the Rest—

Who answer'd—"By no Virtue of my own
Sulayman chose me, but by *His* alone:

Not by the Gold and Silver of my Sighs
Made mine, but the free Largess of his Eyes.
Behold the Grace of Allah comes and goes
As to Itself is good : and no one knows
Which way it turns : in that mysterious Court
Not he most finds who furthest travels for't.
For one may crawl upon his knees Life-long,
And yet may never reach, or all go wrong :
Another just arriving at the Place
He toil'd for, and—the Door shut in his Face :
Whereas Another, scarcely gone a Stride,
And suddenly—Behold he is Inside !—
But though the Runner win not, he that *stands*,
No Thorn will turn to Roses in *his* Hands :
Each one must do his best and all endure,
And all endeavour, hoping but not sure.
Heav'n its own Umpire is ; its Bidding do,
And Thou perchance shalt be Sulayman's too."

One day Shah Mahmúd, riding with the Wind
A-hunting, left his Retinue behind,
And coming to a River, whose swift Course
Doubled back Game and Dog, and Man and Horse,
Beheld upon the Shore a little Lad
A-fishing, very poor, and Tatter-clad
He was, and weeping as his Heart would break.
So the Great Sultan, for good humour's sake
Pull'd in his Horse a moment, and drew nigh,
And after making his Salám, ask'd why
He wept—weeping, the Sultan said, so sore
As he had never seen one weep before.
The Boy look'd up, and "Oh Amír," he said,
"Sev'n of us are at home, and Father dead,
And Mother left with scarce a Bit of Bread :

And now since Sunrise have I fish'd—and see!
Caught nothing for our Supper—Woe is Me!"
The Sultan lighted from his Horse. "Behold,"
Said he, "Good Fortune will not be controll'd :
And, since To-day yours seems to turn from you,
Suppose we try for once what mine will do,
And we will share alike in all I win."
So the Shah took, and flung his Fortune in,
The Net; which, cast by the Great Mahmúd's Hand,
A hundred glittering Fishes brought to Land.
The Lad look'd up in Wonder—Mahmúd smiled
And vaulted into Saddle. But the Child
Ran after—"Nay, Amír, but half the Haul
Is yours by Bargain"—"Nay, To-day take all,"
The Sultan cried, and shook his Bridle free—
"But mind—To-morrow All belongs to Me—"
And so rode off. Next morning at Divan
The Sultan's Mind upon his Bargain ran,
And being somewhat in a mind for sport
Sent for the Lad: who, carried up to Court,
And marching into Royalty's full Blaze
With such a Catch of Fish as yesterday's,
The Sultan call'd and set him by his side,
And asking him, "What Luck?" The Boy replied,
" *This* is the Luck that follows every Cast,
Since o'er my Net the Sultan's Shadow pass'd."

Then came *The Nightingale*, from such a Draught
Of Ecstasy that from the Rose he quaff'd
Reeling as drunk, and ever did distil
In exquisite Divisions from his Bill
To inflame the Hearts of Men—and thus sang He—
"To me alone, alone, is giv'n the Key

Of Love ; of whose whole Mystery possesst,
When I reveal a little to the Rest,
Forthwith Creation listening forsakes
The Reins of Reason, and my Frenzy takes :
Yea, whosoever once has quaff'd this wine
He leaves unlisten'd David's Song for mine.
In vain do Men for my Divisions strive,
And die themselves making dead Lutes alive :
I hang the Stars with Meshes for Men's Souls :
The Garden underneath my Music rolls.
The long, long Morns that mourn the Rose away
I sit in silence, and on Anguish prey :
But the first Air which the New Year shall breathe
Up to my Boughs of Message from beneath
That in her green Harím my Bride unveils,
My Throat bursts silence and *her* Advent hails,
Who in her crimson Volume registers
The Notes of Him whose Life is lost in hers*.
The Rose I love and worship now is here ;
If dying, yet reviving, Year by Year ;
But that you tell of, all my Life why waste
In vainly searching ; or, if found, not taste?"

So with Division infinite and Trill
On would the Nightingale have warbled still,
And all the World have listen'd ; but a Note
Of sterner Import check'd the love-sick Throat.

"Oh watering with thy melodious Tears
Love's Garden, and who dost indeed the Ears

* It was sometimes fancied that the Rose had as many Petals as
her Lover had Notes in his Voice.

Of men with thy melodious Fingers mould
As David's Finger Iron did of old*:
Why not, like David, dedicate thy Dower
Of Song to something better than a Flower?
Empress indeed of Beauty, so they say,
But one whose Empire hardly lasts a Day,
By Insurrection of the Morning's Breath
That made her hurried to Decay and Death:
And while she lasts contented to be seen,
And worshipt, for the Garden's only Queen,
Leaving thee singing on thy Bough forlorn,
Or if she smile on Thee, perhaps in Scorn."

Like that fond Dervish waiting in the throng
When some World-famous Beauty went along,
Who smiling on the Antic as she pass'd—
Forthwith Staff, Bead and Scrip away he cast,
And grovelling in the Kennel, took to whine
Before her Door among the Dogs and Swine.
Which when she often went unheeding by,
But one day quite as heedless ask'd him—"Why?"—
He told of that one Smile, which, all the Rest
Passing, had kindled Hope within his Breast—
Again she smiled and said, "Oh self-beguiled
Poor Wretch, *at* whom and not *on* whom I smiled."

Then came the subtle *Parrot* in a coat
Greener than Greensward, and about his Throat

* The Prophet David was supposed, in Oriental Legend, to have
had the power to mould Iron into a Cuirass with the miraculous Power
of his Finger.

A Collar ran of sub-sulphureous Gold ;
And in his Beak a Sugar-plum he troll'd,
That all his Words with luscious Lisping ran,
And to this Tune—"Oh cruel Cage, and Man
More iron still who did confine me there,
Who else with him* whose Livery I wear
Ere this to his Eternal Fount had been,
And drunk what should have kept me ever-green.
But now I know the Place, and I am free
To go, and all the Wise will follŏw Me.
Some"—and upon the Nightingale one Eye
He leer'd—"for nothing but the Blossom sigh :
But I am for the luscious Pulp that grows
Where, and for which the Blossom only blows :
And which so long as the Green Tree provides
What better grows along Káf's dreary Sides?
And what more needful Prophet *there* than He
Who gives me Life to nip it from the Tree?"

To whom the Tajidar—"Oh thou whose Best
In the green leaf of Paradise is drest,
But whose Neck kindles with a lower Fire—
Oh slip the collar off of base Desire,
And stand apparell'd in Heav'n's Woof entire†!

* Khizar, Prophet and Keeper of the Well of Life; habited always
in the Green which the Angels were supposed to wear; and, whether
from that reason, or some peculiar Phenomenon in the Air, constantly
called Sky-colour by the Persian Poets.

† The Sky is constantly called *Green* in Persian Poetry: whether
because of the Tree of Heaven *Sidra*: or of some fabled Emerald in
Káf on which the World hinges: or because Green has been chosen
(for whatever Reason) for the Colour of *Life* and Honour. The green
tinge of some Oriental Skies is indeed noticed by Travellers: as we see
a little also in our Northern Sunrise and Sunset: but still it must be an

This Life that hangs so sweet about your Lips
But, spite of all your Khizar, slips and slips,
What is it but itself the coarser Rind
Of the True Life withinside and behind,
Which he shall never never reach unto
Till the gross Shell of Carcase he break through?"

For what said He, that dying Hermit, whom
Your Prophet came to, trailing through the Gloom
His Emerald Vest, and tempted—"Come with Me,
And Live." The Hermit answered—"Not with Thee.
Two Worlds there are, and *This* was thy Design,
And thou hast got it; but *The Next* is mine;
Whose Fount is *this* life's Death, and to whose Side
Ev'n now I find my Way without a Guide."

Then like a Sultan glittering in all Rays
Of Jewelry, and deckt with his own Blaze,
The glorious *Peacock* swept into the Ring:
And, turning slowly that the glorious Thing
Might fill all Eyes with wonder, thus said He.
"Behold, the Secret Artist, making me,
With no one Colour of the skies bedeckt,
But from its Angel's Feathers did select
To make up mine withal, the Gabriel
Of all the Birds: though from my Place I fell
In Eden, when Acquaintance I did make
In those blest Days with that Sev'n-headed Snake*,

exceptional Phenomenon. *Blue*, or *Purple*, is rather devoted to Death
and Mourning in the East. As, in this very Poem, one of the Stories
is of the Sea being askt "why he dresses his Waves in Blue?"—And he
answers he does so for the Loss of *One* who never will return.

  * And, as the Tradition went, let the Snake into Eden.

And thence with him, my perfect Beauty marr'd
With these ill Feet, was thrust out and debarr'd.
Little I care for Worldly Fruit or Flower,
Would you restore me to lost Eden's Bower,
But first my Beauty making all complete
With reparation of these ugly Feet."

"Were it," 'twas answer'd, "only to return
To that lost Eden, better far to burn
In Self-abasement up thy pluméd Pride,
And ev'n with lamer feet to creep inside—
But all mistaken you and all like you
That long for that lost Eden as the true;
Fair as it was, still nothing but the Shade
And Out-court of the Majesty that made.
That which I point you tow'rd, and which the King
I tell you of broods over with his Wing,
With no deciduous leaf, but with the Rose
Of Spiritual Beauty, smells and glows:
No plot of Earthly Pleasance, but the whole
True Garden of the Universal Soul."

For so Creation's Master-Jewel fell
From that same Eden: loving which too well,
The Work before the Artist did prefer,
And in the Garden lost the Gardener.
Wherefore one Day about the Garden went
A voice that found him in his false Content,
And like a bitter Sarsar of the North*
Shrivell'd the Garden up, and drove him forth

* Sarsar—a cold Blast.

Into the Wilderness: and so the Eye
Of Eden closed on him till by and by.

—————

Then from a Ruin where conceal'd he lay
Watching his buried Gold, and hating Day,
Hooted *The Owl.*—"I tell you, my Delight
Is in the Ruin and the Dead of Night
Where I was born, and where I love to wone
All my Life long, sitting on some cold stone
Away from all your roystering Companies,
In some dark Corner where a Treasure lies;
That, buried by some Miser in the Dark,
Speaks up to me at Midnight like a Spark;
And o'er it like a Talisman I brood,
Companion of the Serpent and the Toad.
What need of other Sovereign, having found,
And keeping as in Prison underground,
One before whom all other Kings bow down,
And with his glittering Heel their Foreheads crown?"

"He that a Miser lives and Miser dies,
At the Last Day what Figure shall he rise?"

—————

A Fellow all his life lived hoarding Gold,
And, dying, hoarded left it. And behold,
One Night his Son saw peering through the House
A Man, with yet the semblance of a Mouse,
Watching a crevice in the Wall—and cried—
"My Father?"—"Yes," the *Mu*sulman replied,
"Thy Father!"—"But why watching thus?"—"For fear
Lest any smell my Treasure buried here."

"But wherefore, Sir, so metamousified?"   ⎫
"Because, my Son, such is the true outside   ⎬
Of the inner Soul by which I lived and died." ⎭

"Aye," said *The Partridge*, with his Foot and Bill
Crimson with raking Rubies from the Hill,
And clattering his Spurs—"Wherewith the Ground
"I stab," said he, "for Rubies, that, when found
I swallow; which, as soon as swallow'd, turn
To Sparks which through my beak and eyes do burn.
Gold, as you say, is but dull Metal dead,
And hanging on the Hoarder's Soul like Lead :
But Rubies that have Blood within, and grown
And nourisht in the Mountain Heart of Stone,
Burn with an inward Light, which they inspire,
And make their Owners Lords of their Desire*."

To whom the Tajidar—"As idly sold
To the quick Pebble as the drowsy Gold,
As dead when sleeping in their mountain mine
As dangerous to Him who makes them shine :
Slavish indeed to do their Lord's Commands,
And slave-like, aptest to escape his Hands,
And serve a second Master like the first†,
And working all their wonders for the worst."

Never was Jewel after or before
Like that Sulayman for a Signet wore :

* Every Jewel had its special Charm, and so was worn in Ring or
Amulet.

† There is a Story of some one who falling from a Roof, and
wondering what his Turquoise had done for him, was answered, "Well
—you see it has kept itself unbroken."

Whereby one Ruby, weighing scarce a grain
Did Sea and Land and all therein constrain,
Yea, ev'n the Winds of Heav'n—made the fierce East
Bear his League-wide Pavilion like a Beast,
Whither he would: yea, the Good Angel held
His subject, and the lower Fiend compell'd.
Till, looking round about him in his pride,
He overtax'd the Fountain that supplied,
Praying that after him no Son of Clay
Should ever touch his Glory. And one Day
Almighty God his Jewel stole away,
And gave it to the Div, who with the Ring
Wore also the Resemblance of the King,
And so for forty days play'd such a Game
As blots Sulayman's forty years with Shame.

Then *The Shah-Falcon*, tossing up his Head
Blink-"hooded as it was—"Behold," he said,
"I am the chosen Comrade of the King,
And perch upon the Fist that wears the Ring;
Born, bred, and nourisht, in the Royal Court,
I take the Royal Name and make the Sport.
And if strict Discipline I undergo
And half my Life am blinded—be it so;
Because the Shah's Companion ill may brook
On aught save Royal Company to look.
And why am I to leave my King, and fare
With all these Rabble Wings I know not where?"—

"Oh blind indeed"—the Answer was, "and dark
To any but a vulgar Mortal Mark,
And drunk with Pride of Vassalage to those
Whose Humour like their Kingdom comes and goes;

All Mutability: who one Day please
To give: and next Day what they gave not seize:
Like to the Fire: a dangerous Friend at best,
Which who keeps farthest from does wiseliest."

A certain Shah there was in Days foregone
Who had a lovely Slave he doated on,
And cherish'd as the Apple of his Eye,   ⎫
Clad gloriously, fed sumptuously, set high,   ⎬
And never was at Ease were *He,* not by,   ⎭
Who yet, for all this Sunshine, Day by Day
Was seen to wither like a Flower away.
Which, when observing, one without the Veil
Of Favour ask'd the Favourite—"Why so pale
And sad?" thus sadly answer'd the poor Thing—
"No Sun that rises sets until the King,
Whose Archery is famous among Men,
Aims at an Apple on my Head*; and when
The stricken Apple splits, and those who stand
Around cry 'Lo! the Shah's unerring Hand!'
Then He too laughing asks me 'Why so pale
And sorrow-some? as could the Sultan fail,

---

* Tell's Apple, long before his Time: and, by whomsoever invented, a Fancy which (as was likely) would take lasting hold of the Oriental Mind. In Chodzko's *Popular Persian Songs* (Oriental Translation Fund, 1842) is a sort of Funeral Chaunt on Zulfakhar Khan by one of his Slaves; and the following Passage in it: "Your Gun from the Manufactory of Loristan shines like a Cloud gilded by the Rays of the Sun. Oh Serdar! your Place is now empty: you were my Master: Your Gun from the Manufactory of Cabúl shined in your Hands like a Bunch of Roses. Your Ball never missed a Flower put in the middle of my Front Hair."

Who such a master of the Bow confest,
And aiming by the Head that he loves best.'"

Then on a sudden swoop'd *The Phœnix* down
As though he wore as well as gave The Crown*:
And cried—"I care not, I, to wait on Kings,
Whose crowns are but the Shadow of my Wings!"

"Aye," was the Answer—"And, pray, how has sped,
On which it lighted, many a mortal Head?"

A certain Sultan dying, his Vizier
In Dream beheld him, and in mortal Fear
Began—"Oh mighty Shah of Shahs! Thrice-blest"—
But loud the Vision shriek'd and struck its Breast,
And "Stab me not with empty Title!" cried—
"One only Shah there is, and none beside,
Who from his Throne above for certain Ends
Awhile some Spangle of his Glory lends
To Men on Earth; but calling in again
Exacts a strict account of every Grain.
Sultan I lived, and held the World in scorn : ⎫
Oh better had I glean'd the Field of Corn! ⎬
Oh better had I been a Beggar born, ⎭
And for my Throne and Crown, down in the Dust
My living Head had laid where Dead I must!
Oh wither'd, wither'd, wither'd, be the Wing
Whose overcasting Shadow made me King!"

Then from a Pond, where all day long he kept,
Waddled the dapper *Duck* demure, adept

* He was supposed to be destined to Sovereignty over whom the
Shadow of the wings of the Phœnix passed.

At infinite Ablution, and precise
In keeping of his Raiment clean and nice.
And "Sure of all the Race of Birds," said He,
"None for Religious Purity like Me,
Beyond what strictest Rituals prescribe—
Methinks I am the Saint of all our Tribe,
To whom, by Miracle, the Water, that
I wash in, also makes my Praying-Mat."

To whom, more angrily than all, replied
The Leader, lashing that religious Pride,
That under ritual Obedience
To outer Law with inner might dispense :
For, fair as all the Feather to be seen,
Could one see *through*, the Maw was not so clean :
But He that made both Maw and Feather too
Would take account of, seeing through and through.

A Shah returning to his Capital,
His subjects drest it forth in Festival,
Thronging with Acclamation Square and Street,
And kneeling flung before his Horse's feet
Jewel and Gold. All which with scarce an Eye
The Sultan superciliously rode by :
Till coming to the public Prison, They
Who dwelt within those grisly Walls, by way
Of Welcome, having neither Pearl nor Gold,
Over the wall chopt Head and Carcase roll'd,
Some almost parcht to Mummy with the Sun,
Some wet with Execution that day done.
At which grim Compliment at last the Shah
Drew Bridle : and amid a wild Hurrah

Of savage Recognition, smiling threw
Silver and Gold among the wretched Crew,
And so rode forward. Whereat of his Train
One wondering that, while others sued in vain
With costly gifts, which carelessly he pass'd,
But smiled at ghastly Welcome like the last;
The Shah made answer—"All that Pearl and Gold
Of ostentatious Welcome only told:
A little with great Clamour from the Store
Of Hypocrites who kept at home much more.
But when those sever'd Heads and Trunks I saw—
Save by strict Execution of my Law
They had not parted company; not one
But told my Will not talk'd about, but *done*."

Then from a Wood was heard unseen to coo
The Ring-dove—"Yúsuf! Yúsuf! Yúsuf! Yú-"
(For thus her sorrow broke her Note in twain,
And, just where broken, took it up again)
"-suf! Yúsuf! Yúsuf! Yúsuf!"—But one Note,
Which still repeating, she made hoarse her throat:

Till checkt—"Oh You, who with your idle Sighs
Block up the Road of better Enterprize;
Sham Sorrow all, or bad as sham if true,
When once the better thing is come to *do*;
Beware lest wailing thus you meet *his* Doom
Who all too long his Darling wept, from whom
You draw the very Name you hold so dear,
And which the World is somewhat tired to hear."

When Yúsuf from his Father's Home was torn,
The Patriarch's Heart was utterly forlorn,

And, like a Pipe with but one stop, his Tongue
With nothing but the name of "Yúsuf" rung.
Then down from Heaven's Branches flew the *Bird* *
Of Heav'n, and said "God wearies of that word:
Hast thou not else to do and else to say?"
So Jacob's lips were sealéd from that Day.
But one Night in a Vision, far away
His darling in some alien Field he saw
Binding the Sheaf; and what between the Awe
Of God's Displeasure and the bitter Pass
Of passionate Affection, sigh'd "Alas—"
And stopp'd—But with the morning Sword of Flame
That oped his Eyes the sterner Angel's came—
"For the forbidden Word not utter'd by
Thy Lips was yet sequester'd in that Sigh."
And the right Passion whose Excess was wrong
Blinded the aged Eyes that wept too long.

And after these came others—arguing,
Enquiring and excusing—some one Thing,
And some another—endless to repeat,
But, in the Main, Sloth, Folly, or Deceit.
Their Souls were to the vulgar Figure cast
Of earthly Victual not of Heavenly Fast.
At last one smaller Bird, of a rare kind,
Of modest Plume and unpresumptuous Mind,
Whisper'd, "Oh Tajidar, we know indeed
How Thou both knowest, and would'st help our Need;
For thou art wise and holy, and hast been
Behind the Veil, and there *The Presence* seen.

* Gabriel.

But we are weak and vain, with little care
Beyond our yearly Nests and daily Fare—
How should we reach the Mountain? and if there
How get so great a Prince to hear our Prayer?
For there, you say, dwells *The Symurgh* alone
In Glory, like Sulayman on his Throne,
And we but Pismires at his feet: can He
Such puny Creatures stoop to hear, or see;
Or hearing, seeing, *own* us—unakin
As He to Folly, Woe, and Death, and Sin?"—

To whom the Tajidar, whose Voice for those
Bewilder'd ones to full Compassion rose—
"Oh lost so long in Exile, you disclaim
The very Fount of Being whence you came,
Cannot be parted from, and, will or no,
Whether for Good or Evil must re-flow!
For look—the Shadows into which the Light
Of his pure Essence down by infinite
Gradation dwindles, which at random play
Through Space in Shape indefinite—one Ray
Of his Creative *Will* into *defined*
Creation quickens: We that swim the Wind,
And they the Flood below, and Man and Beast
That walk between, from Lion to the least
Pismire that creeps along Sulayman's Wall—
Yea, that in which they swim, fly, walk, and crawl—
However near the Fountain Light, or far
Removed, yet *His* authentic Shadows are;
Dead Matter's Self but the dark Residue
Exterminating Glory dwindles to.
A Mystery too fearful in the Crowd
To utter—scarcely to Thyself aloud—

But when in solitary Watch and Prayer
Consider'd : and religiously beware
Lest Thou the Copy with the Type confound;
And *Deity*, with Deity indrown'd,—
For as pure Water into purer Wine
Incorporating shall itself refine
While the dull Drug lies half-resolved below,
With Him and with his Shadows is it so:
The baser Forms, to whatsoever Change
Subject, still vary through their lower Range:
To which the *higher* even shall decay, .
That, letting ooze their better Part away
For Things of Sense and Matter, in the End
Shall merge into the Clay to which they tend.
Unlike to him, who straining through the Bond
Of outward Being for a Life beyond,
While the gross Worldling to *his* Centre clings, ⎫
That draws him deeper in, exulting springs   ⎬
To merge him in the central *Soul* of Things. ⎭
And shall not he pass home with other Zest
Who, with full Knowledge, yearns for such a Rest,
Than he, who with his better self at strife,
Drags on the weary Exile call'd *This Life?*—
One, like a child with outstretcht Arms and Face
Up-turn'd, anticipates his Sire's Embrace ;
The other crouching like a guilty Slave
Till flogg'd to Punishment across the Grave.
And, knowing that *His* glory ill can bear   ⎫
The unpurged Eye; do thou Thy Breast prepare; ⎬
And the mysterious Mirror He set there,   ⎭
To temper his reflected Image in,
Clear of Distortion, Doubleness, and Sin :
And in thy Conscience understanding *this*,
The *Double* only *seems*, but The *One is*,

Thy-self to Self-annihilation give
That this false *Two* in that true *One* may live.
For this I say: if, looking in thy Heart,
Thou for *Self-whole* mistake thy *Shadow-part*,
That Shadow-part indeed into *The Sun*
Shall melt, but senseless of its Union:
But in that Mirror if with purgéd eyes
Thy Shadow Thou *for* Shadow recognize,
Then shalt Thou back into thy Centre fall
A conscious Ray of that eternal *All.*"

He ceased, and for awhile Amazement quell'd
The Host, and in the Chain of Silence held:
A Mystery so awful who would dare—
So glorious who would not wish—to share?
So Silence brooded on the feather'd Folk,
Till here and there a timid Murmur broke
From some too poor in honest Confidence,
And then from others of too much Pretence;
Whom both, as each unduly hoped or fear'd,
The Tajidar in answer check'd or cheer'd.

Some said their Hearts were good indeed to go
The Way he pointed out: but they were slow
Of Comprehension, and scarce understood ⎞
Their present Evil or the promised Good: ⎬
And so, tho' willing to do all they could, ⎠
Must not théy fall short, or go wholly wrong,
On such mysterious Errand, and so long?
Whom the wise Leader bid but Do their Best
In Hope and Faith, and leave to *Him* the rest,
For He who fix'd the Race, and knew its Length
And Danger, also knew the Runner's Strength.

Shah Mahmúd, absent on an Enterprize,
Ayas, the very Darling of his eyes,
At home under an Evil Eye fell sick,
Then cried the Sultan to a soldier "Quick!
To Horse! to Horse! without a Moment's Stay,—
The shortest Road with all the Speed you may,—
Or, by the Lord, your Head shall pay for it!"—
Off went the Soldier, plying Spur and Bit—
Over the sandy Desert, over green
Valley, and Mountain, and the Stream between,
Without a Moment's Stop for rest or bait,—
Up to the City—to the Palace Gate—
Up to the Presence-Chamber at a Stride—
And Lo! The Sultan at his Darling's side!—
Then thought the Soldier—"I have done my Best,
And yet shall die for it." The Sultan guess'd
His Thought and smiled. "Indeed your Best you did,
The nearest Road you knew, and well you rid:
And if *I* knew a shorter, my Excess
Of Knowledge does but justify thy Less."

And then, with drooping Crest and Feather, came
Others, bow'd down with Penitence and Shame.
They long'd indeed to go; "but how begin,
Mesh'd and entangled as they were in Sin
Which often-times Repentance of past Wrong
As often broken had but knit more strong?"

Whom the wise Leader bid be of good cheer,
And, conscious of the Fault, dismiss the Fear,
Nor at the very Entrance of the Fray
Their Weapon, ev'n if broken, fling away:

Since Mercy on the broken Branch anew
Would blossom were but each Repentance true.

For did not God his Prophet take to Task?
" *Sev'n-times* of Thee did Kárún Pardon ask;
Which, hadst thou been like Me his Maker—yea,
But present at the Kneading of his Clay
With those twain Elements of Hell and Heav'n,—
One prayer had won what Thou deny'st to Sev'n."

For like a Child sent with a fluttering Light
To feel his way along a gusty Night
Man walks the World: again and yet again
The Lamp shall be by Fits of Passion slain:
But shall not He who sent him from the Door
Relight the Lamp once more, and yet once more?

When the rebellious Host from Death shall wake
Black with Despair of Judgment, God shall take
Ages of holy Merit from the Count
Of Angels to make up Man's short Amount,
And bid the murmuring Angel gladly spare
Of that which, undiminishing his Share
Of Bliss, shall rescue Thousands from the Cost
Of Bankruptcy within the Prison lost*.

Another Story told how in the Scale
Good Will beyond mere Knowledge would prevail.

In Paradise the Angel Gabriel heard
The Lips of Allah trembling with the Word

* This paragraph may be omitted, and the two preceding ones
reversed.

Of perfect Acceptation : and he thought
"Some perfect Faith such perfect Answer wrought,
But whose ?"—And therewith slipping from the Crypt
Of Sidra*, through the Angel-ranks he slipt
Watching what Lip yet trembled with the Shot
That so had hit the Mark—but found it not.
Then, in a Glance to Earth, he threaded through
Mosque, Palace, Cell and Cottage of the True
Belief—in vain; so back to Heaven went
And—Allah's Lips still trembling with assent !
Then the tenacious Angel once again
Threaded the Ranks of Heav'n and Earth—in vain—
Till, once again return'd to Paradise,
There, looking into God's, the Angel's Eyes
Beheld the Prayer that brought that Benison
Rising like Incense from the Lips of one
Who to an Idol bowed—as best he knew
Under that False God worshipping the True.

And then came others whom the summons found
Not wholly sick indeed, but far from sound :
Whose light inconstant Soul alternate flew
From Saint to Sinner, and to both untrue ;
Who like a niggard Tailor, tried to match
Truth's single Garment with a worldly Patch.
A dangerous Game; for, striving to adjust
The hesitating Scale of either Lust,
That which had least within it upward flew,
And still the weightier to the Earth down drew,
And, while suspended between Rise and Fall,
Apt with a shaking Hand to forfeit all.

* Sidra, the Tree of Paradise, or Heaven.

There was a Queen of Egypt like the Bride
Of Night, Full-moon-faced and Canopus-eyed,
Whom one among the meanest of her Crowd
Loved—and she knew it, (for he loved aloud)
And sent for him, and said "Thou lov'st thy Queen:
Now therefore Thou hast this to choose between:
Fly for thy Life: or for this one night Wed }
Thy Queen, and with the Sunrise lose thy Head." }
He paused—he turn'd to fly—she struck him dead. }
"For had he truly loved his Queen," said She,
"He would at once have giv'n his Life for me,
And Life and Wife had carried: but he lied;
And loving only Life, has justly died."

And then came one who having clear'd his Throat
With sanctimonious Sweetness in his Note
Thus lisp'd—"Behold I languish from the first
With passionate and unrequited Thirst
Of Love for more than any mortal Bird.
Therefore have I withdrawn me from the Herd
To pine in Solitude. But Thou at last
Hast drawn a line across the dreary Past,
And sure I am by Fore-taste that the Wine
I long'd for, and Thou tell'st of, shall be mine."

But he was sternly checkt. "I tell thee this:
Such Boast is no Assurance of such Bliss:
Thou canst not even fill the sail of Prayer
Unless from *Him* breathe that authentic Air
That shall lift up the Curtain that divides
His Lover from the Harím where *He* hides—
And the Fulfilment of thy Vows must be,
Not from thy Love for Him, but His for Thee."

The third night after Bajazyd had died,
One saw him, in a dream, at his Bed-side,
And said, "Thou Bajazyd? Tell me Oh Pýr,
How fared it there with Munkar and Nakýr*?"
And Bajazyd replied, "When from the Grave
They met me rising, and 'If Allah's slave'
Ask'd me, 'or collar'd with the Chain of Hell?'
I said 'Not I but God alone can tell:
My Passion for his service were but fond
Ambition had not He approved the Bond:
Had He not round my neck the Collar thrown
And told me in the Number of his own;
And that *He* only knew. What signifies
A hundred Years of Prayer if none replies?'"

"But" said Another, "then shall none the Seal
Of Acceptation on his Forehead feel
Ere the Grave yield them on the other Side
Where all is settled?"

But the Chief replied—
"Enough for us to know that who is meet
Shall enter, and with unreprovéd Feet,
(Ev'n as he might upon the Waters walk)
The Presence-room, and in the Presence talk
With such unbridled License as shall seem
To the Uninitiated to blaspheme."

Just as another Holy Spirit fled,
The Skies above him burst into a Bed

* The two Angels who examine the Soul on its leaving the Body.

Of Angels looking down and singing clear
"Nightingale! Nightingale! thy Rose is here!"
And yet, the Door wide open to that Bliss,
As some hot Lover slights a scanty Kiss,
The Saint cried "All I sigh'd for come to *this*?
I who life-long have struggled, Lord, to be
Not of thy Angels one, but one with Thee!"

Others were sure that all he said was true:
They were extremely wicked, that they knew:
And much they long'd to go at once—but some,
They said, so unexpectedly had come
Leaving their Nests half-built—in bad Repair—
With Children in—Themselves about to pair—
"Might he not choose a better Season—nay,
Better perhaps a Year or Two's Delay,
Till all was settled, and themselves more stout
And strong to carry their Repentance out—
And then"—

"And then, the same or like Excuse,
With harden'd Heart and Resolution loose
With dallying: and old Age itself engaged
Still to shirk that which shirking we have aged;
And so with Self-delusion, till, too late,
Death upon all Repentance shuts the Gate;
Or some fierce blow compels the Way to choose,
And forced Repentance half its Virtue lose."

As of an aged Indian King they tell
Who, when his Empire with his Army fell
Under young Mahmúd's Sword of Wrath, was sent
At sunset to the Conqueror in his Tent;

But, ere the old King's silver head could reach
The Ground, was lifted up—with kindly Speech,
And with so holy Mercy re-assured,
That, after due Persuasion, he abjured
His Idols, sate upon Mahmúd's Divan,
And took the Name and Faith of Musulman.
But when the Night fell, in his Tent alone
The poor old King was heard to weep and groan
And smite his Bosom; which, when Mahmúd knew,
He·went to him and said "Lo, if Thou rue
Thy lost Dominion, Thou shalt wear the Ring
Of thrice as large a Realm." But the dark King
Still wept, and Ashes on his Forehead threw
And cried "Not for my Kingdom lost I rue;
But thinking how at the Last Day, will stand
The Prophet with *The Volume* in his Hand,
And ask of me 'How was't that, in thy Day
Of Glory, Thou didst turn from Me and slay
My People; but soon as thy Infidel   .
Before my True Believers' Army fell
Like Corn before the Reaper—thou didst own
His Sword who scoutedst *Me*.' Of seed so sown
What profitable Harvest should be grown?"

Then after cheering others who delay'd,
Not of the Road but of Themselves afraid,
The Tajidar the Troop of those address'd,
Whose uncomplying Attitude confess'd
Their Souls entangled in the old Deceit,
And hankering still after forbidden Meat—

"Oh ye who so long feeding on the Husk
Forgo the Fruit, and doating on the Dusk

Of the false Dawn, are blinded to the True:
That in the Maidán of this World pursue
The Golden Ball which, driven to the Goal,
Wins the World's Game but loses your own Soul:
Or like to Children after Bubbles run
That still elude your Fingers; or, if won,
Burst in Derision at your Touch; all thin
Glitter without, and empty Wind within.
So as a prosperous Worldling on the Bed
Of Death—'Behold, I am as one,' he said,
Who all my Life long have been measuring Wind,
And, dying, now leave even that behind '—
This World's a Nest in which the Cockatrice
Is warm'd and hatcht of Vanity and Vice:
A false Bazár whose Wares are all a lie,
Or never worth the Price at which you buy:
A many-headed Monster that, supplied
The faster, faster is unsatisfied;
So as one, hearing a rich Fool one day
To God for yet one other Blessing pray,
Bid him no longer bounteous Heaven tire
For Life to feed, but Death to quench, the Fire.
And what are all the Vanities and Wiles
In which the false World decks herself and smiles
To draw Men down into her harlot Lap?
Lusts of the Flesh that Soul and Body sap,
And, melting Soul down into carnal Lust,
Ev'n that for which 'tis sacrificed disgust:
Or Lust of worldly Glory—hollow more
Than the Drum beaten at the Sultan's Door,
And fluctuating with the Breath of Man
As the Vain Banner flapping in the Van.
And Lust of Gold—perhaps of Lusts the worst;
The mis-created Idol most accurst

That between Man and Him who made him stands:
The Felon that with suicidal hands
He sweats to dig and rescue from his Grave,
And sets at large to make Himself its Slave.

" For lo, to what worse than oblivion gone
Are some the cozening World most doated on.
Pharaoh tried *Glory*: and his Chariots drown'd:
Kárún with all his Gold went underground:
Down toppled Nembroth* with his airy Stair:
Schedád among his Roses lived—but *where?*

" And as the World upon her victims feeds
So She herself goes down the Way she leads.
For all her false allurements are the Threads
The Spider from her Entrail spins, and spreads
For Home and hunting-ground: And by and bye
Darts at due Signal on the tangled Fly,
Seizes, dis-wings, and drains the Life, and leaves
The swinging Carcase, and forthwith re-weaves
Her Web: each Victim adding to the store
Of poison'd Entrail to entangle more.
And so She bloats in Glory: till one Day
The Master of the House, passing that way,
Perceives, and with one flourish of his Broom
Of Web and Fly and Spider clears the Room.

" Behold, dropt through the Gate of Mortal Birth,
The Knightly Soul alights from Heav'n on Earth;
Begins his Race, but scarce the Saddle feels, ⎫
When a foul Imp up from the distance steals, ⎬
And, double as he will, about his Heels ⎭

* Nimrod.

Closer and ever closer circling creeps,
Then, half-invited, on the Saddle leaps,
Clings round the Rider, and, once there, in vain
The strongest strives to thrust him off again.
In Childhood just peeps up the Blade of Ill,
That Youth to Lust rears, Fury, and Self-will:
And, as Man cools to sensual Desire,
Ambition catches with as fierce a Fire;
Until Old Age sends him with one last Lust
Of Gold, to keep it where he found—in Dust.
Life at both Ends so feeble and constrain'd
How should that Imp of Sin be slain or chain'd?

"And woe to him who feeds the hateful Beast
That of his Feeder makes an after-feast!
We know the Wolf: by Stratagem and Force
Can hunt the Tiger down: but what Resource
Against the Plague we heedless hatch within,
Then, growing, pamper into full-blown Sin
With the Soul's self: ev'n, as the wise man said,
Feeding the very Devil with God's own Bread;
Until the Lord his Largess misapplied
Resent, and drive us wholly from his Side?

"For should the Grey-hound whom a Sultan fed,
And by a jewell'd String a-hunting led,
Turn by the Way to gnaw some nasty Thing
And snarl at Him who twitch'd the silken String,
Would not his Lord soon weary of Dispute,
And turn adrift the incorrigible Brute?

"Nay, would one follow, and without a Chain,
The only Master truly worth the Pain,

F.   30

One must beware lest, growing over-fond)
Of even Life's more consecrated Bond, }
We clog our Footsteps to the World beyond.)
Like that old Arab Chieftain, who confess'd
His soul by two too Darling Things possess'd—
That only Son of his: and that one Colt
Descended from the Prophet's Thunderbolt*.
'And I might well bestow the last,' he said,
'On him who brought me Word the Boy was dead.'

"And if so vain the glittering Fish we get,
How doubly vain to doat upon the Net,
Call'd Life, that draws them, patching up this thin
Tissue of Breathing out and Breathing in,
And so by husbanding each wretched Thread
Spin out Death's very Terror that we dread—
For as the Rain-drop from the sphere of God
Dropt for a while into the Mortal Clod
So little makes of its allotted Time
Back to its Heav'n itself to re-sublime,
That it but serves to saturate its Clay
With Bitterness that will not pass away."

One day the Prophet on a River Bank,
Dipping his Lips into the Channel, drank
A Draught as sweet as Honey. Then there came
One who an earthen Pitcher from the same
Drew up, and drank: and after some short stay
Under the Shadow, rose and went his Way,
Leaving his earthen Bowl. In which, anew
Thirsting, the Prophet from the River drew,
And drank from: but the Water that came up
Sweet from the Stream, drank bitter from the Cup.

* The famous Borak.

At which the Prophet in a still Surprise
For Answer turning up to Heav'n his Eyes,
The Vessel's Earthen Lips with Answer ran—
"The Clay that I am made of once was *Man*,
Who dying, and resolved into the same
Obliterated Earth from which he came
Was for the Potter dug, and chased in turn
Through long Vicissitude of Bowl and Urn:
But howsoever moulded, still the Pain
Of that first mortal Anguish would retain,
And cast, and re-cast, for a Thousand years
Would turn the sweetest Water into Tears."

And after Death?—that, shirk it as we may,
Will come, and with it bring its After-Day—

For ev'n as Yúsuf, (when his Brotherhood
Came up from Egypt to buy Corn, and stood
Before their Brother in his lofty Place,
Nor knew him, for a Veil before his Face,)
Struck on his Mystic Cup, which straightway then
Rung out their Story to those guilty Ten:—
Not to *them* only, but to every one;
Whatever he have said and thought and done,
Unburied with the Body shall fly up,
And gather into Heav'n's inverted Cup,
Which, stricken by God's Finger, shall tell all
The Story whereby we must stand or fall.
And though we walk this World as if behind
There were no Judgment, or the Judge half-blind,
Beware, for He with whom we have to do
Outsees the Lynx, outlives the Phœnix too—

So Sultan Mahmúd, coming Face to Face
With mightier numbers of the swarthy Race,
Vow'd that if God to him the battle gave,
God's Dervish People all the Spoil should have.
And God the Battle gave him; and the Fruit
Of a great Conquest coming to compute,
A Murmur through the Sultan's Army stirr'd
Lest, ill committed to one hasty Word,
The Shah should squander on an idle Brood
What should be theirs who earn'd it with their Blood,
Or go to fill the Coffers of the State.
So Mahmúd's Soul began to hesitate:
Till looking round in Doubt from side to side
A raving Zealot in the Press he spied,
And call'd and had him brought before his Face,
And, telling, bid him arbitrate the case.
Who, having listen'd, said—"The Thing is plain:
If Thou and God should never have again
To deal together, rob him of his share:
But if perchance you should—why then Beware!"

So spake the Tajidar: but Fear and Doubt
Among the Birds in Whispers went about:
Great was their Need: and Succour to be sought
At any Risk: at any Ransom bought:
But such a Monarch—greater than Mahmúd
The Great Himself! Why how should he be woo'd
To listen to them? they too having come
So suddenly, and unprepared from home
With any Gold, or Jewel, or rich Thing
To carry with them to so great a King—
Poor Creatures! with the old and carnal Blind,
Spite of all said, so thick upon the Mind,

Devising how they might ingratiate
Access, as to some earthly Potentate.

"Let him that with this Monarch would engage
Bring the Gold Dust of a long Pilgrimage:
The Ruby of a bleeding Heart, whose Sighs
Breathe more than Amber-incense as it dies;
And while in naked Beggary he stands
Hope for the Robe of Honour from his Hands."
And, as no gift this Sovereign receives
Save the mere Soul and Self of him who gives,
So let that Soul for other none Reward
Look than the Presence of its Sovereign Lord." .
And as his Hearers seem'd to estimate
Their Scale of Glory from Mahmúd the Great,
A simple Story of the Sultan told
How best a subject with his Shah made bold—

One night Shah Mahmúd who had been of late
Somewhat distemper'd with Affairs of State
Stroll'd through the Streets disguised, as wont to do—
And, coming to the Baths, there on the Flue
Saw the poor Fellow who the Furnace fed
Sitting beside his Water-jug and Bread.
Mahmúd stept in—sat down—unask'd took up
And tasted of the untasted Loaf and Cup,
Saying within himself, "Grudge but a bit,
And, by the Lord, your Head shall pay for it!"
So having rested, warm'd and satisfied
Himself without a Word on either side,
At last the wayward Sultan rose to go.
And then at last his Host broke silence—"So?—
Art satisfied? Well, Brother, any Day
Or Night, remember, when you come this Way

And want a bit of Provender—why, you
Are welcome, and if not—why, welcome too."—
The Sultan was so tickled with the whim
Of this quaint Entertainment and of him
Who offer'd it, that many a Night again
Stoker and Shah forgather'd in that Vein—
Till, the poor Fellow having stood the Test
Of true Good-fellowship, Mahmúd confess'd
One Night the Sultan that had been his Guest:
And in requital of the scanty Dole
The Poor Man offer'd with so large a soul,
Bid him ask any Largess that he would—
A Throne—if he *would* have it, so he *should*.
The Poor Man kiss'd the Dust, and "All," said he,
"I ask is what and where I am to be;
If but the Shah from time to time will come
As now and see me in the lowly Home
His presence makes a palace, and my own
Poor Flue more royal than another's Throne."

So said the cheery Tale: and, as they heard,
Again the Heart beneath the Feather stirr'd:
Again forgot the Danger and the Woes
Of the long Travel in its glorious Close:—
"Here truly all was Poverty, Despair
And miserable Banishment—but *there*
That more than Mahmúd, for no more than Prayer
Who would restore them to their ancient Place,
And round their Shoulders fling his Robe of Grace."
They clapp'd their Wings, on Fire to be assay'd
And prove of what true Metal they were made,
Although defaced, and wanting the true Ring
And Superscription of their rightful King.

"The Road! The Road!" in countless voices cried
The Host—"The Road! and who shall be our Guide?"
And they themselves "The Tajidar!" replied:
Yet to make doubly certain that the Voice
Of Heav'n accorded with the People's Choice,
Lots should be drawn; and He on whom should light
Heav'n's Hand—they swore to follow him out-right.
This settled, and once more the Hubbub quell'd,
Once more Suspense the Host in Silence held,
While, Tribe by Tribe, the Birds their Fortune drew;
And Lo! upon the Tajidar it flew.
Then rising up again in wide and high
Circumference of wings that mesh'd the sky
"The Tajidar! The Tajidar!" they cry—
"The Tajidar! The Tajidar!" with Him
Was Heav'n, and They would follow Life and Limb!
Then, once more fluttering to their Places down,
Upon his Head they set the Royal Crown
As Khalif of their Khalif so long lost,
And Captain of his now repentant Host;
And setting him on high, and Silence call'd,
The Tajidar, in Pulpit-throne install'd,
His Voice into a Trumpet-tongue so clear
As all the wingéd Multitude should hear
Raised, to proclaim the Order and Array
Of March; which, many as it frighten'd—yea,
The Heart of Multitudes at outset broke,
Yet for due Preparation must be spoke.

—A Road indeed that never Wing before
Flew, nor Foot trod, nor Heart imagined—o'er
Waterless Deserts—Waters where no Shore—

Valleys comprising cloudhigh Mountains: these
Again their Valleys deeper than the Seas:
Whose Dust all Adders, and whose vapour Fire:
Where all once hostile Elements conspire
To set the Soul against herself, and tear
Courage to Terror—Hope into Despair,
And Madness; Terrors, Trials, to make stray
Or stop where Death to wander or delay:
Where when half dead with Famine, Toil, and Heat,
'Twas Death indeed to rest, or drink, or eat.
A Road still waxing in Self-sacrifice
As it went on: still ringing with the Cries
And Groans of Those who had not yet prevail'd,
And bleaching with the Bones of those who fail'd:
Where, almost all withstood, perhaps to earn
Nothing: and, earning, never to return.—

And first the *VALE OF SEARCH:* an endless Maze,
Branching into innumerable Ways
All courting Entrance: but one right: and this
Beset with Pitfall, Gulf, and Precipice,
Where Dust is Embers, Air a fiery Sleet,
Through which with blinded Eyes and bleeding Feet
The Pilgrim stumbles, with Hyæna's Howl
Around, and hissing Snake, and deadly Ghoul,
Whose Prey he falls if tempted but to droop,
Or if to wander famish'd from the Troop
For fruit that falls to ashes in the Hand,
Water that reacht recedes into the Sand.
The only word is "Forward!" Guide in sight,
After him, swerving neither left nor right,
Thyself for thine own Victual by Day,
At night thine own Self's Caravanserai.

Till suddenly, perhaps when most subdued
And desperate, the Heart shall be renew'd
When deep in utter Darkness, by one Gleam
Of Glory from the far remote *Harím,*
That, with a scarcely conscious Shock of Change,
Shall light the Pilgrim toward the Mountain Range
Of KNOWLEDGE*: where, if stronger and more pure)
The Light and Air, yet harder to endure;
And if, perhaps, the Footing more secure,
Harder to keep up with a nimble Guide,
Less from lost Road than insufficient Stride—
Yet tempted still by false Shows from the Track,
And by false Voices call'd aside or back,

---

* In the original Poem there are *Seven* Valleys of Probation: not
very significant in their Spiritual Outline, as Tholuck implies: and
very confused in their Allegorical Detail, as G. de Tassy admits.
Other great Sufi Doctors distinguished " *The Road* " of Self-perfection
into other Stages, some more, some less in Number than Attar: but
Tholuck tells us *Three* was the usual Scale of Gradation : and, one
must admit, quite enough.

Vulgo tres solent majoris minorisve Perfectionis gradus Muhamme-
dani numerare &c.—Ssufii vel pariter tres vel quatuor Gradus posuere.
I Scheriat, Lex: II Terikat, Iter; III Hakikat, Veritas, quibus adjunx-
erunt quartam aliqui: IV Marifat, Cognitio....In Metsnewi non inveni
Graduum mentionem nisi T. I. p. 72. 'Quum videas Rubrum, aliosque
Colores, qui fit ut non cernas hæc tria Lumina'—Sæpius ut solet prolixe
de Lege, Itinere, Veritate, Attarus cornicatur...nec tamen significat
memorabile quidquam nisi quod perpetuo asserat hos Gradus se in-
vicem quasi in Nuce continere...Sex Gradus constituerat Bajesid, caput
Ruscheniorum: I Lex. II Veritas. III Scientia. IV Appropinquatio.
V Junctio. VI سكونت (indwelling in God) Quies in Deo &c.
Refert doctissimus D. Leyden e Dabistano edocuisse Bajesidum patrem
suum quatuor a Propheta ipso Gradus positos esse &c. &c.

Tholuck's *Ssufismus,* Berol. 1821, p. 325 &c.

Which echo from the Bosom, as if won
The Journey's End when only just begun,
And not a Mountain Peak with Toil attain'd
But shows a Top yet higher to be gain'd.
Wherefore still Forward, Forward! Love that fired
Thee first to search, by Search so re-inspired
As that the Spirit shall the carnal Load
Burn up, and double wing Thee on the Road;
That wert thou knocking at the very Door
Of Heav'n, thou still would'st cry for More, More,
        More!

Till loom in sight Káf's Mountain Peak ashroud
In Mist—uncertain yet Mountain or Cloud,
But where the Pilgrim 'gins to hear the Tide
Of that one Sea in which the Sev'n subside;
And not the Sev'n Seas only: but the sev'n
And self-enfolded Spheres of Earth and Heav'n—
Yea, the Two Worlds, that now as Pictures sleep
Upon its Surface—but when once the Deep
From its long Slumber 'gins to heave and sway— ⎫
Under that Tempest shall be swept away   ⎬
With all their Phases and Phenomena: ⎭
Not senseless Matter only, but combined
With Life in all Varieties of Kind;
Yea, ev'n the abstract Forms that Space and Time
Men call, and Weal and Woe, Virtue and Crime,
And all the several Creeds, like those who fell
Before them, Musulman and Infidel
Shall from the Face of Being melt away,
Cancell'd and swept as Dreams before the Day.
So hast thou seen the Astrologer prepare
His mystic Table smooth of Sand, and there

Inscribe his mystic Figures, Square, and Trine,
Circle and Pentagram, and heavenly Sign
Of Star and Planet: from whose Set and Rise,
Meeting and Difference, he prophesies;
And, having done it, with his Finger clean
Obliterates as never they had been.

Such is when reacht the Table Land of *One*
And *Wonder*: blazing with so fierce a Sun
Of Unity that blinds while it reveals
The Universe that to a Point congeals,
So, stunn'd with utter Revelation, reels
The Pilgrim, when that *Double*-seeming House,
Against whose Beams he long had chafed his Brows,
Crumbles and cracks before that Sea, whose near
And nearer Voice now overwhelms his Ear.
Till blinded, deafen'd, madden'd, drunk with doubt
Of all within Himself as all without,
Nay, whether a *Without* there be, or not,
Or a *Within* that doubts: and if, then *what?*—
Ev'n so shall the bewilder'd Pilgrim seem
When nearest waking deepliest in Dream,
And darkest next to Dawn; and lost what had
When *All* is found: and just when sane quite Mad—
As one that having found the Key once more
Returns, and Lo! he cannot find the Door
He stumbles over—So the Pilgrim stands
A moment on the Threshold—with raised Hands
Calls to the eternal Sáki for one Draught
Of Light from the One Essence: which when quaff'd,
He plunges headlong in: and all is well
With him who never more returns to tell.

Such being then the Race and such the Goal,
Judge if you must not Body both and Soul
With Meditation, Watch, and Fast prepare.
For he that wastes his Body to a Hair
Shall seize the Locks of Truth: and He that prays
Good Angels in their Ministry way-lays:
And the Midnightly Watcher in the Folds
Of his own Darkness God Almighty holds.
He that would prosper here must from him strip
The World, and take the Dervish Gown and Scrip:
And as he goes must gather from all Sides
Irrelevant Ambitions, Lusts, and Prides,
Glory and Gold, and sensual Desire,
Whereof to build the fundamental Pyre
Of Self-annihilation: and cast in
All old Relations and Regards of Kin
And Country: and, the Pile with this perplext
World platform'd, from the Fables of the Next
Raise it tow'rd Culmination, with the torn
Rags and Integuments of Creeds out-worn;
And top the giddy Summit with the Scroll ⎞
Of *Reason* that in dingy Smoke shall roll ⎬
Over the true Self-sacrifice of Soul: ⎠
(For such a Prayer was his—"Oh God, do Thou
With all my Wealth in the other World endow
My Friends: and with my Wealth in *this* my Foes,
Till bankrupt in *thy* Riches I repose!")
Then, all the Pile completed of the Pelf
Of either World—at last throw on *Thyself,*
And with the Torch of Self-negation fire;
And ever as the Flames rise high and higher,
With Cries of agonizing Glory still
All of that *Self* burn up that burn up will,

Leaving the Phœnix that no Fire can slay
To spring from its own Ashes kindled—nay,
Itself an inextinguishable Spark
Of Being, *now* beneath Earth-ashes dark,
Transcending these, at last *Itself* transcends
And with the One Eternal Essence blends.

The Moths had long been exiled from the Flame
They worship: so to solemn Council came,
And voted *One* of them by Lot be sent
To find their Idol.   One was chosen: went.
And after a long Circuit in sheer Gloom,
Seeing, he thought, the TAPER in a Room
Flew back at once to say so.   But the chief
Of *Mothistán* slighted so slight Belief,
And sent another Messenger, who flew
Up to the House, in at the window, through
The Flame itself; and back the Message brings,
With yet no sign of Conflict on his wings.
Then went a Third, who spurr'd with true Desire,
Plunging at once into the sacred Fire,
Folded his Wings within, till he became
One Colour and one Substance with the Flame.
He only knew the Flame who in it burn'd;
And only He could tell who ne'er to tell return'd.

After declaring what of this declared
Must be, that all who went should be prepared,
From his high Station ceased the Tajidar—
And lo! the Terrors that, when told afar,
Seem'd but as Shadows of a Noon-day Sun,
Now that the talkt of Thing was to be *done*,

Lengthening into those of closing Day ⎫
Strode into utter Darkness : and Dismay ⎬
Like Night on the husht Sea of Feathers lay, ⎭
Late so elate—"So terrible a Track !
Endless—or, ending, never to come back !—
Never to Country, Family, or Friend !"—
In sooth no easy Bow for Birds to bend !—
Even while he spoke, how many Wings and Crests
Had slunk away to distant Woods and Nests ;
Others again in Preparation spent
What little Strength they had, and never went :
And others, after preparation due— ⎫
When up the Veil of that first Valley drew ⎬
From whose waste Wilderness of Darkness blew ⎭
A Sarsar, whether edged of Flames or Snows,
That through from Root to Tip their Feathers froze—
Up went a Multitude that overhead
A moment darken'd, then on all sides fled,
Dwindling the World-assembled Caravan
To less than half the Number that began.
Of those who fled not, some in Dread and Doubt
Sat without stirring : others who set out
With frothy Force, or stupidly resign'd,
Before a League, flew off or fell behind.
And howsoever the more Brave and Strong
In Courage, Wing, or Wisdom push'd along,
Yet League by League the Road was thicklier spread
By the fast falling Foliage of the Dead :
Some spent with Travel over Wave and Ground ; ⎫
Scorcht, frozen, dead for Drought, or drinking drown'd. ⎬
Famisht, or poison'd with the Food when found : ⎭
By Weariness, or Hunger, or Affright
Seduced to stop or stray, become the Bite

Of Tiger howling round or hissing Snake,
Or Crocodile that eyed them from the Lake :
Or raving Mad, or in despair Self-slain :
Or slaying one another for a Grain :—

Till of the mighty Host that fledged the Dome
Of Heav'n and Floor of Earth on leaving Home,
A Handfull reach'd and scrambled up the Knees
Of Káf whose Feet dip in the Seven Seas ;
And of the few that up his Forest-sides
Of Light and Darkness where *The Presence* hides,
But *Thirty*—thirty desperate draggled Things,
Half-dead, with scarce a Feather on their Wings,
Stunn'd, blinded, deafen'd with the Crash and Craze
Of Rock and Sea collapsing in a Blaze
That struck the Sun to Cinder—fell upon
The Threshold of the Everlasting *One*,
With but enough of Life in each to cry,
On THAT which all absorb'd—
                              And suddenly
Forth flash'd a wingéd Harbinger of Flame
And Tongue of Fire, and "Who?" and "Whence they
      came ?"
And "Why?" demanded. And the Tajidar ⎫
For all the Thirty answer'd him—"We are ⎬
Those Fractions of the Sum of Being, far ⎭
Dis-spent and foul disfigured, that once more
Strike for Admission at the Treasury Door."

To whom the Angel answer'd—"Know ye not
That He you seek recks little who or what
Of Quantity and Kind—himself the Fount
Of Being Universal needs no Count

Of all the Drops o'erflowing from his Urn,
In what Degree they issue or return?"

Then cried the Spokesman, "Be it even so:
Let us but see the Fount from which we flow,
And, seeing, lose Ourselves therein!" And, Lo!
Before the Word was utter'd, or the Tongue
Of Fire replied, or Portal open flung,
They were *within*—they were before the *Throne*,
Before the Majesty that sat thereon,
But wrapt in so insufferable a Blaze
Of Glory as beat down their baffled Gaze,
Which, downward dropping, fell upon a Scroll
That, Lightning-like, flash'd back on each the whole
Past half-forgotten Story of his Soul:
Like that which Yúsuf in his Glory gave
His Brethren as some Writing he would have
Interpreted; and at a Glance, behold
Their own Indenture for their Brother sold!
And so with these poor Thirty: who, abasht
In Memory all laid bare and Conscience lasht,
By full Confession and Self-loathing flung
The Rags of carnal Self that round them clung;
And, their old selves self-knowledged and self-loathed,
And in the Soul's Integrity re-clothed,
Once more they ventured from the Dust to raise
Their Eyes—up to the Throne—into the Blaze,
And in the Centre of the Glory there
Beheld the Figure of—*Themselves* *—as 'twere
Transfigured—looking to Themselves, beheld
The Figure on the Throne en-miracled,

---

* "*Symurgh*" signifies "Thirty Birds."

Until their Eyes themselves and *That* between
Did hesitate which *Sëer* was, which *Seen;*
They That, That They: Another, yet the Same;
Dividual, yet One: from whom there came
A Voice of awful Answer, scarce discern'd
From *which* to Aspiration *whose* return'd
They scarcely knew; as when some Man apart
Answers aloud the Question in his Heart—
"The Sun of my Perfection is a Glass _
Wherein from *Seeing* into *Being* pass
All who, reflecting as reflected see
Themselves in Me, and Me in Them: not *Me*,
But all of Me that a contracted Eye
Is comprehensive of Infinity:
Nor yet *Themselves:* no Selves, but of The All
Fractions, from which they split and whither fall.
As Water lifted from the Deep, again ⎫
Falls back in individual Drops of Rain ⎬
Then melts into the Universal Main. ⎭
All you have been, and seen, and done, and thought,
Not *You* but *I,* have seen and been and wrought:
I was the Sin that from Myself rebell'd:
I the Remorse that tow'rd Myself compell'd:
I was the Tajidar who led the Track:
I was the little Briar that pull'd you back:
Sin and Contrition—Retribution owed,
And cancell'd—Pilgrim, Pilgrimage, and Road,
Was but Myself toward Myself: and Your
Arrival but *Myself* at my own Door:
Who in your Fraction of Myself behold*
Myself within the Mirror Myself hold

* In one of Jami's Poems, which I can now refer to only by
Memory, he conceives The Deity to have *projected* Creation as a Mirror

To see Myself in, and each part of Me
That sees himself, though drown'd, shall ever see.
Come you lost Atoms to your Centre draw,
And *be* the Eternal Mirror that you saw:
Rays that have wander'd into Darkness wide
Return, and back into your Sun subside."—

This was the Parliament of Birds: and this
The Story of the Host who went amiss,
And of the Few that better Upshot found;
Which being now recounted, Lo, the Ground
Of Speech fails underfoot: But this to tell—
Their Road is thine—Follow—and Fare thee well.

---

in which to behold Himself. And he adds a pretty, but, as usual, faintly illustrative, Story; of some one who, going up from Canaan to Egypt, and wishing to carry "*Yusuf*" the most acceptable Present he can, is counsel'd to carry *a Mirror*: in which looking, Yusuf will see the most beautiful Object in the Universe.

THE TWO GENERALS.

I.

LUCIUS ÆMILIUS PAULLUS.

His Speech to the Roman People after his Triumph over Perseus, King of Macedonia, U. C. 585. Livy xlv. 41. (And unfaithful to the few and simple words recorded in the Original.)

With what success, Quirites, I have served
The Commonwealth, and, in the very hour
Of Glory, what a double Thunderbolt
From Heav'n has struck upon my private roof,
Rome needs not to be told, who lately saw
So close together treading through her streets
My Triumph, and the Funeral of my Sons.
Yet bear with me while, in a few brief words,
And uninvidious spirit, I compare
Beside the fulness of the general Joy
My single Destitution.
                          When the time
For leaving Italy was come, the Ships

With all their Armament, and men complete,
As the Sun rose I left Brundusium:
With all my Ships before that Sun was down
I made Corcyra: thence, within five days
To Delphi: where, Lustration to the God
Made for myself, the Army, and the Fleet,
In five days more I reach'd the Roman Camp;
Took the Command; redress'd what was amiss:
And, for King Perseus would not forth to fight,
And, for his Camp's strength, forth could not be forced,
I slipp'd beside him through the Mountain-pass
To Pydna; whither when himself forced back,
And fight he must, I fought, I routed him:
And all the War that, swelling for four years,
Consul to Consul handed over worse
Than from his Predecessor he took up,
In fifteen days victoriously I closed.
Nor stay'd my Fortune here. Upon Success
Success came rolling: with their Army lost,
The Macedonian Cities all gave in;
Into my hands the Royal Treasure then—
And, by and by, the King's self and his Sons,
As by the very finger of the Gods
Betray'd, whose Temple they had fled to—fell.
And now my swollen Fortune to myself
Became suspicious: I began to dread
The seas that were to carry such a freight
Of Conquest, and of Conquerors. But when
With all-propitious Wind and Wave we reach'd
Italian Earth again, and all was done
That was to be, and nothing furthermore
To deprecate or pray for—still I pray'd;
That, whereas human Fortune, having touch'd

The destined height it may not rise beyond,
Forthwith begins as fatal a decline,
Its Fall might but myself and mine involve,
Swerving beside my Country. Be it so!
By my sole sacrifice may jealous Fate
Absolve the Public; and by such a Triumph
As, in derision of all Human Glory,
Began and closed with those two Funerals.
Yes, at that hour were Perseus and myself
Together two notorious monuments
Standing of Human Instability:
He that was late so absolute a King,
Now Bondsman, and his Sons along with him
Still living Trophies of my Conquest led;
While I, the Conqueror, scarce had turn'd my face
From one still unextinguisht Funeral,
And from my Triumph to the Capitol
Return—return to close the dying Eyes
Of the last Son I yet might call my own,
Last of all those who should have borne my name
To after Ages down. For ev'n as one
Presuming on a rich Posterity,
And blind to Fate, my two surviving Sons
Into two noble Families of Rome
I had adopted—
And Paullus is the last of all his Name.

II.

SIR CHARLES NAPIER.

Writing home after the Battle of Meanee.

(*See his Memoirs*, vol. ii. p. 429.)

[Leaving the Battle to be fought again
Over the wine with all our friends at home,
I needs must tell, before my letter close,
Of one result that you will like to hear.]

The Officers who under my command
Headed and led the British Troops engaged
In this last Battle that decides the War,
Resolved to celebrate the Victory
With those substantial Honours that, you know,
So much good English work begins and ends with.
Resolved by one and all, the day was named;
One mighty Tent, with 'room and verge enough'
To hold us all, of many Tents made up
Under the very walls of Hydrabad,
And then and there were they to do me honour.
Some of them grizzled Veterans like myself:
Some scorcht with Indian Sun and Service; some
With unrecover'd wound or sickness pale;
And some upon whose boyish cheek the rose
They brought with them from England scarce had faded.

Imagine these in all varieties
Of Uniform, Horse, Foot, Artillery,
Ranged down the gaily decorated Tent,
Each with an Indian servant at his back,
Whose dusky feature, Oriental garb,
And still, but supple, posture of respect
Served as a foil of contrast to the lines
Of animated English Officers.
Over our heads our own victorious Colours
Festoon'd with those wrencht from the Indian hung,
While through the openings of the tent were seen
Darkling the castle walls of Hydrabad;
And, further yet, the monumental Towers
Of the Kalloras and Talpoors; and yet
Beyond, and last,—the Field of Meeanee.
Yes, there in Triumph as upon the tombs
Of two extinguisht Dynasties we sate,
Beside the field of blood we quench'd them in.
And I, chief Actor in that Scene of Death,
And foremost in the passing Triumph—I,
Veteran in Service as in years, though now
First call'd to play the General—I myself
So swiftly disappearing from the stage
Of all this world's transaction!—As I sate,
My thoughts reverted to that setting Sun
That was to rise on our victorious march;
When from a hillock by my tent alone
I look'd down over twenty thousand Men
Husht in the field before me, like a Fire
Prepared, and waiting but my breath to blaze.
And now, methought, the Work is done; is done,
And well; for those who died, and those who live
To celebrate our common Glory, well;

And, looking round, I whisper'd to myself—
"These are my Children—these whom I have led
Safe through the Vale of Death to Victory,
And in a righteous cause; righteous, I say,
As for our Country's welfare, so for this,
Where from henceforth Peace, Order, Industry,
Blasted and trampled under heretofore
By every lawless Ruffian of the Soil,
Shall now strike root, and "—I was running on
With all that was to be, when suddenly
My Name was call'd; the glass was fill'd; all rose;
And, as they pledged me cheer on cheer, the Cannon
Roar'd it abroad, with each successive burst
Of Thunder lighting up the banks now dark
Of Indus, which at Inundation-height,
Beside the Tent we revell'd in roll'd down
Audibly growling—"But a hand-breadth higher,
And whose the Land you boast as all your own!"

CAMBRIDGE: PRINTED BY C. J. CLAY, M.A. & SONS, AT THE UNIVERSITY PRESS.